ROUTLEDGE LIBRARY EDITIONS:
URBAN AND REGIONAL ECONOMICS

Volume 5

INDUSTRIALIZATION IN DEVELOPING AND PERIPHERAL REGIONS

INDUSTRIALIZATION IN DEVELOPING AND PERIPHERAL REGIONS

Edited by
F.E. IAN HAMILTON

Routledge
Taylor & Francis Group
LONDON AND NEW YORK

First published in 1986 by Croom Helm

This edition first published in 2018
by Routledge
2 Park Square, Milton Park, Abingdon, Oxon OX14 4RN

and by Routledge

605 Third Avenue, New York, NY 10017

Routledge is an imprint of the Taylor & Francis Group, an informa business

British Library Cataloguing in Publication Data
A catalogue record for this book is available from the British Library

ISBN: 978-1-138-09590-8 (Set)
ISBN: 978-1-315-10306-8 (Set) (ebk)
ISBN: 978-1-138-10188-3 (Volume 5) (hbk)
ISBN: 978-1-315-10326-6 (Volume 5) (ebk)

Publisher's Note
The publisher has gone to great lengths to ensure the quality of this reprint but points out that some imperfections in the original copies may be apparent.

Disclaimer
The publisher has made every effort to trace copyright holders and would welcome correspondence from those they have been unable to trace.

INDUSTRIALIZATION IN DEVELOPING AND PERIPHERAL REGIONS

Edited by
F.E. IAN HAMILTON

CROOM HELM
London • Sydney • Dover, New Hampshire

Croom Helm Ltd, Provident House, Burrell Row,
Beckenham, Kent BR3 1AT

Croom Helm Australia Pty Ltd, Suite 4, 6th Floor,
64-76 Kippax Street, Surry Hills, NSW 2010, Australia

British Library Cataloguing in Publication Data

Industrialization in developing and peripheral
regions.
1. Developing countries – Industries
I. Hamilton, F.E. Ian
338.09172'4 HC59.7

ISBN 0-7099-3827-6

Croom Helm, 51 Washington Street, Dover,
New Hampshire 03820, USA

Library of Congress Cataloging-in-Publication Data

Industrialization in developing and peripheral regions.

1. Industrialization. 2. Economic development.
3. Developing countries–Industries. I. Hamilton,
F.E. Ian.
HD2329.I54 1986 338.09172'4 86-4159
ISBN 0-7099-3827-6

Printed and bound in Great Britain
by Billing & Sons Limited, Worcester.

CONTENTS

CONTRIBUTORS

Sergio Conti, B.A. (Torino), Ph.D. (London School of Economics and Political Science), teaches in the 'Piero e Dino Gribaudi' Economic Geography Laboratory, Faculty of Economics and Commerce, University of Turin, Italy

Pasquale Coppola is Professor in the Political and Social Studies Seminarium of the Istituto Universitario Orientale, Naples, Italy

Evangelia Dokopoulou, Diploma in Architecture (Athens Technical University), M.Sc. in Urban & Regional Planning (Oxford Polytechnic, Oxford, England), Ph.D. (London School of Economics & Political Science), worked as a research assistant at the London School of Economics from 1982 to 1985 and is now Lecturer, College of Humanities, National Institute for Higher Education, Limerick, Ireland

Hunya Gabor is a research fellow in the Institute of the World Economy, Hungarian Academy of Sciences, Budapest, Hungary

Jean-Paul Gabriele, Agrégation Géographie, Doctorat (Université de Paris), formerly a teacher in Chaumont-sur-Marne, is now teaching geography in a school at Feurs, near St. Etienne, France

Lea Goldenstein is Professor in Geography in the Faculty of Philosophy, Letters and Human Sciences, Universidade de Sao Paulo, Brazil

Stela Goldenstein Carvalhaes is currently employed by the São Paulo State Council for the Environment.

F.E. Ian Hamilton, B.Sc. (Econ.), Ph.D. (London School of Economics and Political Science), Senior Lecturer in Geography at the London School of Economics, was Chairman of- the International Geographical Union Working Group on Industrial Geography/Commission on

Industrial Systems 1972-84

Theologos (Lois) Labrianidis, Diploma in Architecture (Thessaloniki), M.A. in Urban and Regional Planning (University of Sussex), England), Ph.D. (London School of Economics and Political Science), is currently scientific fellow in the Centre for Planning and Economic Research of Greece, Thessaloniki, and a consultant on the five-year economic and social plan of Greece relating to Thessaloniki prefecture

Li Wen-Yan is Deputy Director of the Institute of Geography, Chinese Academy of Sciences, Beijing, China

Werner Mikus, Ph.D. (Ruhr Universität Bochum), is Professor of Geography at the Geography Institute of the University of Heidelberg, German Federal Republic

Sam Ock Park, B.A., M.A. (Seoul), Ph.D. (University of Georgia), teaches in the Department of Geography, College of Social Science, Seoul National University, Seoul, South Korea

Roger A. Roberge, B.A., M.A., Ph.D. (Clark University), is currently a member of the International Geographical Union Commission on Industrial Change and Professor in the Department of Geography and Institute for International Development and Co-operation, University of Ottawa, Canada

Anna Segre, B.A., Ph.D. (Torino), teaches in the 'Piero e Dino Gribaudi' Economic Geography Laboratory, Faculty of Economics and Commerce, University of Turin, Italy

Mahindar Santokh Singh, M.A., Dip.Ed. (Malaysia), Ph.D. (University of London), is at present Associate Professor, University of Science, Malaysia, at Penang, and a member of the International Geographical Union Commission on Industrial Change

Antonio Vazquez-Barquero is Deputy Director General of Planning in the Centro de Estudios de Ministerio de Obras Publicas y Urbanismo, Madrid, Spain, and Professor, Universidad Autonoma de Madrid

Peter D. Wilde is Senior Lecturer in Geography, University of Tasmania, Hobart, Australia

ACKNOWLEDGEMENTS

Anna Segre wishes to thank Dr. De Meglio for his assistance in making use of the specialization index in her paper.

Peter Wilde is grateful for the assistance of Ifay Tsang and Kate Charlesworth of the Geography Department, University of Tasmania, and for the comments on an earlier draft made by David Rich.

Pasquale Coppola and Jean-Paul Gabriele wish to thank Ian Hamilton for translating their chapters from French into English.

PREFACE

Industrialization in Developing and Peripheral Regions, together with its companion volume *Industrial Change in Advanced Economies*, contains a selection of revised papers which were originally presented at, or submitted to, the International Geographical Union Commission on Industrial Systems' Symposium in Nébian, near Montpellier, France, in August 1984.

Key aspects of the Commission's activity have been to stimulate new directions of study and to push forward the frontiers of research on an international comparative basis. These functions have frequently been seen to be dominated by researchers from the more advanced industrial economies and from the English-speaking world where work is built on deep and long traditions of theoretical and empirical study of industrial development, adaptation and location. No less important in the Commission's remit, however, has been to foster the interlocking processes of involving participants from less industrialized European countries, centrally-managed economies and developing countries, younger teachers and researchers embarking on their careers, and diffusing to the global community the fruits of both their and the frontier-peoples' findings.

The chapters in this volume are contributed mostly by younger researchers with experience of living and working in developing and peripheral regions and whose concern for the achievements and problems in those areas is of real practical significance. At the same time, the work presented often expresses the state of the art in those countries and regions.

During the 1950s and 1960s and the Second Decade of Development in the 1970s, economists, geographers, regional scientists and international authorities like the United Nations were arguing for the industrialization of less developed countries and areas as a panacea for their poverty, overpopulation and underdevelopment, and as a means of raising people's real living standards everywhere.

With the exceptions of the chapters on the successful newly industrializing countries of South East and East Asia, the broad message of the contributions in this book is one of caution, doubt, even pessimism - about assessing both the achievements of, and the future prospects for, real industrial progress in developing and peripheral regions. The international economic crisis - deepened but not necessarily caused by the oil-price inflation of the 1970s and its multiplier effects - has sharply exposed the weaknesses of previous industrialization attempts and trends in those regions. Not infrequently, unenlightened government policy or State attitudes, bad management or local social structural problems in such regions have exacerbated the recession, prolonged its incidence, or lessened the positive impacts that externally-controlled firms, for all their failings, might have had. A common message is that the developing and peripheral countries and areas exhibit the survival, even growth, of industry mainly as a result of their comparative advantages in lower technology and higher labour-intensive sectors. This seems to underscore the long-term inability of such areas to close the economic gap with the core regions. The exceptions are those economies and regions where strong government has been able to combine political stability with low production costs from large pools of low wage labour in proximity to the most rapidly expanding market and source of foreign investment, namely Japan.

The book falls into several well-defined sections. In the opening chapter, Roger A. Roberge discusses the role of science and technology in economic development from a global perspective while drawing on the experiences of Brazil and Canada, and examines how far the diffusion of capital-intensive, 'appropriate' and foreign-owned technology and their proper adoption can assist in reducing international and interregional disparities.

Chapters 2 to 4 inclusive present contrasting examples of peripheralism in, or adjacent to, developed industrial environments. Peter Wilde casts doubt on the ability of government, industrial organizations and people in Australia to work together with sufficient purpose and co-operation to bring about the industrial restructuring necessary to avoid the peripheralization of the Australian economy within the Pacific Rim. Jean-Paul Gabriele demonstrates how deep-seated isolation interacting with very traditional social structure is hampering significant industrial progress in Haute Marne, France, despite its location between Paris and Lorraine. And Werner Mikus compares the development processes and prospects in border regions in west-central Europe and in the Americas, emphasizing the importance of the specific conditions and their differentiation on both sides of international borders in explaining their diverse industrial experiences.

In chapter 5 Hunya Gabor outlines the processes and patterns of regional change in the centrally-managed east European economies under the conditions of world economic stagnation and search by the east European governments for new ways of stimulating growth and development.

Seven chapters focus on the European 'sunbelt' countries of Spain, Italy and Greece. Antonio Vazquez-Barquero stresses the impacts of the economic crisis on the processes and regional patterns of Spanish industrialization, showing how the country and some of its regions seem to have lost comparative advantages vis-à-vis both newly industrializing and advanced industrial nations. Much the same conclusion is implicit in the chapters on Italy and Greece. Anna Segre outlines how the restructuring of industry in the Biella region of north-west Italy has deepened the local specialization on textile-related activities during the world recession. Sergio Conti examines in depth the quantitative and qualitative loss of industrial vitality in the Mezzogiorno and, with Pasquale Coppola's study of industrial construction in Caserta province north of Naples, concludes that there has been only limited integration between large implanted Italian and foreign enterprises on the one hand and the local small firms on the other. Turning to Greece, in two chapters Evangelia Dokopoulou examines the importance of the role of foreign direct investment in manufacturing in a peripheral EEC host country, Greece, bringing out the pros and cons of multinationals' involvement in local industrialization and analyzing the extent to which their exploitation of Greece as an export platform reflects the country's comparative advantages. Interestingly, she finds evidence of growing forward integration in the aluminium sector between Pechiney and local firms as the internal market expanded and competition in export markets sharpened. Lois Labrianidis studies historical changes in the location of the tobacco industry to demonstrate the complexity of interrelated factors that explain the pattern and process of change.

The final section of the book presents contrasts in the perceptions and assessments of the achievements of industrialization in different Third World contexts. Lea Goldenstein and Stela Goldenstein Carvalhaes graphically portray the bitter environmental and human consequences of capital-intensive industrial development in Cubatao on the coast of Brazil where the social and State power structure has ensured the deprivation of the ordinary workers and their families. In some respects their chapter fittingly follows Labrianidis' who emphasizes the similar low, weak status of the worker. In sharp contrast, the chapters by Mahindar Santokh Singh and Sam Ock Park analyze the patterns and processes underlying the successes of, as well as the constraints on, further progress in the newly industrializing countries in south-east and east Asia. In the last chapter, Li Wen-yan examines the leading regional industrial systems in the Chinese People's Republic and points to some of their problems of modernization. The world awaits the entry of China into the league of newly industrializing economies.

F. E. Ian Hamilton
London, England

CHAPTER 1

PERIPHERAL INDUSTRIALIZATION AND THE TECHNOLOGY TRANSFER PROCESS

Roger A. Roberge

It is only recently that researchers from a variety of disciplines have given more systematic attention to the role of science and technology in economic development. The work of Abramovitz (1956), Schmookler (1966) and Kuznets (1930) has shown that only a small fraction of the total increase in output per worker which has occurred in the American economy since the late 19th century could be explained by increased capital per worker. This 'Residual', as it came to be known, was due not only to technological change but it seems clear that it was certainly an important factor along with education and better allocation of existing factor supplies.

TECHNOLOGY AND THE CHALLENGE OF DEVELOPMENT

The less developed countries (LDCs), having decided to speed the pace of their own development, have adopted strategies which bypass the uncopyable Industrial Revolution in favour of the newer science based technological revolution of the West as is indicated by the preamble of Law #21,617 on technology transfer enacted by the Argentinian government:

> The progress of nations is closely linked with the degree of technical development they have achieved. Hence the extraordinary importance of promoting the technological progress of our country. To achieve it requires a substantial effort, which, if it is to be successful, calls on the one hand for the importation of technologies that are not available in this country, and on the other hand, that they should be accepted and further developed by our

own scientists and researchers.

It is our contention that this transfer of technology has not been adapted to the needs of the importing country as the preamble of the law suggests. As a result, inappropriate forms of production have been introduced which have exacerbated both income and regional disparities. An examination is made of the conditions under which the application of technology to industrial production has taken place in two countries - Canada and Brazil. The first section examines the social and cultural basis for development and argues that underdevelopment in the LDCs is a condition of enduring incapacity to adapt and diffuse technology. Furthermore, it is argued that the inherent complexity of the process as well as the domination of the process by multinational corporations (MNCs) creates a technological dependence on the more developed market economies (MDECs). The next section examines the implications of a dependent technological structure and its relation to patterns of regional development. A final section examines alternatives to patterns of technological dependence for LDCs.

PATTERNS OF TECHNOLOGY TRANSFER: AN HISTORICAL COMPARISON

Since the experience of the MDECs is that science and technology have been major instruments of economic development, it would seem an easy assumption that this would be true also for countries at an earlier stage of economic development. Indeed we might expect that their progress would have been more rapid than has in fact been the case, since the technologies and skills already exist. On the whole, however, and especially in the industrial sector, advance has been slower than desirable. Furthermore, there is evidence to suggest that in many places such benefits as have accrued have been reaped by a privileged minority and concentrated in a few locations. The fact that it has occurred in this fashion is due both to social and political factors as well as the ineffectiveness of the transfer process itself.

The Social Function of Science

In accounting for the failure of science to provide the same benefits to the LDCs as they have in the MDECs, the structuralist view has gained attention.

According to this view, the main weakness of the technological optimist argument is its failure to recognize the way scientific activities relate to the society in which they take place. In a brilliant paper, Herrera (1972) points out that in LDCs science is largely a consumption item whereas in the MDECs it is an investment item. The scientific communities in underdeveloped countries are outposts of advanced country science with very little limited links with the economic and social realities which surround them. In comparison the historical experience of the developed countries is one where the economic demands for innovation influenced the development of science itself.

There are two phases in the development of relations between science and production. In the first, which coincides roughly with the early part of the industrial revolution and the period which preceded it, production technologies were often the source of new scientific discoveries. Later in the second phase which started with the development of the electrical and organic chemical industries, new relationships appeared. The research laboratory became the source of technological innovations and entrepreneurs drew science in closer relationships with production as they began to invest directly in scientific research as a source of potential profit.

Canada, which shares many characteristics with LDCs, has differed in one important respect. Although Canada did import technology, it also had the capacity to adapt this technology to its own requirements. If one looks at the list of important inventions compiled for any one industry, one finds few which have originated in Canada. Yet it cannot be assumed that independent invention was not an important element in the Canadian case. This independent invention was necessary in order properly to apply the technology to new materials, sites and scale of operations. Although some of these adaptations might have been considered obvious by those skilled in the art, they were nevertheless necessary if the industry was to operate at anywhere near the efficiency of the donor country. In many cases, these local adaptations were patented in Canada and as a result we have an historical record of the occurrences which make possible an analysis of the timing, type and location of these adaptive inventions.

This record indicates clearly that the motivation to invention was largely economic. Of the total of 712 inventions patented between 1860 and 1940 in the Canadian pulp and paper industry, a principal components analysis identified a series of groups of invention which reflected the concerns of the industry at that point in time. The dynamic process which lay behind the industry's technical evolution was, following Rosenberg's (1963) terminology, the result of a series of technological disequilibria. A technological disequilibrium occurs when there is a discrepancy between the ability of different steps in a given manufacturing process to equal or exceed expected levels of performance. As a result of this disequilibrium, exploratory inventive activity is initiated. The technical evolution of the pulp and paper industry was seen as stemming from a series of disequilibria which, when technically resolved, created a new technological epoch.

The first indication of the process in the pulp and paper industry is provided by the paper machine which was essentially an attempt to produce paper without a highly skilled labour force. Eventually however an imbalance was created between the paper machine's ability to produce paper and the availability of a source of raw materials which would enable producers fully to utilize the machine's potential. The next technological epoch was defined by its central concern: the development of a commercial process to convert wood into pulp. Given a cheap source of raw materials as well as an expanding market for paper, the concern of the succeeding epoch was the achievement of economies of scale. As a result the new larger and fully integrated mills had a significant impact on the spatial equilibrium of the industry: the newer mills were no longer located near their major markets. Clearly, the problems of production did affect the rate and composition of invention in this industry and as a result it was able to emerge as a world class industry.

The LDCs have not been able to develop this adaptive capacity. This is due to a series of institutional obstacles and can be classified into two groups: [1] cultural obstacles, [2] obstacles connected with the production system.

The cultural obstacles relate to the attitude which is prevalent in many LDCs. These traditional societies mistrust change while in the MDECs, change for change's sake seems almost to be the rule. Poverty also contributes to the poor state of science because of the underdevelopment of human resources. Universities are mistrusted by the political elites of the LDCs as seedbeds of revolutionary change and as a result are kept purposefully weak. In addition, since research and development (R & D) is very expensive relative to basic science, it tends to be rare. In Latin America according to Herrera (1972), the total investment in R & D was approximately 200 million US dollars. These figures can be compared with those for Canada, which spent 400 million US dollars for R & D. Thus Canada, which is near the bottom of the OECD countries in terms of its R & D expenditures, spent twice what all the countries in Latin America spent.

Obstacles related to the Production System

The obstacles related to the production system are due to the fact that the demand for a local technological capability is quite small because of the generally small size of firms. There is also a tendency to downgrade the somewhat inelegant solutions which local innovators may develop in favour of the more sophisticated solutions from abroad. In the short term these imported solutions may be cheaper and quicker to implement than those which have been developed locally, but in the long term, they imply a dependency on the donor country.

Brazil's attempt to develop a pulp and paper industry is a good example of the lack of a technological base for adapting imported technologies. Until the 1960s forestry was popularly regarded as a subject for poets and dreamers. A small handful of men were poorly paid to administer as best they could the vast forest wealth of a Canada-sized nation. It was only in the sixties that forestry schools were set up to train people in this field. On the industrial side an inspection of the patent data at the Institutio Nacional da Propriedad Industrial indicates that few inventions were patented in this area in recent years. During the period when 'import substitution' policies were strongly encouraged, there were attempts reflected in the patent data to develop a paper industry based on a variety of indigenous raw materials ranging from bagasse, rice straw to varieties of softwood. But in recent years these attempts have ceased, and imported varieties of wood, such as eucalyptus and Honduran pine, have largely replaced the local varieties which supply a capital intensive industry concentrated near São Paulo. In turn the recent patent data reflect the advent of this imported technology with large numbers of patents and licences assigned to MNCs. Other independent studies have shown similar direct relationships between the origins of patentees and the level of direct foreign investment. This relationship is examined in more detail in the next section.

TECHNOLOGICAL DEPENDENCE AND THE MULTINATIONAL CORPORATION

Aside from inadequate structures for adapting and generating science, there have been developments in the structure of industrial organization which have made it increasingly difficult for LDCs to generate a self-reliant form of economic development. Canada for instance prior to 1925 depended largely on portfolio investment from British sources and obtained the technology it required by simple franchises or licensing agreements. This type of industrialization did not imply foreign control as long as investors were satisfied with the rate of return of the large multinational corporation. Sunkel (1973), a close associate of Prebisch in the Structuralist School, believes that the technology necessary for development and the means for its continual improvement are lodged in the control of the transnational corporations. As a result international capitalism has become much more highly organized, and governments work closely with these corporations to dominate weaker economies. Research and development is centralized in the home country and foreign users are obliged to buy complete packages of entrepreneurship, management, skills, design technology, financing and market organization at oligopoly or monopoly prices. The result is increasing dependency and a widening of the technological gap.

This situation has arisen because many LDCs have adopted the strategy of welcoming or at least tolerating MNCs in the hope that the transfer of technology will take place. As a corollary they have signed international agreements concerned with technology transfers (Vaitsos, 1972). Today the majority of the members of the International Union for the Protection of Industrial Property are the LDCs of Asia, Africa and Latin America. In signing this agreement, LDCs grant to foreign countries the same patent rights enjoyed by their own nationals. As a result the majority of patents in the LDCs are foreign owned. Ostensibly, the patent rights granted to foreigners have as their objective the stimulation of foreign investment. In fact, as Vaitsos (1972, pp.77-9) points out, the vast majority of these patents have never been worked.

Patents that are neither exploited by the foreigner nor licensed to domestic producers cannot 'transfer technology'. Any transference that takes place is done through contracts relating to know-how, i.e. non-patented technology, and if this technology is secret to the firm, a patent is redundant. If it is not secret then competitors will be willing to sell it and they will be able to do so if its use is not restricted for prospective buyers by a patent held by the original patentee. Thus foreign patents are used to restrain the transfer of technology because it reduces the competition which would otherwise have taken place among foreign sellers of technology (Vaitsos, 1972, p.78).

In some cases local firms are threatened with loss of their licences if they do not agree to takeover by MNCs interested in establishing themselves in LDCs. In some cases patents are taken out in LDCs simply to restrict local producers from engaging in production and thus preserve the market for home producers in the MDECs. In other cases, the protection which the patents provide makes possible monopoly pricing. Vaitsos (1972, p.86) shows that the prices of patented pharmaceutical products imported into Colombia in 1968 ranged from 74 per cent to 5,647 per cent higher than the prices for the same drugs in MDECs.

The implications of international patenting by MNCs can have serious implications for the industrial structure of the host countries. Aside from displacing local concerns, they can be used as means of reducing the level of competition between MNCs in the LDCs. Cross-licensing or patent pooling take place when patent holders (mostly MNCs) 'pool together their patents for competitive products through explicit agreements in order to divide world markets' (Vaitsos, 1972, p.78). An example of such an arrangement was reported to the author in Brazil when Scott Paper granted to Voight Corporation of Germany its patent rights to produce a line of paper tissues.

Forward linkage effects occur when monopoly privileges associated with patented products are applied to areas where patent rights do not hold. Thus patents rights relating to the production of latex can be used to control the industries in which latex will be ultimately used. In addition, the closer the patent is to a final product the more it tends to block the transfer of non-patented technology.

Finally and possibly most important, patents

are not only impediments to the transfer of technology but they can also hamper the adaptation of the technology to the recipient country's requirements. Since patent rights are typically granted for seventeen year periods and since they confer monopoly advantages on foreign producers, there is little chance for domestic producers to familiarize themselves with the process, much less adapt them to their needs. It is conceivable that the abolition of patent rights in certain instances might make it possible for LDCs to adapt these technologies to their own requirements. Italy, in abolishing product and process patents, has been able to develop these technologies and become a technology exporting country in areas where the use of these technologies would have been inaccessible to them if patent rights existed.

Clearly the development of sophisticated technologies has conferred on MNCs certain monopolistic advantages in LDCs which has been detrimental to their own development. It is this aspect of dependence which the structuralist school has singled out for revision. Their critique has had an effect and as a result the Andean Pact countries along with Brazil (Law of December 31, 1971, Code of Industrial Property Law #5772) have put into effect some regulations governing the transfer of technology. The law bans any requirement that the licensee buy capital goods, independent products, raw materials and other technology from any specified source. Clauses restricting the volume of production, prohibiting the use of competing technology, requiring grantbacks of adaptive inventions with respect to the licensed technology and the production of exports of products from the licensee to other countries are all now illegal. This last clause has created a furore with some MNCs since they have long viewed it as their right to act as an exclusive marketing agent for the exports of their foreign subsidiaries (Ebb, 1975). There are however fears that these regulations have been used as negotiation devices, and that countries which are anxious for development may not always apply the laws they have at their disposal. In addition, although these laws do away with some of the excesses of the past, they do little to encourage the development of appropriate technologies for the LDCs. The following section examines the distortion in the spatial structure which the importation of capital intensive technology imposes on the development of LDCs.

TECHNOLOGY TRANSFER AND REGIONAL DISPARITIES

The technological dependence which the inability to modify or disseminate technology produces, along with other domination of the process by large external firms, has implications for the spatial structure of LDCs. One of the most striking changes being wrought in the LDCs is that in less than half a century most of the countries have gone from predominantly rural countries to predominantly urban. In Latin America, which already has a very high overall rate of demographic growth of 2.8 per cent per year, the recent growth rate of the urban sector has been about 7 per cent. In effect this means a doubling of the urban population every ten years. São Paulo itself is projected to have a population of 26.0 million by the year 2000, with Rio de Janeiro adding another 19 million by that year (Beier et al., 1976). Together they account for over two thirds of the industrial employment in Brazil with São Paulo alone accounting for 60 per cent of the total value of Brazilian industrial production although it has only 20 per cent of the population. These disparities in regional development are matched by income disparities where the top 20 per cent of the population earns more than six times the income of the bottom 40 per cent.

To some these disparities are a normal concomitant of the development process. In a report on social development in Latin America, the following rhetorical question is posed.

> The most striking aspect of the social structure of the majority of the Latin American countries is the rapidity of their urbanization process - a seemingly hopeful circumstance, in apparent contradiction with the agricultural bottleneck... Is it not precisely the big city, that is figuratively speaking, the vehicle of modernity (Economic Commission for Latin America, 1963).

Hirschman (1958) also has pointed out that the polarization effects reflected by the high rates of urbanization are 'natural'. In fact he goes further and argues for an unbalanced theory of growth. What is required according to him are massive investments in the capital and technology intensive sectors which are located in the core regions, thus consciously raising the level of regional disparities. No matter how strong or exaggerated the space preferences of the entrepreneurs, once growth takes firm hold in one region, it obviously set in motion certain forces that act in the remaining part. The 'trickling down' effects are the means of transmission of growth to other regions. Among the more important of these effects are the purchases and investments by the growth regions in the less developed region. This will occur according to Hirschman if the two regions are at all complementary. In addition the growth region will absorb some of the disguised unemployment in the lagging regions and thus raise the marginal productivity of labour and per capita consumption in the less fortunate regions. Thus we see the basis for viewing internal migration to the primate city as a modernizing force.

Has it in fact happened the way Hirschman has predicted? An empirical study by Williamson (1965) attempted to identify the pattern of regional disparity in the MDECs as compared to the LDCs. He concludes that regional income inequalities are greater in underdeveloped countries and smaller in developed countries. The time series also indicates increasing regional disparities in the LDCs while they tended to decrease in MDECs. The highest level of disparities for all countries was for Brazil.

Some observers have placed into question models of development such as Hirschman's, which are largely based on the experience of the MDECs. These scholars again point to the dependent character of the development process or as one scholar has put it 'Latin American nations created their dependency at birth' (Schteingart, 1973, p.23). Therefore it cannot be expected, according to the structuralists, that these nations will simply repeat processes that led to the expansion of the societies' originating capitalism which had those other still underdeveloped regions available for their 'take-off' (Kusnetzoff, 1977, p.434). What then are these important differences between the MDECs and LDCs?

Alonso (1968), in discussing industrial location in transitional societies, argues that conditions in large agglomerations tend to be better known than do conditions in the rest of the country and that businessmen making investment decisions are attracted to the place in which uncertainty is minimized. Further, especially in the field of management, conditions in developing countries change rapidly and often unpredictably, as ministries are reorganized, regulations are changed, the cost and availability of funds fluctuate, and relative factor prices change suddenly.

In the transfer of a highly complex technology, another uncertainty is likely to loom as an even more significant factor. The licensee, in establishing a working operation from the patent blueprints, soon discovers that the patents are inadequate. Legal patent descriptions do not show every trick of application and may therefore be practically useless to all but experts in the field. Thus in setting up a branch plant operation, there is a need not only of locally skilled labour supply but also for imported managers and technicians.

In the establishment of an industrial machinery branch plant, foreign investors are likely to minimize these uncertainties by locating or investing in plants which have access to a pool of locally skilled labour. Even in a developed country only the most experienced workmen will regard the clearing of inevitable difficulties of the pilot plant as just another variation within a familiar class of activities. In the transitional societies this kind of labour force is almost always likely to be concentrated in the large metropolitan areas. Universally, imported managers and technicians prefer to live in major cities for obvious personal reasons. Inducements to get them to go to less accessible areas are expensive and likely to be unsuccessful. Needless to say the quality of management and the competence of technicians is likely to be the most important single factor for a branch plant. This is because the uniqueness and fluidity of each situation call for the highest order of personal ability and energy, since prior experience is deficient.

There is also the problem of the transport network. Typically it is not a full lattice covering the entire national territory, but rather tree shaped in which branches converge on a port city or cities. Thus São Paulo and Rio de Janeiro, although apparently peripheral, are nevertheless the most accessible to the nation as a whole. In addition the export and import of products give them an advantage in terms of financial and other high order services which are associated with trans-shipment points.

Some have argued (e.g. Stohr, 1973) in favour of spatial planning to alleviate the problems of the lagging regions. Specifically this type of planning takes the form of intervention in the urbanization process through the selective concentration of development inputs in certain types of centres.

This, it is presumed, will streamline the urban system and encourage a more efficient and rapid diffusion of development outward from the core areas downward through the urban hierarchy. Such a view is associated with the diffusion of modernization approach such as the centre-periphery model, dual societies, regional imbalances and growth poles which when taken together represent a strong effort to limit the development region to its economic spatial determinants. However, as has been pointed out, the problem is also social and cultural. In other words, economic forces cannot function autonomously in space without taking into account the essential factors that condition space - especially the production and dependency relations which have been described in the previous section. Government is sometimes seen as a force which will harmonize and mediate the conflicting interests of regions in the LDCs. This hope, especially in Brazil, has rarely been justified. As we have noted, the transfer of technology by MNCs has been encouraged by that government and even moderate programmes of agrarian reform have not been implemented. Even where attempts at alleviating disparities are made, the results are the same. The SUDENE programme for the north east of Brazil was an ambitious effort of regional development, chiefly industrial, with strong political support since 1959. Various authors agree that in spite, or rather because, of the introduction of highly capital intensive industries, regional disparities were increased, income distribution was not achieved, and a large part of the income generated was returned to the south east of the country. We must conclude therefore that state decisions are reached under strong pressures and control by the dominant sectors of these societies, whose political and economic interests are in constant conflict with the national majorities who are supposed to benefit.

ALTERNATIVES TO DEPENDENCY

The problem therefore may be stated quite simply: what can be done to bring health to the economic life outside the big metropolitan areas where, in Brazil's case, 70 per cent of the population resides! As long as the development effort is concentrated mainly on big cities, where it is easiest to establish new industries, to staff them with managers, and to find finance and markets to keep them going, the competition from these industries will further disrupt and destroy production in the rest of the country, will cause additional unemployment in the smaller import substituting industries, and thus further encourage immigration to the larger centres. How does one then change this depending status?

To solve this problem, one must first accept the fact that there are alternatives to capital intensive industrial development. Hawrylyshyn (1977) has shown that the tendency to use highly capital intensive production techniques is largely the result of non-economic biases. One of these biases is that of the engineer who lived or was trained in the social environment of the MDECs. The standing injunction of this environment - save labour - accords well with the professional instinct of the engineer. If the choice seems inappropriate, it does not naturally occur to the economist to suspect the engineer. In addition there are the biases of the technocrats who argue their own narrow 'professionalism' and are unwilling to entertain low status 'unprofessional' ideas, and insist on 'modern' procedures which utilize 'familiar' methods (Pickett et al., 1974). In the LDCs, the power elites also welcome the modern approach as a 'prestigious facade' which conveniently reinforces the various dependency links keeping the elite in power and the poor, poor.

Empirical evidence from recent studies tends to show that capital intensive techniques are not always necessary. Park finds that many industries offer a high range of choice while Stewart concludes that considerable scope for substitution exists in ancillary activities such as transport, mixing, filling and packing (Park, 1974).

In order to mobilize these forces, however, requires an adaptive technological ability. Since the LDCs have little or no domestically organized and oriented research and development, they have not developed the technology base of skills, knowledge and facilities, and organization upon which further technical progress so largely depends is lacking. No doubt diffusion and unadaptive copying are safer than local invention (Rosenberg, 1963, p.278). Imitation avoids many risks and expenses of testing, and it is therefore less expensive. It has already been shown, however, that invention is a necessary correlate of the diffusion of foreign techology. A country that lacks the kind of technical community found in a well-developed research and development sector lacks a channel to foreign technology. In addition it becomes quite difficult to identify problems clearly and to ask the right questions. Hence, although direct yields to inventive activity may seem low, that is part of the cost of being receptive to diffusion from abroad, of being able to imitate effectively, and in time possibly of being able to improve the technology marginally.

BIBLIOGRAPHY

Abramovitz, M. 'Resource and output trends in the United States since 1870', American Economic Review, vol. 46, 1956, pp.5-23

Alonso, W. Industrial Location and Regional Policy in Economic Development (Center for Planning and Development Research Working Paper 7, Berkeley, 1974)

Beier, G., Churchill, A., Cohen, M. and Renaud, B. 'The Task Ahead for the Cities of The Developing Countries', World Development, vol. 4, no. 5, 1976, p.314

Ebb, L. 'Transfers of Foreign Technology in Latin America: The Birth of Antitrust Law?', Fordham Law Review, vol. 43, 1975, pp.71-9

Economic Commission for Latin America, Report on Social Development in Latin America, May 1, 1963

Hawrylyshyn, O. 'Non-Economic Biases towards Capital Intensive Techniques in Less Developed Countries', Journal of Economics, vol. 37, no. 1-2, 1977

Herrara, A. 'Social Determinants of Science Policy in Latin America', Journal of Development Studies, vol. 9, 1972, pp.19-38

Hirschman, A. O. The Strategy of Economic Development (Yale University Press: New Haven, 1958)

Kusnetzoff, F. 'Spatial Planning and Development in Latin America', Journal of Inter-American Studies and World Affairs, 1977, p.429-44

Kuznets, S. Secular Movements in Production and Prices (Houghton-Mifflin, Boston, 1930)

Pack, H. 'The Employment-Output Trade-Off in LDCs: A Microeconomic Approach', Oxford Economic Papers, 26, 1974, pp.388-404

Pickett, J., Forsyth, D. and McBain, N. 'The Choice of Technology, Economic Efficiency, and Employment in Developing Countries', World Development, vol. 2, 1974

Rosenberg, N. 'Technological Change in the Machine Tool Industry 1840-1910', Journal of Economic

History, vol. 23, 1963
Schmookler, J. Invention and Economic Growth (Harvard University Press, Cambridge, Mass., 1966)
Schteingart, M. Urbanization and Dependency in Latin America (Ediciones SIAP, Buenos Aires, 1973)
Stohr, W. Regional Development, Experiences and Prospects in Latin America (Mouton, The Hague, 1973)
Sunkel, O. 'The Pattern of Latin American Dependence' in V. L. Urquidi and R. Thoys, eds., Latin America in the International Economy (MacMillan, London, 1973)
Vaitsos, C. 'Patents Revisited: Their Function in Developing Countries', Journal of Development Studies, 9, 1972, pp.71-98
Williamson, J. 'Regional Inequality and The Process of National Development: A Description of Patterns' Economic Development and Cultural Change, vol. 13, Part II, 1965, p.84

CHAPTER 2

ECONOMIC RESTRUCTURING AND AUSTRALIA'S CHANGING ROLE IN THE WORLD ECONOMIC SYSTEM

Peter D. Wilde

For more than a decade the Australian industrial system has been undergoing severe upheaval. Most indicators of economic activity now show a much poorer performance than in the early 1970s with unemployment, for example, rising to over 10 per cent for 7 months of 1983 compared with around 2 per cent for at least the quarter century up to 1970. Of particular concern has been the dramatic decline in manufacturing's share of both employment and Gross Domestic Product and the increasing share of the Australian market for manufactured goods which is being taken by imports.

While similar changes are apparent in many other affluent countries, in Australia this restructuring is recognised by many as part of a process which will bring about a reorientation of the nation's role in the global economic system. The author has demonstrated that, for a period dating back from the early 1970s to even before the formation of the Australian federation in 1901, manufacturing in Australia was effectively insulated from the world industrial system, in particular by a very extensive system of tariff protection (Wilde, 1981). Over the past decade, however, circumstances internal and external to Australia have encouraged, and perhaps even forced, the Australian industrial system to become more integrated into the world economy, and in particular to establish a new relationship with the rapidly growing economies of the Pacific region.

What the new orientation will be is far from clear. On the one hand, there are aspirations, evident in a number of government reports commissioned in the 1970s, (for example Australia, Industries Assistance Commission, 1974; Australia, Committee to Advise on Policies for Manufacturing

Industry, 1975; Australian Government, 1977; Australia, Study Group on Structural Adjustment, 1979; Australia, Committee on Australia's Relations with the Third World, 1979; Australia, Senate Standing Committee on Foreign Affairs and Defence, 1980) and at least paid lip-service to by successive governments, to restructure industry in Australia to make it capable of withstanding the pressures of a highly competitive international economy, and to be a base from which Australia could assume a role of political and economic leadership in the Pacific. The basic strategy advocated to effect this restructuring is to allow these Australian industries with high labour costs and low technology to wither away, largely by the removal of tariff protection, while encouraging the manufacture for export of high technology goods at an early stage in the product cycle. On the other hand, however, there are fears that the transformation might be impossible to achieve and that Australia may become an exporter of little more than agricultural and mineral products. Given the changing structure and terms of world trade this in turn could lead to Australia's rapidly losing its place among the most affluent nations of the world.

Change is thus occurring in an environment of uncertainty and insecurity which is engendering an important political debate. This chapter examines some aspects of that debate before reviewing the change in manufacturing which has taken place. In particular it focuses on the brief period since the Labor (social democratic) party was elected to power in 1983 in place of the less reformist Liberal-Country Party coalition.

AUSTRALIAN RESTRUCTURING AND THE WORLD SYSTEM

The new federal Labor government was certainly anxious to pursue new directions for Australia's development and quickly expressed a firm commitment to the three aspects of industrial policy noted above: to become more closely integrated into the economic system of the Pacific region, to reduce dependence on and government support for the weakly competitive industries, and to foster high technology industries and the export of goods and services to the region's industrialising countries. Despite considerable resistance from some left wing party members and some calls for the development of a largely self-contained Australian economy, protected from international competition by even higher tariffs (Crough, 1980; Crough and Wheelwright, 1982), there is more support for the strategy which seeks to revitalise the manufacturing sector and assist parts of it to become internationally competitive and export oriented. This support arises partly from a heightened sense of the vulnerability of an alternative strategy of economic growth based on natural resource exploitation, both because a number of new ventures in mineral and mineral-related activities have failed to come to fruition, including four of the eight aluminium smelters which were planned in the late 1970s (Wilde 1981), and because a widespread drought for three years seriously affected rural exports and profitability, and had well publicised repercussions throughout the economy.

As the recession continues to be felt in Australia well into the 1980s, the rapidly growing economies of the Pacific region have become increasingly viewed as export markets which may help to ensure the growth in the long term of Australia's manufacturing and service industries. However, in order to participate in the growth in the Pacific region, Australia must be willing to absorb greater competition from imports as well as to foster new activities for export. This is because many of the countries concerned, especially the members of the Association of South East Asian Nations (ASEAN), are collectively pressing for reduced protection and improved access to the Australian market in return for access to their markets for Australian mineral, agricultural and manufactured goods. In addition, many of the Asian countries consider bilateral trade balances important, and resist increases in the receipt of Australian exports unless matched by increased imports into Australia of their products, many of which compete with the most heavily protected industries in Australia.

Over the past decade the nations of east and south-east Asia have indeed become increasingly important in both the import and export trade of Australia. This is in contrast to the stability or decline of other countries in Asia, the Pacific and Europe, where the dramatic decline in trade links with the United Kingdom is particularly evident (Table 2.1). While the share of Australia's exports to the nations of south-east Asia has grown more slowly than its share of imports from them, the balance of trade is still markedly in Australia's favour, with exports valued at one-third more than imports in 1982-83. Even so, the increased share of

Table 2.1: Percentage distribution of Australian imports and exports 1972-73 and 1982-83

	IMPORTS		EXPORTS	
	1972-73	1982-83	1972-73	1982-83
Japan	27.9	20.7	31.1	27.0
China, Hong Kong, South Korea, Taiwan	4.7	7.7	4.5	10.7
ASEAN nations [1]	2.5	7.1	6.3	8.9
SUBTOTAL	35.1	35.5	41.9	46.6
South Asia	1.3	0.8	1.1	1.4
Selected Middle East nations [2]	2.4	8.5	1.2	4.9
Papua New Guinea	0.6	0.3	2.1	2.3
New Zealand	3.2	3.1	5.2	5.2
USA	20.9	21.9	12.2	10.2
UK	18.6	6.7	9.7	5.3
Rest of EEC [3]	13.9	13.4	11.1	8.8
All Other	14.0	9.8	15.5	15.3
TOTAL	100.0	100.0	100.0	100.0

[1] Indonesia, Malaysia, Philippines, Singapore, Thailand

[2] Iran, Iraq, Kuwait, Oman, Qatar, Saudi Arabia, Syria, United Arab Emirates, Yemen

[3] Belgium, Denmark, France, West Germany, Greece, Ireland, Italy, Luxembourg, Netherlands

Sources: Australian Bureau of Statistics *Imports, Australia: Annual Summary Tables* (Catalogue no. 5426.0), Australian Bureau of Statistics, Canberra, various issues;

Australian Bureau of Statistics *Exports, Australia: Annual Summary Tables* (Catalogue no. 5424.0), Australian Bureau of Statistics, Canberra, various issues.

Australia's market for manufactured goods which is being met by imports (Table 2.2) is creating such significant problems for manufacturers and their workforces that there are intense pressures to resist change and preserve a manufacturing system insulated from the world by high tariffs.

The trading relations with countries in the Pacific region are constantly changing, not least because of the variations in industrial structure between the newly industrialising countries themselves and the dynamics of their structural change (Edwards, 1982; Linge, 1979a). This change is complex and has vital, but poorly appreciated, repercussions on Australia. For example, pressure is being exerted on Japan, by high energy costs, increasing protectionism in many of its export markets, decreasing demand and the competitive challenges from emerging producers, to shift towards more knowledge and skill intensive activities. As a result, there are very poor prospects of much growth in Japan's demand for minerals and energy, the supply of which is a major, if recently declining, part of Australia's export trade. In addition, the shift in the industrial and export structures of South Korea and Taiwan from light labour-intensive manufactures such as textile products, footwear and electronic products, to products incorporating relatively more raw materials and capital, such as iron and steel, shipbuilding, motor vehicles and metal goods, threatens both the domestic and any export markets of these heavily protected sectors of the Australian economy. Meanwhile textile, clothing, and footwear manufacturers in Australia continue to face penetration of their domestic market, but with Malaysia and most recently Indonesia joining, and beginning to replace, the longer-term suppliers of Hong Kong, Singapore and Taiwan.

Thus the desire to integrate more closely with the Pacific region, both economically and politically, provides a pragmatic political reason for encouraging structural change, difficult and slow though the implementation of this may be. In addition, however, there is substantial evidence that in the present circumstances tariff protection is not serving the Australian economy well. A study of the period between 1968-69 and 1981-82 demonstrated that the most highly protected industries compare very badly with less protected industries in terms of their growth of gross product, their levels of investment, their rates of employment loss and their performance in export and

Table 2.2: Australian imports as a percentage of domestic sales

Industry	1968-69	1973-74	1977-78
Food, beverages and tobacco	4.8	6.1	7.7
Textiles	32.8	40.3	40.3
Clothing and footwear	7.3	17.0	22.8
Wood, wood products and furniture	8.1	10.7	10.9
Paper, paper products and printing	17.1	16.3	17.0
Chemical, petroleum and coal products	24.8	28.4	33.2
Non-metallic mineral products	9.0	9.3	10.4
Basic metal products	7.7	9.2	8.2
Fabricated metal products	8.7	8.4	11.3
Transport equipment	28.2	29.3	30.3
Other machinery and equipment	33.1	35.1	45.4
Miscellaneous manufacturing	20.7	23.0	27.0
Total manufacturing	17.6	19.5	22.9
Rural	n.a.	5.4	10.4
Mining	25.5	13.0	18.3

Source: Industries Assistance Commission (1981) Approaches to General Reductions in Protection, Information Paper No. 3. Australian Government Publishing Service, Canberra.

domestic markets (Australia, Industries Assistance Commission, 1983). In addition, high levels of protection give little incentive to firms to invest in research and development or to adopt new technology (Australia, Industries Assistance Commission, 1982; Slatyer, 1983).

Nevertheless, despite the desire to be actively involved in substantially restructuring the economy, the Labor government was soon faced with political realities which make it all but impossible to effect any restructuring, however desirable, while unemployment, inflation, and public sector deficits remain high (Kahn and Pepper, 1980). The speed of collapse of sectors vulnerable to competition is inevitably greater than the speed with which new sectors can be built up, especially in terms of employment. Moreover, those employers and employees disadvantaged by structural change are usually more easily identified, organised and vocal than those who gain. Adversely affected regions are also very evident and politically sensitive, especially as no effective policy of regional assistance has been developed in Australia, despite the recommendations - usually in very general terms - of several advisers (for example Australia, Study Group on Structural Adjustment, 1979; Australia, Industries Assistance Commission, 1981). In large measure this is because of the jealously guarded rights and responsibilities of the three tiers of government within the Australian federation which are particularly sensitive in matters of regional development. Groups and regions adversely affected by structural change thus exert considerable political pressure to preserve existing jobs or profits and the protection of the domestic market from imports tends to be extended rather than cut back. Thus for example in 1982 the previous government succumbed to lobbying from those opposed to increased competition when it decided not to proceed with a recommended general reduction of tariffs (Australia, Industries Assistance Commission, 1983). More generally, it has been argued that the 'bold gesture' by the previous Labor government in 1973 of imposing a general 25 per cent cut in tariffs made it difficult to discuss further reduction in tariff protection in any forum for many years (Jones, 1983).

Thus, despite well-rehearsed arguments against tariffs and the expressed wish of governments to reduce their level, protection of domestic producers actually increased in the early 1980s. Increasingly instruments of 'administered protection', notably import quotas and regulations, are used rather than the more publicly reviewed and internationally visible tariffs (Australia, Industries Assistance Commission, 1983). It is estimated that in 1977-78 protection represented an effective subsidy by Australian consumers of almost $4000 million. Between that year and 1982 the average rate of effective protection for manufacturing industry as a whole increased from 23 to 26 per cent, for clothing and footwear from 142 to 204 per cent, and for motor vehicles and parts from 88 to 124 per cent. Overall between 1977 and 1982 the real net subsidy equivalent afforded by all forms of protection increased by 10 per cent (Australia, Industries Assistance Commission, 1983).

Decisions by the Labor government early in its term of office with regard to two industries are particularly noteworthy (Australia, Industries Assistance Commission, 1984). In August 1983 a steel industry plan was announced for Australia's monopoly producer, the Broken Hill Propriety Company Limited (BHP). Extensive protection, with import restrictions and bounties on production of up to $70 million a year, was granted for a period of eight years to help the industry regain its internationally competitive position - a task which may be very difficult given the restructuring taking place in the steel industry at a global scale and the competition referred to above from countries such as South Korea. The social and political concerns of the government are readily apparent in the undertakings made as part of the plan by BHP not to make more workers redundant or to close any of the three integrated steel plants, both of which would almost certainly have happened but for government intervention. On the other hand, the possibly conflicting desire of government to have an internationally competitive industry is apparent in the requirement for BHP to make substantial investment during the term of the plan.

Secondly, the troubled car industry has seen yet another change of government policy, although on this occasion there is an apparent toughening of attitude towards the heavily protected industry. The latest motor vehicle plan, which came into force in 1985, aims to create a stable and competitive industry by 1992, primarily by reducing the number of models produced in Australia from 13 to 6 or less, thereby probably reducing the number of local manufacturers from five to no more than three. But despite this plan for the long term reorganisation of the industry, additional import quotas are, in the short term, protecting the domestic producers of some types of vehicle from the need to rationalise. In this case the concern was to prevent immediate job losses in South Australia where the heaviest concentration of the industry occurs. At least one commentator found the plan too weak and would prefer to see the industry forced to restructure rapidly by being exposed to genuine international competition (Australian Financial Review, 30 May 1984: 12), while many fear - or hope - that future governments will not maintain their resolve to restructure the industry when factory closures, retrenchments and company losses begin to be felt. Clearly, any Australian government is faced with a conflict between being foresighted and encouraging industrial restructuring on the one hand and avoiding the short term consequences for some firms' employment and profits that such a policy must have on the other.

Despite the considerable attention paid to protection, in the form of tariffs, bounties, import quotas and the like, it is in fact only one of numerous forms of intervention by governments, oligopolistic corporations and labour unions which tend to preserve the status quo in Australian manufacturing, and in particular to discriminate against exporters and the export development which government is now so anxious to promote (Edwards, 1982; Linge, 1985). Examples of other types of intervention are the shipping regulations and company agreements requiring Australian crews and the foreign exchange regulations which discourage long term offshore warehousing. The present tax structure, which relies on production based taxes, such as payroll, income and company taxes also make exports difficult by raising prices, though proposals currently being discussed (mainly for reasons unrelated to exports) to move towards consumption oriented taxes, such as a sales or value added tax, may ameliorate this. Often too, the monetary and fiscal tools used to manage the domestic economy conflict with the goal of export development, by raising domestic interest rates and discouraging firms from attempting the often risky, low-profit credit-intensive activity of exporting (Edwards, 1982), while the federal structure itself, with the conflicts of interest among the states and between them and the Commonwealth often leads to inefficiency and resistance to change (Linge, 1979b; Wilde, 1981). Unless there is a wholehearted commitment to export development by government, and attention, and perhaps primacy, given to the needs of exporters rather than the needs of the domestic economy, then the restructuring of Australia's economy with a sound export base and its integration with the Pacific region is unlikely to occur. The contrast between Australia and its burgeoning south east Asian competitors in this regard is striking.

While, as seen, the problems associated with reducing tariff protection are immense, those of tackling the intricate and diffuse network of other interventions which inhibit exports have scarcely yet even been thought about in Australia. One exception to this is found in the financial sector. Like manufacturing, the financial system has been beset by protection and regulation which has encouraged it to be remarkably inflexible in its practices and limited in its overseas activities. Recently, however, following reports commissioned by successive governments (Australia, Committee of Inquiry into the Australian Financial System, 1981 and 1984) which strongly recommended deregulation, a start was made to inject more competition, efficiency and innovation into the financial system. On the one hand, many restrictive regulations, such as those controlling bank charges and interest payments, have been removed leading to more competition among banks and between bank and non-bank institutions. On the other hand, in 1984 regulation of foreign exchange transactions was reduced when over 40 non-bank firms were licensed to join the 9 existing banks in this activity, and in 1985 foreign banks were, for the first time, allowed to trade in Australia. At the time of writing 16 such banks, chosen from over 40 applicants and representing some of the world's largest banks, have begun detailed licence negotiations. The 16 are involved in many overseas markets of interest to Australia, with 6 based in the Asia-Pacific area, 6 in North America and 4 in Europe. Moreover, most notably in the case of Japan, a principle of reciprocity has been established by which all 4 major Australian banks will henceforth be able to trade in Japan.

As with manufacturing, a question being asked of the finance sector is whether the reforms have come early enough or gone far enough, given that Singapore and Hong Kong, for instance, have firmly established banking facilities, which are frequently used to float major Australian loans. The series of mergers which took place among Australian banks, reducing the number from 7 in 1979 to 4 in 1983 (Taylor and Hirst, 1983 and 1984) and the acquisition in 1984 of the British bank, Grindlays, by the Australia and New Zealand Banking Corporation which thereby markedly extended its overseas interests in the Pacific region (Hirst and Taylor, 1985), suggest that the Australian banks are taking the challenge of deregulation seriously. But while the direction of intended policy is clear, and important moves have been made despite strong resistance from the left wing of the government party, these moves are clearly insufficient by themselves to fulfil the objective of making Australia a major international financial centre. Indeed the critics from the left and from within the domestic banking system may be proved right and Australia's financial institutions may become powerless pawns in global dealings.

While the apparent severity, in the long term, of the car industry plan, and the easing of banking regulations may be regarded as important signals of a more outward looking economic policy, the general public has probably been made aware of the shift in government thinking as a result of the well-publicised call by the new government for technological advance in industry, both as a means of securing exports and meeting competition in the domestic market.

It is well established that Australia is very dependent technologically on advances made elsewhere and that indigenous development of innovation is consequently very difficult (Fagan, McKay and Linge, 1981; Australia, Industries Assistance Commission, 1983). This is partly because of intra-organisational transfers of technology within foreign owned corporations in a country which probably has the Western world's second highest level of foreign ownership after Canada (Cooper, 1982), and the consequently low, and recently declining, employment in industrial research and development within Australia (Australian Bureau of Statistics, 1983). In addition, the small size of the domestic market and high levels of protection discourage innovation (Australia, Industries Assistance Commission, 1982), while the poor links between the creditable pure science sector of the universities and research organisations on the one hand and the enterprises responsible for industrial innovation on the other reduce commercial applications of scientific developments (Slatyer, 1983). Thus, while Australia is responsible for some 2 per cent of the world's scientific knowledge, it is responsible for only 0.7 per cent of the patents on which commercial innovation is based, only 0.3 per cent of exports of technology intensive goods, and it ranks 23 out of 24 OECD nations in the ratio of the dollar value of technology intensive exports to imports (Australia, Department of Science and Technology, 1983). As a corollary, its export trade remains heavily reliant on crude and minimally processed products of the rural and mining sectors with few gains made over the past decade in the export of technology intensive manufactured products

(Table 2.3)

The Study Group on Structural Adjustment (1979) and the Myer report into technological change (Australia, Committee of Inquiry into Technological Change in Australia, 1980), despite their many weaknesses, both reinforced the desirability of an industrial development strategy which would keep Australia abreast of world technological development and which encouraged specialisation in the manufacture of capital and skill intensive goods for export to the large, dynamic markets of Asia. Although lip-service was paid to these ideas, the debate remained limited and very few policy initiatives based on the reports' recommendations were developed under the Liberal-Country Party government. However, soon after the Labor government came to power, the Minister for Science and Technology, Barry Jones, did an extraordinary job of raising public awareness of and stimulating discussion about technological development. At the same time, the new government introduced various measures to encourage technological development in Australia, for example making grants available for the development of particular innovations, funding technological development proposals in structural adjustment programmes such as the steel and car industry plans referred to above, and establishing a source of venture capital through the Australian Industry Development Corporation to assist the formation of high technology enterprises. In addition, in 1983 the government called a national technology conference with the primary aim of bringing about a 'shock of recognition' of the range and speed of the technological revolution overseas, of Australia's dismal participation in it, and of the urgent need for rapid technological development (Jones, 1983). Subsequently a draft national technology strategy was released (Australia, Department of Science and Technology, 1984) with proposals to increase participation in advanced education and retraining and to adopt, exploit and develop new technology. While the draft strategy was laudable in its aim, albeit more nationalistic and growth-oriented than the Minister's earlier more academic treatment of employment prospects and policies in the post-industrial era (Jones, 1982), its outline proposals for 48 long term and 61 short term actions over the 13 elements of the strategy indicate the huge and wide ranging change needed. It is most unlikely that the necessary reforms can be made against the likely resistance of other

Table 2.3: Commodity structure of Australian exports 1972-73 and 1982-83

Commodity Group	Per Cent	
	1972-73	1982-83
<u>Food, Beverages and Tobacco</u>		
Food of animal origin	17.9	12.2
Other food, beverages and tobacco	14.7	13.8
<u>Crude Inedible Materials</u>		
Metalliferous ores and scrap	11.5	17.5
Mineral fuels	5.6	21.4
Other inedible crude materials (including wool, hides, timber and woodchips)	23.3	11.7
<u>Chemicals and Related Products</u>	4.5	2.1
<u>Manufactured Goods Classified by Material</u>		
Iron and steel	2.9	2.3
Nonferrous metal	4.7	5.8
Manufactures of metal	1.0	0.8
Non metallic manufactures	2.0	1.8
<u>Machinery and Transport Equipment</u>		
Industrial machinery	2.3	2.3
Office, communications and electrical machinery	1.0	1.3
Transport equipment	4.8	1.7
<u>Miscellaneous Manufactured Articles</u>	1.6	2.2
<u>Unclassified</u>	2.2	3.1
Total	100.0	100.0

<u>Source</u>: Australian Bureau of Statistics <u>Exports, Australia, Annual Summary Tables</u>, Catalogue no. 5424.0, various issues.

government instrumentalites and the many entrenched interest groups opposed to different components of the proposed change. Indeed, the revised draft of the technology strategy, due to be published in mid-1985 after a series of delays, will almost certainly carry the caveat that its proposals are not necessarily government policy. In the meantime, Jones has lost his responsibilities for the technology portfolio, which has been added to that of industry and commerce. Although criticised by some (Organisation for Economic Cooperation and Development, 1985) this move was intended to increase the capacity of the enlarged department to encourage industrial restructuring.

The review of Australian science and technology by the Organisation for Economic Cooperation and Development (Organisation for Economic Cooperation and Development, 1985), added to the debate on appropriate technological goals for Australia by recommending in particular the transfer of new technology into the high value added parts of Australian agriculture and fisheries. The pharmaceutical industry was also seen as capable of development, especially if it took advantage of existing strengths and specialisms in Australia, for example by developing products for protection against tropical diseases of humans, animals and plants.

The review also recommended that an appropriate next step in developing a technology strategy was to undertake a series of sectoral studies, in order to establish the great diversity of technological needs. To improve the poor links referred to earlier between pure science and commercial applications it recommended that the Commonwealth Scientific and Industrial Research Organisation (CSIRO) and the potential beneficiaries from their research should be brought closer together by the latter having a greater responsibility for both the funding and the goal setting of the organisation.

While these proposals to introduce high technology industry to Australia and to restructure Australian industry slowly proceed, many companies are in fact increasing Australian integration with the Pacific region by 'going offshore' and establishing manufacturing and service activities in other countries. Between 1969-70 and 1979-80 the distribution of Australian direct investment changed markedly. In the former year 80 per cent of investment was in Papua New Guinea, New Zealand and UK, while by 1979-80 their share of a much increased investment (at current prices) had dropped to 50 per cent and investment in the USA and ASEAN countries had risen to 25 per cent (Waters, Tucker and Bennett, 1982). Just over half of the 226 overseas affiliates of Australian based companies covered by a survey undertaken by the Bureau of Industry Economics were in developed countries and just over half were involved in manufacturing, although direct investment in service activities was increasing more rapidly (Australia, Bureau of Industry Economics, 1983 and 1984). The ASEAN countries were notable for their higher share of affiliates involved in manufacturing (almost 70 per cent of the 48 affiliates involved) and/or the share of affiliates' sales to the host country (75 per cent) rather than to Australia (4 per cent) or other countries (21 per cent). The most frequently noted reason for establishing affiliates in these countries was the growth of the host market (Australia, Bureau of Industry Economics, 1983). Thus, while some companies undoubtedly establish operations in cheap labour countries with the intention of supplying the Australian market, this practice appears not to be particularly widespread. Although direct overseas investment from Australia is of growing importance and is increasingly directed at both developed and less developed countries in the Pacific region, the total outflow of investment funds is still low compared to the inflow (less than one-tenth between 1974 and 1978), and there is evidence of Australia's being used as a stepping stone to peripheral economies by global corporations (Taylor and Thrift, 1981a).

MANUFACTURING CHANGE WITHIN AUSTRALIA

From a peak of 1.3 million in 1973-74 manufacturing employment in Australia declined by 170,000 persons over the next five years and then fluctuated at levels between 1.165 and 1.185 million until its dramatic decline to 1,082,500 in 1982-83 (Figure 2.1). Preliminary figures available after this chapter went to press show that the decline in manufacturing employment continued into 1984. Excluding employment in single enterprise establishments with fewer than four employed, total manufacturing employment in Australia fell by 4.0 per cent from 1,052,905 in 1982-83 to 1,011,947 in 1983-84. Table 2.4 shows the spatial impact of this.

The relative decline has also been substantial and in the early 1980s manufacturing accounted for less than 18 per cent of total employment and contributed scarcely 19 per cent of GDP compared

Table 2.4: EMPLOYMENT IN MANUFACTURING ESTABLISHMENTS[1] 1982-83 AND 1983-84 [2]

States	Persons Employed ('000)			
	1982-83	1983-84	Change	
			No.	per cent
New South Wales	384.6	364.7	-19.9	-5.2
Victoria	363.0	352.8	-10.2	-2.8
Queensland	114.7	111.3	- 3.4	-3.0
South Australia	95.9	91.3	- 4.6	-4.8
Western Australia	65.0	61.8	- 3.2	-4.9
Tasmania	24.1	23.4	- 0.7	-2.9
Northern Territory	2.4	2.4	0.0	0.0
Australian Capital Territory	3.2	3.3	0.1	3.1
	1052.9	1011.0	-41.9	-4.0

Notes: [1] Excludes single establishment manufacturing enterprises with fewer than four employed.
[2] Preliminary figures.

Source: Australian Bureau of Statistics Census of Manufacturing Statistics: Summary of Operations by Industry Subdivision, Australia, 1983-84, Preliminary Catalogue no. 8201.0.

with 28 per cent of both in 1967. Rich (1981) argues that an accelerating rate of productivity increase has not been a primary cause of declining employment levels. Nevertheless, the introduction of new technology and the bias of structural change against labour-intensive industries make most commentators certain that a substantial increase in manufacturing employment is unlikely, whatever Australia's economic future.

Over the 1970s there were substantial changes within manufacturing as production shifted from the highly protected industries mainly producing consumer goods for the domestic market towards activities associated with the exploitation for

Figure 2.1 Manufacturing employment in Australia 1968-69 to 1982-83

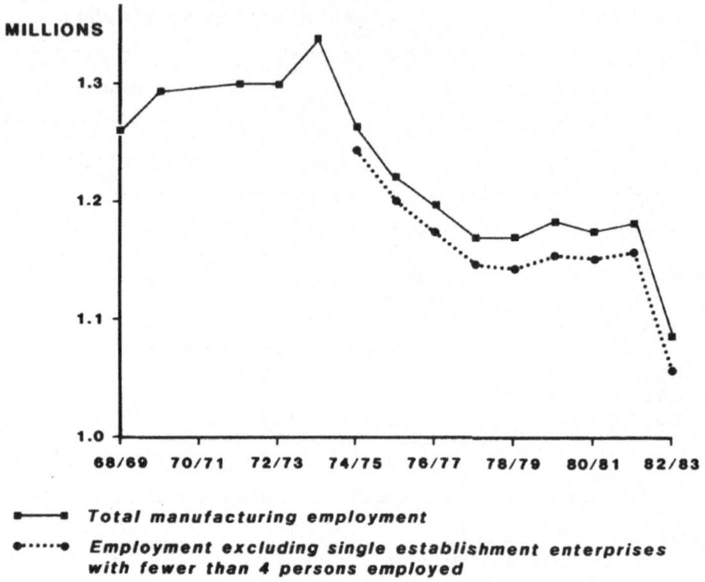

Notes: a) For years after 1973-74 total employment is derived by adding data for average employment over the year for establishments employing four or more workers to figures of end of year employment for single establishment enterprises employing less than four workers.

b) From 1977-78 a revision of the Australian Standard Industrial Classification modified the definition of manufacturing. The change resulted in a reduction in employment classified as manufacturing of about 1,500 persons.

Source: Australian Bureau of Statistics, Manufacturing Establishments: Summary of Operations by Industry Class, Australia, various issues.

export of Australia's mineral and energy resources. Thus textiles, clothing and footwear experienced sharp declines in their share of employment while basic metals, fabricated metal products and food increased their share over the period (Table 2.5). Gibson and Horvath (1983) conclude that in the present restructuring crisis one industry in Australia (petroleum) is industrialising, thirteen are rationalising and nine are deindustrialising.

Different regions react to restructuring at different rates, at different times and in different ways. As a result there is a constantly changing pattern in the areas which are performing better or worse than others. Thus, although the broad distribution of manufacturing employment changed little through the years of decline and remains spatially very concentrated (Figure 2.2), important relative changes have occurred. Wadley and Rich (1983) conclude that decentralisation, as well as occurring on an interstate level seen in the steady decline in the proportion of manufacturing employment located in the major industrial state of New South Wales, is also occurring at other scales. Thus, while the five mainland state capitals continue to account for about three-quarters of all manufacturing employment, the dominance of Melbourne and Sydney is gradually declining, with a combined share of total employment of 55.3 per cent in 1982-83 compared with almost 60 per cent a decade earlier. All state capitals lost mnaufacturing employment between 1973-84 and 1982-83, though at much lower rates in Perth and Brisbane. While the remainder of every state fared better than its respective capital during this period, only the Northern Territory, and non-metropolitan Queensland and Western Australia, countered the national trend and recorded employment gains (Table 2.6). This small measure of decentralisation from the south-eastern core is clearly associated, directly and indirectly, with mineral development. Wadley and Rich (1983) demonstrate that intra-state decentralisation is part of a longer term trend which has persisted through boom and recession. Despite this, some highly specialised, non-metropolitan industrial centres, notably the steel producing cities of Newcastle and Wollongong in New South Wales, have been severely affected by the recession (Stilwell, 1980).

Wadley and Rich also show that within each of the major metropolitan areas geographic dispersion of manufacturing is occurring with the inner city

Table 2.5: Percentage contribution of individual industries to Australian manufacturing employment 1968-69 to 1983-84

Industry	1968-69	1973-74	1974-75[a]	1976-77	1977-78[b]	1980-81	1983-84[c]
Food, beverages, tobacco	14.65	15.25	15.81	16.66	17.07	15.96	16.71
Textiles	4.65	4.08	3.47	3.33	3.25	3.21	3.15
Clothing, footwear	9.68	8.22	7.25	7.15	7.09	6.83	7.04
Wood, wood products, furniture	6.37	6.40	6.27	6.62	6.56	6.86	6.91
Paper, paper products, printing	8.05	8.07	8.28	8.28	8.49	8.90	9.86
Chemical, petroleum, coal products	5.06	5.01	5.14	5.14	5.39	5.21	5.58
Non-metallic mineral products	4.05	4.14	4.09	4.05	4.05	3.99	3.78
Basic metal products	7.00	7.33	7.89	7.98	7.75	8.38	7.64
Fabricated metal products	8.94	8.89	8.85	8.75	9.02	9.81	9.45
Transport equipment	11.46	11.87	11.84	12.18	11.79	11.16	11.53
Other machinery and equipment	14.00	14.87	15.59	14.30	14.01	14.06	12.54
Miscellaneous manufacturing	5.18	5.86	5.52	5.55	5.54	5.62	5.81
Manufacturing	100.00	100.00	100.00	100.00	100.00	100.00	100.00

Notes:
a From 1974-75, excludes employment in establishments with fewer than four employees
b From 1977-798, based on the revised (1978) version of the Australian Standard Industrial Classification
c Preliminary figures

Source: Wadley and Rich (1983) p.16 and Australian Bureau of Statistics, Manufacturing Establishments: Summary of Operations by Industry Class, Australia various issues.

Figure 2.2 Distribution of manufacturing employment in Australia 1973-74 and 1982-83

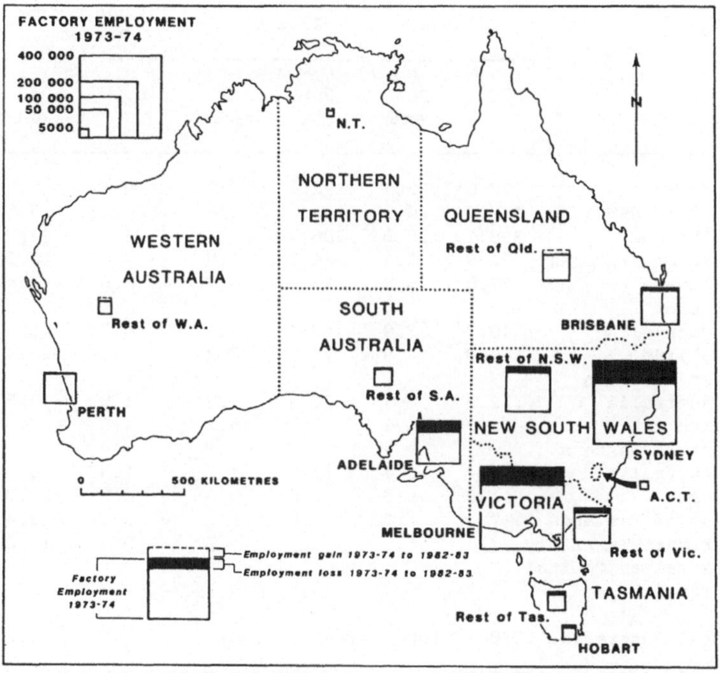

Source: Australian Bureau of Statistics, Census of Manufacturing Establishments: Details of Operations and Small Area Statistics, various issues.

Table 2.6: Regional distribution of manufacturing employment Australia 1973-74 and 1982-83

	1973-74		1982-83		Change in Period	
	'000	Per cent	'000	Per cent	'000	Per cent
Sydney	397.0	29.7	292.6	27.0	-104.4	-26.2
Rest of NSW	119.2	8.9	103.0	9.5	- 16.2	-13.5
Melbourne	398.1	29.8	306.7	28.3	- 91.4	-23.0
Rest of Victoria	71.8	5.4	64.0	5.9	- 7.8	-10.9
Brisbane	77.8	5.8	72.0	6.7	- 5.8	- 7.4
Rest of Queensland	40.7	3.0	47.4	4.4	6.7	16.5
Adelaide	105.8	7.9	77.9	7.2	- 27.9	-26.4
Rest of South Australia	22.3	1.7	20.4	1.9	- 1.9	- 8.5
Perth	58.2	4.3	56.7	5.2	- 1.5	- 2.6
Rest of Western Australia	9.7	0.7	11.0	1.0	1.3	13.4
Hobart	11.9	0.9	9.0	0.8	- 2.9	-24.3
Rest of Tasmania	19.6	1.5	15.8	1.5	- 3.8	-19.4
Northern Territory	2.3	0.2	2.6	0.2	0.3	13.0
Australian Capital Territory	3.7	0.3	3.4	0.3	- 0.3	- 8.1
Total Australia	1338.1	100.0	1082.5	100.0	-255.6	-19.1

Source: Australia Bureau of Statistics Census of Manufacturing Establishments: Small Area Statistics, various issues

areas experiencing substantial job losses and the other suburbs net gains, albeit tempered by some losses in recent years. For example, in Sydney five inner city local government areas lost over 67,000 manufacturing jobs between 1968-69 and 1980-81, while in the same period the outer suburbs gained 16,600 jobs and areas on the metropolitan fringe grew at an even greater rate (Cardew and Rich, 1982; Rich, 1982). Similar trends are identifiable in Melbourne (Linge, 1979b) and Adelaide (Robins, 1981).

Another important change has been the shift in balance between Melbourne and Sydney. At the end of the Second World War Sydney was clearly Australia's major industrial centre with 262,000 employees, almost one-fifth more than Melbourne (Linge, 1979b). Over the next thirty years, however, manufacturing employment increased more rapidly in Melbourne so that by 1973-74 that city, for the first time, had more manufacturing employees than Sydney. During the recession which has followed both have lost substantial numbers of factory workers (Figure 2.2) but Melbourne has continued to fare better than Sydney. Rich (1981) demonstrates that these differences are not explained by differences in employment mix and suggests that the supply and cost of industrial land and the policies of state and local government have been less favourable in Sydney. In addition, recent company restructuring on a national scale has tended to disadvantage Sydney. Despite this, Sydney has grown substantially over the past decade as a centre of finance and corporate control. It is also the location of the head offices of a more diversified and dynamic set of firms and this seems to be enabling it to take over from Melbourne the position of commercial leadership (Taylor and Thrift, 1981a and 1981b). As restructuring and the decline of manufacturing employment continues, performance in management and service activities is likely to be the major determinant of employment levels. In this, Sydney appears certain to be dominant for many years to come.

RESTRUCTURING BY DESIGN OR BY DEFAULT?

A number of writers have applied neo-Marxist interpretations to the crisis of restructuring which besets Australian manufacturing. Taylor and Thrift (1981a) follow Wallerstein (1976) in applying a world system perspective as potentially very useful indeed despite its weaknesses. In this approach Australia is classed, along with a bewilderingly diverse range of countries, as a member of the semi-periphery which helps articulate the relationships between core and periphery in the chain of extraction of surplus value and the generation of unequal development. In relation to the core these countries serve some of the functions of the periphery as they are less technologically advanced and may be a location of profitable investment for producing goods late in the product cycle (Fagan, McKay and Linge, 1981). They are also states descending or ascending the economic ladder, some of which are likely to make gains in periods of crisis. This serves as a demonstration effect and helps to maintain the acceptability and stability of the system as a whole. While questioning whether the terms should be identified with national boundaries, Taylor & Thrift (1981a) found evidence in Australian investment data for a chain relationship between core, semi-peripheral and peripheral economies.

In a more classically Marxist approach, Gibson and Horvath (1983) see the restructuring crisis as resulting from the competition between the emerging global submode of production and the firmly established but crisis-ridden monopoly submode. Aided by recent technological developments in telecommunications and transport, global capital is considerably more mobile than nationally based monopoly capital and can use uneven world development to its advantage. Gibson and Horvath relate the failure of Australian governments to intervene effectively in the economy to the lack of clear leadership by any one dominant fraction of capital. Hence piecemeal, ambiguous and contradictory policies result. Stilwell (1982) emphasises that the general economic imperative of capital accumulation is pre-eminent and that spatial patterns are only varying manifestations of this. There are no spatial imperatives per se causing, for example, convergence or divergence of regional incomes.

While the particular perspective varies, these and other commentators are in clear agreement that the problems in Australian manufacturing today cannot be ascribed to simple, isolated causes such as the domestic industrial structure that developed in the era of protection before the 1970s or the current pressure exerted on Australian manufacturing from Asian imports. Rather the crisis is brought about by complex changes taking place within the world system as a whole, largely caused by the changing strategies of transnational corporations. Because Australia has a dependent semi-peripheral status for trade, investment and technology, it has little autonomy to adjust. An understanding of Australia's development at national or regional scales can only be achieved by a thorough analysis of its international setting and relationships.

There can be no doubt that Australia is undergoing the most intense and significant economic upheaval in its history. The role that Australia is to play in the world economy is in the balance. On the one hand is the possibility of renewed growth and prosperity based on the development of internationally competitive high techology manufacturing and service sectors and close integration with the rapidly emerging Pacific region. On the other hand is the threat of a narrow and vulnerable export economy overdependent on minimally processed agricultural and mining products. Given the evolution of the Australian industrial system to date, the short-term perspective of much of its politics, the lack of informed debate about appropriate directions for Australia to follow (Linge, 1985) and the halting steps taken to face and initiate change over the past decade, it is difficult to see Australian governments, institutions and people working together effectively to bring about that potential prosperity in an economy restructured by design rather than by default.

REFERENCES

Australia, Bureau of Industry Economics (1983), Australian Direct Investment in the ASEAN Countries. Information Bulletin 4, Australian Government Publishing Service, Canberra.

Australia, Bureau of Industry Economics (1984) Australian Direct Investment Abroad: Effects on the Australian Economy. Research Report No. 14, Australian Government Publishing Service, Canberra.

Australia, Committee of Inquiry into Technology Change in Australia (1980) Report. Australian Government Publishing Service, Canberra, 4 vols.

Australia, Committee of Inquiry into the Australian Financial System (1981) Final Report. Australian Government Publishing Service, Canberra, 5 vols. (The Campbell Report)

Australia, Committee of Inquiry into the Australian Financial System (1984) Report of the Review Group, December 1983. Australian Government Publishing Service, Canberra. (The Martin Report)

Australia, Committee on Australian Relations with the Third World (1979) Australia and the Third World. Australian Government Publishing Service, Canberra.

Australia, Committee to Advise on Policies for Manufacturing Industry (1975) Policies for Development of Manufacturing Industry: A Green Paper. Australian Government Publishing

Service Canberra.
Australia, Department of Science and Technology (1983) Australia National Paper for OEDC Conference on International Cooperation in Science and Technology. Department of Science and Technology, Canberra.
Australia, Department of Science and Technology (1984) National Technology Strategy: Discussion Draft. Department of Science and Technology, Canberra.
Australia, Industries Assistance Commission (1974) Annual Report 1973-74. Australian Government Publishing Service, Canberra.
Australia, Industries Assistance Commission (1981) Approaches to General Reductions in Protection; Discussion Paper No. 3; The Regional Implications of Economic Change. Australian Government Publishing Service, Canberra.
Australia, Industries Assistance Commission (1982) Annual Report, 1981-82. Australian Government Publishing Service, Canberra.
Australia, Industries Assistance Commission (1983) Annual Report, 1982-83. Australian Government Publishing Service, Canberra.
Australia, Industries Assistance Commission (1984) Annual Report, 1983-84. Australian Government Publishing Service, Canberra.
Australia, Senate Standing Committee on Foreign Affairs and Defence (1980) The New International Economic Order: Implications for Australia. Australian Government Publishing Service, Canberra.
Australia, Study Group on Structural Adjustment (1979) Report of the Study Group on Structural Adjustment. Australian Government Publishing Service, Canberra, 2 vols.
Australian Bureau of Statistics (1983) Research and Experimental Development: Business Enterprises, Australia. Australian Bureau of Statistics, Catalogue No. 8105.0.
Australian Government (1977) White Paper on Manufacturing Industry, Australian Government Publishing Service, Canberra.
Cardew, R. V. and Rich, D. C. (1982) Manufacturing and industrial property development in Sydney. pp.115-34 in Cardew, R. V., Langdale, J. V. and Rich, D. C. (eds.) Why Cities Change: Urban Development and Economic Change in Sydney. George Allen and Unwin, Sydney.
Cooper, M. (1982) The state of the manufacturing sector, pp.178-86 in Hanley, W. and Cooper, M.

(eds.) Man and the Australian Environment: Current Issues and Viewpoints. McGraw-Hill, Sydney.
Crough, G. (1980) Transnational corporations and the Australian manufacturing industry. Australian Left Review, 75, 6-13.
Crough, G. and Wheelwright, E. L. (1982) Australia: A Client State. Penguin, Ringwood.
Edwards, C. T. (1982) The impact of economic change in Asia or Australia, pp.443-61 in Webb, L. R. and Allan, R. H. (eds.) Industrial Economics: Australian Studies. George Allen and Unwin, Sydney.
Fagan, R. H., McKay, J. and Linge, G. J. R. (1981) Structural change: The international and national context, pp.1-49 in Linge, G. J. R. and McKay, J. (eds.) Structural Change in Australia: Some Spatial and Organisational Responses. Publication HG/15, Department of Human Geography, Research School of Pacific Studies, Australian National University, Canberra.
Gibson, K. D. and Horvath, R. J. (1983) Global capital and the restructuring crisis in Australian manufacturing. Economic Geography 59, 178-94.
Hirst, J. and Taylor, M. J. (1985) The internationalisation of Australian banking: further moves by ANZ. Australian Geographer.16.
Jones, B. (1982) Sleepers Wake: Technology and the Future of Work. Oxford University Press, Melbourne.
Jones, B. (1983) Transition from a resources economy to a skills economy. Labor Forum 5(4), 10-13.
Kahn, H. and Pepper, T. (1980) Will She be Right? The Future of Australia. University of Queensland Press, St. Lucia.
Linge, G. J. R. (1979a) Industrial development in the Pacific basin: competition or complementarity. Unpublished paper presented at the meeting of the International Geographical Union's Commission on Industrial Systems, Erasmus University, Rotterdam.
Linge, G. J. R. (1979b) Australian manufacturing in recession: A review of the spatial implications. Environment and Planning A 11, 1405-30.
Linge, G. J. R. (1975) Australian space and global space. In press.
Organisation for Economic Cooperation and Development (1985) Review of Australian Science

and Technology: Draft Reports. OECD, Paris.
Rich, D. C. (1981) Structural change in Australian manufacturing: An analysis of employment and productivity, pp.143-88 in Linge, G. J. R. and McKay, J. (eds.) Structural Change in Australia: Some Spatial and Organisational Responses. Publication HG/15, Department of Human Geography, Research School of Pacific Studies, Australian National University, Canberra.
Rich, D. C. (1982) Structural and spatial change in manufacturing, pp.95-113 in Cardew, R. V., Langdale, J. V. and Rich, D. C. (eds.) Why Cities Change: Urban Development and Economic Change in Sydney. George Allen and Unwin, Sydney.
Robins, P. A. (1981) The regional impact of structural change in Australian manufacturing industry: The case of South Australia, pp.189-218 in Linge, G. J. R. and McKay, J. (eds.) Structural Change in Australia: Some Spatial and Organisational Responses. Publication HG/15 Department of Human Geography, Research School of Pacific Studies, Australian National University, Canberra.
Slatyer, R. O. (1983) Resources and responsibility: Fostering technological innovation in Australia. Search 14, 192-6.
Stilwell, F. J. B. (1980) Economic Crisis, Cities and Regions: An Analysis of Current Urban and Regional Problems in Australia. Pergamon, Oxford.
Stilwell, F. J. B. (1982) Capital accumulation and regional economic performance: The Australian experience. Australian Geographical Studies 20, 131-43.
Taylor, M. J. and Hirst, J. (1983) The Australian banking system: the current round of rationalisation and restructuring. Australian Geographical Studies 21, 266-71.
Taylor, M. J. and Hirst, J. (1984) Environment, technology and organisation: the restructuring of the Australian trading banks. Environment and Planning A 16, 1055-78.
Taylor, M. J. and Thrift, N. J. (1981) Some geographic implications of foreign investment in the semi-periphery: the case of Australia. Tijschrift voor Economique en Social Geografie 72, 194-213.
Taylor, M. J. and Thrift, N. J. (1981b) Spatial variations in Australian enterprise: The case

of large firms headquartered in Melbourne and Sydney. Environment and Planning A 13, 137-47.

Wadley, D. A. and Rich, D. C. (1983) The Australian Industrial System 1950-81: Review and Classified Bibliography. Occasional Paper No. 13 Department of Geography, University of Tasmania, Hobart.

Wallerstein, I. (1976) Semiperipheral countries and the contemporary world crisis. Theory and Society 3, 461-83.

Waters, D. R., Tucker, K. A. and Bennett, R. B. (1982) What makes Australian companies go overseas? Patterns of and reasons for Australia's direct investment abroad. Unpublished paper presented at the Congress of the Australian and New Zealand Association for the Advancement of Science, Macquarie University, Sydney.

Wilde, P. D. (1981) From insulation towards integration: the Australian industrial system in the throes of change. Pacific Viewpoint 22, 1-24.

CHAPTER 3

INDUSTRY IN HAUTE MARNE: A RURAL BACKWATER IN AN ADVANCED ECONOMY

Jean-Paul Gabriele

Travellers passing through Haute Marne in north-east France are always struck by the very low population density. Closer observation, however, reveals plenty of traces of industry developed in the 19th century in a rural environment. The results of personal surveys, observation and experience in the region, on which this chapter is based, reveal that much of the industry that remains today exhibits strong continuities with the past. Partly for that very reason, entrepreneurs find themselves confronted by severe contemporary economic difficulties to which they are able to respond only slowly and awkwardly.

INDUSTRIAL ADAPTATION IN A PERIPHERAL DEPARTEMENT

A French Backwater

Haute Marne is a 'dead end' in the geography of northeast France, part of the 'desert français'. Inhabited now by some 210,000 people, it has only 33 persons per sq. km. (in contrast to 100 per sq. km. in all France), while in the south-west around Auberive it falls below 5 per sq. km. A long process of rural exodus is to blame, population declining from 259,000 in 1866 to only 181,800 in 1946. Although Haute Marne regained part of this loss after the Second World War, the number of inhabitants has slowly contracted from a peak 214,350 in 1968 to the present figure. Most people live in rural communities, 46 per cent still inhabiting communes with fewer than 2,000 inhabitants. There is no medium-sized, let alone a large, town: St. Dizier has 37,445 inhabitants; Chaumont 29,550; and Langres 11,360. No centre has sufficiently well-developed banking or retailing services, and hence a large enough sphere of influence, to act as an integrating force within the département.

Since the Middle Ages the areas making up present-day Haute Marne formed a frontier between the very distinctive provinces of Champagne, Lorraine, Bourgogne and Franche Comté. Fragmentation continues till today. Inhabitants in the west buy some of their needs in Chalons-sur-Marne, even Reims, those in the south travel to Dijon, while Nancy serves the east. All four cities are outside the département (see Figure 3.1). Integration with Champagne Ardenne (centred on Chalons) is further weakened by the domination of the Regional Council by politicians who favour Marne or Auboise but forget about Haute Marne. And, until recently, the nearest autoroute (A4) bypassed the region en route from Reims to Metz (Figure 3.1).

Long Industrial Traditions

The economic history of Haute Marne centres on the charcoal-iron industry based on the use of local ores, wood and water. Developed first by the Romans, the abbeys and monasteries sustained it through the Middle Ages. By 1847 it was the leading centre of both ore and iron output in France, furnaces being scattered along the rivers Marne, Blaise, Aube and Aujon.

Several factors, however, led to the closure of these furnaces or their conversion into foundries or workshops in the late 19th century. Though some entrepreneurs owned several furnaces, enterprises were very small and found themselves increasingly unable to compete with British iron being produced in coal-fired blast furnaces, French tariffs on imports notwithstanding. Despite the protests of forgemasters meeting in St. Dizier, Emperor Napoleon III signed a treaty for free trade in 1860. Yet in the end it was competition from Lorraine, not Britain, which condemned Haute Marne iron-smelting: the Thomas Gilchrist process enabled Lorraine from 1880 to make iron and steel using its phosphoric 'minette' ores. Forges closed, especially in the valleys, and iron production was concentrated in St. Dizier.

To survive, local entrepreneurs began using Lorraine metals in making higher-value, specialized goods, especially cutlery and glovemaking. Cutlery already had local traditions. Born in Langres in the Middle Ages, cutlery manufacture was relocated to Nogent in the late 18th century and by 1848 employed 6,000 people, mainly in domestic workshops operating on a putting-out basis for Langres and Parisian

Industry in Haute Marne

Figure 3.1: Haute Marne: Towns and Routes

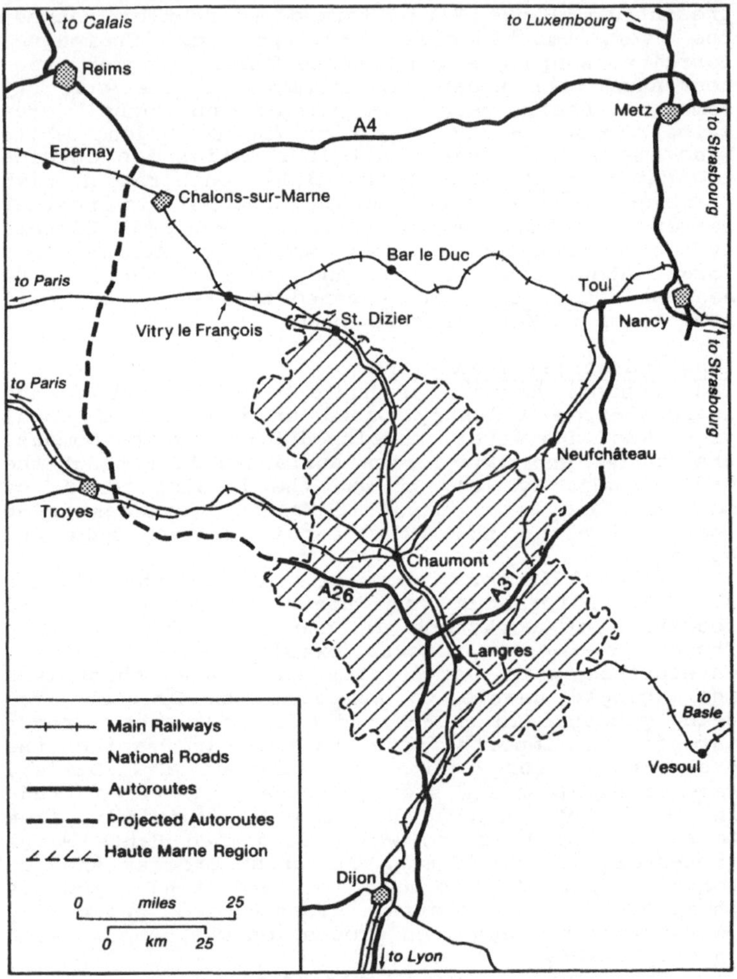

intermediaries. This industry declined, too, from the late 19th century in the face of large-scale factory competition from Sheffield, Solingen and Thiers. Some entrepreneurs turned their attention more to stamping and pressing for armaments, shipping and cycles. Similarly production of gloves in Chaumont became celebrated already in the 18th century but was never large until Trefousse built a factory there in 1829. By 1850 2,000 people were engaged in the industry in Chaumont and a further 5,000 in villages around on a putting-out basis. That activity prospered from exports to Britain and Germany until the 1930s.

Restricted Industrial Revival

The 1950s and 1960s witnessed the growth, from modest beginnings, of two major enterprises in food processing through the efforts of local entrepreneurs. First, the sons of M. Ortiz, a Spanish immigrant who had opened an ice-creamery and parlour in St. Dizier in 1921, purchased automatic machines and in 1957 expanded into factory premises in the town. As business grew they took over other small firms and, from 1970, diversified into frozen food production under the brand name 'Vivagel'. Today, the firm, renowned for 'Miko' ice creams, employs 5,000 workers, 1,200 of them in St. Dizier. Second, in 1946 Jean-Noel Bongrain inherited a small cheesemaking factory in Illoud from his father. In 1957 he invented a new cheese he called 'La Caprice des Dieux', the sales success of which ensured expansion of his enterprise and, from 1967, acquisition of other cheese manufacturers. The firm, now Bongrain-Gérard, in 1983 had a turnover of 4.4 billion FF.

The expansion of these two firms locally, however, could not absorb the growing labour supply of the département. That supply proved to be an attraction for firms seeking to decentralize from Paris or for foreign enterprises seeking European production sites. First to arrive was MacCormick (now International Harvester) from the USA to assemble tractors and manufacture combine harvesters at St. Dizier for the European market. It now employes 1,940 workers and, carrying on the town's metalworking traditions, confirmed it as the main industrial centre of the area (Figure 3.2). Between 1957 and 1964 Langres attracted three firms decentralizing production from Paris: SALEV making lifts, Plastic Omnium producing plastic goods, and Procal manufacturing rubber joints. Labour supplies

Figure 3.2: Haute Marne: Main Industrial Centres

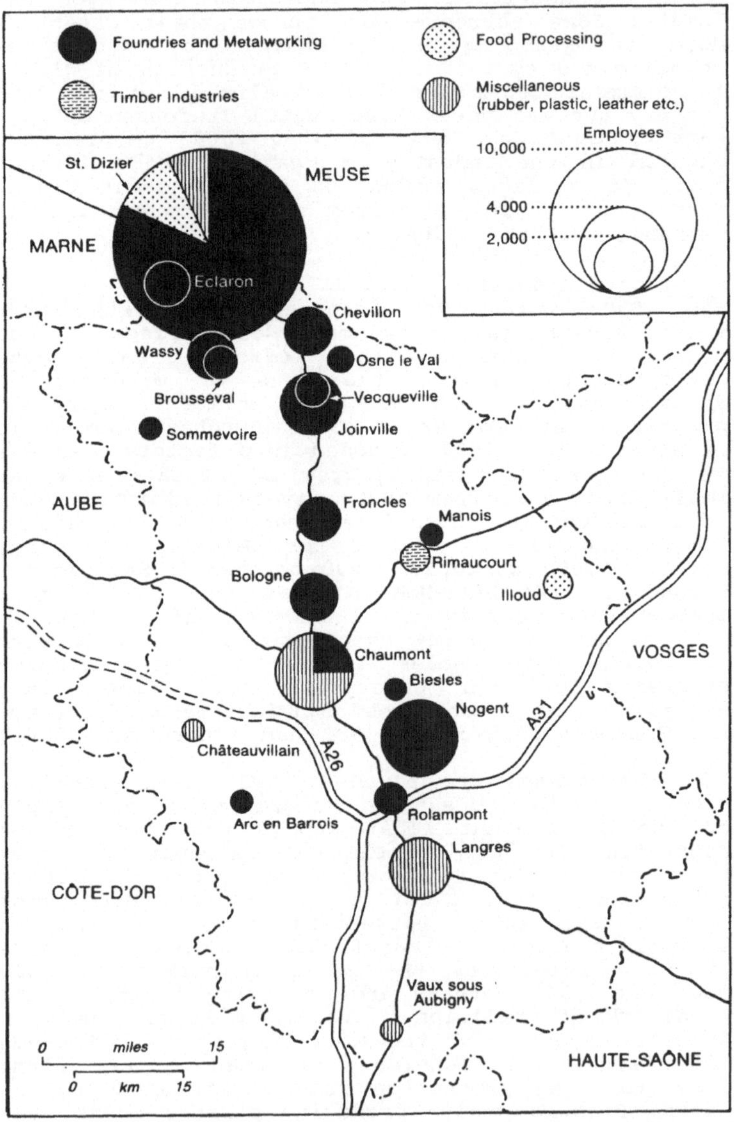

in several rural communities also drew in plants, notably tube-welding at Sommeville, a foundry at Wassy, electronic components at Arc-en-Barrois. The newest lines of production were plywood established at Chamouilley and quality morocco leather goods at Vaux-sous-Aubigny (Figure 3.2).

By contrast, Chaumont suffered the simultaneous effects of the closure of the American air base at Semoutiers and the rundown of the glovemaking, and it remains under-industrialized to this day.

In reality decentralization has involved few plant openings in Haute Marne and has proved to be a process sufficient neither in scale nor diversification to promote real regional development.

WEAKNESSES OF HAUTE MARNE INDUSTRY

Human Environmental Limitations

The most serious consequences of the geographic isolation of Haute Marne from major development poles do not express themselves in technical so much as in human problems.

Regarding transport facilities, local industrial managers are generally satisfied with the ease of truck haulage of their inputs and outputs on the usually quiet national road (routes nationales) system of the region. Indeed, they do not expect major repercussions on freight transport from the construction of the new A26 and A31 autoroutes. By contrast, Haute Marne industrialists suffer from poor passenger transport facilities which seriously constrain their business travel. They are isolated from major airports (Paris, 260km; Mulhouse-Basle, 230km.) and must use the train or their own car to reach either the airport or their final destination. Unfortunately SNCF (French railway) services from Chaumont and St. Dizier do not allow Haute Marne businessmen sufficient working time even in Lyon, Basle or Paris to enable them to return home the same evening. The new autoroutes will help greatly in this respect but local entrepreneurs regret that these highways have arrived too late to benefit them significantly. They also consider that the routes nationales, while adequate for trucks, are not sufficiently well maintained or designed to enable them to drive quickly and safely enough to their business destinations.

A more serious constraint on industrialization is the difficulty of recruiting labour in sufficient numbers and of the right quality in such a rural environment. Poor local education facilities are incapable of training engineers, technicians or managers. The young go to Paris or provincial university cities and rarely return to Haute Marne, a process impoverishing the local labour market, making it impossible to attract or retain advanced and high value-added industrial production. Similarly firms cannot recruit foreign skilled workers or engineers from other French regions because Haute Marne lacks sufficient environmental advantages. The climate has a bad reputation, especially the inhospitable Langres plateau. Skilled workers are unhappy about distance from major cities, the lack of local cultural facilities, social isolation and problems of good schooling for their children. Wives complain that they cannot find employment, entertainment, and must live in inadequate housing.

The results are clear. A foundry in Nogent searched for 2 years for a specialist engineer in the heat treatment of metals. Plastic Omnium found similar difficulties in recruiting skilled workers. These constraints have discouraged Paris-located managements from decentralizing plant to Haute Marne, preferring provincial cities like Reims or places within 150km. of the capital. A location in Haute Marne is usually at best a second or third choice. Furthermore, however, managements of firms which did decentralize from the Paris region such as that for morocco leather goods at Vaux-sous-Aubigny, employing 280 workers, Plastic Omnium (800) and Procal (737) at Langres, said that they prospered only after the closure of SALEV in 1973 and from the trading difficulties of International Harvester (France) at St. Dizier which released industrially-experienced labour for re-employment.

Labour recruitment is also hampered by the workers being deeply tied to the soil in Haute Marne, a powerful legacy of the past. Attachment to their _pays_ is reflected in low levels of commuting to work. As recently as 1975 more than 75 per cent of Haute Marne workers lived and worked in the same commune. Labour market areas from which even larger enterprises draw their workers are predominantly local. Thus 48 per cent of the 1,940 people employed in International Harvester (France) and 60 per cent of the 1,200 working in Ortiz-Miko at St. Dizier live in the commune. Similarly 68 per cent of the 621 employees of the Froncles foundry, 62 per cent of the 479 workers in Ferry Capitain at Vecqueville and 59 per cent of the 335 employed by Forge de

Courcelles at Nogent reside in the local commune. Only the Bologne foundry draws a high proportion of workers (69 per cent of 885) from beyond the commune boundaries.

This attachment also manifests itself in the symbiosis between the world of the worker and that of peasant. According to the French Ministry of Agriculture, in 1980 Haute Marne still had 443 peasant-industrial workers. The roots go back to the 19th century when iron furnace and foundry workers retained parcels of land to supplement their meagre industrial earnings, a phenomenon still apparent amongst some Nogent industrial workers. In the north, the valleys of the Blaise, Marne and Rongeant, such peasant-industrial workers are usually non-farm workers who inherit small sheep runs. Productivity amongst these workers is low, especially when they are preoccupied with the harvest.

Constraints on industrial progress are also imposed by the social structure of local entrepreneurs. Most local enterprises have been family-owned for generations, especially in metalworking where current owners are descendants of 19th century forgemasters. Links between entrepreneurial families are often numerous, not least through marriage, a situation which facilitates integration but equally reinforces isolation from the outside world. The patronal milieu is very strong. Small firms are most prominent in Nogent where 71 enterprises employ 2,285 workers, an average of 32 per firm. A local entrepreneur is more like an artisan in his attitude of mind. Nogent cutlers are especially notorious for neglecting the proper management of their enterprises, running them as if they were family homes. Their individualism is deeply regrettable, often with the result that contracts are lost, sales promotion of products is handicapped by an absence of professional or business cohesion. Individualism is a heritage of times when cutlers worked at home on the orders of Langrés or Parisian merchants. Artisan mentality is reinforced by the grandiose notions of being the 'best workers in France' making the 'best quality products'. While manufacturers should make quality goods they should also respond to the needs of clients. Nogent makers of scissors attach great importance, for example, to polishing the rounded back of the blades but neglect the greater sensitivity of the buyers to the comfort of holding the scissors with the fingers.

The traditionalism of Haute Marne entrepreneurs is also marked by an attachment to 'human scale enterprise' with close interaction with the employees, the patron often working alongside them, getting to know them personally. A director of a larger Haute Marne foundry considers himself, for instance, 'to be the most paternalistic person in the rural environment' as he employs whole families in his enterprise.

Structural Weaknesses of Haute Marne Enterprises

A further historical legacy is metalworking which still dominates Haute Marne industry. This sector in 1983 contained 118 of the 324 firms (36 per cent) that employ 10 workers or more, but accounted for 51 per cent (15,956) of the employment in industry. Enterprises processing local resources - foods, timber, building materials - add some diversity, respectively engaging 2,726, 2,186 and 3,553 workers (8.7, 7.0 and 11.4 per cent). Other manufacturing sectors are either absent or small, pointing to the marginalization of Haute Marne within industrial northeast France.

Table 3.1 emphasizes the dominance of small and medium-sized firms in the industrial structure of the *département*.

Table 3.1 The size structure of Haute Marne industrial firms, 1983

Size (no. of workers)	Haute Marne		France
	Number	Percentage	Percentage
10 - 49	230	71.0	67.2
50 - 199	68	21.0	23.7
200 - 499	18	5.5	5.8
500 +	8	2.5	3.3
Total	324	100.0	100.0

Yet the largest enterprises (with >500 workers) - represented by International Harvester (France), Plastic Omnium, Miko, Bongrain-Gérard, and the Bologne and Froncles foundries - employ 24 per cent of the industrial labour force.

Predominance of small enterprises, associated

with family management and weak financial resources, seriously constrains modernization of production methods or introduction of new products. Most firms are in debt with the banks and unable to raise more capital. Few, like Miko, Bongrain and Plastic Omnium, can raise money through quoted shares on the Paris stock market.

Financial insecurity is compounded by poor management practice. Family control usually means decisions are taken by one person, the head of the family, who is not equally competent in manufacturing, marketing and management. Timber-processing faces special problems in this respect as conflicts arise between the furniture-makers and sawmill owners who both exploit the lumberjacks.

Yet, despite the appearance of independence, isolation and family egoism, which are still very important in Haute Marne, industry is more subordinated to external control than one might expect. Dependency typifies not only the branches of Paris-region firms and of foreign multinationals but also larger local enterprises which have been taken over by French or foreign groups. Metalworking is particularly dependent. Tréfilunion (786 workers at St. Dizier) belongs to SACILOR, a leading French metallurgical combine based in Lorraine. GHM (Générale Hydraulique Mécanique), with 620 employees in three factories located in Wassy, Sommevoie and Val d'Osne, is integrated with the Société Générale de Fonderie. Forges de Froncles is owned by the Belgian group, Cockerill-Sambre, while the US non-ferrous metals giant, Alcoa, controls the Forges de Bologne. Such external control becomes compounded when local entrepreneurs, like Bongrain, move their headquarters to Paris.

Financial dependency is paralleled by technical and commercial dependencies. Forges and foundries work exclusively as subcontractors to bigger firms. Furniture-makers similarly confine their output to parts bought by firms finishing higher value-added furniture outside Haute Marne. Marketing dependence has always been especially strong amongst Nogent cutlers who still supply Langres and Paris wholesalers. So do local surgical-instrument makers who, despite innovation of new products, retain much the same dependence on Paris wholesalers.

THE CRISIS OF HAUTE MARNE INDUSTRY

Until 1980 industry in the region remained sheltered

from the shocks to the French economy and did not sustain serious impacts from the international crisis. Since then difficulties mounted. Freight handled by French railway stations in Haute Marne declined from 250,000 tonnes in 1980 to 216,000 tonnes in 1982. The number of trucks registered in the _département_ shrank in the same period from 47,000 to 45,000. Employment in industry, which almost reached 34,000 in 1975, had decreased to barely 31,000 in 1982. Plant closures and redundancies were to blame, between 1972 and 1982 some 139 enterprises closing (36 in metalworking), a further 149 (104 in metalworking) shedding labour.

Yet because of the large proportion and spatial dispersion of firms so affected, the region did not exhibit dramatic concentrations of the unemployed. But a rise in jobless people from 445 in 1977 to 8,682 in 1983 is a source of concern. Most marked was a 39.3 per cent increase in unemployment in 1981, from 5,500 to 7,670 persons, compared with 18 per cent in adjacent Champagne Ardenne and 21 per cent in France as a whole. A further 1,830 workers lost jobs in 1982. By early 1984 some 10.6 per cent of Haute Marne workers were jobless, but the rate amongst under-25s exceeded 27 per cent, amongst women 15 per cent, in contrast with 8 per cent amongst males over 25 years old.

The experience of individual firms, however, has varied somewhat within this broad downward spiral. Most metal-using firms suffered from the same problem as the steel industry: overpriced metal and shrinking market demand. Tréfilunion has lost money since 1980 and SACILOR, in a similar situation, has been reluctant to rescue it, though it is now undergoing restructuring. International Harvester (France) suffers from depression in the European and wider world agricultural machinery markets and has laid off workers. Foundries which were subcontracting to the automobile industry are hard hit not only by the effects of overcapacity in Renault and Peugeot-Citroën but also by those manufacturers' restructuring policies which involve greater internalization of the production chain. Only Forges de Courcelles at Nogent has succeeded in adapting - by substituting increased business from the West German firm, BMW (Bayerische Motor Werk) for lost work from Renault.

As for other industries in Nogent, the cutlers have lost much business for failing to meet market requirements in design, quality and price in the face of fierce competition from automated producers in other developed European countries and from manufacturers in newly-industrializing countries of South-east and East Asia. Makers of surgical instruments have found themselves victims of both the cuts by the French government in hospital budgets and of competition from highly automated manufacturers in West Germany and Belgium and from very cheap labour producers in Pakistan. Of course, their former buyers, Parisian wholesalers, have substituted imports to maintain their own profit margins.

Haute Marne furniture-makers fared no better, suffering from a sharp drop in market demand and from Italian competition. Similarly building-materials producers face shrunken demand from private housing and industrial sources and from public authorities reducing expenditure on all forms of infrastructure.

Only the food manufacturers, plastics producers and the morocco leather goods maintained their former levels of production, mainly through the quality or specificity of their goods for national and international consumption.

FORCES OF CHANGE

Local authorities and professional bodies in Haute Marne are highly conscious of the need for industrial change to withstand the crisis and to prepare for a modern future society. To achieve this, production methods and product lines must be altered and infrastructure improved.

The Need for New Products and Processes

Change in metalworking industries is particularly tricky. One cannot envisage that larger French or foreign firms would be interested in taking over the bigger independent metalworking firms that are, nevertheless, technically competitive. Forges de Bologne will not be bought out by Alcoa as it is very highly specialized in titanium products. On the other hand, most small enterprises use such traditional methods that larger firms will certainly ignore them.

There seem to be only two promising solutions for the foundries and forges. The first is to promote exports. Two local firms, Ferry Capitain (489 workers) and Forges de Courcelles (335), are spearheading exports as a way of diversifying their subcontractor clientele, especially in the United Kingdom and West Germany. The second solution is the concentration and specialization of production. Even if the foundries can increase value-added with new and final products, they will have to concentrate their production. One should have no illusions that remaining small foundries and forges in the valleys of the Marne and Blaise will have to disappear, their resources pooled more centrally.

Similar concentration is necessary in cutlery-making but is hard to envisage given the intense individualism of the master cutlers. Yet it is precisely this kind of industry that could benefit from grouping resources and operations. Cutlers, quite localized in and around Nogent, could pool their capacity, bring in appropriate specialization, and turn their efforts more towards marketing, especially abroad. They could learn, too, from the brilliant revitalization which a Chaumont firm making surgical instruments achieved by bypassing the Parisian wholesalers and selling direct in bulk to the hard-pressed hospitals at discounted prices. Unfortunately Nogent businessmen are more tied to their old techniques of production and sale; one can only hope that the multiplicity of innovations available nowadays will encourage a younger one amongst them to break with tradition.

Other examples of ingenuity are worth investigation by local entrepreneurs. That structural change must accompany technological change, however, has to be accepted. Haute Marne timber-processing provides an example. Several firms formed a cooperative association to be able to import machinery to trim seats so as to siphon off part of the value-added usually destined for the pockets of local furniture-makers. A polyvalent factory has been set up at Roôcourt La Côte north of Chaumont, but it necessitated a cooperative group organization to finance and operate it. Regrettably this example has attracted too little attention amongst most timber companies, whose owners seem to be simply waiting for the economic crisis to end. Yet the best example of innovation comes from the metalworking industry. The Etablissements Champerois located at Chamouilley, near St. Dizier, a newly-formed collective of local enterprises, in May 1983 exhibited at the 'Inova 83' fair in Paris an automated sweeping and cleaning machine destined for Haute Marne cooperatives, communes and cleansing authorities. The machine, developed with financial assistance from ANVAR (Agence Nationale de Valorisation de la Recherche), has been very successful abroad and is currently being sold in the

Netherlands, West Germany, Israel and Australia.

Infrastructure Improvements
Improved transport facilities are required to encourage local industrial development and stimulate implantation from outside of new activities. Past and present isolation must be broken to facilitate greater business interaction of the *département* with major economic centres in France and abroad.

From this viewpoint, construction of two new *autoroutes* (Figure 3.1), A26 from Calais, and A31 from Metz and Nancy, joining at Humes-Jorquennay between Chaumont and Langres en route to Dijon, offers new opportunities, making Haute Marne a crossroads between northwest Europe and the Rhinelands on the one hand and Switzerland and southern Europe on the other. Though implantation of major service facilities at Humes-Jorquennay are likely, it may be too much to expect that these will lead to any significant industrial development, at least not while the crisis persists. Yet the *autoroutes* will certainly enable local businessmen to develop closer relations with their suppliers and market outlets from their existing locations.

Equally, however, the increase of through traffic on the *autoroutes* gives local manufacturers opportunities both to advertise and sell their products. It is remarkable, for instance, how many French people are unaware of Nogent cutlery. One can propose that Haute Marne entrepreneurs open shops or use sales outlets at convenient service points along the *autoroutes* and display their distinctive cutlery, furniture, basket-ware and ironwork. Similarly the growth of tourism, recreation and lodging facilities can help the local economy and offer a further medium for marketing manufactures.

By making the region better known nationally and internationally, the improved transport facilities could attract more entrepreneurs from outside the region. Yet the problems of education and training for the young still remain serious.

FROM BACKWATER TO CROSSROADS?

Haute Marne industry already survived one grave crisis in the late 19th century by a slow process of restructuring, involving abandonment of iron-smelting and geographic concentration of new production lines. Since 1980 it has faced another, this time of international magnitude from which none of the locally-, French-, or foreign-owned firms located in

Haute Marne have been immune. Their difficulties, however, have revealed more clearly than ever before the isolation of the *département* and its social structural consequences as major handicaps to development. In present conditions the capacity for Parisian enterprises to set up branches is very limited and, in any case, few are likely to locate a major plant in Haute Marne. Public authorities tend to concentrate their welfare services in regions of highly localized, large-scale unemployment like Lorraine; Haute Marne can expect little assistance of this type. The most likely solution to the region's problems will be found in exploiting to the maximum the opportunities offered by the new *autoroutes* in converting the *département* from a French backwater into a European crossroads and enabling it to modernize its productive and social structure.

CHAPTER 4

INDUSTRIAL SYSTEMS AND CHANGE IN THE ECONOMIES OF BORDER REGIONS: CROSS CULTURAL COMPARISONS

Werner Mikus

To explain the structure and the development of industrial systems in border regions it is necessary to take into account factors of history, geographical policy and regional development. Processes of the formation of branch plant economies, expansion and mobility of certain industrial groups such as footloose industries and changes in the importance of site factors for industry cannot be left aside. Of especial importance is the sort of border and how strongly it influences regions with different levels of development. The growth of core regions has generally resulted in regional disparities and, above all, in the increase of centre-periphery contrasts.

THE PROCESS OF BORDER INDUSTRIALIZATION

Only in exceptional cases have border regions been integrated into the process of industrialization, and usually if they possessed mineral or other natural resources worked in situ. A few examples in Europe demonstrate this. Industrial regions based on coalfields on the borders of Belgium and northern France, of the Netherlands and the Federal Republic of Germany, of the Saarland and Lorraine or, prior to 1939, in the Upper Silesia industrial region on the Prussian German-Polish border. A natural resource, like hydro-electricity from border rivers, which is used internationally, is another basis for industrialization. Often, however, exploitation is impeded by complicated international arrangements. Agricultural production, too, might foster the process of industrialization in border regions if the processing of the crops takes place in the same area, though in these cases the location near the border plays a less important role.

Viewed historically, border regions could hardly be taken into consideration for industrial development during times of a national oriented economic policy. Above all, the risk of a military conflict kept industries away from border regions. Thus the development or rather the promotion of border regions has hardly ever been an object of industrial policy. Moreover, the agglomerative tendency of industry itself is an important factor which underlines the disadvantages of location in border regions so that in many countries these areas suffered from very strong, centre-periphery differences. Moreover, the influence of the border on potential sales was often significant for industrial enterprises, making it difficult for them to expand their markets.

Few attempts were made at international political cooperation after World War I so that no economic consequences worth mentioning were achieved in relation to the experience of border regions. World War II brought a decisive change in this. More peripheral areas, among them border areas, became industrialized, favoured by an increased mobility in the choice of site, the expansion of multi-branch companies, the reinforcement of industrial and regional policy measures to advance the economies of peripheral areas. Dispersal of industrial sites, the intensification of transnational cooperation within various economic systems, the international division of labour and the exploitation of foreign neighbour markets all meant better utilization of advantageous inter-regional sites including those in peripheral or border regions.

The increased number of international 'common market' systems must be emphasized as a force which provided the basis for the economic development of border regions, albeit with differential effects. Most especially in western Europe international cooperation, which was assumed to have positive effects for the development of border regions, has been intensively promoted, with the result that areas long neglected have been integrated to a greater extent into the process of industrialization. Areas along the Franco-German border and along the Belgian border offer additional location benefits because of their advantageous centrality in relation to the markets of several EEC countries. It is very surprising that this new locational advantage has only been used by a relatively small number of companies. It shows the inertia or continuity in the persistent location of industry, especially of head offices, and plants in traditional core areas. More branch-plants have been established either by their parent firm in border regions, in their own country, or in a neighbouring country near the border. Both of these location types have to be distinguished from the autochthonous development of border industries. The particular problems of development, planning and cooperation in border areas, which have partially been compensated by special planning organizations, have attracted increased attention in literature since World War II (Hansen, 1983; Stoddard, 1983).

STRUCTURAL PROCESSES AND BORDER INDUSTRIES

To explain industrial development and structure one has to look at the specific factors of the settlement pattern and development and which conditions favour location and development, and which important conditions do not exist. Are there disadvantages for industry in such areas? Some conditions in border regions may have a positive effect:

1. favourable labour market conditions, namely wage advantages;
2. state support for investments such as tax relief;
3. price differences, which appear in the form of cost advantages;
4. the opening up of new market areas.

The last-mentioned factor particularly, however, may turn out to be disadvantageous if the influence of the border is associated with unfavourable customs regulations. Frequently, the necessary capital, locational activities, top management and adequate potential of highly skilled people are missing from border regions and thus do not facilitate industrialization. Negative factors arise from poor traffic systems, as in general infrastructure is less well developed. Certain industrial sectors are clearly deterred by that. Additionally, one has to take into account the fact that unfavourable socio-geographical factors associated with minorities occur in many border regions.

The sharpest contrasts in terms of extremely disadvantageous conditions have developed on the East-West frontier in middle Europe where there are, at the same time, marked divergences in political and economic systems between the CMEA socialist countries on the one side and capitalist ones with freer markets on the other. These compound the above-mentioned borderland problems.

Political systems and their dynamics play an important role in the development of border regions. In very centralized countries the activation of border regions follows a different path from that in federal countries, where regions are less dependent on the central government. Differences between Switzerland and France illustrate this. In various countries the problems of integration of border regions result from centralist politics. As a result of the differences in the development of neighbouring countries there are, however, comparative cost advantages and disadvantages which are most sharply evident in border regions. Over the years, these differences might, of course, change.

Structural features of border industries are often exemplified by the domination of certain industrial sectors. According to the development stage of border regions, different advantages will be exploited. Wage differences encourage the location of labour intensive sectors across borders, especially textiles or watchmaking. Power plants have created a great number of connections across boundaries among energy cooperatives, a trend increased by the building of nuclear power plants built in border regions partly for safety, and partly for environmental and political reasons. Most significant is the high proportion of branch plants in border regions. As a result there are hardly any administrative, research and development departments present in border region industries, creating a specific dependence on the head plants and offices. This often has negative influences on the structure of labour markets in border regions as the dominating function of producing goods requires employment of only a segment of the labour market; jobs for the highly skilled are virtually unavailable.

Summing up, advantages are to be found for industrial location in border regions, but these, however, are exceeded by the disadvantages resulting from the general development of the region and from the specific demands of industrial enterprises moving to border regions. In addition, there are manifold criteria for the analysis of border industries, such as the kind extent of cross-border connections and the production processes caused by the installation of twin plants and retail facilities. The increased flexibility of footloose industries in their choice of site as well as the ability and preparedness of industrial managements to engage in locational splitting of production have favoured the border regions' chances of development. This raises certain questions, such as: which conditions have stimulated the migration of a firm to the periphery? Which conditions have favoured or hindered industrial production in peripheries? How relevant has the neighbourhood effect been in border regions?

Statistical comparisons of the structure and development of border industries are hardly possible because of differences of data gathered at different times for different purposes by different countries in different ways. Nevertheless, the following examples examine core, semi-periphery and periphery. Worldwide there are different forms and types of development of border regions within these categories. Border industries operating transnationally occurred in Europe for the first time in the Swiss-German border region after the Zollverein had been founded in Germany in 1834 (Weh, 1932). Today, this very region shows various kinds of connections: daily commuter migrations, power stations with transborder services, and plants of Swiss and German-based firms operating on both sides of the border. A similar situation exists in parts of the borders of Switzerland-Italy-France and France-Belgium-Federal Germany-Netherlands (Weber, 1977). In recent years new means of transport, namely pipelines, have created new transnational links across national boundaries.

BORDER AREAS IN THE EUROPEAN CORE: BADEN - ALSACE - NORTH ITALY

Basically there have been disparities between Switzerland on one side and Italy, France and West Germany on the other side for a number of years. Common to all four countries is their location in the centre of Europe. Only in some areas has this, however, led to a substantial improvement in, or completion of, traffic networks. The polycentric structure of these countries is reinforced by the divisive effects of national boundaries. The provision of rather poor services of various kinds for peripheral areas is especially a result of this. Location features common to all these border regions are mostly the periphery disadvantages: relatively great market distances and unfavourable infrastructure. Figure 4.1 illustrates the capital

Fig. 1 Model of border Industrialization in central Europe

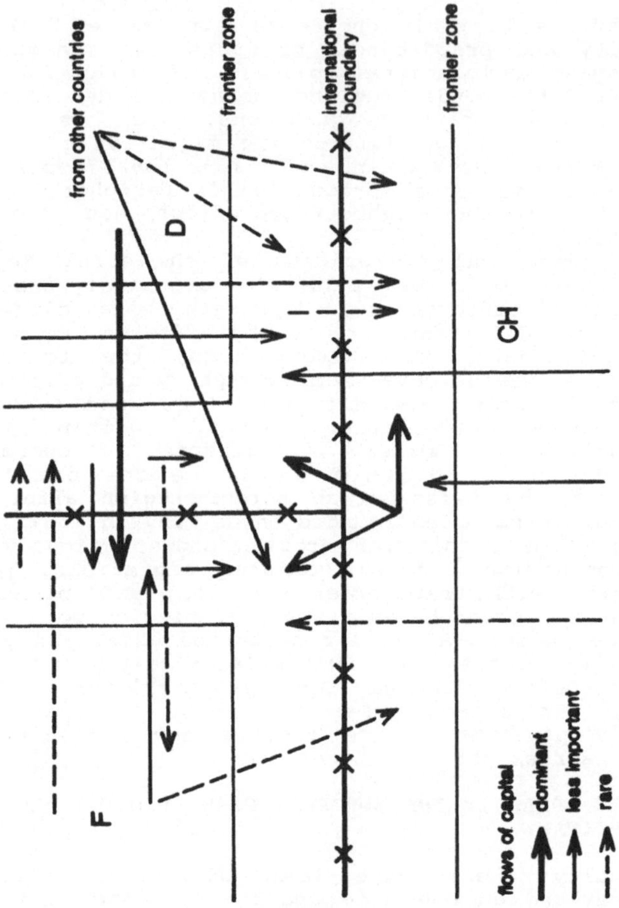

flows in this region.

Higher running costs are caused by additional expenses for transport and communication due to longer distance from agglomerations mainly situated in the national core regions. On the German side of the 'Hochrhein - Bodensee Region' along the Swiss border, 39 per cent of the total (295) of industrial enterprises are subsidiary firms or branch plants employing 67 per cent of the total industrial workforce of the region, according to a PROGNOS-study (Bullinger and Furler, 1982, p.13). Swiss influence on the industry of this region is quite considerable, as some 30 per cent of the industrial work force are employed by chemical companies based in Basle, Switzerland (Polivka, 1984; Mikus, 1979; Gallusser and Muggli, 1980). As a result of this, control of an enormous proportion of the regional industry lies with the concern's head offices in the neighbouring country. There are, however, no significant differences compared with independent local enterprises as regards supplies. Only a small proportion of the production of the branch plants in Germany is meant for export to Switzerland. By far the highest proportion is destined for the EEC. Hence these plants on German territory can be regarded as Swiss production bases for the EEC.

For a long time there has been a suction effect on the border labour market in Germany which is especially notable in the Lörrach area (Mohr, 1982). This results from the attractiveness of the great variety of jobs available in Switzerland demanding higher qualifications and offering higher wages. This had led to a shortage of labour in some segments of the local German labour market. Such selective influences emanating from Basle, Zurich/Baden and Schaffhausen, in the form of job market competition, were bound to affect the level of wages and labour costs on both sides of the border. Most important, however, is the risk factor in times of recession and, above all, economic and political crises arising from the threat of the Swiss government to take measures to reduce the number of German commuters, for example, by not renewing expired work permits. The risk and the continuing dependence of communities on the German side on the decision of Swiss concerns are specific characteristics of this border region.

Different features can be illustrated by reference to the French-German border industries. The development of border industries in this region is more recent, as the region had been consciously avoided by industrialists up to World War II because of tensions between France and Germany. Since 1945 various transnational networks have been established there, mainly by transnational investments (Albrecht, 1974; Marandon, 1977). Alsace is the region with the second highest proportion of foreign investments in France, there being about 400 foreign enterprises as opposed to 1,000 French industrial companies (Bullinger et al., 1983, VIII f.). With 45 per cent, the German companies dominated other foreign investors, followed by Swiss firms with 26 per cent. Between 1955 and 1984, 481 industrial enterprises had been founded in Alsace: 206 of these are foreign, employing about 20,000 workers; 252 are French with 40,000 employees; 23 are joint ventures (see Table 4.1).

Swiss companies in the French border region belong to chemical and plastic industries, most German companies to the textile or building materials industries. From both Switzerland and Germany companies in metal processing, electrical and mechanical industries have settled in this region (Table 4.2). German companies are usually based in neighbouring federal states or Bundesländer such as Baden-Württemberg, Saarland and Rhineland Palatinate. Their plants have been built in Alsace for various reasons, mainly because of the proximity of consumer markets or industrial customers.

In such core regions as these, transnational commuters have gained great importance. While in 1963 there were only about 8,000 commuters to Switzerland and Germany per day (Arnold-Palussiere, 1983, p.210) the number had increased to about 26,000 in 1977 and reached 37,000 in 1982, some 21,000 commuting to Switzerland, about 16,000 to West Germany. The increase demonstrates the rise of the attractiveness of Switzerland as a labour market. About half of the commuters are female; of these about half are unmarried and under 26. The most important employers are in the chemical, metal-processing and building industries, with only 15 per cent being in the service sector. This illustrates the great importance of labour market potential for the industrial development of border regions. The main regional target centres for French commuters are: Basle, Freiburg, Karlsruhe, Rastatt and Offenburg/Kehl. Topping this list is the City of Basle with 6,000 commuters from Baden and about 13,000 from Alsace. A further 1,400 German and 4,000 French commuters were coming in 1981 to the outer

Table 4.1 Enterprises and Employees created by French and Foreign Capital in Alsace 1955-1982

	Number of enterprises			Number of employees		
Origin	Bas-Rhin	Haut-Rhin	Alsace	Bas-Rhin	Haut-Rhin	Alsace
National	119	133	252	11,518	27,991	39,509
Foreign Countries	116	90	206	20,442	13,030	33,472
FRG	90	49	139	12,799	6,636	19,435
Switzerland	1	24	25	49	2,812	2,861
U.S.A.	15	11	26	6,080	3,302	9,382
Netherlands-Belgium	-	1	1	-	41	41
Great Britain	-	1	1	-	23	23
Others	10	4	14	1,514	216	1,730
French-Foreign C.	14	9	23	1,503	835	2,338
French-German	11	2	13	1,348	546	1,894
French-Swiss	1	5	6	148	196	344
Others	2	2	4	7	93	100
Total	249	232	481	33,463	41,856	75,319

Source: ADIRA, 1983, p.65

Table 4.2 Industrial Jobs Created in Alsace by Industrial Sectors 1954-1978

Industrial Groups	Jobs created	Share of the industrial group %	Share of jobs created %	Foreign capital %	Capital of FRG %
Food processing, beverages	3,215	14.4	4.2	45	14.6
Energy, mineral oil, gas	779	75	1	-	-
Electric energy, water	73	2	0.1	-	-
Non-ferrous metals	709	43	0.9	-	-
Metallic minerals	840	30	1.1	7.5	-
Material of construction	1,492	11	2	63.5	40.5
Glass	134	12	0.2	-	-
Foundries	4,092	24	5.4	20.2	16.3
Machinery	12,894	44	17.1	71	44.3
Electric, electronic	7,276	45	9.6	58.7	33.8
Automobile	17,599	97	23	20	6.9
Basic chemicals	5,567	83	7.3	43.5	-
Other chemicals, pharmaceutical	1,286	45	1.7	88.6	6.6
Plastic, rubber	2,706	53	3.6	45.1	32
Paper, cartons	3,008	42	4	6.2	4.3
Textiles, clothing	6,494	20	8.5	51.5	38.9
Leather, shoes	2,717	52	3.6	84.2	81.2
Wood products, furniture	1,784	17	2.3	42.4	41.2
Printing, publishing	249	3	0.3	20.9	-
Building	2,761	5	3.6	20.1	20.1
Total	75,675	30	100	45.4	14

Source: R. Kleinschmager, 1982, p.86

areas of Basle. Likewise, Greater Basle is the centre for female commuters. In some areas transnational commuters make up more than 20 per cent of the labour force as, for example, in northern Alsace Wissembourg, Lautemburg, Selz, and southern Alsace Huningen and Verret (Bullinger, 1983, IX). The number of German commuters to France is, by contrast, insignificant, amounting to only 300-400 persons.

Further examples of the development problems of borderland industries are provided by some alpine valleys. Worth mentioning are some attempts at industrialization in the south Tyrol of north Italy which have been promoted by manifold support, such as financial aids and less restrictive control on capital transfer (Pixner, 1983). The selection and development of numerous industrial areas had created several decentralized poles which themselves have triggered off new agglomerations. Ethnic as well as linguistic conditions - similar to the situation in the Upper Rhine region - have promoted rather than hindered transnational investments. Two-thirds of foreign investment come from West Germany as a result of the tendency, beginning in the late 1950s, to establish branch plants more often in areas with a large labour force potential. Important for investors in south Tyrol was the neighbourhood-effect: the majority of companies originating in neighbourhood regions from across the West German boundary (Bavaria and Baden-Wurttemberg).

By contrast the structural weakness of border regions can be illustrated by the closures of firms in northern Italy, Alto Novarese, which were exclusively specialized on watchstone perforation. Various reasons, such as the innovation of the use of lasers and concentration processes in the industry took their negative toll (Mikus, 1982), see Figure 4.2.

BORDER INDUSTRIES IN SEMI-PERIPHERAL AREAS: THE 'FRONTIERZONE' ON THE RIO GRANDE, THE USA AND MEXICO

In no other continent does there exist such a long border dividing North from the South, separating a highly industrialized and a Third World country, as between Mexico and the USA. This zone had only few raw materials and other natural resources to offer industrialization: some coal, iron-ore, non-ferrous metals for refining, some farm products like cotton, fruit, vegetables and corn. Textile manufacturing had been introduced there in the 1930s but the real

Figure 4.2: Closures of Firms in Alto Novarese, Italy

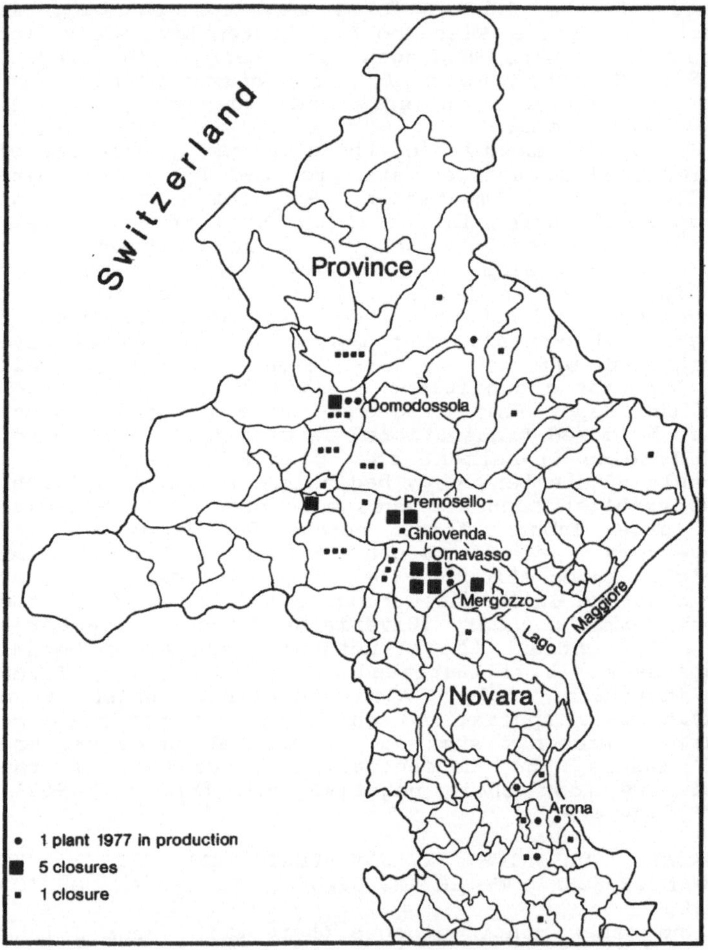

stimulus for development, however, did not come before the 1950s (Stoddard, 1983).

For historical reasons, Mexico pursued protective policies in its border regions but these were abolished in 1965 by the introduction of the Border Industrialization Program (BIP). This was a response to the worldwide trend, which had begun in the early 1960s, to transfer more and more labour-intensive production to developing countries, such as Taiwan, Korea, the Philippines, Singapore and Puerto Rico. Thus, the Mexican government decided after decades of restrictive and nationalistic policies, to attract industry (mainly from the USA) to northern border towns. After an initial phase of import-substitution policies, export-orientated industries gained intensive promotion in the course of the industrialization programme. During the early years it was only possible to establish plants within a 20km. border zone, but in 1971 and 1972 the previously excluded 50km. coastal zone was included, and the same conditions were granted for the whole of Mexico (Commercio Exterior, 1978, p.409). Finally, restrictive ownership regulations concerning foreign enterprise were abolished in 1977. An additional attraction for new foreign investment was the adoption of the industrial park policy by many border towns. Some towns like C. Juarez or Matamoros, even built two industrial parks (Dillman, 1976, p.142) and there are differences in infrastructure and services from place to place. The numbers of enterprises and employees grew dynamically. In 1965, 12 plants employed 3,000 workers in the zone; by 1974 the number of plants had risen to 455, the labour force to 76,000; in 1982 there were 585 plants with some 127,000 employees, despite interruption to development by a recession in the mid-1970s.

Table 4.3 shows the development of plants, number of employees, proportion of female labour force and the regional share of Baja California from 1975 till 1982. The latter has strongly decreased in comparison with the Rio Grande border region where the towns show different tendencies. In September 1977, 88 per cent of the 531 plants promoted by BIP were located in towns in the border region (House, 1982, p.219; Secretaria, 1983, p.1). They included 197 firms in the electrical-electronics industry, 134 in the textile and garment industry, 37 in transport machinery, 32 in furniture, 13 in food processing, 19 in the service sector and 98 in other

Table 4.3 Development of Border Industries (Maquiladoras) in Mexico 1975-1982

	Plants	Employment	Female %	Blue Collar %	Engineers %
A. Total					
1975	454	67,214	78.3	86.1	8.8
1976	448	74,496	78.8	86.8	8.3
1977	443	78,433	78.0	86.9	8.1
1978	457	90,704	76 8	86.6	8.3
1979	540	111,365	77.1	86.0	8.6
1980	620	119,546	77.3	85.3	9.1
1981	605	130,973	77.4	84.5	9.6
1982	585	127,048	77.3	82.9	10.5
B. Examples					
1. Cd. Juárez					
1975	86	19,775	69.1	87.5	6.9
1976	81	23,580	69.8	87.6	6.7
1977	80	26,792	69.6	87.9	6.9
1978	92	30,374	69.3	87.9	7.0
1979	103	36,206	69.0	86.0	8.3
1980	121	39,402	68.0	85.4	8.7
1981	128	43,994	67.3	85.2	8.7
1982	129	42,695	65.9	82.7	10.3
2. Matamoros					
1975	40	9,778	72.6	87.2	7.8
1976	39	10,966	72.9	86.8	9.3
1977	37	11,357	70.5	86.2	9.8
1978	40	13,443	70.1	86.6	9.1
1979	46	15,894	70.7	87.1	8.5
1980	50	15,231	70.5	85.7	9.6
1981	46	15,607	68.7	85.3	9.6
1982	41	14,643	63.0	84.9	9.6
3. Baja California (Ensenada, Mexicali, Tecate, Tijuana without La Paz)					
1975	182	15,285	68.2	87.1	8.2
1976	181	15,279	68.5	87.6	7.5
1977	178	14,396	67.9	88.9	6.2
1978	179	16,115	66.6	88.5	7.0
1979	203	19,689	67.9	88.8	6.9
1980	230	20,418	66.6	87.5	7.9
1981	215	23,182	65.7	85.1	9.8
1982	200	22,233	65.2	84.2	10.4

Source: Secretaría de Programacíon y Presupuesto: Estadistica de la Industria Maquiladora de Exportacion 1974-1982, Mexico 1983, pp.1-7

industrial branches.

These plants were called Maquiladoras. The Spanish term maquila, in its original usage, referred to the share of flour retained by the miller as payment for grinding someone else's grain. In 1972 the definition of maquiladora was enlarged to include also an industrial plant, already operating to serve the Mexican market, which developed an export function, providing that the direct cost of the exported product should not exceed 40 per cent of the total production (Urquidi and Villareal, 1975, p.157). The term 'in-bond' refers to the bond (fiunza) which had to be deposited by the US firm, determining the maximum number of items permitted free entry at one time (House, 1982, p.216).

Their share of employees increased, compared with the other industries, showing significant regional differences (Revel-Mouroz, 1973, p.215). The Maquiladoras exploit a vast labour force potential with its widely differing wage levels between one-third and one-sixth of the US levels. There have been some changes which brought a relative rise, reaching uniformly about one-third of the US labour costs in the 1970s, a higher rate of increase in comparison with the Far East where labour costs remained a tenth of the US level. Due to the currency devaluation in the 1980s, however, wage costs have declined to the Singapore level (Martinez del Campo, 1983, p.148). This trend towards increased wage advantages has been brought about by increasing the female workforce (78 per cent, see Table 4.3), and unmarried young people in the 17-23 age group (85 per cent). Plants have been established mainly as branches where wages make up 50 per cent or more of the overall production costs (Dillman, 1976, p.143). This enabled US companies to deliver cheap products to European and Latin American markets. It is one example of the so-called 'springboard-effect'. Even by comparison with branch plants in the Far East locations on the Mexican border provided advantages with regard to faster distribution to the US market and less complicated communications. By applying the so-called 'twin-plant' or 'dual-plant' concept, a significant division of the plants' function has been achieved (Mitchell, 1977). Jobs demanding higher skills, such as 'goods inventory, incoming inspection, materials control, technical support, working, distribution-communication centre, and management advice ...' were located in the USA, while in Mexico 'the labour-intensive materials turnover operation, with high-volume and long run work' were installed. In other words, assembly requiring labour-intensive use is completed on the Mexican side, while machining, capital intensive production, and operations with no Customs advantages remain within the USA (House, 1982, p.218). The capital : wages relation in the Maquiladoras has been as follows: drink 2.7; transport machinery 1.5; furniture 1.5; leather 1.4; technical engineering 1.26; electrical engineering 1.1; garments 0.74. These rates are in general below those of other industrialized regions in Mexico. The majority of BIP firms are the last link in a production chain. Changes in various fields, like increasing labour costs, increasing number of strike days or revaluation of the Mexican currency are likely to increase the number of re-migrations (Suarez Villa, 1982, p.1131, and 1983, p.960).

Not all companies in the border region, however, operate on a twin-plant basis. Some take advantage of Mexican commuters working in plants on the US side of the border region. And finally there is the very great number of Mexicans who migrated legally to work in the USA (chicanos).

Meanwhile the realization of the BIP has been viewed with regard to its positive and negative economic and social perspectives. This is because of an extreme dependence on foreign companies, showing single features of neo-colonial exploitation, combined with great vulnerability of the industry caused by its dependence on US-trade cycles. The multiplier effect has been very limited, as the anticipated integration with the Mexican economy has hardly been achieved. Only 1.5 per cent of the materials or consumable inputs are of Mexican origin. Negative, too, have been the consequences on the labour market where the selective effect of a dominant female workforce, required for routine work, has been noticeable. In addition, only a small contribution to the financing of social costs comes from BIP firms. By offering mainly jobs for unskilled workers there is a minor training effect, though the percentage of white collar workers and engineers has increased in the early 1980s. Positive advantages have been namely the effects on income (König, 1979, p.18) and, with growing exports, on the balance of payments (Martinez del Campo, 1983, p.1948).

These and other reasons have caused Mexican economists to try to achieve more backward linkages to process more Mexican raw materials, raise the diversification of BIP firms and increase their integration with the Mexican economy (Newman, 1979, p.295).

BORDER INDUSTRY IN DEVELOPING COUNTRIES: PERU AND ANDEAN PACT COUNTRIES

The development of the border regions is a major aim in developing countries, as well as in industrialized countries. This has often not proceeded yet beyond an initial planning phase. Only a few firms have been founded so far in such regions, yet there, too, attempts are being made to manage the development of the periphery through the use of legal regulations and state policies.

Prospects for development of border industries in Third World countries have to be seen in the context of the present location structure of industry. Urbanization and industrialization as interdependent, intensifying processes have primarily influenced metropolises. Accumulation of capital, consolidation of infrastructure (and other reasons proved important by migration research) have led to an enormous population concentration, causing various agglomeration disadvantages. Not only the vast number of firms and employees but other agglomeration features, such as the concentration of management, research and distribution centres of companies, stress the dominant role of the major cities. Structural and regional problems, manifold disparities between centre and periphery, which might become even more differentiated are symptomatic. The degree of industrial concentration is very high in some countries: in Brazil 80 per cent of industrial firms are concentrated within the São Paulo - Belo Horizonte - Rio de Janeiro triangle. Concentration in other countries is similar: in Peru, where 70-80 per cent of all industrial enterprises are situated in the agglomeration of Lima (including Callao).

To explain the sparse industry outside the agglomerations one has to consider the locational basis of the various enterprises. The industrial processing of agricultural products and mineral resources is quite important in this respect. Basically industry meets extremely unfavourable conditions in peripheral areas within developing countries, especially in border regions without major cities, infrastructure or natural resources. The industrialization of these countries is, to an essential extent, under the influence of foreign investments, which are also concentrated in agglomerations, neglecting the border regions. And foreign companies use various methods in the spheres of labour inputs, management, types of operation, technology transfer and participation of investments from different countries which make location in border areas difficult.

Worldwide, foreign investments have increased more in industrial countries than in developing countries (Hamilton, 1985). This has affected South American developing countries, too, where in comparison with other developing continents, such as Africa, Asia, and especially the Middle East, even less had been invested (Junta, 1979). Furthermore, in Latin America the Andean Pact countries were the most neglected by foreign investors, who were primarily interested in participating in joint ventures exploring, exploiting and processing natural resources. They participated in firms in major cities, mainly to promote the import of products and only to a very small extent did they invest in processing imported materials as, for example, in Venezuela. US companies are the main investors in the Andean Pact countries, with more than 50 per cent of the total foreign investments (Junta, 1979). A classification of the investments by sectors shows the predominant position of the mining and energy sector with more than 50 per cent, though local resources raise this in Peru and Venezuela to a higher level than in Colombia.

The reasons for such little interest on the part of foreign investors in the Andean states are many. Prime amongst them are: (1) the peripheral countries' situation; (2) small local markets; (3) long distances, meaning high transportation costs for developing inland markets and for transnational marketing with its still difficult customs barriers; (4) the need for transnational cooperation between the Andean Pact countries; (5) the traditional orientation of the EEC countries to African and Asian developing countries as a result of stronger post-colonial connections; (6) the lack of financial support from Spain, the major former colonial power in Latin America; (7) domination by the USA, leading to one-sided development exploiting resources and processing raw materials to only a very small extent; (8) a preference for investment in Brazil, Mexico and Argentina in Latin America instead of the Andean countries; (9) low Japanese investment, but expanding imports from Japan; and (10) especialy high political and social instability in some countries.

In some border areas in Latin America the neighbouring countries have not yet settled their conflicting claims on territory, a factor which has prevented investments and created altogether adverse conditions for the development of border regions. Concepts to decentralize industry were developed in Peru primarily in the 1950s and since the 1960s have been increasingly applied in other Latin American countries. Huge projects have been planned, some of which are under construction, whilst others show hardly any signs of realization. In some locations industrial parks have been installed at enormous cost. Diversity of industry, both in spatial and structural terms, was supposed to change the traditional specialization on exploiting resources and on the limited range of consumer goods industry and to diminish dependence on foreign, namely industrial, countries. At the same time, planning in the context of the international division of labour was taken up and the concept of the industrial parks eventually became a constitutent part of the process of industrialization within developing, urbanizing poles (Indupol after Boisier, 1974, p.402)

As early as 1959 Peru began to use legal degrees to stimulate industrial settlements outside agglomerations. One of the first measures was the construction of an industrial park in Tacna on the border with Chile. Further border locations considered for industrial development and partly realized have been at Juliaca, Pumo, Sullana, Pto. Maldonalo on the Bolivian border, and Tumbes, Talara, Jaen and Bagua on the Ecuadorian border.

The fact that the main efforts are in the Peruvian coastal region, however, shows how immobile the production agents (capital investors, entrepreneurs, labour force) are.

One major problem of industrialization by means of industrial parks is the high cost of the establishment of the infrastructure, leading to high expenditure per job created. The great economic problems current ever since the mid-1970s have affected the opportunities for the development of border regions, too. Although various sources, like Banco Industrial in Peru, grant financial support and some attempts of industrialization had been made, most projects failed (Jameson, 1979; Mikus, 1984). In Tacna, for example, only a few firms were founded, some being twin-plants and branch establishments of public enterprises, as in fish

Table 4.4 Regional differentiation of industry in Peru 1976

Areas Departamentos		Enterprises		Employment			Gross Product	Input from Abroad
		total	%	total	%	Blue collar %	%	%
Total		8,185	100	270,435	100	70.2	100	35.1
Lima and Callao		5,817	71.1	199,814	73.9	69.8	69.0	40.6
Remaining central P.		765	9.3	24,626	9.1	71.4	10.3	22.3
Northern Peru		708	8.7	24,225	9.0	67.9	13.8	22.3
Southern Peru		591	7.2	15,220	5.6	72.3	5.6	38.4
Eastern Peru		304	3.7	6,550	2.4	74.5	1.3	17.5
Amazonas	(p)	13	0.2	192	0.1	76.0	0.2	3.2
Ancash		49	0.6	8,906	3.3	67.4	2.5	37.5
Apurimac		7	0.1	71	0.0	60.6	0.0	4.0
Arequipa		334	4.1	10,937	4.0	73.2	4.4	44.3
Ayacucho		16	0.2	161	0.1	63.4	0.1	5.2
Cajamarca	(p)	61	0.8	647	0.2	67.2	0.3	8.7
Prov. Callao		461	5.6	27,085	10.0	68.7	15.2	58.7
Cuzco		135	1.7	2,388	0.9	70.7	0.8	17.3
Huancavelica		8	0.1	120	0.0	77.5	0.0	26.0
Huanuco		82	1.0	1,002	0.4	67.0	0.2	8.8
Ica		186	2.3	2,975	1.1	70.0	0.9	27.1
Junin		241	2.9	6,438	2.4	81.2	4.5	1.9
La Libertad		258	3.2	10,422	3.9	72.4	4.6	28.4

Lambayeque		188	2.3	6,263	2.3	78.7	3.0	20.0
Lima Metrop.		5,356	65.4	172,729	63.9	70.0	53.7	34.1
Prov. Lima		136	1.7	4,498	1.7	67.3	2.1	27.6
Loreto	(p)	304	3.7	6,550	2.4	74.5	1.3	17.5
Madre de Dios	(p)	16	0.2	221	0.1	74.7	0.0	17.1
Moquegua		9	0.1	90	0.0	63.3	0.0	15.8
Pasco		47	0.6	526	0.2	72.4	0.1	36.8
Piura	(p)	150	1.8	5,925	2.2	48.2	5.9	20.2
Puno	(p)	35	0.3	699	0.3	67.8	0.2	4.7
San Martin		28	0.3	613	0.2	69.2	0.1	7.8
Tacna	(p)	55	0.7	814	0.3	70.8	0.2	9.7
Tumbes	(p)	10	0.1	163	0.1	76.1	0.0	6.2

(p) = Peripheral Departamentos

Source: Ministerio de Industria, Turismo e Integracíon: Estadistica Industrial 1976. P EE - 16, Vol.1-11, Lima

canning or milk processing industries, while the remainder were only small businesses just serving or producing for the local market. The processing of available local resources varies from region to region: in Tacna olives are processed, in Iquitos timber is sawn. This occurs, however, only to a very limited extent without reaching a more sophisticated level of processing. A survey of some industrial aspects of the departments in Peru (Table 4.4) shows the concentration in Lima, dispersion in several other areas, and the general absence of industry from border areas like Tacna.

Despite some developing countries' aims to integrate border regions into their national economies the influences of isolation, discontinuity and instability are particularly effective in preventing this happening. The relatively higher risks make entrepreneurs hardly prepared to regard border regions as possibilities for their enterprises - except if attracted by opportunities for raw material processing.

PLANNING THE FUTURE DEVELOPMENT OF BORDER INDUSTRIES

Measures for the development of border regions require international cooperation at national, regional and local levels to reduce the separatist effects of national boundaries. Disparities and accompanying comparative cost advantages for industrial production and marketing are important location factors which must be included to a higher degree in industrial planning. Better integration of peripheral areas with the core is one result of establishing border industries, transferring dynamic industrial processes into other regions and regional development with multiple dependencies on core regions. Disadvantages in border regions can be offset by lower production and transfer costs, subsidies or tax concessions, improvement of many forms of transport and of services, such as the financial and educational infrastructure. Yet most attempts at industrialization of such regions have only been of short duration; closures resulted and only a small proportion of firms survived. Border regions remain a challenge.

BIBLIOGRAPHY

Adira Strasbourg (ed.) 'L'Alsace économique', no.73 spécial de la Conjoncture Alsacienne, July 1983

Albrecht, V. 'Der Einfluss der deutschfranzösischen Grenze auf die Gestaltung der Kulturlandschaft im südlichen Oberrheingebiet', Freiburger Geographische Hefte, 4 (Freiburg, 1974)

Arnold - Palussiere, M. 'Die grenzüberschreitende regionale Zusammenarbeit auf dem Gebiet der Raumordnung', Akademie für Raumforschung und Landesplanung, 71, (Hanover, 1983)

Banque de France, Secrétariat Régional d'Alsace (ed.) 'Les participations étrangères dans l'industrie alsacienne', January 1978.

Boisier, S. 'Industrializacíon, urbanizacíon, polarizacíon: Hacia un enfoque planificado' in M. Nolff (ed.), El desarrollo industrial latino-americano, Lecturas 12, (Mexico, 1974) pp.402-29

Bullinger, D. and Furler, M. 'Abschlussbericht "Standortstudie Hochrhein-Bodensee". Gutachten über standortverbesserte Massnahmen für die gerwerbliche Wirtschaft in der Region Hochrhein-Bodensee', PROGNOS, Project 122-1549 (Basel, 1982)

Bullinger, D. et al. 'Diagnostic Quantitatif des Flux Transfrontaliers. Etude de Prospective Economique de la Région Alsace', PROGNOS, Project 122-1871, (Basel 1983)

--- 'L'Alsace vue d'Outre-Rhin. Note de Réflexion. Etude de Prospective Economique de la Région Alsace', PROGNOS, Project 122-1871/al, (Basel 1983)

--- 'Les Structures Economiques et les Conditions-cadre du Development Economique dans le Contexte Rhénan. Diagnostic Historique et Actuel. Etude de Prospective Economique de la Région Alsace.' PROGNOS, Project 122-1871/al, (Basel, 1983)

Cassidy, J. C. 'The Location of Foreign Direct Investment: The U.S. Offshore Electronics Industry in Mexico.' (University of Pennsylvania, Philadelphia, 1979)

Comercio Exterior 'La Industria Maquiladora: Evolucíon Reciente y Perspectivas', XXVIII, 4 (1978), pp.407-14

Dillman, C. D. 'Maquiladoras in Mexico's Northern Border Communities and the Border Industrialization Program', Tijdschrift voor Econ. en Soc. Geografie, 67, 3 (1976), pp.138-50

Gallusser, W. A. and Muggli, H. W. 'Grenzräume und internationale Zusammenarbeit. Beispiel: Region Basel', Fragenkreise (Paderborn, München, 1980)

Hamilton, F.E.I., 'Multinational Enterprise: Spearhead or Spectre?', chapter in C. Dixon and D. Drakakis-Smith (eds.), Multinationals in the Third World (Croom Helm, Kent), forthcoming

Hansen, N. 'International Cooperation in Border Regions: An Overview and Research Agenda', International Regional Science Review, Vol.8, 3 (1983), pp.255-70

House, J.W., 'Frontier on the Rio Grande', Oxford Research Studies in Geography, (Oxford, 1982)

Institut National de la Statistique et des Etudes Economiques, Direction Régionale de Strasbourg (INSEE) (ed.), Chiffres pour l'Alsace, 4 (1982)

Jameson, K.P., 'Designed to Fail: Twenty-five Years of Industrial Decentralization Policy in Peru', The Journal of Developing Areas, 14, (1979), pp.55-70

Junta del Acuerdo de Cartagena, 'Evaluacíón de la Inversion Directa Extranjera en el Grupo Andino y de la Administracíon de la Decisíon 24', Anexo Tecnico, 4, (Lima, 1979)

Kleinschmager, R. 'Toute l'Alsace. L'Activité Industrielle', Wettolsheim, 1982)

Konig, W. 'Efectos de la Actividad Maquiladora Fronteriza en la Sociedad Mexicana', Simposia Nacional sobre Estudios Fronterizos, (El Colegio de Mexico - Faculdad de Filosofía y Letras de la UNAL Monterrey: N. Leon, 1979)

Marandon, J.-C., 'Auslandische Industrieansiedlungen in Grenzgebieten. Ein Vergleigh Baden-Elsass', Berichte zur deutschen Landeskunde, 51, (1977), pp.173-203

Martínez del Campo, M., 'Ventajas e Inconvenientes de la Actividad Maquiladora en Mexico', Comercio Exterior, 33, 2 (Mexico, 1983), pp.146-51

Mikus, W. et al., 'Industrielle Verbundsysteme', Heidelberger Geographische Arbeiten, 57, (Heidelberg, 1979)

Mikus, W., 'Types of Spatial Interactions in Industry with Examples of Northern Italy', Società di Studi Geografici, Scritti Geografici (Florence, 1982), pp.727-36

--- 'La Planificacíon de los Parques Industriales', Boletin de Lima, 31 (Lima, 1984), pp.38-48

--- 'Räumliche Verflechtungen der Wirtschaft - Kriterien, Typen, Beispiele', in H. Elsasser, D. Steiner (eds.), Räumliche Verflechtungen in der Wirtschaft, Zuricher Geographische Schriften 13 (Zurich 1984), pp.53-76

Ministerio de Industria, Turismo e Integracíon,

'Estadistica Industrial 1976'

Mitchell, J.A. 'Preliminary Report on the Impact of Mexico's Twin-plant Industry along the US-Mexican Border', El Paso: Organization US Border Cities (1977)

Mohr, B. 'Elsässische Grenzgänger in der Region Südlicher Oberrhein', Industrie- und Handelskammer Südlicher Oberrhein, Sitz Freiburg (ed.) (Freiburg, 1982)

Newman, J.L. 'Mexico's Maquiladora Program. Business in Mexico', Mexico City: American Chamber of Commerce in Mexico (1979)

Pixner, A. 'Industrie in Sudtirol. Standorte und Entwicklung seit dem Zweiten Weltkriet', Innsbrucker Geographische Studien, 9, (Innsbruck, 1983)

Polivka, H. 'Die chemische Industrie in Raume von Basel', Basler Beiträge zur Geographie, 16 (Basel, 1974)

Revel-Mouroz, J. 'L'Industrialisation de la Frontière Mexique-Etats-Unis per les "maquiladoras"', Cahiers des Amériques Latines, 7 (1973), pp.202-21

Ricq, C. 'Les Travailleurs Frontaliers en Europe; Essai de Politique Sociale et Régionale', (Paris, 1981)

Secretaría de Programacíon y Presupuesto 'Estadistica de la Industria Maquiladora de Exportacíon 1974-1982' (Mexico, 1983)

Stoddard, E.R., Nostrand, R.L. and West, J.P. (eds.), 'Borderlands Sourcebook. A Guide to the Literature on Northern Mexico and the American Southwest', (University of Oklahoma, 1983)

Suárez Villa, L. 'La Utilizacíon de Factores en la Industria Maquiladora de Mexico', Comercio Exterior, 32, 10 (Mexico, 1982), pp.1129-32

--- 'El Ciclo del Proceso de Manufactura y al Industrializacíon de las Zonas Fronterizas de Mexico y Estados Unidos', Comercio Exterior, 33, 10 (Mexico, 1983), pp.950-60

Urquidi, V.L. and Villarreal, S.M. 'Importancia Econǫmica de la Zone Fronteriza del Norte de Mexico', Foro Internacional, XVI, 2 (1975), pp.149-74

Weber, H.-U. 'Landeskunde und Raumordnung einer Grenzregion der Europäischen Gemeinschaft', Berichte zur deutschen Landeskunde, 51 (1977), pp.155-71

Weh, M. 'Die Landesgrenze als Sandortfaktor, Untersucht an der oberbadisch-schweizerischen Grenzindustrie', Zur Theorie der

Staatswirtschaft und Besteuerung, 4 (Bonn, 1982)

CHAPTER 5

RECENT EAST EUROPEAN REGIONAL DEVELOPMENT EXPERIENCE

Hunya Gabor

The location of existing economic activities, natural resources and settlements form a kind of environment for economic policy, yet all economic decisions by market forces or by central planners have their regional impacts. Economic development everywhere proceeds at an uneven economic pace: there have always been favoured and neglected regions. On the other hand, socialist political thinking - both in East and West - demands equality of standard of living in various regions and settlements types. This ideological starting-point has led to the pursuit of social and economic goals of a regional nature. Although regional policy does have some influence on redistributing income and locating economic activities, decisions taken without regional considerations have had much stronger effects in the EEC (Yuill et al., 19 0) and, in Eastern Europe where regional capital allocations by the Five-Year-Plans are simple regroupings of the objectives decided for the national economies as a whole. As the regional dimension of the economy is all-embracing on the one hand, yet secondary on the other, its treatment by geographers and economists has been divergent. The former tend to consider regional issues and inequalities in abstract from the political and economic characteristics of the country, whereas the latter usually neglect regional variations between different parts of a country.

The following chapter evaluates economic development in selected East European countries from the regional perspective. Stress is laid on industrial development which has been a focal issue in these countries, though this is not intended to be an expression of a one-sided view of social and economic development based merely on industrialization as a development strategy. Is there a special, East European, way of socialist regional economic development? While economic development in a capitalist economy is limited by the demand for its products, a socialist economy faces constraints of the supply of resources. Profit orientation in the former related to capital ownership and a soft efficiency control in the other determines differences in economic regulation. Regional development differs accordingly: in Eastern Europe costly investments are often located in economically backward regions and tend to reduce regional inequality at a rapid rate during industrialisation phases. During socialist modernisation, resources are absorbed rapidly and since at a particular date countries differ in the quantity and quality of their natural and human resources, their development levels differ accordingly. Yet socialist development paths have been challenged since the mid-1970s and new tendencies have emerged to modify regional development.

THE END OF THE 'TRADITIONAL' EAST EUROPEAN DEVELOPMENT PATH

The economic development of Eastern Europe reached a new phase in 1978-79. The traditional path ceased to be viable, its potential having mostly been exhausted. Economic mechanisms and policy decision-making were not flexible enough to change the economy rapidly to a path of growth required by new regional and global circumstances. Although this situation was not unexpected, the countries were unprepared for it. Theoretically it was realised in the early 1970s,with different emphasis from country to country, that the resources that had supported extensive growth had been exhausted and that the economy could be developed further only by intensive methods of raising productivity. This conclusion was drawn mainly as a consequence of the emerging shortage of labour, and the problem was thereby considered as simple as that.

In practice, the extensiveness of economic growth in Eastern Europe implied a wasteful use not only of labour but of all other resources as well. The main goal was the maximum rate of economic growth, and within that of industry, and not rational resources management. A high rate of accumulation, a high proportion of productive investments (including industrial ones) and increasing specific use of materials and energy were also features of the extensive growth path. From the mid-1970s raw materials and energy became dearer, due both to an increase in import prices and to a rise in domestic costs of exploitation. On-going investments, increasing costs of agricultural production, strains on the transport sphere, and consumer market hardships caused by the increasing divorce of purchasing power from market supply escalated the costs of economic expansion. The relative scarcity of domestic resources initially resulted in an increasing import intensity of economic growth. As East European countries engaged external financing of both development and on-going production, they became more indebted.

Borrowing provided a new means of continuing earlier economic policies, however, as structural policy and economic mechanisms were not adapted to the environment from which an increasing share of resources came. Consequently, no internal conditions were established for the depreciation of loans. Later, not only were new loans impossible to obtain but also debt servicing faced difficulties which were aggravated by unfavourable recessionary changes in the world markets and the tightening of money markets after 1980. Then, the last remaining source of extensive economic growth - foreign credit - also dried up. Almost simultaneously, the Soviet Union discontinued raw material and energy deliveries on favourable terms, so that the use of further resources from that direction became impossible, too.

The late 1970s was thus a period of increasing strain, lost momentum on the earlier path of growth and, simultaneously, a failure of the economic policies designed to parry external impacts - all manifest in every country in the drastic decline in the rate of economic growth. In the early 1980s the strains increased and led to crises (Poland, Romania), acute balance of payments problems (Hungary, GDR), loss in international competitiveness and supply problems. Economic growth and investment became negative, stagnant, or continued to slow.

Measures to overcome these problems or for alleviating their effects were restrictive or of short-term nature. It became clear that long-term economic growth was only feasible through economic management of resources involving novel economic mechanisms and institutions, and entailing wide-ranging political, social and individual consequences.

POLISH EXPERIENCE AND REGIONAL INEQUALITY

The Economic Setting

The Polish leaders of the 1970s came into power following worker demonstrations of December 1970 which exposed the political and economic discredit of the earlier leadership. They sought solution of a number of pressing political, social and economic problems through accelerated economic growth. Import-sustained economic growth began, financed mainly by capitalist loans, to modernize industry. Targets approved in the early 1970s set deadlines mostly in 1990 and required vast investments. The growth of accumulation and an intensive process of capitalist-related indebting lasted until 1974, resulted in rapid economic growth and large-scale creation of new jobs which removed the problem of putting to work the population generation born in the postwar baby boom.

Strains created by the fast growth became manifest in 1975. As a result of mistaken structure-related decisions, slow adaptation of the western technology and protracted building of projects, no domestic productive basis was established for the repayment of credits. Centralized economic mechanisms impaired the chances of active integration with the world market, and the slowdown in capitalist economies added external economic strains. But strained growth went hand in hand with a fast increase in the purchasing power of the households, for whose socially acceptable regulation no instruments have been created up to the present day. No suitable commodity supply mechanism came into being, as the performance of agriculture fell short of target: in the later 1970s there was 2 per cent less farm production per capita compared with the early 1970s. Agricultural policy, which aimed neither at collectivization nor at overall modernization of small farms, led to stagnation. Production in the state and co-operative sectors attracted most investment, increased essentially more slowly than costs and, to repay credit, went mostly for export.

The big economic boom came from external financing, not from increased internal capacity for accumulation, and at the price of having left unsolved such fundamental social problems as the relationships between leaders and masses, the economic mechanisms and the future of agriculture.

These problems led again in 1976 to open social clashes over price rises.

No solution was found in the late 1970s to either the new strains ensuing from import-induced growth or the sharpening fundamental social problems. Leaders were unable to make an essential revaluation of development aims and continued to set unrealistic goals. From the end of 1976 several party plenums were concerned with the 'new economic manoeuvre', but this only contained general restrictions and lacked future-oriented ideas. Investment activity declined, the construction of several important projects was suspended, imports were restricted and much coal production was committed in the long term as exports to the West to finance credits. Efforts were made to improve food production, housing and consumer market stability, to prevent deterioration in the social climate. But the superficial measures - as, for example, increasing meat production in the socialist sector of agriculture at the expense of growing grain imports - operated against the fulfilment of other goals, including the improvement of the external balance. Continual postponements in finding proper solutions and the spiral of increasing tension led in August 1980 to a massive outbreak of worker discontent.

These events are reflected in economic growth rates. Annual increases in industrial output declined from 9-10 per cent in 1974-75 to 5 per cent in 1978, and zero in 1980. Agricultural output and building (connected to investments) showed similar trends. In consequence, national income had stopped growing by 1979 and in 1980 decreased to the level of 1976. Investments peaked in 1977, but in 1980 were already 20 per cent lower. The curb on investments affected manufacturing most of all.

Regional Impacts 1970-80

The spatial structure of Poland is still basically determined by the 19th century division which set the framework for the industrial revolution and its modern urban consequences. The former Prussian-German west and southwest is the most developed industrial region with a dense transport network focusing on Silesia. The former Russian areas around Łódź received machine and instrument industries after 1950 to diversify its textile industries, while Warsaw developed into a modern machine-manufacturing centre, yet the hinterlands of these two cities are thinly populated, devoid of significant towns and industry, and typified by underdeveloped agriculture as the main activity. South-eastern Poland, historic Galicia, has low level industrialization, the high density of peasant population and the farm fragmentation being most conspicuous features.

The great early 1970s' boom resulted in a spatial spread of industrialization. The key development programmes determined directly the development of one or more voivodships (provinces) and the raw material related industrial programmes producing directly for export have remained operative ever since. Several of these need elaboration here.

The Legnica-Głogów district of copper mining and metallurgy developed rapidly and in the late 1970s per capita investment here was the highest in Poland. This south-west Silesian voivodship, earlier relatively less industrialized, experienced manifold development. By contrast, the development of the Lublin coal basin suffered long-term procrastination because of the infrastructural under-development of eastern Poland and the unfavourable location of the coal away from markets. But production and export have been launched in the early 1980s. Exploitation of the Bełchatów lignite fuel and energy field has been fast because it is in the vicinity of Łódź. As a result, by the late 1970s, the less industrialized voivodship of Piotrkow Tribunalski attracted more investment and in the early 1980s replaced Legnica-Głogów as the area with the highest investment per inhabitant.

Development of the Vistula river system is involving regulation downstream of Warsaw in connection with the 1960s and 1970s location there of several major chemical plants yielding fast development in the voivodships of Włocławek and Płock. No special programme was launched for the other lignite producing districts in central Poland (e.g. Konin), but thanks to the energy programme they also progressed fairly fast while the sulphur-producing area of Tarnobrzeg also developed rapidly because of its export-orientation.

The Upper Silesian agglomeration was the scene of a priority programme connected with construction of the new Katowice steelworks and, from the mid-1970s, an increase in export-orientated coal production which became of primary national economy significance. These priorities explain why this area was the only Polish urban agglomeration to maintain high per capita industrial investment as late as

1980.

At the time of the preparation of ambitious industrial programmes in the early 1970s, a concept was designed for the development of the settlement network up to 1990. Emphasizing the historical potentialities, the advantages of agglomerations, and the importance of infrastructure, it attributed top priority to the use of natural resources which has practically been the main factor of spatial structure formation ever since. No special plan was drawn up for the development, the industrialization of the underdeveloped eastern part of the country, but it was stressed that the development of infrastructure may promote progress there. Industrialization of these agricultural areas is the function - in addition to the demand for labour - of a socially acceptable programme for the improvement of agriculture. Because of a lack of such a programme industrialization began, with no particular preferences, generated urban employment in Galicia but the peasant families did not give up their farms, preferring to commute to work.

In 1975 a comprehensive administrative reform was introduced in Poland. The earlier 17 voivodships and 5 towns enjoying voivodship rights were replaced by 49 voivodships. The largest cities are now treated together with their agglomeration and gravitation zones, embracing also belts void of industry and towns. This reorganisation was not followed by decentralised industrialization as occurred in Romania or by upgrading the underdeveloped voivodships through centrally-located large-scale projects. There were several reasons for this: a subsequent decline in investments leading to selective concentration on 'important' projects in Poland; and the emphasis in Polish spatial planning on efficiency of location and urban networks in contrast to ideological commitment of Romanian leaders to industrialization of less developed areas. Yet there was similarity in the two countries in the growth of the new centres of administration in which population increased rapidly.

Problems and Patterns since 1980

A rapid decline in economic performance between 1980 and 1982 was halted in 1983. Decline most affected manufacturing and building, the former hit hardest by import restrictions on capital equipment to save hard currency. Extractive activities working for export were sustained at a relatively high level.

Agriculture increased output after 1981, encouraged by higher State purchase prices, the favourable political climate established for the private farmer, and government endeavours to establish parity between industrial and agricultural incomes.

Employment in industry has been decreasing since 1978, but the drastic fall in production has not led to large-scale lay-offs because enterprises prefer to keep reserves. The government foresaw this and in 1981 reduced the retiring age by five years, so considerably decreasing the employment ratio, particularly in towns with a greater proportion of aged people. Yet as industrial activity declined, the number of people working on farms increased, and rural-urban migration has lost much momentum.

In 1980 the unsolved socio-economic problems led again to worker demonstrations (Pajestka, 1982). The strongest bases of the Solidarity trade union were traditional, developed, manufacturing centres (Gdańsk, Wrocław, Poznań, Warsaw and its environs), where the investment and developed programmes of the early 1970s promised more (up to date jobs, better living conditions) but where the lost momentum of growth and the production strains emerged soonest, industrial production (and probably efficiency) already declined before 1981, and investments were cut to the greatest extent in the late 1970s.

Since the crisis, investment activity has decreased so much that, according to various Polish opinions, even existing technological standards cannot be sustained. The amounts allotted to mining, agriculture and housing have been cut relatively less. From the spatial perspective, the mining districts receive relatively more and the manufacturing industry centres less.

Under military rule since 1982 the Polish United Workers' Party lost much leadership, leading positions of state administration changed hands frequently, and most voivodship leaders were replaced. The military leaders and commissaries, however, have even recently experienced low efficiency and corruption in local management, which they are now trying to overcome by their own means.

The long-term impacts of these recent years will be manifest in, among others, the results of the economic reform. In 1981 plan directives were eliminated and industrial associations wound up to yield increased enterprise autonomy which, in a geographical sense, implies increasing independence of the centre but also intensifies the criticial importance of co-ordination in the territorial hierarchy.

The 1982 law on planning (Łukasiewicz, 1983) declares that it is necessary to increase local autonomy. If fixed locations are at issue, the leading executives of the voivodship or city must be involved in making decisions on investments. If the industry is footloose, the local authority's consent should be required for the investment. Voivodship leaders and managers of enterprises operating in their territories must co-ordinate their respective actions in each other's interests. Projects which have implications beyond the voivodships' boundaries must be handled by strengthened macroregional planning.

Owing to data limitations, the spatial impacts of financial flows can be gauged only from the geography of retail trade. County differences were in a ratio of 1 to 2 in both 1975 and 1980, the lowest values being recorded in the eastern underdeveloped counties, the highest in Warsaw. The ratio declined to 1 to 1.5 in 1982, reflecting some income equalization mainly by the rationing of consumer goods. The regional statistics do not reveal either the effects of above-average benefits granted to miners or the regional distribution of the very considerable US dollar turnover within the population and PEWEX shops (Hamilton, 1983), mainly the better-off people.

The level of industrialization, calculated as the number of employed per thousand inhabitants, decreased in the period, while there was also greater regional uniformity. A similar process took place in Hungary. But the Katowice agglomeration, with nearly four million inhabitants and the largest concentration of population and industry in East Central Europe with its vertically integrated coal-steel industry-heavy machinery system, still plays a dominant role. In the 1980s, it enjoyed development priority and was thus less affected by the decline in production than manufacturing regions.

The spatial differences in the degree of industrialization were reduced because of new raw material discoveries in less industrialized voivodships. The periphery's gradual closing of the gap was not so much due to fast creation of jobs as to a slower increase in the number of employed.

The voivodships may be classified into three groups on the basis of level, structure and character of economic development: (1) industrial areas with long-standing manufacturing and big towns; (2) new mining and chemical centres; (3) less industrialized areas. The changes that have taken place since 1975 have altered the balance between these areas as follows:

(Poland = 100)	1975			1982		
	(1)	(2)	(3)	(1)	(2)	(3)
Population	49.9:	16.9:	33.4	50.1:	16.7:	33.1
Industrial employment	62.8:	14.5:	22.5	61.0:	15.3:	23.7
Industrial output	61.9:	14.1:	21.2	52.8:	18.3:	28.7

(Because of rounding the figures do not add up to 100).

As is evident, the less developed areas have gained relatively favourably, but many problems of inequality still await solution.

SPATIAL ECONOMIC CHANGE IN ROMANIA

The Industrialization Drive

In the early 1970s Romanian leaders committed themselves to pursue the East European type policy of strained industrialization to overcome the country's continued underdevelopment. Priority was given to fast growth involving grandiose schemes and ignoring those advocating balanced growth aimed at economic efficiency. The society looked on all this peacefully, because living standards were improving until the late 1970s, a bureaucratically over-regulated environment fostered a refined sense for enforcing individual interests, and no traditions existed for the organization of common social thinking. In this way, keeping in view its goals, the leadership could increase without social limit the rate of accumulation to the very limit of economic endurance, while in case of crises it could protect the interests of production by curbing household consumption.

Between 1971 and 1978 the Romanian economy achieved an annual rate of growth above 10 per cent, the rate of accumulation growing from 32 per cent in the early 1970s to 36 per cent in the late 1970s, reaching a peak of 42 per cent in 1980. This was mostly financed by productive reinvestment and resource flows from agriculture to industry. This source gradually lost significance as the agricultural crisis unfolded, giving way to the increasing role of external credits used mainly for financing growing energy imports.

The demand generated by industry for labour was not satisfied by high natural population growth rates and drew labour away from agriculture. Since farm incomes were half those in industry, masses of people gave up farm work, especially the younger people. State policy encouraged this process through both wages and investments, endeavouring to regulate it by imposing restrictions on residence in towns.

Farm employment decreased by 1 million in the early 1970s and industrial employment increased by 833,000. Greater emphasis than in the 1960s was placed on manufacturing, particularly engineering, textiles and clothing which permitted relatively dispersed location. The coefficient of localization of industrial output, and within it of engineering output, decreased.

Regional Change in the 1970s

Investment priority was given - in addition to the traditional centres of manufacturing in Brasov and Timis counties - to the counties of the southern Carpathian foothills (Argeş, Vilcea). Less prominence was given to traditional primary material producers (Prahova, Bacau) and to the capital, Bucharest. No special attention was paid, for the time being, to the country's northern, underdeveloped half. From 1975 to 1980 nearly twice as much was invested in money terms as in the previous five-year plan period and served to further development of existing industrial centres just as much as the underdeveloped areas. Industrial counties received a similar proportion of investments as in the previous five years, but a rearrangement did occur amongst the newly developing ones. The counties that in the first half of the decade had received a priority share of investments, now, having received basic developments, lost significance. More attention was paid to counties previously neglected in development terms.

The amount assigned to industrial development decreased or stagnated (cf. the early 1970s) in Argeş, Ialomiţa, Mehedinţi, Teleorman, Vilcea, their share declining from 15.2 per cent to 8.3 per cent. By contrast industrial investments tripled in Bistriţa-Nasaud, Salaj, Calaraş, Botoşani and Dolj, rising from 4 per cent to 8.6 per cent.

Changes in distribution of industrial output between 1975 and 1981 can be evaluated with less accuracy than previously, chiefly because no comparable figures of prices are available after

1980. The change of producers' prices increased the production value mainly of counties specialized in energy. In 1981, 34.8 per cent of the industrial output of Prahova county (in which Ploieşti is located) was accounted for by energy. From 1975 to 1981 it increased its share of Romanian output in value terms by 1.5 percentage points.

Two other oil-drilling counties, Argeş and Bacău, where energy accounted for 30 per cent of output, gained 0.6 and 0.4 percentage points. Similar growth occurred in Gorj county, where lignite mining made up 26.8 per cent of output.

Counties with a declining share of industrial output are headed by Bucharest, registering a 1.5 per cent decline, Brasov with 1.1 per cent, Cluj and Sibiu with 0.5 per cent. These are counties mainly specialized in the highest phases of processing, and their loss of relative importance was solely due to the price changes (Gabor, 1982).

Development cannot be interpreted unambiguously by geographical regions. What appear to be determining factors are the production pattern and previously-achieved levels of development. Areas of fast growth according to these criteria are: the southern Carpathian foothills, the Black Sea region, northern Transylvania and the Szekler country. Slow development is manifest in previously developed southern Transylvania (the Braşov-Sibiu zone) and the capital, Bucharest.

Job opportunities expanded nationwide in the late 1970s. The rate was particularly fast in most backward counties where creation of even a few thousand new jobs resulted in a considerable growth above a low base. Despite decreasing dispersion of industrially employeed per 1,000 inhabitants, rates of growth in northern Transylvania, the southern Carpathian foothills and southern Danubian counties were double those in southern Transylvania. These trends reflect state policy for spatial convergence in accordance with the 1972 national planning resolutions. Two regional development priorities in the 1976-80 national economic development plan were the upgrading of counties classified as under-developed by per capita industrial output and the increasing of the number of towns, including new industrial towns. These goals expressed an industry-orientated and quantitative approach to the whole problem. According to the plan, every county was to achieve a minimum 10-billion-lei value of industrial output by 1980. However, because of delays in project realization and other shortfalls, this plan was not achieved: eight counties remained below the 'magic limit'.

Although the less developed counties increased their industrial output faster than average, growth could not be distributed evenly over the territory of the counties, because big investments were located in the county seats, generally towns around 50,000 population with under-developed infrastructure - like Bistriţa, Zalău and Botoşani - while other towns in the same counties (with few exceptions) did not grow.

The regional development plan adopted as part of the 1981-85 five-year plan was more comprehensive than the previous one. It contained a county-based summary of general and sectoral plan targets, including but few territory-related goals in the strict sense. Less industry-orientation was manifest in comparison with the 1976-80 plan, the main goal being to achieve by 1985 a per capita output totalling 70,000 lei. Every county should achieve an industrial production value of at least 15 billion lei. The plan also specifies various quantitative targets for the population's food supply, the development of the local industry and services, and the amount of raw materials and energy to be saved.

The Romanian plans are quantitatively-orientated, adjusted to ideological commitments which overstrain finances and favourable for creating a territorially uniform economic structure. There is no need for complicated regional economic calculations to provide a reason for the selection of a particular location. Often, not even the fundamental natural conditions exist. For example, the location of the Bistriţa steel-works is arbitrary insofar as no local raw materials, professional skills or markets are available, and the large scale of the plant creates problems of labour training, transport and water supply, but in the long term, the plant already plays a role as a factor of location for other industries, as it is to be the raw material supply base for northern Transylvania and Cluj-areas hitherto lacking a steel industry and machine-manufacturing capacities. It is a sign of circumspect application of the industrial diffusion policy that heavy machinery plants have been located evenly throughout the country. In the early 1970s such a plant was set up in Wallachian Craiova, centre of Oltenia, in southwest Romania, while in the late 1970s another was built in east Moldava, in Iasi. A plant in Cluj supplying all Transylvania will soon reach full capacity.

For want of statistics, regional trends in the early 1980s may only be approximated. Preliminary plans were unrealistic as early as the moment of their announcement. Economic strains grew so acute by 1980 as to cause a crisis hard to handle. The spatial aspects of economic development probably lost importance in the list of priorities. Restoration of equilibrium in the external balance of payments became the main task to be achieved by all means, urged by the International Monetary Fund, too.

Investments stagnated between 1980 and 1983; on the whole capitalist imports were halved, while in 1982 a US $1.5 billion trade surplus was achieved. A cut of one-third in oil imports brought restrictions in energy use. But the cumulative effects of a mistaken agricultural policy for decades was that farm production could not meet domestic demand, but neither could exports be sacrificed either. A radically new situation came into being with the need to avoid the paralysing effect of strains not in an expanding economy but in one for which only contracting resources are available. The leadership did not protect the population from the crisis and, what is more, even laid greater emphasis on production, necessitating rationing of food, energy and fuels.

Introduction of austerity is linked with an ideology of economic reform, which, while not giving up the earlier centralization, urges the lower echelons to assume greater responsibility. Self-financing, self-management and self-sufficiency are the triple slogans of this campaign.

Self-financing means that counties and cities have to rely in the future on their own resources to cover their costs. Central government contributions to county budgets are to decrease year by year but the income the county must generate on its own territory is determined centrally in each case separately. Self-management should mean autonomy for county councils in managing their own affairs. Since the organizational system ensures sovereignty to the party secretary on all levels, and the local party secretary and the president of the council are one and the same person, their economic role has been increased.

Self-sufficiency is to strengthen the same tendencies, with priority for the food self-sufficiency in the villages and the counties.

In the past the equilibrium of the food market was upset by villagers appearing as buyers in the towns, a possibility which is now limited by a number of rationing and other procedures.

A certain measure of county-level self-sufficiency has always been an aim in East European countries, following the Soviet example. Previously, state purchases and retailing had well-defined territorial patterns in Romania, but now, inter-county exchanges and allocations from central reserves have been even more circumscribed and there are signs that self-sufficiency is strictly enforced. Different meat-rationing systems are operated in various counties, the amount that can be bought changing from month to month. Regional specialization in agricultural output has decreased so that Timiş grows more potatoes, Hargita more maize to ensure local supply at all costs.

The strengthening of this type of territory-oriented approach entails a lot of deleterious effects and a deterioration in efficiency. While it probably is not intended as a long term measure, curbs on consumption continue through 1985 and, given that the country's economic situation will not improve much in this decade, strict prescription-based management is unlikely to be eased.

The current five-year plan requires massive production-orientation of investment with increasing shares of agriculture, mining and energy. In addition to oil fields and lignite mines in the Carpathian foreland, mines are being sunk in numerous minor coalfields. Manufacturing industry plants able to export, most usually those in the regions having long-standing traditions, may be in an advantageous position as indicated by the fact that in the last two years President Ceauşescu has mainly paid visits to these. The supposition that the decentralization of industrial production has slowed down considerably will be borne out by statistical evidence only in several years' time. Yet at settlement level a more favourable tendency has started, the opening of local small-scale plants and mines since 1980 and the commencement of sideline producer co-operatives may enhance the economic stability of many villages and small towns.

BULGARIA: AN ECONOMY UNDER LESS STRAIN

Following a decade of rapid structural changes and a high rate of accumulation, Bulgaria in the 1970s carried out relatively less strained, extensive industrialization. The proportion of farm workers was halved between 1950 and 1970 in the country's employment structure, but in the 1970s only a slow decline was envisaged. Already in 1970 the leadership sought intensive economic development, trying to increase productivity and to spread manufacturing systems, featuring low material intensity and applying advanced technology. Investment went into reconstruction rather than expansion. Favouring such a policy was the fact that the spatial structure of Bulgarian industry had been fairly balanced from the 1950s and 1960s so that it was unnecessary to disperse new plants amongst the major regions for the purpose of creating jobs and intensifying the presence of industry.

Unfortunately, economic performance usually fell short of target as no mechanisms encouraged economic use of resources or facilitated fast - but not strained - microstructural changes. In the late 1970s internal tensions appeared in the economy and growth was slowing. Though agricultural employment was reduced from 27.6 per cent to 23.7 per cent, a labour shortage emerged in agriculture, worsened by an ageing workforce.

The Bulgarian economy is heavily dependent on foreign markets, above all the Soviet Union. For this reason it could increase oil imports on favourable terms; even the freeze in 1980 occurred for it on a higher level than for other countries. Thanks to this and a fast nuclear power station building programme, energy supply expanded dynamically, and the changeover to more economic uses could be delayed. Refined oil products were exported to restore the stability of the capitalist-related balance of payments in 1979-80 so facilitating increased imports of advanced technology.

Most of the numerous constraints on growth affecting the other East European countries were in subdued evidence in Bulgaria. However, this also contributed to delays in increasing efficiency. The dynamism of the growth of industrial output and national income weakened from 8-10 per cent in the early 1970s to 6-7 per cent in the late 1970s, and 4 per cent in the first years of the 1980s.

Patterns, Policies and Problems of Industrialization

The country's industrial development led in the second half of the 1970s to an increasing significance of the material-intensive branches, especially chemicals, near the two main Black Sea ports, Varna and Burgas, and in northern and central Bulgaria, in Pleven and Sliven. Of late, exploitation of lignite increased again, accelerating in Stara Zagora county while Vratsa county achieved a high rate of development as a result of the location there of the nuclear power station.

The policy of changing industrial structure is also orientated towards high technology sectors, especially electronics, but this strengthens the traditional industrial centres like Sofia. By contrast traditional industries are most developed in the peripheral counties, although the less industrialized northern counties expanded output at an above-average rate throughout the 1970s.

Industrial employment has been dispersed in Bulgaria for historical reasons. Manufacturing industry traditions are entirely non-existent. No concentrated industrialization occurred under 19th century capitalism. Towns were trading centres dotted evenly throughout the country's territory. No agglomerations came into being, nor did the capital - Sofia - acquire primacy. Besides the towns, other factors of industrial location - lignite, non-ferrous metals, harbours - are also evenly distributed throughout the country.

Even so industrialization has, as yet, little affected the region along the Danube, Dobrudja, the eastern and southern mountain regions. (Smolyan county is an exception, thanks to its ore mining and metallurgy.) Underdeveloped districts are relatively thinly populated but not dominated by major towns.

Not surprisingly interregional income differentials are small. The annual average is 10 per cent higher than the national average only in Sofia and Pernik county, whereas the less industrialized counties record a figure no more than 10 per cent below average. The location of heavy industry and agriculture's lesser significance are the main explanations of the deviations.

Large-scale depopulation of the country's mountainous and hilly districts in the course of industrialization is particularly evident in interior eastern Bulgaria outside the coastal region, where there are hardly any towns, and an underdeveloped transport network and unfavourable natural conditions make extensive stock-raising the only practical economic activity. The problem is aggravated by the fact that part of the area is inhabited by Turks, whose more wealthy and educated stratum emigrated to Turkey in the early 1970s.

In 1982, following a resolution of the Central Committee of the Bulgarian Communist Party (Robotnichesko Delo, May 20, 1982) a large-scale campaign was launched for the 'rejuvenation' of the borderland and of the underdeveloped areas. About 45 per cent of the country's territory was classified into this category. Only 20 per cent of the population lives there. Emphasis is being laid on settling people in these districts and improving living conditions, though no particular location of industry is envisaged. Allocation of flats on favourable terms, the assurance of kindergarten places, and higher wages have already attracted many young applicants, indeed more than the number for whom suitable arrangements have been made (Trud, June 23, 1983). It is still hard to foresee what will remain of this programme once the campaign loses momentum.

As an economic entity and intermediate link in the territorial hierarchy of administration, the county, particularly through its party committee, pursues a direct co-ordinating role. Worthy of mention here are the county foreign exchange councils established in 1979. The local counterpart of a similar central body (functioning under the direction of Todor Zhivkov), this type of council convenes monthly for the county's first secretary of the Bulgarian Communist Party to hear the managers of production enterprises report on their fulfilment of the export plan and their possibilities for saving on imports. As the needs arise he contacts the competent industrial sector minister in Sofia urging elimination of any bottleneck hindering the fulfilment of the export target or calling for a modification of specific economic regulators. A similar organ keeps an eye on energy conservation.

Self-financing of the counties and major cities forms part of the 'new economic mechanism' introduced since 1979. A report of the 1971 Congress of the Bulgarian Communist Party expressed the view that it was necessary to ensure a tax-based income for settlements and a share, as a further source of income, of the profits of the industry operating on their territories, so that it should not be necessary to expect central financing. Previously, there had been no such local income. In practice, however, the central organs continue to determine the framework of local income and expenditure. Local authorities strive to acquire the right to collect more taxes which they can now spend with more autonomy than previously.

CZECHOSLOVAKIA

After 1969 prudence characterized every domain of Czechoslovak economic policy. This was evident in relations with the West - the only limited recourse to borrowing and licence purchases - and in avoiding internal reforms. Programmes to increase efficiency and improve products were mostly unfulfilled in the 1970s as a result. But overspending on investment and growing energy intensity enabled the country to sustain the rate of economic growth until the mid 1970s. The 1976-80 five-year plan aimed at a 5 per cent annual increase in national income by improving the structure and efficiency of economy. Unfavourable impacts of world economic changes were to be contained by increasing agricultural self-sufficiency, intensifying coal production and eliminating administratively world market oscillations. This defensive approach continued to weaken international competitiveness, which had declined over a long period, and to widen the technological lag behind leading nations.

Financial difficulties emerged after 1980 despite relatively low debt servicing. National income decreased after 1975 to 4 per cent, then to 3 per cent and, from 1980, to between 2 and 0 per cent. Of late, intensified criticisms have been voiced on economic peformance, energy and economic mechanisms. That the debate has become more open has so far resulted in only partial and not particularly consistent revision of the mechanism and of the progress so far made (Csaba, 1981).

Czechoslovak structural policy gives high priority to coal and electric energy production. These sectors received an annually growing share of industrial investments from 1976 to 1980 amounting to 25 per cent. Some 35 per cent had been envisaged in the early 1980s but already in 1981-82 the sector had 47 per cent of the investments launched. At first only an increase in domestic coal production was at issue, but later a programme of nuclear power station construction was added. Both required development of related domestic engineering, thus indirectly tying up an even larger share of investments. Simultaneously, less was available for chemicals and steel and very little for modernization of most manufacturing industries.

Regional Impacts

The geographical impacts of these policy shifts are clear. The brown coal mining area of Most in the northern Czech area received 9 per cent of the country's investments in 1975, 11 per cent in 1980, and following Prague and Bratislava, had the highest investment per inhabitant in the country, exceeding the national average by some 30 per cent. Moreover, mining entails devastation of the natural environment and requires numerous ancillary investments. The town of Most and part of the road and railway network had to be relocated.

Similarly the proportion of investments located in the northern Moravian hard coal mining district increased where, in the Ostrava basin, mining costs continually rise. Industrial output in Ostrava and Karvina increased slowly in the late 1970s and decreased in 1981. Known reserves will be exhausted in 20 years, so that this agglomeration urgently needs a new development path.

Oil processing was stepped up after 1970 using Soviet imports, but because of problems of procurement in 1979 the petrochemicals programme was withdrawn from the plan. After 1980 there were no possibilities for increasing oil imports and, as a result, the industrial development of Bratislava, where the largest refinery is located, came to a halt and began to decline.

The 1981-85 plan still includes a development of the timber industry, which necessitates investment mainly in less developed Slovakia and southern Bohemia. Faster development of light industries having long-standing traditions, but having been technically neglected, is also foreseen in the plan and may assist development in the northern Czech territories. The general industrial policy targets adopted in the 1981-85 plan give priority to economic sectors indispensable for conditions of austerity: rationalizing energy and metal uses, the manufacture and diffusion of microelectronic devices, semi-conductors and robots; modernization of transport and materials handling.

More rapid job creation in the late 1970s could not prevent a significant slowdown in industrial production. However, a relationship is evident in that industrial production increased faster in districts where industrial employment also grew, principally in Slovakia and the southern Czech district where industrial employment still fell short of the national average. What was happening was the drawing of the locally resident population into industry.

Equalization between the districts measured by the number of industrially employed per 1,000 inhabitants slowed after 1975, but the coefficient of dispersion was already of a very low value. Industrial output increased at an above average rate in less industrialized districts and in Prague. By 1980 industrial output was more evenly distributed throughout the country than five years earlier. Yet a difference remained manifest between the northern and southern Czech territories. The former, accounting for 32 per cent of the area of Czechoslovakia, produce 53 per cent of industrial output and contain 44 per cent of the population (1981 figures). There are more than 200 industrially employed per 1,000 inhabitants. The region contains two coal basins (Kladno and Most) a traditionally industrialized zone between them, and Prague, the capital. Least suitable for extensive economic development, and because reconstruction was not carried out, this region recorded the slowest industrial development in the 1970s (the situation resembles that in the south-eastern GDR).

From 1970 wages in the socialist sector and retail trade grew fastest in the two capitals, Prague and Bratislava, although a slow catching up process is occurring in the Slovak districts. The differences have increased in the Czech lands, though it should be noted that industrial wages in Czechoslovakia since 1955 have been more egalitarian than in other East European countries. A 15 per cent nationwide rise of wages between 1975 and 1980 was distributed unevenly from the spatial perspective. Clerical workers in Prague and miners received more than anyone else. Above-average building industry wages may also be instrumental in this distribution. There is hardly any deviation in per capita annual average income in non-capital districts. Yet it was 39 per cent above the national average in Prague in 1975, 42 per cent higher in 1980, whereas in Bratislava wages were 60 per cent above in both years.

According to all economic indicators, however, the biggest regional differences in development continue to be manifest between the western Czechoslovakia inhabited by Czechs and eastern inhabited by the Slovaks, a result of pre-1945 history.

Differences in industrial structure are not negligible between the two regions. Although the balance of light and heavy industry became uniform in the 1970s in the two regions, Slovakia has greater importance in petrochemicals, building materials, timber-processing, manufacture of electric machinery related to specialization in activities processing local raw materials, materials imported from the Soviet Union (due to the region's eastern location) and with higher labour-intensity. In productvity Slovak industry no longer lags behind that of the corresponding Czech plants.

Central policy envisages convergence in the economic and welfare levels of the two regions through accelerated development of Slovakia involving an increasing share of investment (34.3 per cent in 1981). Slovakia has a permanently negative difference between the generation and use of national income, still offset in the early 1970s by Bohemia's contribution. Later, however, both regions exhibited deficits upsetting the equilibrium of the whole national economy, and requiring financing by foreign credits.

Traditionally Slovakia was the leader in the growth of industrial output but this slowed and the early 1980s feature an identical rate in both regions (Brhlovic, Kodaj and Krc, 1982). The cause lies hidden in the structure of the Slovak industry. The amount of Soviet oil processed in Bratislava cannot be increased further, and a similar situation holds for the Soviet iron ore treated at Kosice. In other words, the raw material import problem slowing the economic growth of Czechoslovakia expresses itself mainly in Slovakia.

After 1981 the regional issue lost its significance in the face of the country's general economic problems. The priority objectives no longer include accelerated Slovak development, largely because Slovak industry continues to increase its share of exports and approach the Czech level, i.e. Slovak industry has become significantly more export-orientated.

In earlier years the fast growth of Slovak industry was sustained mainly by extensive local labour reserves and the increased involvement of capital and raw materials. Even today the economic mechanism favours extensive growth advantageous to Slovakia. Czech industry would have required intensive development featuring efficiency-orientation based on reconstruction not expansion. But no suitable economic policy and mechanism has been established for this. As a result, Czech industry fell behind in international competitiveness and resources were partly transferred to Slovakia, a process definitely strengthened by the Slovak leadership's interests.

The present economic situation, however, affects Slovakia just as much as Bohemia. With the contraction of certain sources of growth, greater emphasis has been placed here, too, on efficiency, which may lessen - differently from the 1967-68 situation - local resistance to a possible reform of the economic mechanism. A trend contrary to this, on the other hand, results fom the high rate of natural increase of population, expanding the labour force and so requiring more creation of jobs.

GERMAN DEMOCRATIC REPUBLIC

Indebtedness, decreased competitiveness and poor agricultural output contributed in the late 1970s to slower economic growth in the GDR.

Against a historic background of a stagnant labour force, economic policy had had to expand industrial output through increased productivity. On the other hand, extensive sources of growth were an increase in material and energy intensity and foreign credits. These sources were exhausted by the late 1970s and hence, the economy of imported materials and energy came to the fore in economic policy; the measures taken to achieve savings are termed 'complex rationalization' in the literature. Despite this, energy and metallurgy took more investment because efforts were made to increase the domestic production of energy as an import-substitution measure. The results were slight, as the production costs of brown coal soared rapidly. By contrast, though investment was cut, production increased fastest in the manufacture of machines, transport equipment and electronic products. Electronics and related electrical industries were declared priority sectors in 1979 together with the diffusion of automation and robotics designed to save labour.

After 1980 every rationalization programme was carried out with greater intensity which is reflected in investment. The theory and practice of economic policy seem to be more in harmony with each other than previously. Yet the economic machanism set constraints. Complex rationalization generally implies a system of technical and organizational programmes designed to reduce specific costs, to eliminate losses not normally evident. Because of the uncertainty of the accuracy of calculations, it is hard to get a real picture of the results of rationalization.

Another priority of complex rationalization after 1979 was the efficient spatial organization of production and improved working and living conditions in different areas through use of local reserves. Earlier developments had been unilaterally sector-orientated and the organizational concentration of production did not result in contraction of industrial location. Elimination of duplicate capacities and of the unprofitable transport serving them is now the goal of territorial rationalization and involves the transfer of labour to the more productive locations. Reinforced local party and state machinery was made responsible for this rationalization between economic units. Several plants pooled their resources for jointly building heat or power plants, social institutions and infrastructure.

The campaign for spatial rationalization was connected with changes in economic organization. Industry and construction were reorganised into 'combines' to co-ordinate the whole vertical line of manufacture of specific end-product groups, including the necessary research and development. Combines were organized also for local industry, one for each district. Concentration in one location of the plants belonging organizationally to one and the same combine went ahead to save transport and operation costs. This led of course to an increase in commuting and is one of the reasons why in the 1980s it is necessary to increase housing mainly in the southern industrial districts (Leipzig, Karl-Marx-Stadt, Dresden and Plauen).

The principles of the 1981-85 economic plan were a perfection of rationalization and the intensification of the national economy, calling attention to the need for better plan preparation and combines taking initiatives. The development priorities (microelectronics, robotics, computing techniques, fine metallurgy and chemicals industry) were designed to provide the technical basis for intensification. Regional development programmes were also drawn up for every district and for a number of major urban agglomerations.

Regional Trends

In the early 1970s industrial production grew fastest in the least industrialized northern and eastern districts, mostly an extensive spread of industry to absorb available labour reserves. In the

Cottbus district lignite mining, energy production and chemicals grew rapidly. New capacities were built in the Frankfurt-an-der-Oder district for the treatment and processing of the oil, iron ore and timber shipped from the Soviet Union. Thuringia, too, exhibited an above-average rate, an industrial area with traditions, where fragmented, small-scale plants were replaced by new combines and where electronics were located. Dresden also attracted this new industry.

After 1975 Neubrandenburg and Schwerin in the north and east, where the labour-absorbing industrialization was already completed, ceased to show an above-average rate of growth. Though the share of agriculture in employment still appears high, the density of population is low and the number of workers per hectare is much lower than in the south. Industry slowed drastically in the Cottbus district where coal mining remained the main activity. Amongst previously fast developing districts Frankfurt-an-der-Oder, Gera, Erfurt and Suhl preserved their positions in 1980. Since then there has been hardly any increase in Soviet raw material deliveries and the dynamism of production in Frankfurt is probably declining now.

The spatial structure of the GDR's economy is characterized by a heavy concentration of production and population in the south, yet per capita indicators show large-scale equalization.

Nearly half of the industrially employed and of production are in the south-east. Long standing industrial regions, urban agglomerations and raw material sites adjoin one another. There are more than 200 industrial workers per 1,000 inhabitants. A well-developed transport network serves the region. Yet many problems are raised by this concentration: little open space; industrial and drinking water in short supply; polluted water and air. And the economic management system favours expansion rather than modernization.

The problem of these agglomerations came to the fore in the early 1970s. The rationalization drive was mainly directed at these areas, but no integrated approach was adopted in the early 1970s, except for housing and infrastructure. At that time, however, fast industrializing areas, not the southern agglomerations, had enjoyed priority. From the late 1970s, when infrastructure again received less investment, top priority was given to the most spectacular goal, housing, an undoubtedly important trend, as the big towns have lots of unhealthy flats. On its own, however, this programme was by no means sufficient for improving the environment. Most of the economic development occurred in the peripheral regions of the agglomerations, where crowding and environmental deterioration are not yet advanced. Thuringia and some parts of the district of Dresden are such areas.

The significance of the capital, Berlin, increased in the GDR's life. It is the biggest city and housing supply per head the highest. Improved living standards are evident in the growth of retail trade. In a country featuring a centralized management of economy and society the increased role of the capital to the detriment of the provincial big towns is logical but not advantageous, but it is a trend which has been one of the government's objectives in the early 1980s.

EAST-CENTRAL EUROPE IN TRANSITION

Just one indicator proved to be suitable for measuring spatial industrial development: industrial employment. Although data are available for industrial output and investment, too, they are not comparable with certainty even within a country, still less between countries, because of frequent price changes (see Table 5.1).

The spatial pattern of Bulgarian industry is more balanced than that in the GDR and Czechoslovakia. Bulgarian industrial development is practically exclusively a product of the socialist period; there is here no sign at all of past polarization resulting from capitalist industrialization. In the other two countries, significant differences do occur and show considerable stability. The spatial structure of Poland also results from earlier industrial development typified by large towns and agglomerations; these have not been essentially altered by development after 1945. By contrast, Romania, by pursuing rapid industrialization deliberately decreases the interregional differences.

The slowdown in economic development in the late 1970s led in each country to less regional change. The typical 'traditional' path of socialist economic growth got into crisis and possibilities for expanding the sources of further growth became exhausted. Former extensive development meant that the areas with material and labour resources always experienced more rapid development. In the later

Table 5.1: Number of industrial workers per 1,000 inhabitants, weighted according to the proportion of population

Country	Number of administrative units	1968	1975	1980
Bulgaria	27	0.31	0.22	0.18
Czechoslovakia	11	0.28	0.22	0.21
GDR	15	0.31	0.26	0.29
Romania	40	0.67[1]	0.47	0.40
Poland	49	-	0.48	0.45
Hungary	20	0.50	0.34	0.26

[1]1970 figure

Source: For 1968: I. Koropeckij, 'Equalization of regional development in socialist countries, Economic development and cultural change, vol.21, no.1, pp.68-86, 1975.
1980: author's calculations

1970s three sources of growth played a critical role: labour, raw materials and material imports.

Labour supplies became scarcer in each country, and this factor lost its absolute and relative significance. Development of domestic raw material sources gained priority investment in each country. Where only old material sites were viable, investments did not produce the expected results. Where possible, new raw material sources were brought into production, as in Poland, and the prosperity of the mining districts was the main factor in narrowing the gaps in the levels of development between regions.

After 1975 imports increased rapidly in each country, and, due to the increasing energy intensity of their economies and to the simultaneous construction of chemicals' capacities, the import mainly of oil and later of natural gas grew rapidly. From 1980 there has been no increase in oil imports. As most countries imported from the USSR processing plants were located in the eastern regions: the district of Frankfurt-an-der-Oder, Slovakia, the Black Sea coastline. These areas grew rapidly at the time of expanding material imports, being the most dynamic areas of the respective countries, but after the freezing of deliveries they lost their dynamism.

In the late 1970s development depended less on internal sources and more on the East European countries' balance of payments and foreign credit imports. The constraints affected the less developed areas, industrial dispersion being taken off the agenda. The economic dynamism of the northern GDR, Slovakia, northern Transylvania and eastern Poland fell back to the national average, a tendency which will be even more in evidence in the 1980s. Most success was recorded by the GDR in development through modernization and a more economic management of resources, yielding faster growth in the developed manufacturing industry districts of the south.

The decreasing availablity of resources in each country required stricter distribution control, even rationing. Greater emphasis was placed on increasing producers' and population's awareness of the need to save and on local initiatives. In Romania and Bulgaria an increasing role was played by the county party organs in all domains from supply to the population to the fulfilment of the export plans, while in Czechoslovakia and in the GDR they have greater say in the guidance of agriculture and management of inter-plant linkages. In a period of increasing shortages in the field of consumption the supply of, and the incomes in, the capital cities increased more than in the other regions of the countries. Though the role of local authorities has increased, in a legal sense no decentralization of the decision authority has occurred. To all this Poland is an exception: there these tendencies were more characteristic of the mid-1970s, and the crisis broke out sooner, launching reform-oriented changes.

Most countries exhibit a slowing in urbanization. Cutbacks in industrial development meant fewer people moving to the towns, a trend reinforced as governments began to pay greater attention to the villages to solve farming problems. The tendency for concentration in agricultural organization came to an end. So did the former strength and guiding role of just a few central settlements, while the village as an economic unit gained in significance, both through large-scale socialism and, in the early 1980s in most countries, also though the support of small-scale production.

Eastern-Central Europe is currently in a period

of transition. No clear economic concepts have so far been formulated to further future progress. The same applies to the plans of regional development. An efficiency-oriented path of economic development would call for an efficient utilization of the spatial pattern of the economy.

BIBLIOGRAPHY

Brhlovic, G., Kodaj, M. and Krc, R., 'Zdaje a faktory dehodobeho razvoja Slovenska v jednotneg ekonomike CSSR', Pravda, 1982, Bratislava

Csaba, L. 'A csehszlovak iparpolitika iranyzatai' (Trends in Czechoslovak industrial policy) Iparpolitikai Tajekoztato, 1981, pp.10-11

Gabor, H. 'A roman iparfejlesztes teruleti kerdesei' (Spatial Issues in Romanian Industrial Development), Iparpolitikai Tajekoztato, 1982, no.5, pp.

Hamilton, F.E. Ian, 'Regional Policy in Poland: A Search for Equity?', Geoforum, 13 (2), 1983, pp.121-32

Łukasiewicz, A. 'Reform of planning system in Poland', Oeconomia Polonica, 1983, p.2

Pajestka, J. 'The Polish crisis of 1980-1', Oeconomica Polonica, 1982, pp.3-4

Yuill, D., Alen, K. and Hull C. Regional Policy in the EEC, Croom Helm, London, 1980

CHAPTER 6

THE TRANSFORMATION OF THE INDUSTRIAL SYSTEM IN SPAIN

Antonio Vázquez-Barquero

During the last thirty years the industrial space in Spain has passed through continuous transformation, from a situation where modern industrial activity was focused on advanced industrial and metropolitan areas (1950s) to another where, despite intensification of the concentration process, a diffusion began towards the intermediate industrial areas (1960s and 1970s). The spatial changes have not ended, insofar as a new pattern is tending to take shape. Since the late 1970s the Spanish industrial system appears to be taking on multipolar characteristics. The causes are to be found in the strong de-industrialization of the traditional industrial centres and in the impact that processes such as productive decentralization, endogenous local development and functional decentralization exercise over industrial location.

This chapter analyses Spanish industrial changes and leads to the explanation of factors of development and of the current crisis in the Spanish economy. It continues with a definition of industrialization and de-industrialization processes, identifies the changes of the industrial system on the territory and ends with some comments on the latest tendencies in the Spanish industrialization pattern.

FROM DEVELOPMENT TO CRISIS

Since the 1950s the Spanish economy has passed through two clearly differentiated periods. The first was one of growth (from 1957-59 to 1973) in which a strong production expansion occurred with an annual GDP growth rate of 7 per cent (1961-74) and in which the unemployment rate was very low (1.6 per cent). The second is a period of crisis from

1974-75 onwards, in which the GDP growth rate fell (2.3 per cent during 1975-78; 1.1 per cent during 1979-83) and the unemployment rate increased progressively from 7.4 per cent in 1978 to 18.1 per cent in 1983.

It is easy to establish the factors that promoted Spanish industrial development, since it has been an object of attention of Spanish and foreign researchers (Garcia, 1980; Hudson and Lewis, 1984).

A key element was the 'liberalization' of the Spanish economy, begun in 1959 with the Stabilization Plan. Modernization and expansion of the Spanish productive system was consolidated only with the progressive integration of the Spanish economy into the international economy after the late 1950s, facilitating the attainment of foreign and domestic balance in the growth process.

Structural change was made possible because the economic and social conditions in Spain favoured a profit accumulation, which was most attractive to private foreign and national investors. Low costs of energy and raw materials combined especially with a socially-controlled labour market with an abundant labour supply, few social conflicts and low salary levels, all permitted low production costs. High protection levels of the domestic market assured the sale of manufactured goods in an expanding market.

Add to this a high degree of oligopolization within the markets, permissive monetary policy, allowing for a certain degree of inflation and an economic policy favouring growth through subsidies and incentives, and one may conclude that the conditions for capital accumulation were very favourable.

On the other hand, the 'liberalization' of the economy allowed for the growing presence of multinational firms and improvements in technology, stimulating the rise in productivity, particularly in industry (Muñoz et al., 1978; Vázquez, 1981B). A high domestic savings rate (more than 23 per cent of the GNP during 1961-74) was a great force in structural change. Yet foreign capital has played a strategic role, not only because more than 20 per cent of the gross industrial investment between 1960 and 1973 came from foreign savings, but also because the multinational firms have stimulated the utilization rate of entrepreneurial capacity.

Lastly, the 1960s growth process owes its success to the specific conditions of its foreign balance, that could only be made under an international economic situation of economic expansion. Spain has shown a continuous tendency towards a trade deficit because of its expanding need for imported capital, intermediate and consumer goods (even of agricultural products). The progressive rise in exports of processed agricultural and manufactured products by multinational firms has mitigated, not eradicated, this imbalance. Only remittances by emigrants, the flows from tourism and foreign investments brought the Balance of Payments into balance, and therefore have favoured the consolidation of the structural changes of the period.

The pattern of industrialization and growth described above embodies important limitations and deficiencies. First and foremost, it lacks the capacity for productively using all available human resources. Second, the industrialization model entrenches an uneven sectoral structure by favouring the final goods industries and basic industries with old-fashioned technology. Finally, the industrial system has a high level of foreign dependence, on both the productive and organizational level, and financial and technological levels (Vázquez, 1980; Segura, 1983).

However, during the 1970s the favourable conditions changed and the constraints became far more decisive in shaping the new situation. Most authors agree in defining the Spanish economic crisis as one of crisis of its industrial system, but it is difficult to make a diagnosis. One hypothesis notes that the supply of industrial products has been dissociated from national and international demand. Not only has the demand diminished in many products and has focused towards 'new' products, but besides this the international supply has increased as the growth of the NICs poured industrial goods into international markets. This has caused a reduction of demand for Spanish key products (textiles, ships, iron and steel, durable consumer goods). Thus, many industrial plants suffer overcapacity and need to adjust to the present conditions of the national and international markets.

A second hypothesis indicates that cost increases in raw materials, energy and mainly wages, has lowered the entrepreneurial surplus (43 per cent of GDP during 1961-74; 37 per cent during 1975-83) and has deteriorated the capability of industry to accumulate capital. It is not so much that the oil price shocks increased energy costs in Spain but, above all, that liberalization in the labour market since 1975 has put pressure on rising average wages (an increase of 15 per cent during 1961-74: 22 per cent during 1975-78 and 12.7 per cent during 1979-83), simultaneously as the rate of increase in productivity was reduced by half (6.4 per cent during 1961-74; 3 per cent during 1979-83). The problem is especially serious when new investments are required to make firms more competitive.

A third hypothesis refers to deficiencies in the institutional framework that characterizes the system of enterprise financing. The majority of Spanish firms have low self-financing levels that make them rely on bank and public financing. Problems in this sphere are very serious. The powerful private banks have low efficiency levels; they have raised financial services' costs because of an excessive business expansionist policy and have paid more attention to speculative, rather than industrial, operations. Public financing is limited, has serious functional defects and operates through privileged financial channels that block access to official funds for most firms. These defects in financial markets have increased the difficulties of the Spanish industrial system.

INDUSTRIALIZATION AND DE-INDUSTRIALIZATION

The phases of development and of crisis in the Spanish economy correspond to the operation of industrialization and de-industrialization processes (Table 6.1). Industrial production grew the fastest amongst the economic sectors during the development period (10.3 per cent during 1961-74), raising the share of the industrial sector in the GDP from 28 per cent in 1954 to 32 per cent in 1974. After 1974 there was a progressive reduction of the growth rate of industrial activity (2.4 per cent in 1975-78; 0.6 per cent in 1979-83), decreasing the share of industry in total production to 28 per cent in 1983.

Unfinished Industrialization

Manufacturing firms were the most dynamic force in the economy in the development period. Not only did manufacturing production grow at high rates, above those of industrialized countries (12 per cent annually from 1958-60 to 1964-66) but the intersectoral change has been large in scope, particularly since the mid-1960s. The coefficient of similarity (UNECE, 1972) that correlates the distribution of manufacturing production (at the 2

Table 6.1: Indices of Industrial Production 1972 and 1981

Branches	1972 (1962 = 100)	1981 (1973 = 100)
Food, beverages and tobacco	353	148
Textiles, clothing and leather	358	92.4
Wood and furniture	315	99.8
Paper and printing	463	135
Chemicals and allied	421	139
Non-metallic mineral products	535	110
Iron and steel and basic metals	475	106
Metal products, machinery and transport equipment	429	114

Source: INE and Banco de Bilbao

digit level of the ISIC classification) between 1958-60 and 1973-75 was 0.93 (0.92 between 1964-66 and 1973-75).

Nevertheless, intersectoral changes have not been sufficiently profound to convert Spanish industry to the pattern of the more advanced countries. Despite the fact that manufacturing industry no longer focuses on making traditional consumer goods, it has not developed the capital goods industries sufficiently well and retains a relatively high share of basic industry (Table 6.2). On the other hand, the structure of Spanish manufacturing industry continues to exhibit important differences from those of advanced countries (Vázquez, 1980).

The strategic sectors in industrial growth processes have been basic industries, chemicals, metal products, machinery and transport equipment. During the postwar period, basic industry was the main focus of interest of the government's autarchic policy, a situation continued in the most recent decades. It is only since the 1960s that private national and international initiatives (supported by the State) have widened productive structure to include the chemical, durable-consumer goods and

Table 6.2: Changes in the Structure of Production in the Manufacturing Sector (per cent)

	1958-60	1973-75
Industries of Non-Durable Goods [1]	47.4	32.9
Industries of Intermediate Goods [2]	29.9	40.6
Industries of Capital Goods and of Durable Goods [3]	22.7	26.5

[1] Food, beverages, textiles, clothing, shoes, furniture
[2] Paper, cork, chemicals, petroleum and coal products, non-metallic minerals, basic metallurgy
[3] Metal products, electronic equipment, machinery, transport material

Source: INE

machinery sectors. Dualism, however, is an important constraint in the Spanish industrial system.

Even though some manufacturing production has reached high productivity levels comparable to those in advanced countries, especially machinery, motor cars and shipbuilding, most manufacturing activities have important technical and organizational deficiencies, and thus low productivity. Industrial dualism reflects a clear technological dualism in the industrial system and analysis of the firms' system provides new information that backs this hypothesis.

Expansion of modern productive activities has been made possible thanks to the penetration of multinational firms in the productive system, especially in chemicals and durable-consumer goods sectors and to the development of State-owned firms, mainly in the basic sectors. The active role of these firms has combined with the incentives offered by State industrial policies to favour a certain concentration of the productive activity in large plants, particularly since the early 1960s. This fact nevertheless has not altered the system of small firms that is essentially a legacy of the previous industrialization pattern. In this way, entrepreneurial dualism has been strengthened by the process of industrial development.

De-industrialization

During the last decade de-industrialization and restructuring became the two dominant processes in the Spanish industrial system. De-industrialization is a proven fact, evident even in the unreliable Spanish statistics. During the period 1973-81 industrial employment (including construction) declined by 16.7 per cent, a loss of 815,183 jobs, and manufacturing employment by 15.3 per cent or 517,150 net jobs. Nevertheless, de-industrialization was followed by a restructuring of firms that still continues, increasing productivity in all sectors (Table 6.3).

De-industrialization has been a response to both the reduced and changed character of demand and to a drop in the profit rate. According to Alcaide, 1984, the net surplus of industry dropped by 41 per cent during 1973-71. Wages, energy and raw materials' prices increased, yet market constraints meant that firms were unable to transfer the whole rise in input costs into output prices. Hence, the mortality rate of firms increased to a high rate, though it is unknown precisely, while the birthrate has risen less due to reduced expectations from entrepreneurial profits. Nevertheless, the importance of the informal economy in traditional (and even in new) production covers up the extent of the amplitude of the process (Ybarra, 1982).

Firms that were able to resist the first impacts of the crisis have restructured themselves, differentiating production and introducing new technologies in the productive process. Productive reconversion has largely been spontaneous, even though the State has helped some firms and sectors since the early 1980s (Aranzadi et al. 1983; Ortun et al. 1983).

The crisis is most intense in the basic industries, machinery, durable consumer goods, as well as the traditional textile, leather and shoe industries. Base metals and iron and steel industries have not been restructured up to now, partly because they could continue their businesses during the decade with the aid of State subsidies. Despite their apparent smooth running, with an annual production growth rate of 4 per cent during 1972-82, the firms find themselves with progressively burdensome financial problems which prevent them from carrying out necessary restructuring themselves to become competitive.

Table 6.3: Shifts in Industrial Production, Employment and Productivity in Spain Annual Growth Rate 1973-81

Branches	Value added at constant prices	Employment	Productivity (1)
Food, beverages and tobacco	5.03	-2.21	7.4
Textiles	-1.12	-4.18	3.2
Clothing and leather	-0.88	-3.40	2.6
Wood and furniture	-0.02	-2.29	2.3
Paper and printing	3.82	-1.40	5.3
Chemical and others	4.20	-0.69	4.9
Non-metallic mineral products	1.15	-0.76	1.9
Iron and steel, base metals	0.76	-1.74	2.5
Metal products, machinery and transport equipment	1.67	-1.69	3.4
Total	1.99	-2.06	4.14

Source: Alcaide, 1984
(1) Value added per worker

Reductions in domestic sales by firms making equipment, shipbuilding and construction materials have been compensated by an increase in exports at prices under production costs, which caused serious deficits in the firms. Despite the high rise in production costs during the last decade, the changes of the domestic and international demand and the rising competitiveness of the NIC, the firms have not been restructured or modernized. On the contrary, the public funds have been used for keeping them artificially in the marketplace.

The crisis has affected activities such as machinery, durable-consumer goods and transport equipment in different ways. Some production, such as electronic equipment for audio-visual purposes (annual growth rate of 4.9 per cent during 1972-82) and motor cars (4.9 per cent) have increased, thanks to the differentiation of production through the introduction of new technology and - to the maintenance and renovation of the demand. Others, such as computers and new office machines, have increased and diversified production to meet new demands, though their importance is not known. On the contrary, shipbuilding (-4 per cent), construction machinery (-1.8 per cent), railroad equipment (-1.6 per cent), domestic appliances (-0.9 per cent) have contracted because of changes in demand. The adjustment has come late in general, while in shipbuilding it still has to be made and its consequences are not well known.

The textile (annual growth rate of 0.8 per cent during 1972-82), clothing and shoes (-1.1 per cent) activities suffered seriously during the crisis as a result of international competition by the NICs and of some industrialized countries, such as Italy. At first, the reaction of most firms was to keep up with the activity and with the profit rates through the informal economy (Ybarra, 1982). Other firms, however, have closed. Nevertheless, since the late 1960s some firms, particularly in clothing, began to restructure, introducing new equipment and production methods and improving the design of their products. In this way, their share in national and international markets has been partially regained. Overall thus far, however, the adjustment has been limited.

Other activities have experienced generally positive tendencies during the crisis with a considerable rise in production and productivity. The rise in costs of energy and raw materials considerably stimulated the mining and petroleum industries, which expanded output between 1972 and 1982 at an annual rate of 5.7 per cent. The food, beverages and tobacco industries underwent important restructuring, with an outstanding rise in the production and productivity of those manufactures that include higher value added, such as canned foods (annual rate of 6.2 per cent) and non-alcoholic beverages (8.1 per cent). Introduction of new production methods and the differentiation of products has allowed adjustment of production to the changes in demand.

Lastly, there has been surprising adjustment in the chemical industry, which sustained an annual growth rate of 3.4% during 1972-82), though pharmaceuticals, fertilizers and pesticides have been incapable of altering their production structure in the face of changing and decreasing demand. Production of plastics (6.2 per cent), final chemicals (5.7 per cent) and intermediate chemicals (4.9 per cent) has improved thanks to restructuring by firms to increase their productivity.

Finally, the system of firms has altered during the crisis.

Public firms lost their dynamism during the past decade, whereas multinational and local private firms have restructured their production systems and introduced new products and higher efficiency. State concerns in the iron and steel and shipbuilding industries have found adjustment difficult because of too much bureaucracy and a lack of entrepreneurial capacity. Multinational firms, particularly those making motor cars and plastics, and in agri-business, have increased their penetration of Spanish markets as a result of their marketing and technology strategies. Local firms in turn, especially in the textile, shoe-making and machinery industries, went through a period of intensive restructuring and are beginning to act as dynamic agents in finding a way out of the crisis.

On the other hand, firms have adjusted in response to profound changes in production systems. New technologies have favoured functional decentralization in activities such as motor cars, electronics, durable-consumer goods, plastics and textiles. Progressive introduction of decentralized production systems based on networks of small production units is being intensified, while introduction of new equipment has raised productivity.

TRANSFORMATION OF INDUSTRIAL SPACE

The processes of industrial development and crisis have had significant spatial impacts. The forces generated by industrialization and de-industrialization have influenced industrial location and altered the spatial distribution of activity and employment. Thus, in the last thirty years the Spanish regional and urban pattern has been passing through on-going transformations. Two distinct phases can be observed: the first was industrial diffusion linked to urbanization; the second, industrial and urban decentralization.

Industrial Diffusion and Urbanization

Until the late 1950s industrial activity focused

mainly on the regions of old industrialization, the Basque country, Asturias, Catalonia and Madrid (see Figure 6.1) (Ferrer and Precedo, 1981). Factors such as commercial and industrial traditions (except in Madrid), locational advantages, agglomeration economies and, in the case of Madrid, the advantages of being the country's capital favoured the location of basic industry, machinery, metal products and transport equipment in these regions.

Except in the case of Valencia, where certain industrial activities, such as the manufacture of toys, shoes, furniture, ceramics, were developed to take advantage of a strong handicraft tradition and local resources, the rest of Spain made up the industrial periphery of the Spanish economy. The only modern industrial sites were in coastal cities and a few in the interior (such as Valladolid and Zaragoza) while handicrafts remained in rural areas. In general, these activities supplied regional and local markets.

During the 1960s there began a strong spatial diffusion process of industrial activity, particularly around the traditional industrial centres of the late 1950s (Lasuen, 1976). It spread to the area defined by the triangle formed by Madrid, the Basque country and Catalonia, and more specifically in the belt that extends between Asturias and Valencia.

The factors that explain the ensuing concentration-diffusion process are numerous. Not only were the proximity of markets, agglomeration economies, resource availability, the commercial and entrepreneurial tradition shaping the location of industry in the period of development, but so too were Spanish economic policy and the strategies of multinational firms.

The reduction of inter-regional disparities was not the main objective of economic policy but, instead, the concentration-diffusion process favoured by the market forces were supported by political measures. The goals of agricultural, industrial and infrastructure policies conditioned not only public investment but, to a lesser degree, private investment in that direction. As Richardson (1975) points out the spatial distribution of growth has been influenced by an implicit regional policy, more than by an explicit regional policy.

At the same time, public firms did not develop a systematic policy of location geared towards the development of poor regions, but instead followed the same locational criteria as the private firms.

Figure 6.1:

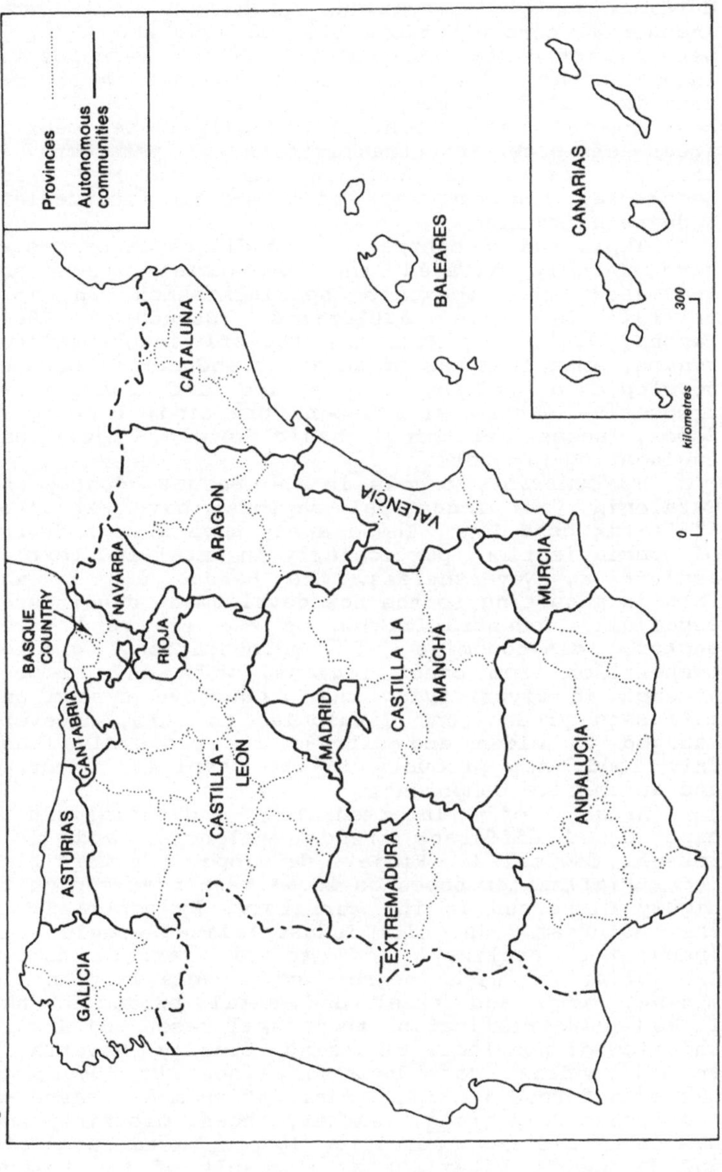
Provinces
Autonomous communities
GALICIA
ASTURIAS
CANTABRIA
BASQUE COUNTRY
NAVARRA
RIOJA
CASTILLA - LEÓN
ARAGÓN
CATALUNA
MADRID
CASTILLA LA MANCHA
EXTREMADURA
VALENCIA
MURCIA
ANDALUCIA
BALEARES
CANARIAS
0
300
kilometres

Multinationals' location behaviour favoured industrial concentration. Between 1960 and 1972, 72 per cent of direct foreign investments were located in the areas of advanced industrialization (36 per cent in Madrid, 26 per cent in Catalonia and 10 per cent in the Basque country) and only 16 per cent in areas of weak industrialization (7 per cent in tourist activities and in the Huelva pole, Andalucia) and the rest in areas of intermediate industrialization.

Thus, the concentration and diffusion processes have largely altered the industrial space and increased the region's specialization in more capital intensive activities (Escudero, 1984; Mancha, 1984). Only Madrid, a recently industrialized region, amongst areas of advanced industrialization, developed a modern, diversified and competitive productive system with paper, printing, chemicals, foods, shoes, clothing, basic metals, metal and engineering products.

By contrast, trends in the Basque country and Catalonia (old industrial regions) have exhibited different behaviour. These areas have a high degree of specialization, particularly in metal and textile activities. Nevertheless, the Basque country was late in adjusting to the new development conditions, especially decentralization of the iron and steel sector, diseconomies of agglomeration, greater competition from other regions, with only a weak attempt at diversifying the productive system and diffusing production. Catalonia, in turn, however, managed to widen and diffuse its productive base into food, new products in the chemical industry, and automotive components.

Areas of intermediate industrialization experienced different trends. Valencia, and to a lesser degree La Rioja, developed diversified industrialization based on local resources and quite highly dispersed in the territory. By contrast, in the Asturias, an old industrialized region in industrial decline, and to a lesser degree Cantabria, a high degree of specialization in mining, iron and steel and metal products, has linked industrialization to natural resources and to the flow of non-local financing. Finally, Navarra is an intermediate case because, since the 1960s, it has transformed its industrialization model based on local resources (food, leather, shoes, clothing) and has developed new activities (paper, metal products and transport material) as a result of the Basque spread effect.

Lastly, in areas of weak industrialization, the growth of modern chemicals and metals industries has blocked the development of an industrialization process based on local resources and has not yet achieved completion of the industrialization process and a break with underdevelopment. Industrializing regions (Andalucia, Aragon, Murcia and Galicia) have a greater specialization in food, energy and mining; they combine centres of modern industrial concentration in cities with diffused rural industrialization around and maintain large intra-regional imbalances. The less industrialized regions (Castilla-Leon, Castilla-La Mancha and Extremadura) specialize in mining, wood and cork, cement and ceramics in modern industrial locations in some cities, like Burgos, Valencia and Valladolid and isolated focal points of local industrialization. These have been progressively depopulated.

Finally, since the 1950s urbanization and the formation of large metropolitan areas have accelerated. Urban population rose from 57 per cent of the total population in 1960 to 74 per cent in 1980, with an annual growth rate of 2.6 per cent during 1960-70 and of 2.2 per cent during 1970-80. The annual growth rate of the greater metropolitan areas was 3.4 per cent in 1950-60 and 1960-70 and 2.8 per cent during 1970-75. These high growth rates in urban population are due to the high migration flows that during 1960-73 involved 4.2 million persons, of whom 60 per cent were inter-provincial migrants and 40 per cent intra-provincial migrants (Santillana, 1984).

The explanatory factors for these processes have been industrialization and modernization (Gaspar, 1984), though urban growth has also been conditioned by other factors such as the increase in tertiary activities, tourism and fishing and by the dynamics of the traditional urban system (Ferrer and Precedo, 1981). It is true that the largest industrial centres are next to the biggest cities and that during the industrial development period the industrial and urban concentration has increased. Yet urbanization of provincial capitals and in smaller towns strengthened despite the relative absence of industrial activity.

Industrial and Urban Decentralization

The industrial crisis initiated a structural change in the productive system in which mainly the recently industrialized regions (i.e. Valencia, La Rioja and Navarra) acquired a greater role by adjusting themselves more quickly to changes in demand and in technology while the regions of traditional industrialization in decline (the Asturias and Basque country) appear incapable of reconverting their industries. This defines a new situation in which the concentration of industrial activity decreases and the industrial system becomes more diffused.

De-industrialization affects all regions but the fall in industrial production growth rate and in industrial employment has an uneven incidence within the territory (Table 6.4). Greatest losses occurred in industrial employment in the regions of advanced industrialization (Catalonia 177,100 during 1973-81; Basque country 75,500, and Madrid 53,600) and in some areas with weak industrialization such as Andalucia (74,800).

Table 6.4 Variation of the Industrial Production and Industrial Employment (per cent) 1973-1981

Regions	Industrial Production	Industrial Employment
Andalucia	19.4	-21.4
Aragon	22.3	-13.6
Asturias	1.6	-11.1
Baleares	22.4	-21.9
Canary Islands	13.8	-22.0
Cantabria	1.0	-10.8
Castilla-La Mancha	24.3	-12.0
Castilla-Leon	35.4	- 4.6
Catalonia	15.9	-18.8
Extremadura	8.6	-25.7
Galicia	35.2	- 6.1
Madrid	24.0	-12.7
Murcia	37.7	-13.1
Navarra	40.2	- 8.8
Basque country	1.4	-20.3
Rioja	56.0	-11.8
Valencia	31.0	- 7.0
Spain	19.3	-14.8

Source: Banco de Bilbao

The impact of the industrial crisis in the national space can, to an extent, explain the transformations under way of the industrial system.

A final assessment cannot be made due to the lack of statistical information and because the process is not yet complete. But, the process of change in the industrial space can be better understood by comparing the location of the activities that have gone into crisis with that of sectors that withstood it better (Banco de Bilbao, 1981, 1984 and Mancha, 1984).

The textile crisis is particularly serious in Catalonia and to a lesser extent in Valencia, regions in which more than 80 per cent of the value added in that industry was localized (Banco de Bilbao, 1981). The crisis in clothing and shoes has had the same effect in Catalonia, Valencia and Madrid (more than 60 per cent of value added in 1981) as well as in other regions. The crisis in printing and publishing has had a greater impact in Catalonia than in Madrid, and this fact has changed the location pattern. The iron and steel crisis is felt in the Basque country, Asturias and Valencia. The shipbuilding crisis affects, above all, Galicia, Andalucia, the Basque country and Cantabria. The crisis of the equipment goods and metal products industries mostly affects the Basque country, but also Andalucia, Catalonia, Madrid and Valencia.

The food and beverage industry has done well, particularly in Catalonia (20 per cent of value added in 1981). The chemical industry, least affected by the crisis, increased its concentration in Madrid and Barcelona (48 per cent) due to improvements in demand for plastics and final chemical products, and lost shares in Andalucia and to a lesser degree in the Basque country. Although the statistical information raises serious doubts, the most positive changes in mining seem to have taken place in Catalonia. Finally, the automotive industry has reconverted rapidly to the new national and international conditions and stays active in Galicia, Valencia, Aragon and Castilla-Leon.

During the crisis period a new pattern of industrial space starts to be defined. Important changes are already perceptible in the areas of advanced industrialization. Madrid, and to a lesser extent Catalonia, where there is a textile crisis, are adjusting quite well to the new conditions through rationalization, investments and growth of the informal economy. The Basque country, however, feels the impact of the crisis most directly not only because the old propulsive industries (iron and steel and shipbuilding) have an uncertain future, but also because the equipment goods and metal products industries must be restructured before reaching their maturity as they have lost competitiveness and markets.

The adjustment to the crisis has been uneven in the areas of intermediate industrialization. In regions where a high degree of specialization exists and with an industrial development supported from the outside (Asturias and Cantabria) the industrial crisis is profound (in mining, iron and steel and shipbuilding) and the available indicators point out that their industrialization path is no longer viable. Nevertheless, the regions where industrialization was based principally on the development of local initiatives (Valencia, La Rioja and to a lesser extent Navarra) adjustment to the crisis has been better and the restructuring of local industry has been more efficient, although occasionally the informal economy grew too much, as in the production of shoes, for example.

Lastly, areas of weak industrialization have experienced less impact of the industrial crisis, if one excludes Andalucia (9 per cent of the value added in Spanish industry in 1981) where during 1975/81 losses in employment were 21,931 in food, beverages and tobacco and 22,294 in the metal industry. One notices a profound restructuring of certain traditional activities in the industrializing regions (food and clothing in Murcia, Andalucia and Galicia), the crisis of subsidized sectors (shipbuilding in Andalucia and Galicia, for example) and a certain rebirth of local activities. As occurred in Aragon, today's crisis offers the regions an opportunity of completing their industrialization process by taking advantage of their local potential. The same comments can be made about Castilla-Leon, for it has increased its share in industrial value added during the crisis by 5 per cent in 1975 and 6 per cent in 1981.

Finally, since the mid 1970s one can observe important changes in the urbanization process, as the urban population growth rate and migration flows drop (Borja and Serra, 1984).

Provincial capitals increased their relative importance in the provinces' population to a lesser degree than in the early 1960s. The medium-size cities (defined as those between 20,000 and 180,000 inhabitants) grew the fastest. Given their relatively even distribution in Spain and their number (approximately 200), the strengthening of the medium-sized cities may yield a consolidated system of cities that breaks with today's urban hierarchy, as long as tendencies for industrial decentralization and service sector development mature in the present decade.

By contrast, metropolitan areas are going through a period of change of unknown characteristics. Though they retain a high growth potential as a result of their youthful population, itself a result of previous migration, their demographic share has stabilized (Madrid, Barcelona, Bilbao, 25 per cent of total population in 1981) and is even tending to diminish. The reason is that central metropolitan areas have stagnated due largely to de-industrialization and change in the service productive activity. Besides this, since the early 1970s and particularly in the 1980s, this regression also affected the neighbouring towns. These transformations can be explained not only by a loss in the growth rate but also by factors that benefit deconcentration such as the saturation of urban centres, the better housing supply in medium-sized towns and migration toward residential areas with better environmental conditions.

TOWARDS THE FUTURE

The economic crisis in Spain is a process that is still not complete and results from a complex set of causes. It is difficult, therefore, to define exactly what the future outcomes will be. Nevertheless, the behaviour of the economic agents during the last ten years indicates some important changes with respect to the preceding period.

First, industrial and agricultural sectors appear to be losing their former importance in the productive system. Industrial reconversion and reindustrialization are making a profound change in industrial structure; old products lose their markets, differentiated production appears in old industries, and new products are introduced with a greater technological content.

Yet secondly, the services sector becomes more and more complex. Low productivity activities (public administration, small businesses, etc.) continue to increase, but what is really new is the increasing growth of modern services with high productivity levels involving the use of computers, telematics and entrepreneurial services.

It seems clear that industry will not continue to be the propulsive sector of structural change in Spain. In the next few years, productivity will continue to rise in the industrial activities, but the recuperation of industrial employment will not take place. In the near future new industrial goods will be produced, but the present transformations of the industrial system are an irreversible process because of the use of labour-saving technologies in productive processes and the increasing competition from the NICs and industrialized countries.

It appears that small firms tend to recuperate their dynamic role within the Spanish industrial system. The new technologies allow for greater flexibility in the production system and can be used by small firms and plants to produce goods that are custom-made and more adapted to the specific demands of the firms and of the consumers. The changes under way point towards a restructuring of the pattern of the entrepreneurial hierarchy with the development of a multipolar system in the organization of production and with the introduction of multiproduct systems on the enterprise level.

The spatial impact of the industrial crisis is now very important. De-industrialization is more relevant in areas of advanced industrialization and it seems that multiregional and multinational firms are changing their location criteria. They no longer prefer to establish their plants in metropolitan centres and in areas of advanced industrialization but instead consider more and more the non-metropolitan, rural areas and zones of intermediate and weak industrialization as more convenient.

Research on new industrial plants' location patterns now being formed maintains the hypothesis that multiregional and multinational firms in Spain have changed their criteria of location to reduce production costs and improve competitiveness. Non-metropolitan areas and regions with intermediate and weak industrialization offer relatively better conditions such as lower labour costs and less social conflict, the availability of industrial land at lower prices and with tax benefits, a lack of agglomeration diseconomies. The available technology allows non-metropolitan location to take advantage of information economies and of functional decentralization of the productive process.

Yet, since the early 1970s the potentials for local industrialization are growing, mainly in areas of intermediate and weak industrialization areas (Vázquez, 1983 and 1984). What is different about these processes is that they group the following characteristics: they have developed without direct State intervention; they do not result from the location of the multiregional or multinational plants; they started through the development of the areas' own resources; they were located in small towns, and in any case in non-metropolitan areas.

The factors that explain endogenous local development vary from place to place and can comprise: a certain industrial (artisan) or commercial tradition; the urgency of overcoming a crisis in the local economy; the availability of a certain amount of savings mostly from agricultural or commercial activity; unlimited supply of labour; the existence of small urban centres with a minimum of services available. During the 1970s these experiences of local industrialization took on greater impulses, because the industrial crisis and urban deterioration gave a differential value to this industrialization pattern.

Despite the fact that adjustment to the crisis has been accomplished with delay by comparison with the industrialized countries, and even though the crisis is more profund in Spain, the economy is overcoming the crisis. Important transformations are taking place in the industrial system, and it seems that a new spatial pattern is tending to take shape. Doubts arise though about Spain's future position in the new international division of labour which has not yet been defined. The problem is not only that there are evident signs that the Spanish economy has lost some comparative advantage in international markets compared with certain NICs (Donges, 1983) but there are also important constraints on Spain's consolidating a position as an intermediate economy with comparative advantages in certain types of industrial products as opposed to advanced countries and the NICs. Uncertainty arises above all from the fact that Spain's entry into the EEC may change the conditions that favour the present transformation of the spatial industrial system and thus define a new situation. In any case, a margin exists so that Spanish policies may impinge on the future industrial system in Spain.

BIBLIOGRAPHY

Alcaide, J. Estructura y Evolucion del Sector Industrial en la Crisis Economica, Fundacion FIES de la CECA, Madrid

Alfonso Gil, J. 'Estado y Desarrollo Economico. El Caso Español. 1940-1975', Ph.D. thesis, Universidad Autonoma, Madrid, 1979

Aranzadi, C., Fanjul, O. and Maraval, F. 'Una Nota sobre Ajuste y Reindustrializacion', Papeles de Economia Española, no.15, Madrid, 1983

Banco de Bilbao, La España de las Autonomias, Espasa-Calpe (ed.), Madrid, 1981
Banco de Bilbao, Renta Nacional de España y su Distribucion Provincial, Madrid, 1984
Borja, J. and Serra, J. Notas sobre Urbanizacíon y Sociedad en la España Actual, UIMP Pazo de Mariñan, La Coruna, 1984
Boyer, M., 'La Empresa Publica en la Estrategia Industrial Española. El INI', Informacíon Comercial Española, no.500, Madrid, 1975
Donges, B.J., 'El Reto de los Nuevos Paises Industrializados para la Economia Espanola', Economia Industrial, no.234, Madrid, 1983
Escudero, M. 'Los Planes Economicos Regionales como conjunto de Politicas Estrategicas a Desarrollar a Medio Plazo', Meeting on Economic Planning, PSOE, 8 and 9 June 1984, Madrid
Ferrer, R.M. and Precedo, L.A. 'El Sistema de Localizacion Urbano e Industrial', Banco de Bilbao, 1981
Garcia Delgado, J.C. 'Crecimento y Cambio Industrial en España. 1960-1980 Viejos y Nuevos Problemas', Economia Industrial, no.197, Madrid, 1980
Gaspar, J. 'Urbanization: Growth, Problems and Policies', in Williams, A. (ed.), Southern Europe Transformed (Harper and Row, London, 1984)
Herbert M. and Vázquez, A. 'The Simultaneous Crises of the Spanish Economy and Polity', to appear in Hudson, R. and Lewis, J. (eds.), Dependent Development in Southern Europe, (Methuen, London, 1984)
Hudson, R. and Lewis, J. 'Capital Accumulation:The Industrialization of Southern Europe', in Williams, A. (ed.), Southern Europe Transformed (Harper & Row, London, 1984)
Lasuen, J.R. Ensayos sobre Economia Regional y Urbana, (Ariel Publishers, Barcelona, 1976)
Mancha Navarro, T. 'Perfil Industrial de las Regiones Españolas', Informacion Comercial Española, no.609, Madrid, 1984
Munoz, J., Roldan, S. and Serrano, A. 'La Internacionalizacíon del Capital en España, (Cuadernos para el Dialogo Publishers, Madrid, 1978)
Ortun, P. and Sanchez-Junco, J. 'La Politica de Reconversion Industrial en España hasta 1983', Economia Industrial, no.229, Madrid, 1983
Richardson, M.W. Regional Development Policies and Planning in Spain (Saxon House/Lexington Books,

1975)
Santillana, I. 'Las Migraciones Internas en España. Necesidad de Ordenacíon', Informacíon Comercial Española, no.609, Madrid, 1984
Segura, J. 'La Crisis Economica como Crisis Industrial. La Necesidad de una Estrategia Activa', Papeles de Economia Española, no.15, Madrid, 1983
United Nations Economic Commission for Europe 'Some Aspects of Manufacturing in Southern European Countries', Economic Bulletin for Europe, vol.20, no.2, New York, 1982
Vazquez-Barquero, A. 'Los Paises de la Europa del Sur ante la Nueva Revolucíon Industrial', Papeles de Economia Espanola, no.5, Madrid, 1980
Vazquez-Barquero, A. 'Hacia una Nueva Estrategia Economica para España', Cuadernos Universitarios de Planifacacíon Empresarial, vol.VII, no.3-4, Madrid, 1981A
Vazquez-Barquero, A. 'Dipendenza Tecnologica e Sviluppo di Transizione. Il caso dei Paesi Sud-europi', Economia Marche, no.8, Bologna, 1981B
Vazquez-Barquero, A. 'Industrialization in Rural Areas. The Spanish Case.' OECD Intergovernmental Meeting, Senigallia, June 7-10, 1983, TECO. CT/RUR/LL/06
Vazquez-Barquero, A. 'Derarrollo con Iniciativas Locales en España', Informacíon Comercial Española, no.609, Madrid, 1984
Williams, A. (ed.), Southern Europe Transformed, (Harper and Row Publishers, London, 1984)
Ybarra, J.A. 'Economia Subterranea. Reflexiones sobre la Crisis Economica en España', Informacíon Comercial Española, no.218, Madrid, 1982

CHAPTER 7

CHANGE IN A TEXTILE INDUSTRIAL AREA IN NORTHERN ITALY

Anna Segre

Discussions of industrial restructuring have pointed out its marked spatial form and the creation of a new spatial and social order as a consequence of productive and regional decentralization processes. Until relatively recently, the industrialization problems of areas which appeared to be recipients of so-called 'counter-urbanization' processes were considered to be of marginal importance as compared with those suffered by the large industrial and business service agglomerations (Cencini, Dematteis and Menegatti, 1983). In Italy, the so-called peripheral economy has been the subject of much research and debate concerning its role in national development. Recent studies have paid increasing attention to the spatial consequences of intra-firm organizational and other requirements which involve and transform the functions of major regions to ever greater degrees (Bagnasco, 1977, Bagnasco and Garofoli, 1978; Messon, 1975; Rua and Zacchia, 1983).

AREAS OF SPECIALIZATION

The location of areas considered to be peripheral as compared with central, marginal and intermediate areas, raises many questions of their definition and typology.

As a rule, peripheral areas are recognized as having several common features: dispersed presence of small and medium-sized firms; substantial specialization in lines of production which are usually considered to be backward; high activity rates associated with low productivity agriculture; high rates of turnover of firms (births and deaths) and labour mobility (Garofoli, 1983; IRER, 1981). All these features permitted the peripheral areas to maintain a certain level of vitality and to react positively to the economic crisis for a much longer period than the central and, with varying capabilities, the intermediate areas.

The work published by the Istituto Regionale di Richerche per Lombardia (IRER) (1981) distinguishes three different types of local productive structure in peripheral regions:

a) specialized areas characterised by the predominance of one sector typified by a high level of competition between producers of the same or similar products on account of the lack of substantial vertical linkages between firms which could yield inter-firm division of labour within the sector;
b) local productive systems which differ from the specialized areas in that, while they are 'mono-sectoral', more inter-relationships exist between firms in the sector through subcontracting arrangements, and the production system appears to be more integrated;
c) system areas where a remarkable division of labour has been created by firms engaging in diversified activities through both inter-industry and intra-industry exchanges.

Sometimes in these areas a sector is even created to produce capital equipment to be used in finished goods production, in this way guaranteeing the control, if not for technologies, at least for production techniques.

According to IRER classification, that last type would appear to the more developed productive specialized area, composed of small and medium-sized firms, able to have a self-sustaining growth and development process.

The hypothesis proposed in this case study of the Biella area production system based on the textile industry foresees the existence of upper level system-areas which, because of their limited production size, a certain narrowness in linkages outside the area relationships and inertia in the introduction of both technological innovations and widened production systems, cannot be considered as central areas within a functional hierarchy. Nevertheless, these areas have shown, also in recent years, aspects much closer to the dynamism of local productive systems than to central area crisis, although sharing some common overall structural features with these latter ones. This hypothesis introduces new criteria into regional and national spatial understanding and allows further reflection on opportunities for different industrial policy interventions.

Research on other European countries allowed the definition of local production systems which show dynamics similar to Italian ones, emphasizing some trends through a comparative analysis. Areas analyzed, however, are not always indentical to those studied in Italy as the starting conditions of the production structure are different, although the situations are not too different.

In France, for instance, productive specialization areas have been identified as (Garofoli, 1983):

a) highly articulated and complex local productive systems;
b) recently founded and expanding local productive systems;
c) older specialized areas suffering progressive crisis;
d) areas of spatial decentralization.

Also in the United Kingdom, although the productive structure is mainly based on medium and large-size firms, some very strongly specialized areas exist usually from olden times. In West Germany, instead, diffuse industrialization areas are less important, as well as in smaller countries like Belgium, the Netherlands, Denmark and Ireland. Anyway, in all those countries, specialized areas are dominated by major sectors which are traditional, with a clear prevalence of textiles.

From the same sources, it would also appear that specialized areas have had an increasing importance, apart from Italy, in the southern European countries (Spain, Portugal, Greece). This is quite important, as development occurs in response not only to local prospects but also to the structure of the new international labour division. In those countries specialized areas are usually concerned with traditional or low-technology manufacturing fields (such as shoes, toys, or pottery, etc.) generally not considered suitable any more for major industrially developed countries.

The textile field, taken as an example of older, traditional production in developed countries and therefore based on a mature technology, has been exposed to great and growing competitiveness from newly industrialized countries during the 1960s and 1970s. Nevertheless, the theory that such fields can still find suitable localization also in more advanced countries seems to be acceptable, especially for sophisticated production stages and in those areas which have been able to diversify production to attain two goals: (a) creating or increasing a sector which is validly supporting the main field and allowing it to control the technologies, at least partially, and (b) creating an area which is sufficiently diversified from the productive point of view to draw also some service activities from outside and make it less dependent for 'inputs' in the regional and national contexts and, on the other hand, more open regarding 'outputs' in those same contexts. A detailed analysis of these kinds of problems is made for Manchester by Gibbs (1983).

THE BIELLA REGION

Biella is one of the older textile industry districts of Italy. Located in the valleys of the Alpine foothills, it initially had all necessary productive localization factors: plentiful water, wool from sheep breeding, availability of manpower and the capital of some wealthy local families.

Italian textile districts which competed historically and compete still with Biella are Schio-Valdagno in Venetia, whose production however was cotton-based, at least initially, and Prato in Tuscany, whose products are mainly made not from raw materials but from rags, broken and recycled as yarns and then woven. The Biella region has always specialized in higher quality woollen products that, starting with very fine Australian and South African wools, led to the weaving of high-quality fabrics. Thus, since its early industrialization it has been a very highly specialized area, not only in the textile field but also within the woollen sector. In fact, the Biella region shares these features of specialization in common with the Lille, Roubaix, Tourcoing, Armentières, Lione-St. Etienne, Chamond-Tarare and Mulhouse areas in France; the Krefeld area in West Germany; the Lancashire cotton area and Yorkshire woollen area in Britain; the Verviers-Eupen woollen area, the cotton and linen area around Ghent, and in several dispersed centres in western Flanders, in Belgium; the area between Almelo, Hengelo and Enschede in the Netherlands; and the

Veile, Herning and Ikast areas of Denmark.

The region occupies, within Piedmont, a mountain area comprising: the head of the valley where industry was installed first and which still maintains its original productive characteristics; a lower hilly area, crossed by the valley, where bigger centres are located; and a foothill area, where the main town, Biella, and plain are areas of recent dynamic industrial structure.

Total population and population active in manufacturing have both been decreasing in the 1971-81 period, mainly in the mountain and hilly areas and the chief town.

That could be a signal for two separate phenomena: population departure from higher valleys where a production decrease occurred; and the service sector in Biella, as well as a 'counter urbanization' process (Dematteis, Di Meglio and Lusso, 1984), as the population decreases in Biella and by increases in neighbouring municipalities' data, where the growth of residential population can be disconnected from new working communities and connected to better environment conditions.

As a rule, considering the whole area, a phenomenon of partial down-valley shift of productive activities is remarkable and connected to sectoral transformation and, therefore, to the change in the relative value of some classical location factors.

METHODOLOGY AND RESULTS

Population and industrial variables for the period 1971-81 (ISTAT, 1971A,B, 1981A,B) have been analyzed to reveal the industrial, occupational and demographic structure of the Biella region. Using data of employment in the two leading industrial sectors, textiles and engineering, it was possible to classify the municipalities in the region into four types:

a) expanding, in which growth of employment occurred in manufacturing as a whole and in both sectors;
b) municipalities in which the expansion of engineering alone contributed to some overall industrial employment;
c) stable, where no fundamental changes occurred; and
d) municipalities in a crisis where industries of both sectors, and overall, were

declining in those years.

Table 7.1 presents the results of the analysis. The first observation is that the textiles sector, prevailing in 1971 in most municipalities, continues to be the leading sector also in 1981, while the engineering sector, second in 1971, also maintains its position in 1981. The number of cases where it is not second any more is equivalent to the number where it is newly developed. Besides the addition of some new sectors in municipalities where the secondary sector changed, what seems to be remarkably important is the quantitative variation, which indicates greater productive diversification. Note, in this connection how the specialization index has decreased in 35 of the 59 municipalities. This index has been calulated by the following formula: SI = (per cent of first sector employees)^2 - (per cent of second sector employees)^2 - ... (per cent n sector employees)^2. Those include both the chief town, Biella, with a low index percentage variation (-5 per cent), and as many other municipalities where the indices show that such a process is much stronger (Borriana -23 per cent; Cossato -22 per cent; Gragia -23 per cent; Mosso S. Maria -14 per cent; Verrone -28 per cent and Zubiena -22 per cent).

With regard to sectors, textiles was the leading one in 53 municipalities in 1971 and in no fewer than 55 municipalities in 1981, although in the same period its importance had decreased in 37 municipalities, as expressed in a lower percentage of active population in the textile industry sector. The opposite occurred for the secondary sector, its share of the active population having increased in 34 municipalities, in 25 of them the mechanical engineering industry accounting for that growth. Such trends are particularly noticeable in some major municipalities and in Biella town itself. Indeed, Biella goes with Cossato, where textile employees have decreased by 41.7 per cent and mechanical engineering employment has risen by 34 per cent; Cerreto Castello, where the percentages respectively are -38 per cent and +17 per cent; Occhieppo Inferiore, with -13 per cent and +121 per cent; Tollegno, with -33 per cent and +418 per cent; and Vigliano Biellese, with -21 per cent and +68 per cent. It should be noted that sectors with less than 2 per cent of all employees in manufacturing have been excluded as have municipalities with less than 30 employees at both census dates.

Table 7.1 Specialization Index (SI) and Importance of Leading and Secondary Industrial Sectors in the Municipalities of the 'Biella Region' 1971-1981

Munici-	1971								1981							
			Leading Sector			Secondary Sector					Leading Sector			Secondary Sector		
palities	SI	EM[1]	Sec.	Emp.	%	Sec.	Emp.	%	SI	EM[1]	Sec.	Emp.	%	Sec.	Emp.	%
Type 1A																
Camburzano	76.9	145	T	110	76.0	M	11	7.5	70.6	205	T	136	66.3	M	49	24.0
Candelo	83.2	742	T	613	82.6	M	63	8.4	76.7	992	T	747	75.3	M	135	13.6
Cosapinta	97.2	70	T	68	97.1	-	-	-	87.7	87	T	76	87.3	M	7	8.0
Cavaglia	72.9	644	M	454	70.5	SR	113	17.5	73.8	996	M	716	71.9	SR	153	15.4
Crosa	78.8	114	T	87	76.4	M	22	19.3	85.0	152	T	127	83.6	M	24	15.8
Curino	81.0	35	T	28	80.0	NFM	4	11.5	87.4	100	T	87	87.0	NFM	8	8.0
Dorzano	81.6	51	T	42	80.8	M	5	9.7	89.1	88	T	78	88.7	M	7	8.0
Lessona	94.0	740	T	695	94.0	M	26	3.6	89.9	1,066	T	954	89.5	M	103	9.2
Pettinengo	97.9	651	T	637	97.9	-	-	-	97.0	727	T	705	97.0	M	15	2.1
Piatto	-	-	-	-	-	-	-	-	89.6	65	T	58	89.3	M	5	7.6
Pollone	95.1	682	T	648	95.1	M	19	2.8	89.4	738	T	658	89.2	M	29	4.0
Ponderano	73.8	373	T	266	71.4	M	67	18.0	66.9	541	T	342	63.3	M	97	18.0
Salussola	55.1	58	T	28	48.3	M	10	17.3	78.6	189	T	147	77.8	M	14	7.5
Veldengo	86.1	714	T	612	85.8	M	39	5.5	90.2	938	T	844	90.0	M	48	5.2
Valle S. Nicolao	54.7	39	T	17	43.6	M	11	28.2	71.3	104	T	72	69.3	M	16	15.4
Type 1B																
Borriana	87.3	115	T	100	87.0	M	8	7.0	67.3	230	T	136	59.1	CL	72	31.3
Castelletto Cervo	49.1	48	L	16	33.3	W	11	22.9	62.7	106	T	60	56.6	NFM	24	22.6
Cerrione	92.0	557	T	512	91.9	M	28	5.1	78.4	923	T	709	76.8	NFM	140	15.2
Donato	72.9	24	T	16	66.7	W	7	29.2	84.8	63	T	53	84.2	M	5	8.0

Mottal- ciata	82.2	337	T	274	81.4	P	37	11.0	75.5	469	T	345	73.6	M	60	12.8
Quaregna	90.6	676	T	611	90.4	M	34	5.1	82.4	771	T	628	81.5	SR	78	10.2
Roasio	70.2	158	T	107	67.7	M	18	11.4	63.4	307	T	182	59.3	F	58	18.8
Verone	98.7	1,027	T	1,013	98.7	-	-	-	71.3	2,409	MV	1,474	61.1	T	891	36.9
Type 1C																
Netro	77.1	98	MET	74	75.6	M	13	13.3	87.8	104	M	91	87.5	T	5	4.9
Sandi- gliano	76.8	1,062	T	794	74.8	CL	154	14.6	84.1	1,831	T	1,526	83.4	M	199	10.9
Type 2A																
Andorno Micca	69.4	551	T	372	67.5	M	72	13.0	68.8	566	T	379	67.0	M	80	14.1
Benna	72.9	496	T	349	70.3	M	69	13.9	77.8	395	T	299	75.6	M	73	18.4
Biella	71.6	10,388	T	7,257	69.8	M	1,622	15.6	68.1	9,305	T	5,976	64.2	M	2,084	22.3
Bioglio	92.5	146	T	135	92.4	W	6	4.1	78.1	125	T	96	76.8	W	13	10.4
Camadona	89.0	54	T	48	88.8	M	3	5.5	80.0	30	T	23	76.6	M	7	23.3
Cerreto Castello	91.7	1,110	T	1,014	91.4	M	90	8.1	82.0	780	T	636	81.5	M	106	13.6
Cossato	81.2	3,210	T	2,570	80.0	M	418	13.1	63.5	2,559	T	1,499	58.6	M	561	21.9
Gaglianico	76.4	967	T	715	74.0	M	180	18.7	68.4	1,096	T	695	63.5	M	268	24.5
Occhieppo Inferiore	82.1	689	T	561	81.5	M	66	9.6	74.7	688	T	492	71.6	M	146	21.3
Pralungo	92.2	431	T	397	92.2	M	11	2.6	87.0	350	T	303	86.6	M	29	8.3
Tollegno	97.7	1,638	T	1,599	97.7	-	-	-	93.3	1,166	T	1,086	93.2	M	57	4.9
Trivero	95.1	3,850	T	3,658	95.1	M	101	2.7	93.5	3,329	T	3,113	93.5	M	132	3.9
Valle Mosso	91.3	2,918	T	2,657	91.1	M	194	6.7	87.9	2,640	T	2,311	87.5	M	209	8.9

Table 7.1 (cont'd)

Munici-palities	1971								1981							
			Leading Sector			Secondary Sector					Leading Sector			Secondary Sector		
	SI	EM[1]	Sec.	Emp.	%	Sec.	Emp.	%	SI	EM[1]	Sec.	Emp.	%	Sec.	Emp.	%
Vigliano Biellese	91.1	2,721	T	2,473	90.9	M	150	5.6	83.5	2,384	T	1,972	82.8	M	253	10.6
Type 2B																
Graglia	71.9	68	T	48	70.6	M	6	8.9	56.0	99	T	38	38.4	CL	36	36.4
Type 3A																
Masserano	74.8	640	T	461	72.1	NFM	124	19.3	69.1	644	T	426	66.2	NFM	110	17.1
Mezzano M.	69.1	54	T	36	66.7	M	7	13.0	70.3	62	T	42	67.8	M	10	16.2
Mongrando	83.3	692	T	569	82.3	M	87	12.6	79.9	674	T	531	78.8	M	86	12.8
Roppolo	88.1	49	T	43	87.8	M	3	6.1	89.3	45	T	40	88.9	M	4	8.8
Soprana	84.9	45	T	38	84.5	CL	3	6.7	75.6	46	T	34	74.0	V	6	13.1
Viverone	54.6	43	F	16	37.2	M	12	27.9	64.4	38	M	22	57.8	F	10	26.2
Zuiena	75.3	34	W	25	73.5	T	4	11.7	59.0	34	T	18	52.9	W	6	17.6
Zumaglia	80.5	74	T	59	79.5	M	7	9.4	85.0	72	T	61	84.7	M	4	5.5
Type 4A																
Callabiana	98.0	154	T	151	98.0	-	-	-	97.3	113	T	110	97.3	-	-	-
Mosso S. Maria	89.0	672	T	596	88.7	F	49	7.3	76.8	394	T	297	75.4	F	52	13.2
Occhieppo Superiore	79.3	885	T	689	77.9	M	123	13.9	72.8	757	T	536	70.9	M	89	17.8
Sagliano Micca	63.9	647	T	346	53.5	CL	222	34.4	77.2	428	T	326	76.2	CL	40	9.1
Sordevolo	73.5	264	T	187	70.9	M	50	19.0	70.5	226	T	151	66.9	M	47	20.8

Strona	97.7	1,374	T	1,342	97.7	-	-	-	95.6	650	T	621	95.6	M	16	2.5
Veglio	99.2	460	T	456	99.2	-	-	-	98.6	278	T	274	98.6	-	-	-
Type 4B																
Massazza	84.1	973	T	804	82.7	CL	152	15.7	96.8	436	T	422	96.8	M	14	3.2
Miagliano	96.6	382	T	369	96.6	CL	8	2.1	94.4	231	T	218	94.4	M	8	3.9
Not included in the previous typology																
Brusengo	61.5	257	T	136	53.0	M	76	29.5	63.9	335	T	202	60.2	M	62	18.5
Roneo Biellese	75.5	254	T	186	73.3	NFM	44	17.4	78.5	300	T	232	77.4	NFM	35	14.9

[1] EM = employed in manufacturing

T = Textile
M = Mechanical Engineering
CH = Chemical
NFM = Non-ferrous metals
P = Paper
CL = Clothing
L = Leather
W = Wood
F = Food
MET = Metallurgy
SR = Synthetic Rubber
MV = Motor Vehicle

Thus the first verifiable phenomenon is that industrial restructuring in the Biella region has resulted from a clear textile industry contraction and a mechanical engineering industry growth. This fact seems to be quite important in defining this 'integrated system area'. In fact, even if last census data (1981) do not allow it to be asserted definitively, as disaggregated data are not yet available, it is assumed that mechanical engineering industry, which had such growth, is that related to textiles. From other sources (U.I.B.) it can be deduced that engineering employment increased by 28,634, a growth of 74 per cent during the 1971-80 period. If the 1,700 employees of the Lancia car manufacturing plant installed in Verrone in 1973 are subtracted from this figure, more than 1,100 new employees remain, most of them due to the expansion of the textile-related mechanical engineering sector in the form both of machinery manufacturing and direct and indirect suppliers of spare parts and maintenance services.

The Biella region that substantially remains a textile-manufacturing area is thus having its structure completed by a main sector-related mechanical engineering industry more than in the past. Such inter-sectoral relationship is certainly one of the main reasons allowing the area to face the crisis, either through the possibility of shifting labour from one sector to another, or through greater control of production cycle technology - itself allowed by the presence in the same area of capital goods using and manufacturing industries. This adaptation or adjustment is more marked in the southern zone of the region, which seems to be the part that faced the crisis better. In fact the major sectors still maintain their importance inside it. Thus the plains area is the most dynamic one in the sense that sector variation or new sector appearance occurs more frequently.

The secondary sector, usually the textile-related machine industries, maintains or increases its importance more significantly than textiles' decline mainly in Biella and in more traditionally textile valleys. That means that a productive reconversion based on a long-consolidated sector allowed these municipalities to avoid unemployment.

Crisis occurs in both main sectors only near the heads of the valley on the mountain borders. Yet in lowland municipalities the crisis assumes a different meaning, often insofar as greater agricultural activity has compensated for the industrial job losses.

The Biella textile area thus maintains its productive specialization features in an almost 'more specialized' form since it demonstrates a strengthened 'bi-sectoral' character. Trends noted at the municipal level are quite differentiated and certainly important inside the area, revealing an anomalous feature of the area, notably the maintenance of certain production dynamics even in less attractive or accessible areas. Actually, it is quite difficult to find major disequilibria in the area and that could be considered as further evidence of diversification and as another feature of this integrated system-area.

AN INTERMEDIATE AREA

In conclusion, the Biella region case study provides evidence of the presence of areas which play an intermediate role between the true central areas and those local productive systems that may never be able to surpass a certain threshold of complexity and integration. Those areas experience inner demographic dynamics, economic vitality expressed in both a certain sector specialization and wider diversification and the capacity to attract tertiary functions (Segre, 1983). Thus they become quite differentiated functionally as regional sub-poles partly dependent on central areas and yet with a certain autonomy of the local integrated system-area. They occupy an intermediate position in the regional economic and urban-functional hierarchies.

BIBLIOGRAPHY

Bagnasco, A. Tre Italie. La Problematica Territoriale dello Sviluppo Italiano (Il Mulino, Bologna, 1977)

Bagnasco, A. and Messori, M. Tendenze dell'economia Periferica (Valentino, Turin, 1975)

Cencini, C., Dematteis, G. and Menegatti, B. (eds.) L'Italie Emergente. Indagine Geo-Demografica sullo. Sviluppo Periferico (Franco Angeli, Milan, 1983)

Dematteis, G., Di Meglio, G. and Lusso, G. 'Fine della Marginalità Alpina? Un'Inchiesta presso le Comunità Montane del Piemonte', CCIAA Cronache Economiche, no.2, 1984, pp.17-26

Fua, G. and Zacchia, C. (eds.) Industrializzazione sensa Fratture (Il Mulino, Bologna, 1983)

Garofoli, G. (ed.) Ristrutturazione Industrie e

Territoria (Franco Angeli, Milan, 1978)
Garofoli, G. 'Aree di Specializzazione Produttiva e Piccole Imprese in Europa, Economia Marche, no.1, June 1983, pp.2-88
Gibbs, D.C. 'The Effect of International and National Developments on the Clothing Industry of the Manchester Conurbation', in F. E. Ian Hamilton and G. J. R. Linge, (eds.) Spatial Analysis, Industry and the Industrial Environment, vol.3: Regional Economies and Industrial Systems (Wiley, Chichester/New York, 1983), pp.233-54
IRER, Industrializzazione Diffusa in Lombardia. Sviluppo Territoriale e Sistemi Produttivi Locali (Franco Angeli, Milan, 1981)
ISTAT, 11° Censimento Generale della Popolazione, 1971a
ISTAT, 5° Censimento Generale dell'Industria e del Commercio, 1971b
ISTAT, 12° Censimento Generale della Popolazione, 1981a
ISTAT, 6° Censimento Generale dell'Industria e del Commercio, 1981b
Segre, A. 'Le Consequenze della Ristrutturazione Industriale sul Settore dei Servizi per le Imprese nell'Area Biellese', Associazione dei Geografi Italiani, Atti del XXII Congresso Geografico Italiano, vol.II, no.III, 1983, pp.489-504

CHAPTER 8

THE DYNAMIC OF THE INDUSTRIAL SYSTEM IN A BACKWARD REGION. CRISIS AND INDUSTRIAL INNOVATION IN THE ITALIAN MEZZOGIORNO

Sergio Conti

UNDERLYING WEAKNESSES

Of all the depressed areas of western Europe, southern Italy stands out for its lack of historical industrial experience, for it has had little connnection with the modern and contemporary history of the Italian peninsula as a whole. Moreover, both at the end of the Second World War and after three post-war decades of extraordinary State intervention, underdevelopment in the South was not comparable with that in other backward European regions, with respect to the size of either the area or the population involved. The development processes that took place in the South until the 'crisis' of the 1970s were rooted in an export-led growth model adopted for the Italian economy as a whole. It resulted in a significant discrepancy between the traditional sectors and those in which the country had major advantages due to lower wages and the lack of foreign competition, in turn implying a decided imbalance between the various regions, above all between North and South.

The starting point of this analysis lies in some concepts widely accepted by recent analyses of the problem of the South, which generate much lively debate. At the descriptive level the structure of southern Italian industry at the beginning of the 1970s exhibited important weaknesses, for, while industrialization was reaching its peak (see Figure 8.1), there were serious signs of imbalance in the size of plants, their spatial distribution and sectoral composition.

Despite two decades of extraordinary State intervention which fundamentally transformed manufacturing industry in the South, in 1971 there were only limited numbers of large plants, and it

Figure 8.1: Industrialization Trends in The Mezzogiorno

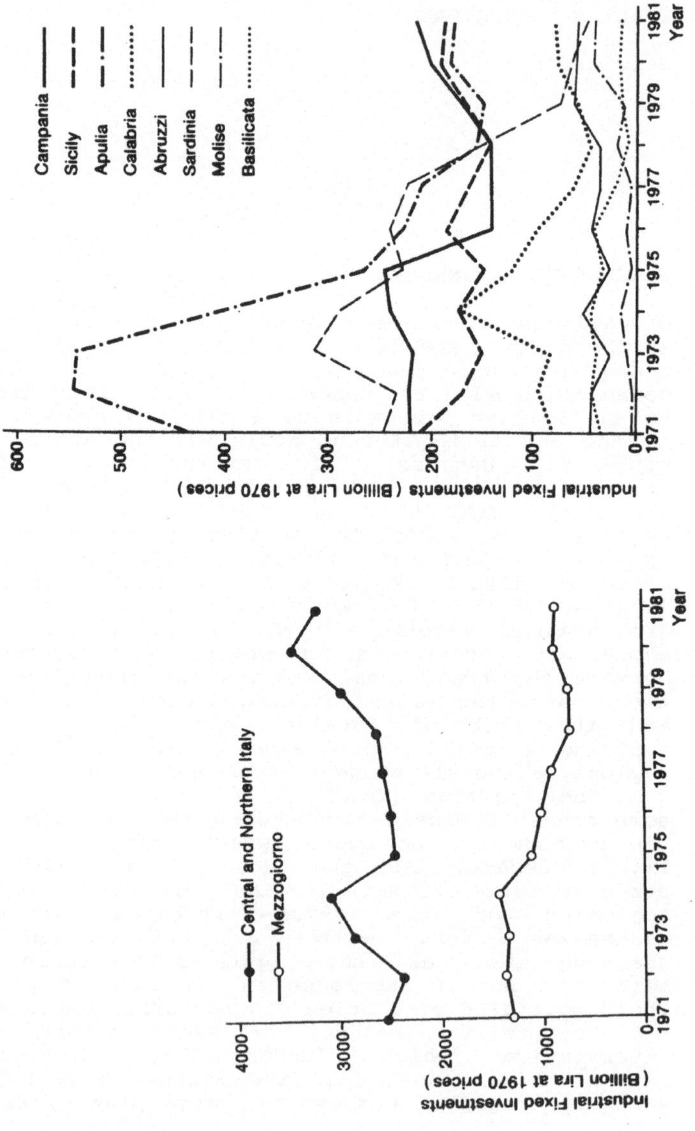

still predominantly comprised small and very small firms. There was a definite lack of medium-sized firms to bridge the gap between these two extremes and create an integrated structural network. The census of 1971 established that 95.7 per cent of locally-owned units employed less than 10 workers (as against 87.2 per cent in the Centre-North), which corresponded to 40.8 per cent of all workers employed in industry in the South (as against 20.7 per cent in the Centre-North) (ISTAT, 1973). At the sectoral level large plants generally operated in capital-intensive sectors, incapable of providing either high levels of employment or of significantly stimulating industrial self-sufficiency. Moreover, the small firms generally working in traditional sectors and incapable of facing up to the competition of products located outside the region seemed destined to succumb to a gradual process of disintegration. The third outstanding problem facing the South was in part a synthesis of the first two: the concentration of investment in a few, very large, firms, highly integrated technologically and productively, resulted in marked territorial imbalance between a limited number of growth 'poles' and the rest of the territory with a burden of economic and social structures historically and functionally far removed from them. Between 1961 and 1971, 69.7 per cent of the low-interest funds granted to southern industry for various reasons concerned investment initiatives of over 3,000 million lire, 19.1 per cent between 500 and 3,000 million lire and only 11.2 per cent under 500 million lire. Figure 8.1, though based on the administrative units, illustrates the unequal distribution of industrialization over the region.

REGULARITIES AND ANOMALIES OF SOUTHERN ITALY

The descriptive aspects synthesized above would however be of little moment were they not accompanied by, first, an analysis of the most recent transformations and processes going forward in southern Italian industry, and second, the embedding of the analyses in their methodological and theoretical contexts.

Two phenomena of crucial importance came to light during the 1970s concerning process. First, a phase characterized by a fairly high rate of transfer of Italian industry to the South; this had been most spectacular in the first four years of the decade but was interrupted in 1974 (Biondi and

Coppola, 1974; Conti, 1982). Financial stimuli had played a decisive role in those years, and it was not by chance that the capital-intensive sectors were becoming ever more frequently the protagonists of the industrialization of the South. Between 1971 and 1973 the basic sectors of the South absorbed altogether 77 per cent of low-interest loans (D'Aponte, 1976). Industrial investment in the South reached a peak of 44 per cent of the national total in 1973 (Graziani and Pugliese, 1979), after which it declined dramatically both in absolute values (by about 40 per cent in the three year period from 1975 to 1977) and in percentage of the total investments made by the entire Italian industry (from 44 per cent in 1973 to 30 per cent in 1975 and to 24 per cent in 1977) (Compagna, 1978).

This process of long term regression is common to many peripheral European areas, as a result of the economic stagnation of the 1970s which had a profound effect on the economies of the weaker regions. In France, for example, the unemployment rates of the problem regions (Midi-Pyrénées, Nord, Pas-de-Calais, Languedoc, Provence-Côte d'Azur, Aquitaine, Bretagne) from 1973 on, went up to levels that could no longer be attributed to cyclic variations in supply of, and demand for, labour (Idrac and Laborie, 1976). Analogous phenomena can be found in Great Britain, where traditional assistance strategies for the more backward regions had decreasing success rates (Keeble, 1977) and in West Germany itself, where territorial imbalance in the levels of economic development is traditionally less marked than in other European countries (Nicol, 1979). Various explanations have been suggested as lying at the root of this change in the development pattern of Western industrial nations. Essentially they can be traced to the worldwide stagnation of economic growth, accompanied by the changing international divison of labour and the tendency towards saturation in domestic demand for consumer goods in industrial countries (Freeman, 1978; Carney and Lewis, 1980). For reasons closely linked with one another the weaker regions have borne the brunt of this situation. On the one hand, the crisis in the Keynesian-type economic mechanisms is connected with the breakdown of traditional regional economic policies which were based primarily on financial incentives. Southern Italy was no exception to the rule, as the trend in easy-term loans, after reaching a peak in 1975, shrank in the following years to a half and sometimes to a third of the figure for the early 1970s.

Under these conditions public programmes became residual and had to be concentrated more in large conurbations where unemployment was rising and technological restructuring of the productive apparatus being carried out most intensively. Furthermore, a radical transformation of the industrialization process was about to take place. The success of regional policy in previous decades had been ensured by a high degree of mobility amongst industrial firms and corresponded to their demand for additional production capacities. Under the new conditions of the 1970s, a policy of 'extensive' industrialization was replaced by an 'intensive' type of industrial development, emphasizing modernization of the means of production. The degree of urbanization began to play a prominent part in these processes, in that the productive potentials lending themselves most readily to an 'innovation-oriented' policy were localized in the urban districts. From this view point, too, transformations in the economy of the South in the 1970s conformed to this greater regularity: within the framework of the whole Italian territorial system, the gap between the South and the Centre-North areas tended to widen, as is shown, albeit indirectly, by a number of aggregate figures. From 1975 on, the investment trend (-21.9 per cent for the whole system) was already lower in the South than in the Centre and the North (-22.6 per cent, as against -21.5 per cent). Later, the trend of the previous years - during which the South gradually gained a larger share of industrial investment - was even reversed, continuing to fall very rapidly in all sectors, and did not recover, or only picked up very slightly, until 1979. In other parts of the country there were obvious, though moderate, signs of recovery as early as 1976, which became more definite towards the end of the decade. Investments fell by 7.2 per cent in the South in 1976, by 11.9 per cent in 1977 and by 21.8 per cent in 1978; recovery was slight in 1979 (+0.8 per cent), notable in the following year (+17.1 per cent), but data are once again negative in 1981 (-2.0 per cent). In contrast, in the Centre-North, the trend of industrial investment was as follows: 1976, +2.2 per cent; 1977, +3.3 per cent; 1978, +1.0 per cent; 1979, +14.4 per cent; 1970, +14.3 per cent; 1981, -6.6 per cent (elaboration of ISTAT data). The analysis of some structural data also contains an evaluation, albeit indirect, of the processes of transformation endogenous in the industrial system in the various regions. It is well-known that in the 1970s there was a considerable modification of industrial strategy everywhere, yet this was not homogenous from the sectoral, and much less so from the territorial, point of view.

All industrialised countries (Centro Ricerche Economica del Lavoro, 1977) reduced the quota allocated to fixed investments, while they increased investment for plant modernization and, at the same time, diverted new investments to the traditionally industrialized areas. The modification of the process of accumulation thus assumed well-known forms - the introduction of more advanced technology, the transfer of production into more competitive sectors and development of R&D within firms. Yet geography has rarely been able to provide systematic, quantitative and qualitative analyses of these processes since, in many countries including Italy, they generally elude the usual collection of statistics, only case studies being able to provide satisfactory insights.

Thus it is necessary to use indirect and relatively approximate information to build up a picture by keeping the quota of industrial investment allotted to machinery and equipment separate from that allotted to plant construction, assimilating the former to a process of 'intensive' growth of the productive capacity and the latter to the formation of additional production capacity (expansion investment).

Figure 8.2 shows the trend of the relationship between these two types of investment in major Italian territorial divisions and in separate regions of the South. This brings out how advanced the reconversion process is in the traditionally industrialized regions of the industrial triangle (Piedmont, Lombardy and Liguria) where, from the mid-1970s investment in machinery and new equipment was constantly greater than investment in new production capacities, whereas the 'extensive' policy continues to be given precedence in the two other areas of the country.

These results have an essentially qualitative value since they bring out the structural nature of the new industrial investment and its dynamic trend, and tell us nothing about the quantity of investments made. Nevertheles, by comparing these elements with those previously outlined, it can easily be deducted that, albeit at the level of the

Figure 8.2: Machinery and Plant Investment in Italy

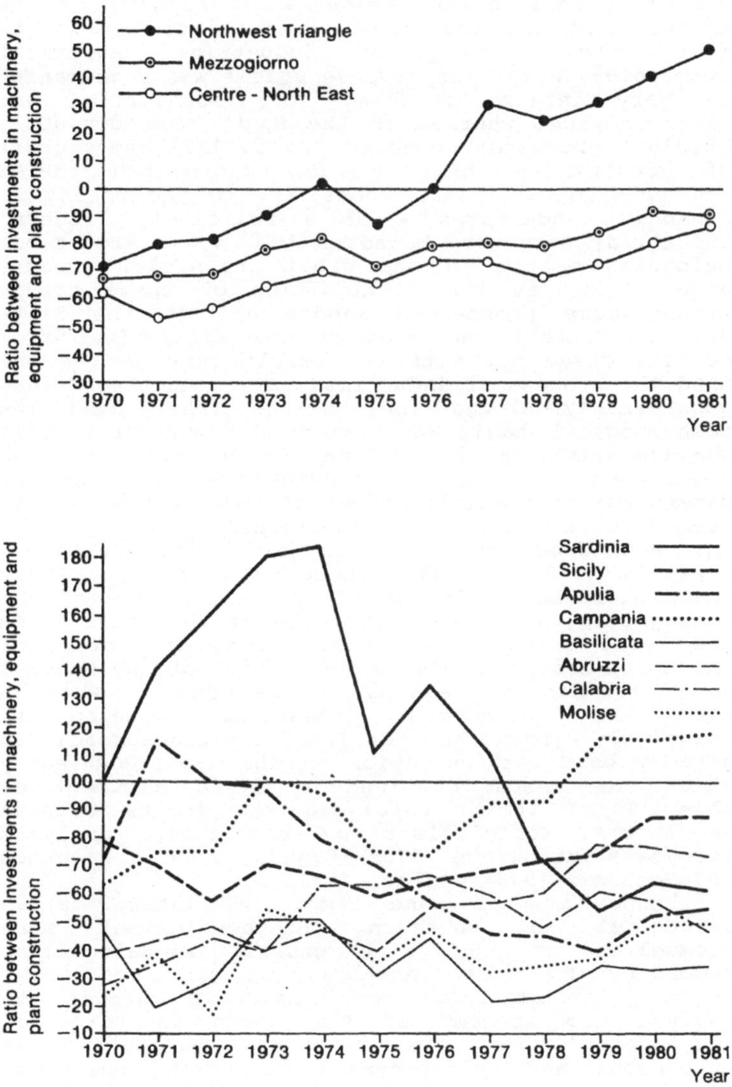

macro-regions, the Italian industrial system is facing profound transformations which are taking on different forms in the various macro-regions of the country. In the industrial triangle of the North-West, the recovery of industrial investment immediately after the 1973-74 crisis was accompanied by very intense processes of reconversion and restructuring, whereas in the South some decidedly original processes appeared. Up to 1974 the process of industrialization of the Mezzogiorno had induced the creation - thanks above all to the policy of financial incentives - of a relatively 'modern' industrial structure based on few, very large firms belonging mostly to the great industrial groups. After 1974, as the difficulties of these groups became more pronounced (above all in the State Holding Sector) the flow of new initiatives from outside dried up, with the result that on the one hand the process of industrialization in these areas considerably slowed and on the other hand the technological basis of investments made previously was not essentially modified. On the contrary, the development of new undertakings of smaller dimensions on the initiatives of local entrepreneurs seemed to take on growing importance.

According to some authors (for instance, Lizzeri, 1980 and 1983) these data bring out very novel elements in the social-economic tissue of the Mezzogiorno, where the new force of the small firms and local entrepreneurs would bring many areas of the South nearer to the image we have of the Central and North-Eastern regions of the country, where a kind of autonomous industrial development, relatively dynamic and territorially widespread, had already been set in motion in the 1960s and early 1970s. The issues involved in the development of this 'Third Italy' catalyzed the debate between economists, sociologists and territorial analysts for years during the 1970s (Bagnasco, 1977; Bagnasco and Messori, 1976; Goglio, 1982).

Hence at the same time, the interpretative categories of southern underdevelopment were themselves to undergo a general re-definition. According to these authors, it was no longer correct, or at least not completely correct, to analyse the economy of the South in terms of 'dependency' (on the northern regions) since autonomous and self-propelling growth phenomena were to emerge.

It is from this point of view that the economy of a typically backward area such as the Italian

Mezzogiorno would reveal features that were anomalous with respect to other European areas. If, indeed, in most regions which have been receiving assistance, the regional policy of the 1960s produced an extensive growth pattern of industries making primarily standardized products, industrialization in the Italian South had been carried out on an essentially intensive pattern (i.e. a few very large firms) and based on relatively advanced technology and historically far removed from the socio-economic context of the region. It was not called 'industrialization without employment' by chance. With the advent of the 1970s, while these backward regions were more affected by the reduction of industrial employment in all the Western countries, the Italian South once more produced a divergent, dynamic pattern. Industrial employment developed between 1971 and 1981 at a rate above the national average in all the southern regions, with particularly high peaks in the Abruzzi and Molise (55.3 and 75.1 per cent respectively). The average for the whole of Italy was +11.1 per cent; Abruzzi, +55.3 per cent; Campania, +20.2 per cent: Apuglia, +30.4 per cent; Basilicata, +36.8 per cent; Calabria, +18.4 per cent; Molise, +75.1 per cent; Sicily, +20.1 per cent; Sardinia, + 29.0 per cent (ISTAT).

Notwithstanding this, the unemployment rate throughout the South was still higher than in any other part of Italy (and it is getting worse). The Mezzogiorno still has a large commercial deficit, while the situation in the other territorial divisions has improved from this point of view.

The unemployment rate in the South in 1980 was 11.4 per cent, as against a national average of 7.6 per cent (Borzaga, 1982). In these circumstances it is therefore admissible to ask what the essential nature of southern industrialization was in the years of stagnation.

METHODS AND HYPOTHESES FOR A STRUCTURAL ANALYSIS. THE INNOVATIONS-ORIENTED REGIONAL POLICY

In the face of the progressive decline of the regional economy and the fact that traditional policies concerning backward regions have been brought into question, gradually more emphasis in international debate has been placed on the search for solutions which favour qualitative processes of industrial development. Such solutions tend to emphasize the importance of an alternative strategy based on the development of the indigenous technological potential to be found in industrialized countries. It is generally maintained that an innovation-oriented regional policy can help a region to win the fight for survival in a time of structural change (Ewers and Wettman, 1980; Martin, 1976).

The debate on the relationship between innovation and regional development has grown more heated in recent years. It is indeed true that in neo-classical analyses the models of regional economic growth only included technology as a residual factor (Malecki, 1983) and technological standards were seldom seen as a source of inequality among the regions (Williamson, 1980). In this connection, however, the conceptual models of Pred (1977) and Krugman (1979), who start from the concepts of cumulative causation and agglomeration economies, the 'optimistic' models based on the concept of diffusion (Hagerstrand, 1979), and those somehow derived from the conceptualization of growth poles (to name only the most important), are all pillars of an extremely important mode of conceptual thought. But all have been only partially demonstrated empirically. As Malecki (1983, p.96) has pointed out these studies have perforce treated technological change as a homogeneous process within industries or nations. And when research on R&D processes was eventually taken up seriously, analysis of aggregated inter-industry differences and the influence of firm size and of market structure were once more given pride of place.

The result is that this type of research also has only limited regional implications. At the risk of over-simplification, if the first-named body of research made important conceptual contributions, the second was significant primarily in terms of the geography of enterprise. In any case from all these studies, it emerges that the concepts of innovation and technology are now recognized as a fundamental field of research for regional economy. In fact they constitute one of the most important single influences on regional change, though so far both the micro-economic and macro-economic analyses, though not made sufficiently in terms of spatial factors, have excluded systematic analysis (Planque, 1983).

In reality, very complex issues arise in attempting to define the concept of innovation. To start with, a variety of definitions has been suggested for it (Hoover, 1971; Mansfield, 1968).

Moreover, the theory of the firm itself has elaborated no 'certain' analytical instruments to identify the firms and the sectors that produce innovation within a given economic system. Hence, from the empirical point of view, the path chosen was to fall back on indirect formulations which are only partially based on the nature of technology, while they try, indeed, to favour the functions which a given sector or a given firm exerts on the dynamics of the wider industrial system (for example, the factors that make certain sectors more competitive than others, particularly at the international level).

As the Italian economic system is characterized by a marked specialization in traditional products and at the same time is progressively losing ground where products of advanced technology are concerned (G. Conti, 1978), the identification of innovating sectors would involve pin-pointing the precedence given by certain firms and sectors to flexibility and the capacity to adapt swiftly to changes in international markets (Onida, 1978). (Italy's position has however improved recently in several non-traditional sectors, including machinery construction.)

To transfer these formulations into a hypothesis for research would have two great advantages, on both the theoretical and the empirical levels. It would allow one to show up the inadequacy not only of the 'orthodox' theories of international trade and their neo-classical formulations, but the most recent interpretations based on the 'theory of the product life cycle' as well. Particularly the latter, which gives precedence to technology because it determines international specialization and groups of products on the basis of their 'technological age', has been found to be excessively simplified, incapable of grasping either superstructural features which influence industrial policies or the growing complexity of the intermediary and mature products (Azzolini, 1981) or even to allow verification at the sectoral level. On the contrary the answer of specialists in industrial economics would lie in the identification of the sectors that act as pillars of the system by means of aggregating non-sectoral categories.

From the empirical point of view a solution has been reached by a procedure of aggregation regarding the structural articulation of Italian industry and consequently working on a relatively flexible concept of 'innovation industry' not directly dependent on technological content but with reference to the position of the products in the matrix of the structural interdependencies of industry -- such as to define the position and the specialization of an industrial structure with respect to others (for example, Italy's position with respect to other industrialized countries).

In examining the structural transformations of southern Italian industry, it is thus necessary to apply precisely this criterion since it emphasizes and verifies not only the transformations endogenous to the regional economy, but the very relationships that are being set up between the South and the Italian economic system as a whole. In other words, two distinct groups of sectors must be kept separate - key sectors (Table 8.1) and non-key sectors (Averitt, 1968; Del Monte and Fotia, 1980; Del Monte, 1980) - deriving them from the classification laid down by the OECD for export sectors as far as the principal industrialized countries are concerned (apart from Italy these are the USA, Japan, West Germany, France, United Kingdom, Spain and Sweden). The former would seem to carry out particularly important functions in the economy; the latter generally appear to belong to the category of traditional goods.

Whether or not a sector belongs to the key activities depends on the presence of at least two of the following requisites at the same time: (a) technological convergence, (b) industries producing capital goods, (c) industries that induce noteworthy linkages, (d) sectors growing at a rate much higher than the national average, (e) highly research-intensive sectors, (f) sectors whose price variations have outstanding influence on prices in other sectors, (g) sectors which, by failing to develop, create bottlenecks in the economy, (h) sectors where the trend of wages influences that of other sectors. A procedure of this kind was first applied to the American economy by Averitt (1968).

The sectors thus identified have in their turn been submitted to a two-fold verification. The first is very simple and indirect in relation to the sectoral inter-dependence of Italian economy (Pilloton and Schachter, 1978), the second carried out with reference to the Commission of European Communities (Commission des Communautés Européennes, 1979) whose object was structural aggregations similar to those taken into consideration here. The latter verification led to the exclusion of those products with a very low content of skilled labour for which Italy has to face great competition from countries only just becoming industrialized, so that she has to make a considerable outlay for reconversion and restructuring and keep production costs down as much as possible. This concerns the radio, tyres and inner tubes, synthetic fibres, iron and steel sheeting sectors. The 38 sectors thus identified, which form the basis for the elaboration to follow, are listed in Table 8.1.

INDUSTRIAL SYSTEM-AREAS, INNOVATION AND REGIONAL POLICY IN THE 1970s

The hypothesis is that these key sectors carry out a 'strategic' function in the evolution of Italian industry, at the same time constituting a virtually innovatory factor in a given regional productive structure. The data utilized refer to all the new industrial enterprises that were set up in the South between 1971 and 1983, taken from the annual IASM-CESAN report, which is the only one that gives information of decisive interest for this analysis: (1) the date when the factory was built and (2) a high degree of disaggregation in 397 sectoral categories which cannot be found in other statistical sources. The area analysed is that where the Cassa per il Mezzogiorno intervenes, while, for obvious reasons, productive units employing less than 10 workers have been excluded.

The concept of 'innovation' utilized is thus only 'pure' insofar as it does not take into account the crucial elements that define a process of innovation (spatially, as well). That process is complex and diversified, constituted by interdependent factors of different functions, sometimes separated or split up geographically. These elements include the flow of information, training of the work-force, the role of communications, the economies of agglomeration. Presented here is an attempt to qualify a process of industrialization structurally, trying at the same time to provide indications which will open up new discussions on the problem of the function of the South in the national economic system. This last objective is implicit in the very nature of the analysis and the criteria that led to the selection of the sectors on which the analysis is centred. For 'strategic' sectors of the Italian industrial system, verified according to data from the sectoral interdependencies, would provide indications from which the relationship between the South and the

Table 8.1 The Key Industrial Sectors

Cast iron
Iron bars
Office machinery
Machinery for building trade
Transformers
Telecommunications apparatus (excluding radio and telephone apparatus)
Telephone apparatus
Cars
Planes
Cosmetics
Plastic and resinous materials
Dyes and colouring products
Chemical elements and composites
Basic chemical products
Electric household appliances
Electric medical appliances
Electric component parts
Elaborators
Iron and steel bars and sections
Iron and steel tubes
Generators
Agricultural machinery
Machines for working metal
Machines for textile and leather industries
Machines for printing industry
Heating appliances
Pumps and centrifuges
Maintenance machine equipment
Machine tools not classified elsewhere
Appliances for measuring and checking electricity
Equipment for the distribution of electricity
Scientific, optical appliances, etc.
Scientific measuring instruments
Pharmaceutical products
By-products of oil
Chemical products not classified elsewhere
Explosives
Fertilizers

other territorial economic formations of the country could be redefined both empirically and theoretically.

Of the 3,661 plants analysed, a significant number (1,437, equal to 39.2 per cent) belong to the key sectors. In employment terms their contribution is even more important, almost equalling the number of workers employed in the second group of plants (88,393 as against 89,910). The first deduction from these overall figures is relatively obvious and implicit in the different nature of the two groups of sectors: the average size of the plants is decidedly greater in the key group (61.5 workers employed). At the same time, it is easy to recognize macro-regional differentiation of spatial dynamics.

The 38 provinces of the Mezzogiorno form the basis of the regional analysis. Parts of the province of Rome, of which only the southern one is included in the areas where the Cassa per il Mezzogiorno intervenes, are considered here. Figure 8.3 shows the character of the processes of industrialization in the period under consideration. The horizontal axis gives the figures of additional employment in the non-key sectors with respect to the total new employment figures. The vertical axis gives the employment figures for the key sectors. The graph therefore gives an immediate idea of how far the first or the second group has affected industrialization in the southern provinces between 1971 and 1983. The further a province is from the diagonal axis, the greater is the dominance of one sector over the other. The key sectors will be more important if it is above, the non-key sectors if it is below the axis.

Some very significant observations can be made at once: first, the most macro-scale observation is that there is still a condition of productive-economic stagnation in a conspicuous number of provinces, in some cases involving whole regions (Calabria, Basilicata, most of Sicily and Sardinia). This is demonstrated by the behaviour of the two groups of sectors, figures for which are particularly low in both cases. Even when the group denotes a greater incidence with respect to the 'traditional' part, the increase in employment figures is so small that one cannot speak of any industrial 'take-off' worthy of note (areas A and B).

Secondly, equally significant is the behaviour of the provinces which include an urban centre of high rank (Naples, Bari, Palermo) and are also the only 'historical' urban centres in the Italian Mezzogiorno. Indeed in the first two (Naples and Bari) there is a fairly significant increase in employment (the two provinces alone absorb practically 20 per cent of the newly employed). None the less the incidence of the traditional sectors is significantly greater than that of the key sectors.

Figure 8.3: Process of Change in the Mezzogiorno

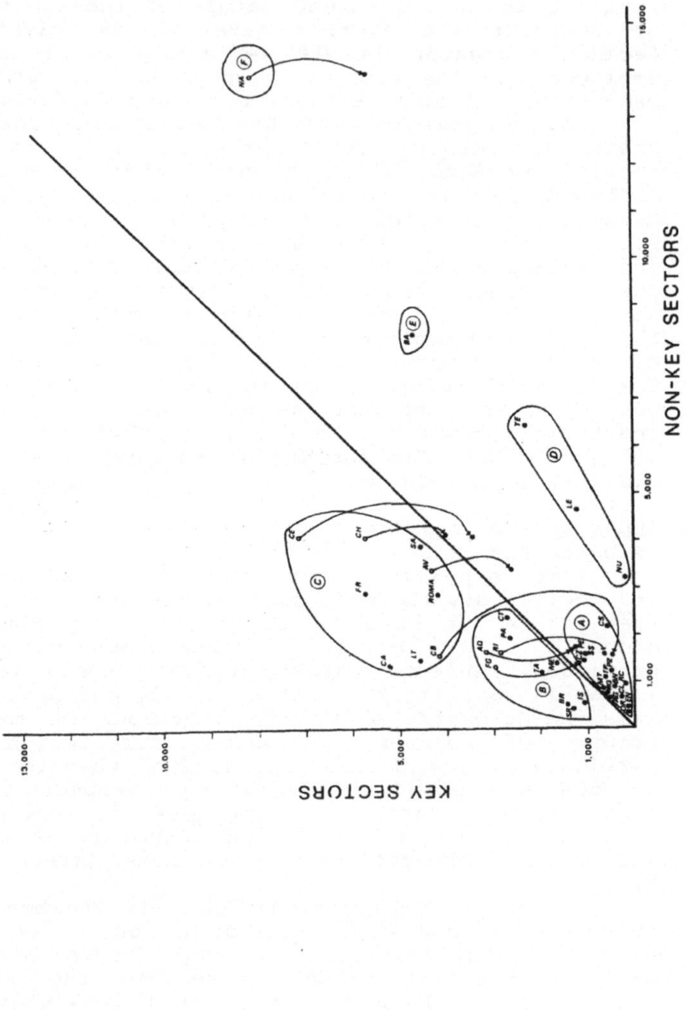

This is a result that could hardly have been foreseen, since it would have been legitimate to expect that the urban economy could activate a process of more advanced industrialization.

Thirdly, quite to the contrary, but in line with the points made above, is the whole region of Apulia (and, in part, of Sardinia) which, as Figure 8.1 shows, in the early 1970s especially, received a considerable proportion of the investments made in the southern regions. In these cases, the key group reveals particularly limited increases, especially in relation to previous tendencies.

Fourthly, the weight of the key sectors is however evident in provinces where there are medium-sized urban centres. Within area C, except for Cagliari, there is in fact no chief regional centre (Rome, as has been pointed out, is a separate case). If one examines the group of provinces placed above the diagonal axis (areas A and B), there are only Cagliari and Palermo (the chief towns in Sicily) whose values are particularly low.

Lastly, a device has been utilized on the same graph to define the dynamics of the phenomenon more precisely. The employment figure in the key sectors of the sample of the large firms has been shown separately, and the arrows in Figure 8.3 indicate the new location that the province would be given. Obviously this is rather an arbitrary procedure, of value essentially for purposes of verification, even though there are good reasons for adopting it. As is well known in the history of the industrialization of the South, the large firms have played a fundamental role, absorbing most of the financial assistance and determining the productive structure of wider geographical areas. Our survey, which tends to exclude the plants that employ over 1,500 workers, modifies the location of certain provinces - such as Caserta, Chieti and Avellino - which drop below the axis in the figures. However in these cases the presence of relatively sound industrialization is confirmed by the considerably high residual values. The case of Campobasso is quite the opposite, for the check has brought out how a large firm - in this case Fiat - was practically alone in directing the process of industrialization of the 1970s.

In any case, as a whole the analysis leads to the hypothesis of a substantial differentiation within the Mezzogiorno, where, from amongst the stagnation of most of the territory, a few significant industrialized areas emerge, some of them 'modern' and 'innovative', others characterized by a repetition of the traditional type of industrial structure. The former, relatively most numerous, have the merit of showing significantly high values.

The next step consists in going beyond the administrative aggregation referred to so far and exploring more deeply the territorial dynamic. Figure 8.4 presents a detailed picture of the different behaviour of the two groups of sectors and is thus the best way of showing the territorial patterns of industrialization in the 1970s. For the sake of convenience, the values have been grouped commune by commune, yet the disaggregation is such that definite territorial 'modules' can be identified.

The first clear observation is the segmentation and fragmentation of the industrial network of the South. The concentration of the group of key sectors in specific geographical areas is a marked feature, counterbalanced by their negligible presence in an extremely large part of the Mezzogiorno, in particular, being largely absent from areas where a considerable process of de-industrialization had taken place in the previous decades. Actually, the description of the processes operating can be reduced to a minimum by an examination of the map. Hence, here only a few quantitative details are added to elaborate the descriptive details more clearly. The emergence of certain areas of 'new' industrialization, such as Frosinone, Caserta, Latina, Salerno, Cagliari and Chieti is the most striking phenomenon. It reveals unquestionably the formation of spatio-industrial systems that modify the territorial organization of the region. In other words, the 'historical' nuclei of industrial development - the urban centres of Naples, Bari and Palermo - where 56 per cent of the workers employed in manufacturing in the South were concentrated in 1951 (productive units with more than 20 workers) and still around 45 per cent in 1971, now employ less than 35 per cent of these workers. On the other hand, the newly industrialized areas mentioned account for more than 30 per cent.

Obviously the influence of the large firms has often continued to be decisive, yet the formation of relatively integrated structures, albeit spatially limited, is a phenomenon that can no longer be neglected in some southern areas. The fact that the process of industrialization is still largely led by entrepreneurs who are outsiders in the South is

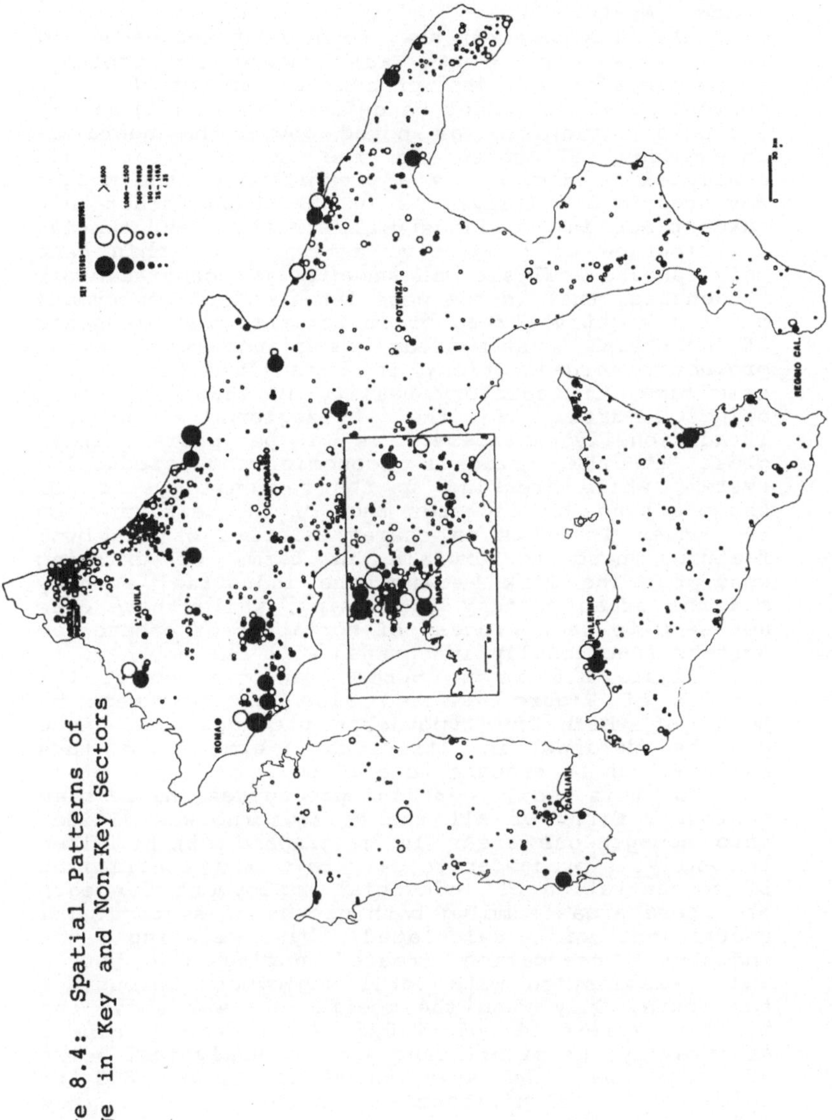

Figure 8.4: Spatial Patterns of Change in Key and Non-Key Sectors

another matter.

All this confirms how, throughout the decade of the crisis, the South was undergoing profound transformation of its productive structures, the content of which cannot be defined so much in macro-economic variables (as noted above the quota of investments allocated to the South after 1974 continued to decline as a proportion of the amount invested in all Italy), as in the changes that have taken place in the industrial structure and spatial distribution of productive activity. In this case only spatial analysis can show the two contradictory tendencies, that is the positive trend of employment and the negative trend of investment. The emergence of industrial 'system-areas' with innovation in the productive organization, is a tangible but at the same time contradictory reality in that it somehow brings parts of the Mezzogiorno territory (traditionally considered as a peripheral area) close to the national economic and productive system, while breaking up the regional system. On the one hand, it isolates much of the territory, on the other it takes on characteristics of its own, features hard to explain in terms of existing concepts. The link between the industrial economy and the urban economy is missing, while there does not seem to be a process of formation of productive systems functionally integrated with one another.

Figure 8.5 is a 'pure' transposition of the details of Figure 8.4 and also an instrument by means of which the hypothesis previously advanced can be defined in structural terms, and this analysis can be brought to a close.

To this end, certain procedures have been followed. First of all the Mezzogiorno was divided into homogeneous areas in geographic extent. Then the analysis proceeded to calculate the coefficient of concentration of industrial employment for each of these areas summing both groups of sectors. The coefficient was calculated by relating the industrial occupation created during the period under examination with total employment throughout the South. Only when the coefficient was above the minimum threshold of 0.025 (considered, albeit arbitrarily, as significant from an analytical point of view) was the area shown in Figure 8.5 to indicate 'significant' areas of new industrialization.

Within each of these industrial 'system-areas' 'innovative' sectors were identified with respect to employment as a whole, arranging the areas in a

Figure 8.5 'Industrial System Areas' in the Mezzogiorno

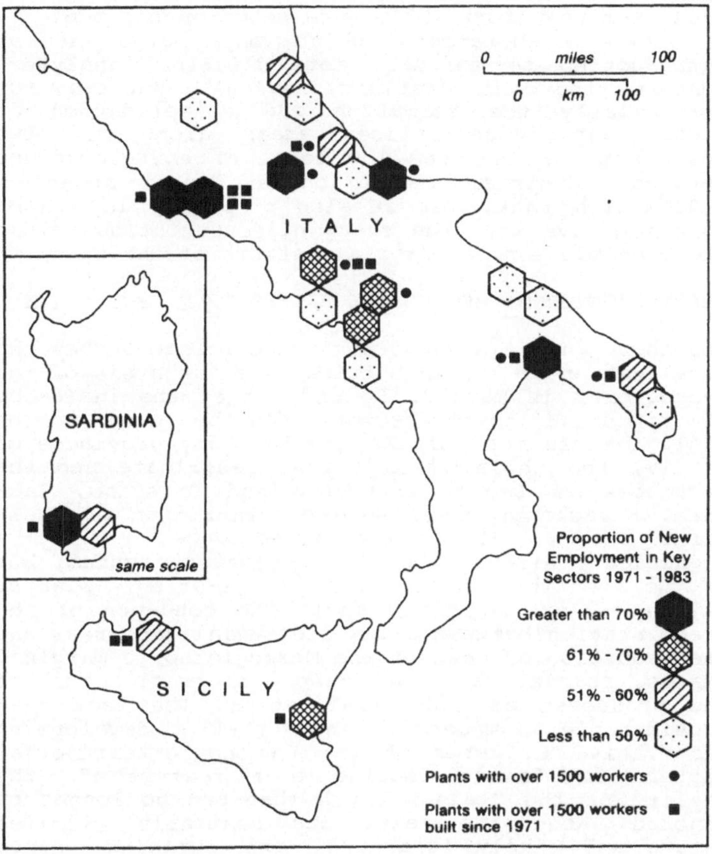

four-level hierarchy, three of which concern the non-key group of sectors. Lastly, all the large firms at present operating in the South, including those set up before 1971, were shown on the map.

This elaboration, which may serve as an introduction to further, more detailed, analyses, confirms the considerations previously put forward, particularly the formation and consolidation of significant industrialized areas along the two coastal axes; and the low level of correspondence between industrial innovation and urban areas of medium-high rank. Yet it also proposes, in a much more incisive way, the sharp differentiation within the economic and territorial network of the South.

THE MEZZOGIORNO: REGRESSIVE RATHER THAN PROPULSIVE

The above analysis shows first and foremost that the localization of key industries in a few areas of the Mezzogiorno is marked. By and large, the incidence of firms in these sectors can be said to be negligible in most of the region. Many provinces of Sicily, the whole of Calabria, Basilicata and the provinces of Lecce, Benevento and Oristano, lack them. Elsewhere, where some concentration of these firms occurs, it is the consequence, not of a significant diffusion of the innovatory system, but of the localization of a few, large-sized plants. This does not so much repeat the concepts of the fragmentation between a few industrialized areas and the reduction of most of the Mezzogiorno to marginal status, as elaborate more deeply the real nature of the processes of industrialization. The fact that considerable modern industrial development (innovative in terms of the economic-territorial pattern) has found a footing is a feature of the reality of the Italian South than can no longer be ignored. None the less, its spatially limited nature and likely 'weakness' are striking, since the urban nuclei generally represent a 'spurious' element in these industrial systems.

Secondly, from Figure 8.5 one can identify the induced effects of the large firms previously established in the region. The areas of greatest innovation do not usually correspond to those of leading industrial localizations. Striking examples of this are the multiple petrochemical plants at Pisticci (Basilicata) and Gela (Sicily) and most of the car factories set up in the Mezzogiorno in the early 1970s at Termini Imerese (Sicily), Termoli (Molise) and Sulmona (Abruzzi). In all these cases the choice of site for new firms in the respective areas is still of negligible importance. Less dramatic conclusions can be drawn, however, from the petrochemical plant in Priolo (eastern Sicily) and the metallurgical plant in Taranto, as they seem to have created very little capacity for innovation in their regions, being extremely slight in the former case, though it involves a number of places on the coast of eastern Sicily, more intense in the latter case, though it is concentrated notably around Taranto.

It is more difficult to interpret the cases where the industrialization of the 1970s has brought about the formation of interpolar axes of industrialization. The reciprocal welding together of the centres of Campania would at first sight seem to be confirmed, yet on closer examination a number of controversial factors emerges. Naples reveals a weakness not easily predictable, given the relatively high levels of industrialization previously achieved there. It would seem incapable of giving impulses to a structural transformation of the productive system of the region, which by and large presents an image of relative general stagnation that confirms the backwardness of its industrial structures (see Coppola's chapter in this book). In the Neapolitan conurbation, only a little over 30 per cent of the new jobs have been created in the key sectors, which is a figure decidedly lower than the average for the Mezzogiorno as a whole.

The situation in the strip of the Adriatic coast gravitating to Bari appears still more serious. Previously it registered industrial drives so strong that it was predicted a polycentric functional structure would be solidly established both within the region (the much-debated Bari-Brindisi-Taranto triangle) and in the direction of the Ionian area as well as northward along the Adriatic coastline. The limited base of key sectors, their essentially local, urban market orientation, and their frailty in northern Apulia and the Basilicata region as a whole are all factors which confirm, for the Apulian system, a productive system with: little claim to dynamic or modern features; and the termination of timid attempts at economic-spatial integration which had seemed to be emerging in previous years.

By contrast, the processes of industrialization brought about along the Adriatic coast of the Abruzzi and to the south of Rome, help to establish the most significant examples of real industrial transformation in the Mezzogiorno. In these areas the investments in 'innovative' sectors are not confined only to the larger urban centres, but seem to foreshadow a well-knit polycentric functional structure, branching out into the hinterland on the one hand and on the other involving both the small and medium-sized urban centres (see also Coppola's chapter in this book). Finally the relationship between urban structure and innovative industry confirms once more the problem of the functional crisis of the cities of the South. Apart from the macro-geographic example of Naples, there is a re-emergence of the dramatic dichotomy between a limited number of relatively dynamic centres and most of the urban south which is incapable of exerting a stimulating effect on the surrounding territory. These issues have been fully dealt with by Italian geographical research (Becchi Collida', 1976; Cinatempo, 1976; Brusa and Scaramellini, 1978). Much of the urban Mezzogiorno, with the exception of small industrial areas, has failed to reveal any ability to bring about a sophistication of regional structures and continues to hover on the verge of industrial change, 'backward' in its productive structures and 'regressive' with regard to the social - economic equilibrium of the region.

BIBLIOGRAPHY

Averitt, R. T. The Dual Economy: The Dynamics of American Industry Structure (Northon, New York, 1968)

Azzolini, R. 'Aspetti del Commercio Esterno Manifatturiero dell'Italia e dei Principali Paesi della CEE dopo la Prima Crisi Petrolifera', in L. Pennacchi (ed.) L'Industria Italiana. Trasformazioni Strutturali e Possibilità de Governo Politico (Angeli, Milan, 1981)

Bagnasco, A. Tre Italie. La Problematica Territoriale dello Sviluppo Italiano (Il Mulino, Bologna, 1977)

Bagnasco, A. and Messori, M. Tendenze dell'Economia Periferica (Valentino, Turin, 1976)

Becchi Collida', A 'La Città Meridionale', in F. Indovina (ed.) Mezzogiorno e Crisi (Angeli, Milan, 1976).

Biondi, G. and Coppola, P. Industrializzazione e Mezzogiorno. La Basilicata (Istituto Geografico Università Napoli, Naples, 1974)

Borzaga, C. 'Lo Sviluppo Regionale Italiano Durante gli Anni '70', in S. Goglio (ed) Italia: Centri e Periferie (Angeli, Milan, 1982)
Brusa, C. and Scaramellini, G. 'Armatura urbana e Industrializzazione nel Mezzogiorno', in E. D'Arcangelo and D. Ruocco (eds.) Atti del XXII Congresso Geografico Italiano (Salerno 18-22 Aprile 1975), vol.II, Tomo II (Istituto Geografico Italiano, Naples, 1978)
Carney, J. and Lewis J. (eds.) Regions in Crisis (Croom Helm, London, 1980)
Centro Ricerche Economic del Lavoro L'Evoluzione della Congiuntura Internazionale e i Riflessi sulla Crisi Italiana (CREDL, Rome, 1977)
Commission des Communautés Européennes L'Evolution des Structures Sectorielles des Economies Européennes depuis la Crise du Pétrol, 1973-1978 (Economie Européene, numéro spécial, Brussells, 1979)
Compagna, F. 'Il Mezzogiorno davanti agli Anni '80', in C. Muscara (ed.) Mezzogiorno e Mediterraneo (Muscara, Venice, 1978)
Conti, G. 'La Posizione dell'Italia nella Divisione Internazionale del Lavoro', in Specializzazione e Competitività Internazionale dell'Italia (Il Mulino, Bologna, 1978)
Conti, S. Un Territorio senza Geografia. Agenti Industriali, Strategie e Marginalità Meridionale (Angeli, Milan, 1982)
D'Aponte, T. 'Incentivi Territoriali e Sviluppo Industriale: L'Esperienza del Mezzogiorno' Nord e Sud, vol.14 (1976), pp.33-53
Del Monte, A. 'Settori Maturi e Settori Innovativi nell'Industria Meridionale' Quaderni Sardi di Economia, vol.2 (1980) pp.181-202
Del Monte, A. and Fotia, G. Struttura Industriale e Specializzazione Internazionale dell'Italia (Università Napoli, Naples, 1980)
Ewers, H. J. and Wettman, R. W. 'Innovation-oriented Regional Policy' Regional Studies, vol.14 (1980) pp.161-79
Freeman, C. 'Technical change and employment'. Paper presented at a Workshop on the relationship between Technical Development and Employment, Six Countries Programme Secretariat, Delft, Netherlands (1978)
Ginatempo, N. La Città del Sud. Territorio e Classi Sociali (Mazzotta, Milan, 1976)
Goglio, S. (ed.) Italia: Centri e Periferie (Angeli, Milan, 1982)
Graziani, A. and Pugliese, E. (eds.) Investimenti e

Disoccupazione nel Mezzogiorno (Il Mulino, Bologna, 1979)
Hagerstrand, T. Innovation Diffusion as a Spatial Process (University of Chicago Press, Chicago, 1979)
Hoover, E. M. An Introduction to Regional Economics (Akhoff, New York, 1971)
Idrac, M. and Laborie, H. P. 'L'Economie du Midi-Pyrénées en Crise. Revue Géographique des Pyrénées et du Sud-Ouest, vol.47, 1, (1976), pp.9-30
ISTAT Censimento dell'Industria e del Commercio (ISTAT, Rome 1973)
Keeble, D. E. 'Spatial Policy in Britain: Regional or Urban?' Area, Vol.9 (1977), pp.3-8
Krugman, P. 'A Model of Innovation, Technology Transfer and the World Distribution of Income' Journal of Political Economy, vol.87 (1979), pp.253-66
Lizzeri, G. Il Mezzogiorno in Controluce (Enel, Rome, 1980)
Lizzeri, G. (ed.) Mezzogiorno Possibile. Dati per un Altro Sviluppo (Angeli, Milan, 1983)
Malecki, E. J. 'Technological and Regional Development: A Survey' International Regional Science Review, vol.7, no.2, (1983), pp.89-125
Mansfield, E. Industrial Research and Technological Innovation (Norton, New York, 1968)
Martin, F. The Regional Factor in the Diffusion of Innovation (Economic Council of Canada, Ottawa, 1976)
Nicol, W. R. 'Relaxation and Reorientation: Parallel Trends in Regional Disincentive Policies' Urban Studies, vol.16 (1979), pp.333-9
Onida, F. Industria Italiana e Commercio Internazionale (Il Mulino, Bologna, 1978)
Pilloton, F. and Schachter, G. Input Output Italia (Svimez, Northeastern University Press, Boston, Mass., 1978)
Planque, B. Innovation et Développement Regional (Economica, Paris, 1983)
Pred, A. City-systems in Advanced Economies (Wiley, New York, 1979)
Williamson, J. G. 'Unbalanced Growth, Inequality and Regional Development: Some Lessons from U.S. History', in V. L. Arnold (ed.) Alternatives to Confrontation (Heath, Lexington, 1980)

CHAPTER 9

INDUSTRIALIZATION NORTH OF NAPLES: PROBLEMS OF SECTORAL AND SPATIAL CONNECTIVITY

Pasquale Coppola

A great amount of literature examines the evidence of deep disequilibria between the distribution of population and economic activities in Campania (Abignente et al., 1978). The disparities are described in the terms la polpa (flesh) and l'osso (bone) introduced in research on the Mezzogiorno to describe the contrast between localization of production in parts of the coastal strip and underdevelopment in the interior. The extent and depth of the latter and local population pressure on the region's infrastructure greatly weaken the developmental potential of the highly urbanized zone around the Gulf of Naples. Consequently Naples appears poverty-stricken, racked by severe economic marginalization, disorderly urban form and great service bottlenecks (Coquery, 1963; Rao, 1967).

A REGION IN TRANSITION

Despite these negative phenomena, the attraction of the leading regional city and its immediate hinterland as a development pole for industry and urban expansion has persisted for want of regional alternatives. Until the 1960s industrialists found new building sites in inner north-east suburban Naples, fashioning this district into an embryonic growth pole (Mazzetti, 1966). Yet this assisted the processes of thinning the population of the historic core, creating new middle-class residential quarters on the hills and State-financed housing for the less privileged in the western and northern suburbs. Frantic building operations led to displacement of people from inner areas to dormitory towns to the south-east along the coast. The poorer industrial zones tended to attract labour from all areas of Campania except touristic places on the

Gulf of Naples, Sorrento peninsula and leading local centres like Salerno and Caserta.

During the past 20 years government policy for Mezzogiorno development has combined with spontaneous trends to alter the spatial structure, bringing new areas into the development process. The major industrial nucleus in north-east Naples began to decline in the early 1960s, unable to generate new entrepreneurial capacity or adapt to changing regional needs on account of capital shortages, saturation of sites practically uncontrolled by city legislation, and the obsolescence of infrastructure for regeneration purposes. The chief industrial concentration of Campania became degraded mainly to subsidized activities or a marginalized black economy (Boccella, 1982).

Yet by the late 1960s the first effects of the policy to industrialize the Mezzogiorno, inspired by the Perroux model of polarized development, began to be evident (Biondi and Coppola, 1974) in a network of numerous industrial sites provided with infrastructure, served by autostrade, and where public policy offered a wide range of financial incentives to Italian and foreign firms to locate. Some sites in the interior, however, remained peripheral, unable to attract modern firms, lacking local initiatives and hence not achieving the aims of the development strategy for such areas. But where concentrated investment created considerable job opportunities, factories stimulated social change, the pace of life and contributed - together with modern communications - to new patterns of consumption, modernization and urbanization. Dynamic forces emerged close to the overcrowded coastline as a result of the location there of modern industries serving inter-regional markets and assisting national decentralization processes (D'Aponte, 1976A).

Gradually the 'intermediate' Campania emerged (Biondi, 1983) as the core in regional development strategy and the re-establishment of spatial equilibrium, even though its potential role was overestimated by government expectations. The zone in which this upgrading occurs extends from the periphery of Naples (Fralliciardi et al, 1983) to: Capua and Caserta in the north; the countryside around Acerra; the interior valleys as far as Avellino: the industrial zones of southern Lazio, encompassing overpopulated Sarno (D'Aponte', 1976B); and extends from Salerno to Eboli, 80km from Naples (Figure 9.1). Solofra is an interior industrial

Figure 9.1: The Province of Caserta

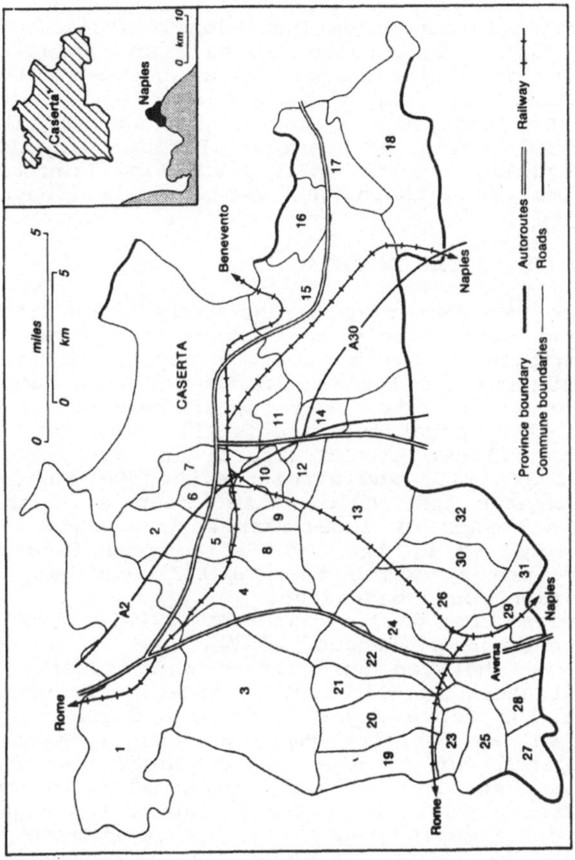

The communes of the province of Caserta are: (1) Capua, (2) S. Prisco, (3) S. Tammaro, (4) S. Maria Capua Vetere, (5) Curti, (6) Casapulla, (7) Casagiove, (8) Macerata Campania, (9) Portico di Caserta, (10) Recale, (11) S. Nicola la Strada, (12) Capodriso, (13) Marcianise, (14) S. Marco Evangelista, (15) Maddoloni, (16) Cervino, (17) S. Maria e Vico, (18) S. Felice a Cancello, (19) Villa di Briano, (20) Frignano, (21) Casaluce, (22 Teverola, (23) S. Marcellino, (24) Carinaro, (25) Trentola Ducenta, (26) Gricagnano di Aversa, (27) Parete, (28) Lusciano, (29) Cesa, (30) Succivo, (31) S. Arpino, (32) Orta di Atella.

oasis which is consolidating (Biondi, 1984).

The most favourable sites for industrial development in southern Italy lie between Aversa and Caserta. They enjoy a very special situation between the great Naples market and the network of medium-sized towns in central Latium served by modern highways - towns where industrial traditions long existed in spinning and weaving silk (Coppola, 1983).

THE BASES OF MODERN INDUSTRY

There were few factories in the early 1960s between Aversa and Capua. Only silk spinning and weaving were significant, having been developed in French style 'industrial colonies' founded by Ferdinand IV of Bourbon after 1760. Putting-out remained a key part of the operations and still engaged 1,500 people in villages around Caserta in 1938. Decline set in after 1945, and efforts either to penetrate markets beyond the region with cheap silk or to maintain a corner of local markets in quality silks were constrained by the lack of a local financial infrastructure by which the capital necessary for modernization could be raised.

Despite the decline in the cultivation and processing of hemp (Ruocco, 1957), some integration was achieved between agriculture and industry and still continues. By 1930 beet cultivation provided a basis for the Capua sugar refinery and tobacco was being cured, an activity which was greatly extended by the opening of a large tobacco factory at Santa Maria Capua Vetere in 1957. The seasonality of work, however, meant that mostly female labour was engaged from the villages in production. The experience they gained in factories, however, later became an important attraction to entrepreneurs of new industries involving assembly operations like Sit-Siemens (now Italtel) making telephones at Santa Maria Capua Vetere. Yet most of the industrial initiatives taken in this region in the late 1950s did not emanate from traditional sectors - foods, shoes, clothing - that generally served only the regional market.

The 1950s saw the laying of the foundations for stimulating industrial initiatives in the Mezzogiorno. The band of countryside separating clusters of centres around Aversa and between Marcianise and Caserta soon came into the public planning eye for development. (Much more recently other centres were proposed for growth near Capua and San Felice a Cantello.) The first spatial planning hypothesis for the region, advocated in 1953, designated the gravitation zone of Caserta as a zone with good growth potential (Caputi-Forte, 1977). Introduction of State aid for southern industry led immediately to the installation of firms to tap the advantages of excellent location, abundant cheap labour and the lack of labour troubles in local enterprises (D'Aponte, 1976C).

The presence in the zone of Caserta, the provincial capital, of medium population size, with administrative bureaux, schools, lycées and a hospital, was important, and one should not underestimate the role in development of the network of smaller but densely-clustered centres like Aversa and Santa Maria Capua Vetere, which raised the infrastructural level of the extraordinarily underdeveloped non-metropolitan space in the Mezzogiorno.

Moreover, these centres had plentiful development land which could enable enterprises to operate without suffocation from the insufficient space, congestion and functional disorder existing in Naples. Furthermore the infrastructure of the provincial centre offered longer-term opportunities for training skilled cadres and raising service provision closer to a metropolitan level.

The key element in the take-off of large-scale industrialization was the zone's accessibility. Part of the plain of Campania between Aversa and Capua was traversed by the direct Naples-Rome route, a prolongation of the ancient Via Appia. Accessibility was greatly increased in the early 1960s by the inauguration of the autostrada de la sole (Catandella, 1968), that provided three exits near the industrial sites. Further improvement is occurring in the 1980s by the opening of the A30 that offers better connections with other industrial nodes in Campania, like Pomigliano d'Arco, Avellino and Salerno, and in Puglia. Proximity to Naples-Capodichino airport has emerged as a factor of importance in movements of engineers and managers. This transport network structure came to favour the location primarily of foreign industrial enterprises requiring fast connections with north and central Italian markets.

THE PHASES AND CHARACTER OF INDUSTRIALIZATION

The industrial pole between Aversa and Capua already proved to be decisive in the region's development after 1957 in attracting foreign multinational investment.

Saint-Gobain opened a glassworks in Caserta and Pierrel Pharmaceuticals a plant at Capua in 1958. The American 3M Corporation established a chemical plant on the edge of Caserta in 1960. Following shortly after were major electronics and telecommunications firms: Sit-Siemens (now Italtel) with 4,000 employees at Santa Maria Capua Vetere and branches of Texas Instruments at Aversa, Face Standard at Maddaloni, and GTE at Marcianise, all employing more than a thousand workers each. Others, engaging more than 500 workers, like that making heavy machinery on the outskirts of Ponte Selice, and a State railway engineering works, were also put into operation. Later, at the end of the 1960s, two other foreign multinationals opened chemicals plants in the region, Union Carbide (Elettrografite Meridionale) from the USA, and Air Liquide (SIO) from France, both at Santa Nicola La Strada. Several Italian firms opened branches for processed foods near Caserta and shoes near Aversa, while Olivetti established an electronic calculating machine factory.

Most 1960s' investments were in modern sectors, mainly chemicals, electrical, electronics and engineering, with a high level of foreign participation. Between 1961 and 1971 about 10,000 new jobs were created, a 67 per cent increase, a relatively modest rise. The inflow of investment was sustained through the early 1970s by both Italian and foreign manufacturers. Indesit built an electrical appliances factory at Teverola, near Aversa, Coca-Cola a drinks-bottling plant in San Marco Evangelista, where Kodak also set up a film-processing laboratory. Installation of the Alfasud car assembly plant at Pomigliano d'Arco, employing 15,000 workers, attracted a number of firms to the Caserta area: Gallino-Sud (a joint venture between ITT and the public corporation, SME), Keller-Sud (belonging to the Swiss firm, Uni Keller), Fata-Sud and Worthington (both US subsidiaries) (Benetti et al., 1973).

These multinational and national firms were attracted by the economies of agglomeration on offer in the region. They confirmed the dominant role in shaping regional industrial structure of modern sectors, usually in the hands of big corporations externally-controlled beyond the region (and Italy in most cases) and serving markets outside the Mezzogiorno (Cotugno et al., 1981). The multiplier effects locally of these large firms, however, have been limited. Only in electronics has any subcontracting to small and medium-sized firms occurred. Most new locally-owned enterprises use traditional methods and mainly produce light machinery, building materials, foods, furniture and shoes to meet local demand, which has grown with rising living standards.

Investment in the region remained high in the second half of the 1970s but not on account of local entrepreneurial initiatives or new plant construction by externally-controlled firms. Rather, it resulted from complex restructuring and modernization of existing plant to raise labour productivity or replace labour by installing more modern technological equipment. Redundancies and short-term working became more frequent: between 1978 and 1980 the Cassa Integrazione Guadagni, a public fund set up to pay the wages of workers temporarily unemployed in Caserta, paid out for the equivalent of 10 million man-hours lost by employees of the engineering, glass, chemicals, ceramics and textile industries (Zollo, 1982). Overall, large firms cut their labour forces by an average of 10 per cent and introduced new production structures. Olivetti, for example, detached and expanded its robotics division. Amongst other firms, Saint-Gobain, Union Carbide, 3M and Keller-Sud altered their production organization, reducing staff and unleashing short-term labour disputes. Yet, in general, employment has been maintained, technological levels improved, quite unlike in other areas of the Mezzogiorno. Indeed, about 11,500 industrial jobs were added in the Caserta area between 1971 and 1981, a rise of 46 per cent as compared with 38 per cent in the whole province and 26 per cent in the entire Mezzogiorno. Despite recent contractions in the labour force 12 enterprises still employ more than 70 per cent of Caserta industrial workers.

INDUSTRIAL SPACE OR INDUSTRIAL SYSTEM?

Caserta province is certainly now one of the most 'industrialized' in the Mezzogiorno. Figure 9.2 shows that the index of industrialization (the number of industrial employees per 1,000 population), which averages 80 for the whole province, varies substantially from area to area, being around the average in the central communes of Caserta, Maddaloni, Santa Nicola La Strada,

Figure 9.2: Index of Industrialization, Caserta Province

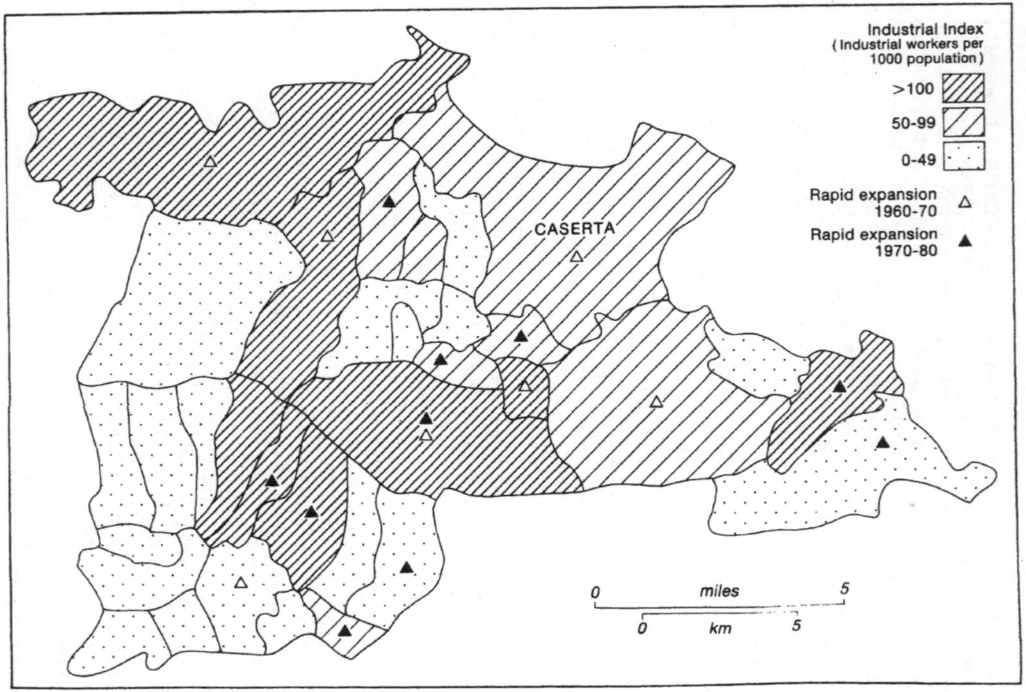

Capodrise, S. Prisco, Casapulla and Casa Giove; and substantially above it along the Aversa-Capua axis in Casaluce, Teverola, Carinaro, Marcianise, Santa Maria Capua Vetere and Capua. The extreme south-east, San Felice a Cancello, and the western zone around Aversa (Santo Tammaro, Villa di Briano, Frignano, Santo Marcellino, Trentola-Ducenta, Parete, Lusciano, Cesa, Succivo and Orta di Atella) are very much less industrialized. Teverola, near Aversa, where Indesit is located, records the highest concentration, with more than 200 industrial workers per 1,000 population.

In general big plants have not hindered the development of the local economy as much as they have elsewhere in the Mezzogiorno, in areas where industrialization has been virtually entirely new. Figure 9.3 shows that in employment the leading industries are electronics and telecommunications equipment, followed by: textiles, clothing, leather and fur; building materials; and chemicals. The importance of electronics is positive insofar as it provides a modern regional economic and technological basis, but negative to the extent that policies of the electronics firms have been to use intermediate or second-hand technology or to confine their operations to simple segments at the end of the production chain.

Furthermore, there is a high risk of industrial disinvestment from the region because most of the larger manufacturing firms have decision centres located outside the Mezzogiorno, not just in northern Italy but mostly outside Italy in the USA or Western Europe. The foreign-owned firms restrict the level of integration of their branch plants with the peripheral region economies to the very minimum sufficient to present an acceptable image locally (Biondi and Coppola, 1979). This usually means a level of integration insufficient to generate multiplier effects of substantial magnitude and long-term duration in the local economy, the branches being mere assembly units run by foreign managers, in fact (Sciarelli and Maggioni, 1975), generating more multiplier effects through very strong backward supply linkages in products and services outside the region and outside Italy. Subcontracting work is often the best, albeit inadequate, form of integration that can be expected between the local and the externally-controlled firms (Del Monte, 1982).

The recent development of local industry in Caserta province does not constitute real progress

Figure 9.3: Major Industrial Sectors, Ownership and Employment, Caserta Province, 1984

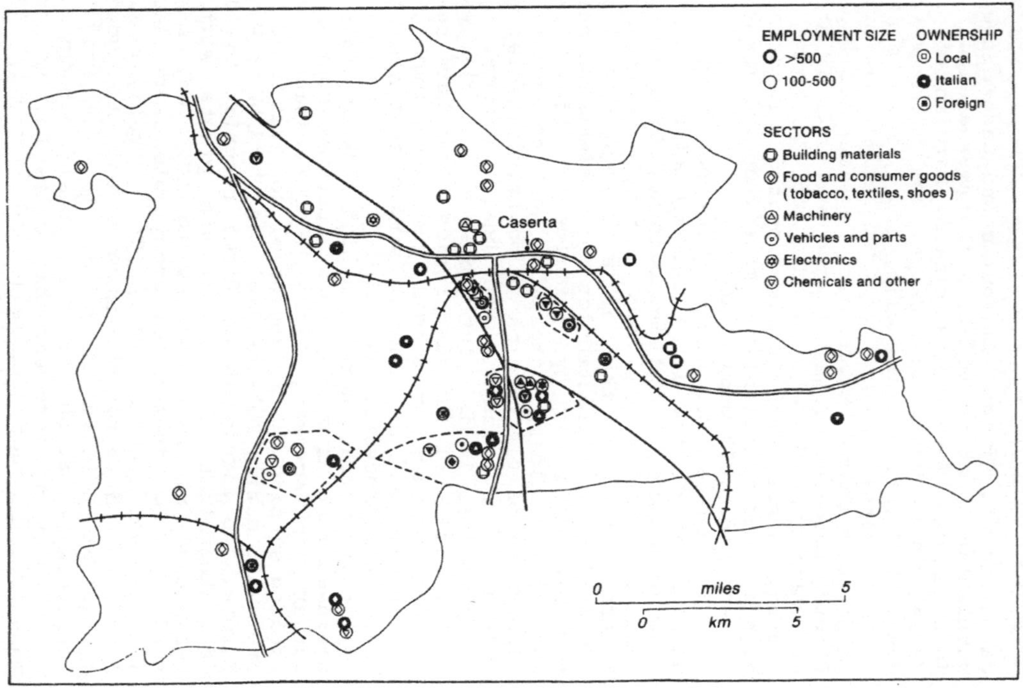

in the integration of industrial sectors but rather comprises the rise of local micro-industrial systems on the margins, in the micro-spatial sense, of major industrial sites (Pontarello, 1983). Any local autonomous propulsive mechanisms are submerged under the disparate diversity of new firms, their persistently high death rates, their backward technologies and their strong tendencies to form part of the black economy - all characteristics rooted in the extremely segmented labour market (Cotugno, Di Luccio and Pugliese, 1981). The clustering of local activities on the fringes of modern industrial sites is an utterly nebulous form of integration exemplified by the shoe firms between Aversa and Sant'Arpino or around Santa Maria a Vico. Figure 9.3 illustrates the distribution of major industries in Caserta province. It shows that most clusters of manufacturing comprise diverse sectors, and combinations of local, Italian-owned and foreign-owned firms. Research has demonstrated the lack of linkage in many cases between them either within individual clusters or between different areas of the province (Diglio and Bencardino, 1983; Sciarelli, 1979; Sciarelli et al., 1982).

The real problem is the absence of positive integration between the foreign and local industrial enterprise: somewhat more, though still limited, exists between Italian-owned and local firms. Generally there is simply a juxtaposition of industrially-used spaces, each space experiencing its own specific path and rate of change without inter-industry connections, imitative learning or sharing of experience in the organization, stages and character of work. Under these conditions there is no guarantee that industrial development will take root and forge the inter- and intra-industry linkages that define a 'local production system'. Dualism is already very deep. The risks are that future development towards a more integrated provincial (and Mezzogiorno regional) economy will be hindered by increasing disorder and delays in urban services and infrastructure; that Caserta will reproduce the conditions that afflict Naples.

BIBLIOGRAPHY

Abignente, M. Territorio e Risorse in Campania (Guida, Naples, 1978)
Benetti, M., Ferrari, M. and Medori, C. Il Capitale Straniero nel Mezzogiorno (Coines, Rome, 1973)
Boccella, N. Il Mezzogiorno Sussidiato (Angeli,

Milan, 1982)
Biondi, G. 'L'emergere di una Campania Intermedia', Orizonti Economici, no. 37 (1983), pp.9-15
Biondi, G. Mezzogiorno Produttivo. Il Modello Solofrano (ESI, Naples, 1984)
Biondi, G. and Coppola, P. Industrializzazione e Mezzogiorno. La Basilicata (Istituto di Geografia Economica dell'Università di Napoli, Naples, 1974)
Biondi, G. and Coppola, P. 'Il Lavoro Fuggente. Multinazionali e occupazione in Campania', Orizonti Economici, no.22 (1979), pp.109-30
Capute, P. and Forte, F. La Planificazione Territoriale nelle Regioni del Mezzogiorno (Angeli, Milan, 1977)
Catandella, M. 'Il Tronco Roma-Napoli dell'Autostrada del Sole e La Localizzazione delle Industrie', Bolletino Società Geografia Italiana, vol.CV, pp.357-71
Coppola, P. 'Geografia di Uno Spazio Emergente', in G. Ragone (ed.), Economia in Trasformazione e Doppio Lavoro (Il Mulino, Bologna, 1983), pp.33-71
Coquery, M. 'Aspects Démographiques et Problèmes de Croissance d'une Ville "Millionaire": Le Cas de Naples', Annales de Géographie, vol.393 (1963), pp.572-604
Cotugno, P. et al, Mezzogiorno e Terza Italia: Il Modello Casertano (ESI, Rome, 1981)
Cotugno, P., Di Luccio, L. and Pugliese, E. 'Classe Operaia e Industria in un'Area Periferica: Il Casertano', Politica e Economia, vol.3 (1981), pp.77-89
Del Monte, A. Decentramento Internazionale e Decentramento Produttivo. Il Caso dell'Industria Elettronica (Loescher, Turin, 1982)
Diglio, S. and Bencardino, F. 'Primi Risultati di una Ricerca: I Rientri in Campania', in M. L. Gentileschi and R. Simoncelli (eds.) Rientro Degli Emigrati e Territorio. Risultati di Inchieste Regionali (Istituto Grafico Italiano, Naples, 1983), pp.369-99
D'Aponte, T. 'Incentivi Territoriali e Sviluppo Industriale: L'esperienza del Mezzogiorno', Nord e Sud, no. 14 (1976A), pp.33-53
D'Aponte, T. La Piana del Sarno (Istituto di Geografia e de Geografia Economica dell'Università di Napoli, Naples, 1976B)
D'Aponte, T. 'Aspetti Geografici della Politica di Inventivazione Finanziaria per lo Sviluppo Industriale del Mezzogiorno', Italian

Contributions to the 23rd International Geographical Congress 1976 (CNR, Rome, 1976), pp.259-71

Fralicciardi, A. M. et al. 'Prime Valutazioni sulla Dinamica Demografica in Campania', in C. Cencini, G. Dematteis and B. Menegatti (eds.) L'Italia Emergente. Indagine Geo-Demografica sullo Sviluppo Periferico (Angeli, Milan, 1983), pp.479-97

Mazzetti, E. Il Nord del Mezzogiorno (Comunita, Milan, 1966)

Pontarello, E. 'Una Politica Industriale per Il Mezzogiorno', in G. Lizzeri (ed.), Mezzogiorno Possibile (Angeli, Milan, 1983)

Rao, A. L'Area di Influenze di Napoli (ESI, Naples, 1967)

Ruocco, D. 'La Coltura della Canapa in Campania', Atti del XVII Congresso Geografico Italiano, vol. 3 (1957), pp.555-60

Sciarelli, S. 'L'industrializzazione in Campania: Realtà e Prospettive', Nord e Sud, vol.XXVI, no.8 (1979), pp.270-90

Sciarelli, S. and Maggioni, V. 'Un'industria Acefala: Primi Risultati di una Indagine Svolta in Campania', Rassegna Economica, vol.XXXVIII (1975), pp.1493-1511

Sciarelli, S., Maggioni, V. and Stampacchia, P. L'Industria in Campania all'Inizio degli Anni Ottanta (Federazione Regionale Industriale della Campania, Naples, 1982)

Zollo, G. 'L'industria Casertana degli Anni Ottanta', Punto 4, vol.2 (1982), pp.12-18

CHAPTER 10

FOREIGN MANUFACTURING INVESTMENT IN GREECE, COMPETITION AND MARKET STRUCTURE

Evangelia Dokopoulou

The main question examined in this chapter is the extent to which the activities of the multinational enterprises (MNE) in Greece have caused a concentration in its industrial structure and what are the determining forces in this process. In this context, the discussion focuses on: (1) the problems of measuring and evaluating the concentration of MNEs in the manufacturing structure of a less developed country; (2) the concentration of foreign subsidiaries in Greece's industrial structure; and (3) factors determining the pattern of concentration.

THE IMPORTANCE OF MULTINATIONALS

The dramatic rise in the activities of MNEs since the Second World War and their growth in the share of world industry has led to arguments that MNE control and power over the host country economy and politics is expanding. Broader discussions relate the rise in foreign direct investment since the mid 1970s to the strategy of firms to intensify expansion abroad as an adaptive response to the recession and the economic crisis; and further that this phenomenon guides a process of centralization (Michalet, 1982). Other opinions support the notion that a growing share of MNEs in the manufacturing production of host advanced countries is associated with the concentration of sales in a decreasing number of larger enterprises. According to this, the first impact of a MNE subsidiary entering the host country and the changes which follow in the industrial structure will be towards a concentration of control in sectors which it has penetrated. Most recent evidence has established that there is indeed a resurgence in the role of MNEs since the early to mid 1970s (United Nations, 1978). In fact, in both current and real terms the stock of foreign direct investment abroad by MNEs expanded more sharply during 1975-80 than in the period 1961-75. Foreign direct investment abroad from developed countries expanded during 1971-80 faster relative to the growth of product and exports of their countries compared with the 1967-71 period (Dunning and Stopford, 1983).

The growing importance of MNEs has provoked the comments on the counterveiling power of MNEs over host government policies (Vaitsos, 1976). The major credit to this thesis is given by the evidence on the increased control over technology trade within groups of subsidiaries of MNEs possessing ownership advantages and by the evidence of intra-group transfer pricing. In fact trade has mostly increased amongst subsidiaries of MNEs with higher research intensity products than amongst those with lower intensity products (Leroy, 1978).

The resurgence of MNEs' investment stock abroad and the observed tendency towards industrial concentration of the world's major industrial firms (Dunning and Pearce, 1980) coincided with other features and changes in the world economy in which host governments have played a pivotal role. To a great extent this chapter argues that governments in less developed countries, like Greece, have become more central to the strategies of MNEs than the MNEs are for the host governments. For instance, there has been a retreat of MNEs from the exploitation of natural resources and the development of public utilities in less developed countries because of the trends towards nationalization of MNEs' assets without compensation; changes in the economies of scale in industries and the industrial organization; the shift of MNE investments to trade and services; the formation of free trade blocs; and changes in the institutions of host countries affecting adversely the protection of foreign direct investment. All these factors influence the direction of foreign direct investment flows between industries and their geographic distribution between the developed and developing countries. They also pose difficulties in both the periodization of foreign direct investment (FDI) flows and the evaluation of the effects of MNE entry into the host country's industrial structure.

The impacts of the MNE during its entry into the host country's industrial structure will primarily depend on the existing structure of the latter (Fishwick, 1982; Parry, 1979). First, if the MNE enters a new and modern sector not yet existing in the host, less developed country it increases the number of firms, diversifies the industrial structure towards more modern sectors and reduces concentration. Secondly, if it chooses to take over existing nationally-owned or other foreign-owned firms there may be not an initial effect on the diversification and concentration because there will be no change in the number of existing firms. But there will be organizational linkage concentration between national capitalists' corporate structures and the MNE. Thirdly, if the MNE enters a sector dominated by few nationally-owned firms, it increases specialization but decreases the number of sellers, though there might be collusion subsequently and price setting. So, practically this may not reduce concentration and the power of oligopolies to set prices.

Subsequently, there are three more possible changes from the MNE's entry. First, concentration and diversification may increase if less competititive nationally-owned firms operating inefficiently and in a protected environment lose market shares to the MNE. They may also close down or merge. Because MNEs will operate in a small developing economy there will be little room for expansion of new firms unless they are, or become, export orientated. Moreover there will be little opportunity for new firms to enter the market and compete with established MNEs. Secondly, other foreign firms may choose to enter a sector with oligopolistic structures motivated by the prospects of collusion. In this case there will be increased concentration and specialization. Finally, a diversification and decentralization may take place through the entry of backward and forward linked firms to the foreign sector. For instance, the establishment of an aluminium smelter may increase investments from other nationally-owned and foreign firms in packing and aluminium processing (see Figure 10.1).

Evidence from the effects of MNE entry in certain developed countries has refuted or held inconclusive the assertion that there is a causal relationship between MNEs' operations and industrial concentration in the host manufacturing structure. Also the methods of measurement of the centralization of control of MNEs in host countries have come under criticism (Gilman, 1980; Ghertman and Allen, 1984).

The following analysis of the Greek case is

based on partial use of a questionnaire survey supported by interviews in 1982 in 118 MNE subsidiaries located in Greece. (The survey was designed for the author's Ph.D. thesis [Dokopoulou, 1985].)

PROBLEMS OF MEASURING CONCENTRATION: MNEs IN GREEK INDUSTRIAL STRUCTURE

The methods of measurement of the impact of the MNE entry in the host industrial structure include: the seller and buyer concentration in branches penetrated by MNE; the size and concentration of assets and of gross and net profits; and the relative importance of FDI to the GNP in, and exports from, a host country. In a less developed country like Greece the difficulty of measuring concentration originates in the features of her industrial structure. First, it is characterized by a dualism. There is a substantial proportion of output in the hands of the 'informal' sector which usually comprises the smaller sized firms. The MNEs in Greece have little interaction with it and cannot easily take market shares from it for reasons described later. In certain sectors like clothing, olive pressing and processing, dairy products, metal working, electrical engineering and transport goods, it is extremely difficult to measure market shares of small firms since a large proportion of them does not declare transactions.

Secondly, there is an intensification of linkages between the subsidiaries of different MNEs and between the former and nationally-owned ones (Figure 10.1). These linkages cannot be measured because they are organizational, interlocking directorates and exchanges of materials and of various services. Sometimes, MNEs take over a firm belonging to a nationally-owned corporation. Joint ventures are also set up with local entrepreneurs owning a corporation with diversified activities like tourism and shipping.

Thirdly, assets of certain foreign subsidiaries in Greece have grown more by borrowing from local banks than from a transfer of capital from the parent. This is because they have a relatively greater ability than domestic firms to absorb funds and finance their operations.

Fourthly, the concentration of control by MNEs can result from linkages between the parents of foreign subsidiaries. MNEs cooperate in joint R&D projects in developed countries because some of them

Figure 10.1 Organizational links in the aluminium industry in Greece, 1960-1979

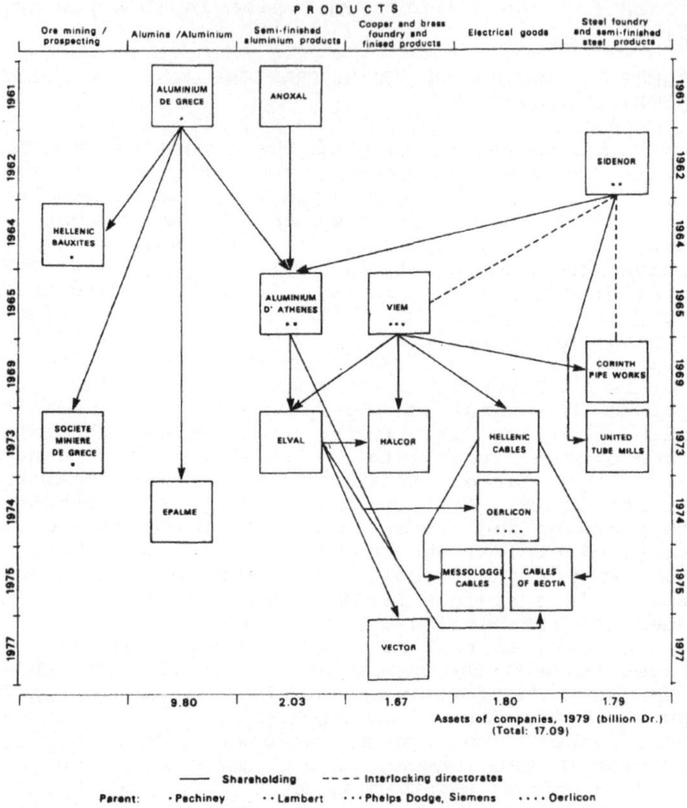

Sources: ICAP Financial directory of Greek companies, 1981. J.M. Stopford, J.H. Dunning and K.O. Heberich, The World Directory of Multinational Enterprises, Macmillan Reference Books, 1980. Who Owns Whom 1982, Europe, Dun and Bradstreet Ltd., London, 1982

require costs on a grand scale as in transformer technology; so, costs are undertaken jointly. Further, such linkages are followed by agreements between MNEs for market shares for supplies of components in public investment projects of several countries developing their infrastructure as the Middle Eastern ones, and also in large technological projects jointly undertaken between EEC countries.

In consequence, there are several ties and agreements for sharing product markets and controlling prices in less developed countries between several subsidiaries whose parents have joint R&D projects. Such agreements for sharing product markets and setting prices do exist in Greece in telecommunication components and transformers, products exclusively purchased by the public corporations. Thus, apparently, the seller concentration may not increase but the network of linkages will be intensified. In this case, the few foreign sellers in Greece will collude, fearing the clash in larger markets. In fact, the governments in less developed countries which have shortage of funds to finance public investment projects are tied to credit from MNEs. Sometimes credit is supplied from foreign banks which credit MNEs. For this reason, they may allow entry to many MNEs in the same field and split orders between them. This is the case for mechanical equipment and electrical goods.

CONCENTRATION OF FOREIGN SUBSIDIARIES IN GREECE.

The most appropriate data for measurement of concentration of foreign subsidiaries in Greece's industrial structure are the share of assets in total manufacturing. Gross and net profits are misleading indicators because there are variations in the accounting practices between companies and because of the impact of the regional development subsidies on them. The latter tend to reduce net profits due to the increased depreciation allowances. Sales figures are not published. The share of foreign subsidiaries in Greece's manufacturing for the years 1970, 1975 and 1979 in Table 10.1 indicate a decreasing importance of foreign subsidiaries in the stock of Greek manufacturing investment since the early 1970s. This decrease has been sharpest since 1975. The share of firms with a foreign shareholding over 50 per cent in Greece's manufacturing assets was 31.5 per cent

Table 10.1: Distribution of Employment and Assets of Foreign Manufacturing Subsidiaries in Greece, 1979

	Assets					Employment			No.
	% of Directory 1970 - 1975		Dr.b	% of Directory 1979		000s	% of Directory 1979		1979
Shareholding over	50%		15%	15%	35%	15%	15%	35%	15%
Sectors	(1)	(2)	(3)	(4)	(5)	(6)	(7)	(8)	(9)
Food	13.2	16.3	5.3	7.3	5.6	5.53	14.2	12.7	19
Drinks and beverages	11.8	13.9	4.7	27.4	27.4	2.86	32.1	32.1	4
Tobacco	..	9.8	-	-	-	-	-	-	-
Textiles	5.1	5.3	10.0	9.2	2.0	5.96	23.4	3.7	20
Clothing	9.0	13.5	1.7	9.6	9.6	4.92	18.9	16.7	20
Wood	38.3	32.8	0.5	5.1	2.5	0.31	5.3	2.9	4
Furniture	-	-	-	-	-	-	-	-	-
Paper	21.4	16.7	3.2	16.7	14.4	1.17	13.7	12.0	9
Printing	..	0.4	0.1	..	..	0.08	..	..	3
Leather	5.6	12.5	0.4	13.8	13.8	0.22	20.5	13.8	3
Rubber and plastic	44.2	30.4	3.5	18.4	17.1	2.08	16.4	14.9	13
Chemicals	61.4	45.7	16.0	35.7	34.3	7.21	29.0	25.7	46
Oil and coal	83.9	97.0	4.2	10.2	10.2	0.30	9.1	9.1	2
Non-metallic minerals	8.5	6.8	5.8	12.8	6.2	3.98	15.5	9.4	18
Basic metals	58.6	47.0	23.9	61.7	52.7	6.11	60.1	52.9	8
Metal products	23.4	11.2	5.1	12.5	10.4	3.39	13.1	8.4	20
Non-electrical machinery	8.3	6.5	2.5	29.2	17.3	1.47	24.8	10.2	21
Electrical goods	35.6	40.0	13.2	48.2	42.0	7.79	46.4	42.1	35

Transport equipment	54.8	62.3	13.8	23.3	23.3	3.11	12.1	12.1	6
Miscellaneous	64.7	32.5	4.2	57.6	55.8	1.15	45.2	24.0	11
Total	31.5	28.6	118.1	19.6	16.1	57.3	17.8	134.2	255
x	27.3	25.0	5.9	19.9	20.0	2.9	19.9	15.1	
s	25.2	23.5	6.21	17.9	16.7	2.5	15.7	13.7	
Coefficient of variation	92.0	94.2	105.0	89.9	83.3	88.1	78.7	90.7	

.. = nil
\- = negligible

Sources: Columns 1 and 2, Giannitsis, A., 'Economic Integration of Greece in the EEC and Foreign Direct Investment', in M. Nikolinakos (ed.), EEC, Greece and Mediterranean, Nya Synora, Athens, 1978 (in Greek).
Columns 3 and 4, E. Dokopoulou, 'Foreign Investment in Manufacturing in Greece: Linkages and Spatial Impacts', Ph.D. thesis submitted to the University of London, 1985.

in 1970 and declined to 28.6 per cent in 1975. By 1979, the share of assets of subsidiaries with a shareholding over 15 per cent in Greece's manufacturing had declined to 19.6 per cent. Between 1970-75, the share of assets of subsidiaries with a shareholding over 50 per cent declined in 9 out of 19 sectors in which they had invested. Between 1975-79 the share of foreign investment seems to have declined in 13 out of 19 sectors. But the indications in Table 10.2 suggest that there was a shift of foreign operations in Greece towards the establishment of export platforms rather than investments to serve the local markets. The number of foreign subsidiaries in Greece's major 200 exporting companies in manufacturing and mining, rose from 45 in 1973 to 55 in 1979 and 1980. It would be reasonable to accept that the prospect of Greece's full EEC membership in 1981 has accelerated the role of Greece as a 'bridge' for MNEs to establish export platforms to serve the Middle East markets.

The concentration of foreign subsidiaries in products output and markets in Greece is shown in Tables 10.3 and 10.4. Table 10.3 distributes the main products of 87 subsidiaries by their share in output and market in Greece. The number of foreign subsidiaries involved in the manufacture of each product does not exceed 3. The 87 subsidiaries appear to have an oligopolistic control on the output and market of the majority of their principal products. They control more than half of the output in 61 out of 91 products (66 per cent), and concentrate more than half of sales in Greece in 36 out of 65 of their main products (55 per cent). In only 10 products (11 per cent) out of the 91 they share less than one quarter of output and in only 9 products in 65 (14 per cent) their market share is less than a quarter.

Table 10.4 shows a seller concentration amongst foreign subsidiaries which sell over 10 per cent of their output in Greece. Some food processing, pharmaceutical, textile and clothing companies were excluded because there is a lack of disaggregated census statistics in their products. In a sample of 59 subsidiaries, 37 (63 per cent) concentrate more than 50 per cent of output in one of their principal products. In a sample of 46 subsidiaries, 23 (50 per cent) concentrate more than 50 per cent of the market sales in their product. One subsidiary may have an oligopolistic control on more than one product. Only one tenth of the sample of the

Table 10.2: Foreign Subsidiaries in the 200 Major Exporters in Greece; Selected Years

Year	Number of Subsidiaries
1973	45
1976	50
1978	56
1978	55
1980	55

Source: Elaboration from the list of the top 200 exporting companies published in Bulletin, (Deltion) Federation of Greek Industries, various issues

Table 10.3: Product output and Market Share of 87 Foreign Manufacturing Subsidiaries, Greece, 1981

Output share*	Products No.	%	Market share*	Products No.	%
Over 50%	61	66	Over 50%	36	55
25-49%	21	23	25-49%	20	31
10-24%	7	8	10-24%	7	11
Up to 9%	3	3	Up to 9%	2	3
Total	91	100	Total	65	100

* The number of subsidiaries in each product does not exceed 3.

Source: Interviews

Table 10.4: Concentration of Foreign Subsidiaries in Product Output and Market Shares

Output share	Subsidiaries No.	%	Market share	Subsidiaries No.	%
Over 50%	37	63	Over 50%	23	50
25-49%	22	37	25-49%	22	48
10-24%	22	17	10-24%	13	28
Up to 9%	6	10	Up to 9%	5	11
Total	59	100	Total	46	100

Source: Interviews

respondents have less than 10 per cent in a product output and market. The figures in Tables 10.3 and 10.4 are revealing not only because they suggest an oligopolistic concentration in Greece in products penetrated by MNEs. In fact, with the exception of the aluminium smelter, none of the foreign companies operating in Greece, even the largest in the sample, has any plant of an optimum size, and they are all the smallest concerns in their group of affiliates operating in European countries. So, the need to realize economies of scale in production has not been a deterrent to enter the market.

The foreign manufacturing subsidiaries enjoy substantial proprietary advantages vis-à-vis nationally-owned enterprises, especially over the smaller 'informal' firms. They have a superiority in the use of technical processes, supplies of cheaper inputs from affiliates, efficient organization, management and marketing and financing facilities from the parent plant and local banks. Despite this, the smaller nationally-owned firms with their marginal efficiency, maintain substantial market shares in Greece and compete effectively with the large foreign subsidiaries. This situation is shown in Table 10.5. More than two-thirds in a sample of 78 foreign subsidiaries enjoy a monopoly or oligopoly position. Twelve subsidiaries (15 per cent) are monopolies, and only 6 of these employ more than 80 workers. There are 25 subsidiaries (32 per cent) with one to five competitors in Greece. More than one third of the sample's subsidiaries operate in a dualistic market, sharing it with a few larger firms and with many smaller ones, the 'informal' sector. The characteristics of the 'informal' sector vary amongst sectors. It is composed of firms privately owned and under family control. They operate in labour intensive processes, like the assembly of solar energy panels, TV, boilers, electrical and mechanical goods and transport equipment, and in clothing and food processing. They lack capital to finance modernization and the purchase of materials and labour to carry out larger scale operations. They have an inefficient family control and management, backward techniques and lack information of markets beyond their boundaries. Evidence from two subsidiaries in the vehicle assembly sector is that, although the 'informal' sector firms have a high birth and death rate, their numbers have not been reduced and they maintain their market shares at the expense of the foreign owned firms.

Table 10.5: Number of Competitors for 78 Foreign Manufacturing Subsidiaries in Greece, 1981

Competitors*	Subsidiaries No.	%
None	12	15
1-2 large	18	23
3-5 large	23	29
1-4 large and many small firms	13	17
Only many small and medium sized firms	12	15
Total	78	100

* Subsidiaries sell more than 20 per cent of their output in Greece.

Source: Interviews

Table 10.6: Competition from Imports for 75 Foreign Manufacturing Subsidiaries in Greece, 1981*

Competition	Subsidiaries No.	%
Yes, in the same and differentiated products	38	51
Impossible or difficult to import similar products or substitutes	28	37
Yes, only in specialized products	9	12
Total	75	100

* Excludes pharmaceutical subsidiaries and includes subsidiaries with more than 10 per cent of their sales in Greece.

Source: Interviews

There are several factors which assist the 'informal' sector firms to retain large profits vis-à-vis the foreign firms and to prevent a concentration of market in the hands of few foreign sellers. First, they extensively avoid taxation. Secondly, a large proportion of their output is distributed through kinship ties, especially in food processing. Thirdly, some 'informal' firms have lower production costs compared with foreign-owned ones. This is due to the absence of codes for the standardization for many products in Greece. This allows for bad standards and unreliable and low quality of product. Foreign-owned firms have to conform to some standard of the parent plant. 'Informal' firms spend negligible amounts on the quality control of their output; they sell unstandardized products, and there is no mechanism to enforce the protection of consumers and environments. The public corporations purchase supplies from the 'informal' sector. But these do not have to conform to some code or standard.

Fourthly, family-owned firms produce at lower costs relative to foreign-owned because they employ unpaid family members and have low overheads. Yet there is no evidence that the foreign firms have influenced the 'informal' sector towards a concentration of greater efficiency or economies of scale.

FACTORS EXPLAINING CONCENTRATION OF FOREIGN SUBSIDIARIES IN GREEK INDUSTRIAL STRUCTURE

There are three important issues in the concentration of industrial structure of Greece, following entry of MNEs. First, subsidiaries can develop most of their market potential in the urban areas rather than in towns and rural districts which are dominated by the 'informal' sector. So there is a limit to the concentration which may be created. MNEs tend to locate near high localized urban markets, like Athens, to minimise transport costs. Their distribution costs increase in the countryside because of the distance of markets and because of the great dispersal and the poor accessibility of the Greek towns. The 'informal' sector has a fair proportion of its activity in the countryside and is protected by the high transport and distribution costs.

Secondly, protection from cheaper imports in Greece is weak for many of the products of MNEs. Cheaper imported substitutes take market shares from the formal sector and from foreign firms and affect to a lesser extent the 'informal' sector's market. This decreases concentration. Table 10.6 distributes 75 foreign subsidiaries according to their protection from imports in Greece. Despite the fact that two-thirds of the sample were earlier found to be monopolies or oligopolies, fewer subsidiaries are in fact very much protected. The overwhelming majority of the subsidiaries' respondents, 38 out of the 75 (51 per cent), finds competition in Greece from a wide range of differentiated and specialized substitutes. Fewer subsidiaries are protected, only 28 (37 per cent).

MNEs have in the past achieved from governments in Greece a protection from cheaper imports, but this was for a limited period of time and due to the bargaining power of MNEs. Although Greece has become since 1981 a formal member of the EEC it has still in force non-tariff barriers, like numerous taxes and duties imposed at the customs on the CIF price of imports of manufactured goods; bureaucratic procedures which cause delays at customs; prohibitions of authorities on the importers' manufacturers to accept credit from the exporting firms abroad. Most imports enter the country through Athens, the principal market of MNEs, and are consumed there because of the high transport and distribution costs involved in selling the products in the markets of the rural periphery which suffer from bad accessibility. Partly accountable for this pattern of lessened protection from imports in Greece is the policy of the government to allow the entry of trading subsidiaries of MNEs in the hope that they will in the near future set up small plants as soon as a minimum market share is achieved. But in sectors where there are long established, national, capitalist interests, like in denim production, the government has enforced insurmountable barriers to imports. The protection from cheaper imports in Greece was also weakened by the dumping practices of plants located in other Mediterranean countries. This was largely the result of the intensification of competition due to the recession.

Some of the imports come from the Socialist countries and are purchases of the public corporations. The State uses purchases of the public corporations in barter trade with the centrally-planned economies to exchange for surplus agricultural production. Such policies of the government cause the exit or diversification of subsidiaries from one sector dominated by State purchase to another, or a shift to the export processing. For instance, Philips selling components to the Public Telecommunication Corporation had a declining share of orders because the Corporation shifted its purchases to the Socialist countries. So Philips set up in 1981 a plant for TV assembly, and pharmaceutical firms shifted to cosmetics.

Table 10.7: Origins of Investment of 118 Foreign Manufacturing Subsidiaries operating in Greece in 1981/2

Origin	Subsidiaries No.	%
Sales Office	44	37.2
Partnership with Greek businessmen	41	34.7
of which:		
Joint ventures	26	22.0
of which with Greek businessmen living abroad:	15	12.7
Takeovers	15	12.7
State promoted	8	6.7
Total	118	100.0

Source: Interviews

Thirdly, State purchases have been an important factor for the entry of MNEs in Greece, and the government policies on public investment projects and purchase of supplies had been the major force in the change in the industrial concentration in Greece. Despite the fact that the governments have been increasingly purchasing from Socialist countries components of technically advanced goods, at the same time they also allowed entry to as many competitors as wished to set up production for the public corporations. They give a preference to the Greek-made manufactures, even if these are proving more costly than imported ones. The public corporations split orders between firms operating in Greece. The result is an overcapacity, and this is observed in the production of drugs, telecommunications components and transformers and transport equipment.

Fourthly, as shown in Table 10.7, the majority of

foreign subsidiaries entered Greece as either a trading subsidiary with a sales office or going directly to production (for export platforms). The smallest proportion of the projects (6.7 per cent) was promoted directly by the State. Forty-one subsidiaries, a third, commenced in cooperation with local entrepreneurs. Of these, fifteen projects (12.7 per cent) originated in takeovers of shares of an existing Greek-owned firm. Gradually the shareholding was increased and the management passed into the hands of the foreign shareholder, even if they had not the majority of shares. Twenty-six projects (22 per cent) started as joint ventures with Greek industrialists and of these 15 were initiated by Greek businessmen living and working abroad for a long period. Amongst the 41 subsidiaries which involved a cooperation with a Greek entrepreneur, 13 (11.0 per cent), are affiliated to a Greek corporation. This pattern indicates increased linkages between MNEs and Greek corporations.

LINKAGES

Linkages between foreign and nationally-owned corporations have been intensified also because some of them share a joint production facility and others subcontract work in their laboratories, especially in pharmaceutical and veterinary products and cosmetics. Some Greek-owned and foreign firms share both sales and administration and laboratories as well.

The previous discussion suggests that MNE entry increased the capital supply from the nationally-owned corporations and intensified linkages with Greek- owned corporations. It also suggests multiplier effects inter-sectorally and intra-sectorally and some industrial diversification. Figure 10.1 illustrates this case. It shows the impact on Greece's industrial structure of linkages created after the building of the aluminium smelter by Pechiney in 1961. The project of the aluminium smelter has created from 1961 to 1979, in 16 years, 15 more projects, 13 of which are forward linked with aluminium as primary or secondary metal or with shareholding and interlocking directorates. From 1962 to 1979 there were 13 more companies created in four industrial branches involving engineering and metal processing. The assets of the original project of the smelter were in 1979 Dr.b.9.8. The assets of the forward linked 14 firms were Dr.b.7.29, which represent 74.4 per cent of the initial project investment.

BIBLIOGRAPHY

Dunning, J. H. and Pearce, R. D. The World's Largest Industrial Enterprises (Gower, Farnborough, 1982)

Dunning, J. H. and Stopford, J.M. Multinationals, Company Performance and Global Trends (Macmillan, London, 1983)

Fishwick, F. Multinational Companies and Economic Concentration in Europe (Gower, London, 1982)

Ghertman, M. and Allen, M. An Introduction to the Multinationals (Macmillan, London, 1984)

Gilman, M. G. The Financing of Foreign Direct Investment: A Study of Multinational Enterprises (Pinter, London, 1980)

Leroy, G. 'Technology Transfer within the Multinational Enterprise' in M. Ghertman and J. Leondiades (eds.), European Research in International Business (North Holland, Amsterdam, 1978)

Michalet, C.A. 'Multinationals: Change of Strategy in the Face of Crisis', Institute for Research and Information on Multinationals Conference, Paris, November 1982

Parry, T. G. 'Competition and Monopoly in Multinational Corporate Relations with Host Countries', in R. G. Hawkins (ed.), The Economic Effects of Multinational Corporations (Jai Press, Greenwich, Conn., 1979)

Vaitsos, C. 'Power Knowledge and Development Policy: Relations between Transnational Enterprises and Developing Countries', in G. K. Helleiner (ed.), A World Divided (Cambridge University Press, Cambridge, 1976)

CHAPTER 11

MULTINATIONALS AND MANUFACTURED EXPORTS FROM THE ENLARGED EEC PERIPHERY: THE CASE OF GREECE

Evangelia Dokopoulou

This chapter discusses the changing role of multinational enterprises (MNE) in the manufactured exports from Greece following the entry of Greece into the EEC. It focuses on two questions: whether the pattern of MNE exports reflects the country's comparative advantages; and how that pattern affects the position of Greece in the international divison of labour.

Three main points are argued. First, Greece plays a role in the southern EEC periphery as an export platform of MNEs attracted there by the country's comparative advantages following Greece's association with the EEC since 1962. Secondly, the pattern of MNE exports has been changing since the recession of 1974 and has been affected by the political relations between Greece and her export markets and within the broader region of the Mediterranean basin and the Middle East. Thirdly, Greece's industrial restructuring depends to a significant extent on the decisions of the MNEs that have established export platforms in the country. The case of the aluminium industry illustrates this.

ENLARGEMENT OF THE EEC AND ANTICIPATED BEHAVIOUR OF MULTINATIONALS

The discussion rests on the recognition that the industrial system of a small country depends on exports overtly because its market is too small to support an efficient size of plant, especially in a variety of sectors and products. Hood and Young (1979, pp.173-5) argue that the integration of a country in a customs union such as the EEC may, because of the abolition of tariffs, enlarge the size of its foreign market area and thus stimulate foreign investment. They also suggest that it can influence the choice of MNEs in favour of a subsidiary production in the country rather than maintaining exports to it. Finally, such enlargement can encourage MNEs to etablish export platforms and to rationalize production facilities to serve the total market from a smaller number of plants of a minimum efficient scale.

The position occupied in the international divison of labour by a small country integrated in the EEC will be affected in several ways by the choice of MNEs to establish production affiliates there for exports. First, a diversification of the host country's industrial structure may result from a wider variety of products which can be manufactured for export to an enlarged market than could be before the integration. Secondly, MNE processing for exports may or may not reflect the host country's comparative advantage and subsidiaries may or may not be endowed with such characteristics as to create a good export performance. The difficulty of evaluating the MNE export performance is due to transfer pricing widely practised by the MNEs (Roumeliotis, 1978; Rugman, 1985). Thirdly, a significant proportion of world trade is carried out as intra-group transactions (Dunning and Pearce, 1981; Hood and Young, 1983). This means that the industrial restructuring in a small country would be an integrated part of the organization of global production of a corporation. And the corporation's priority will be to achieve the complementarity of functions and the internalization of transactions in technology, materials and managerial expertise between subsidiaries rather than responding to markets (Caves, 1982; Rugman, 1981 and 1982; and Vaitsos, 1980). In other words, the corporations attempt to optimize their internal division of labour.

For some years prior to Greece's full membership within the EEC in 1981 - association with the EEC took place in 1962 - much discussion supported the idea that the effect of the southern enlargement of the EEC would be an increase in the export-processing investment by MNEs, especially by the US-based ones which would take advantage of the cheap labour of peripheral economies and low cost inputs from EEC affiliates to export to either EEC or Third World countries. Giannitsis (1978, p.135) maintained that this tendency was evident in Greece between 1970-76.

Opposite views were expressed, such as by Murolo (1982, p.217), Tsoukalis (1981, p.47) and

Vaitsos (1982, pp.159-60), who argued that MNEs had already been present in Greece; that they did not depend on southern Europe to expand their activities in the less developed countries because they had already penetrated them with imports using their sales subsidiaries. Further, that affiliates in Third World countries produced the same lines of goods as in southern Europe, and US subsidiaries were already predominant in advanced EEC countries.

The research presented in this chapter is based on partial use of a questionnaire survey supported by interviews with personnel of 118 MNE subsidiaries operating in Greece in 1982. The survey was designed for the author's Ph.D. research (Dokopoulou, 1985). Additional information has been collected from the annual reports of the subsidiaries and from the list of the top 200 exporting mining and manufacturing companies that is published in the Bulletin of the Federation of Greek Industries.

THE CHANGING POSITION OF GREECE IN THE INTERNATIONAL DIVISION OF LABOUR

Greece typifies a newly-industrializing country which experienced rural transformation and impressive economic growth rates for most of the 1960s and until the recession of 1974 (Table 11.1).

Table 11.1: Percentage annual changes in Greece

	1965-75		1975-1981	
	Greece	OECD	Greece	OECD
GDP	6.3	4.0	3.5	2.3
Manufacturing	9.7	4.0	4.0	3.7
Fixed investment	4.5	3.3	1.0	1.5
Inflation	7.3	6.3	17.7	10.3

Source: OECD, Economic Surveys, Greece 1982, OECD, Paris, 1983

During the period of growth, the share of rural sector in the GDP declined from 23.2 per cent in 1973 to 14.8 per cent in 1973 and 13.7 per cent in 1980. The proportion of employees in agricultural occupations declined, too, from 53.8 per cent in 1961 to 30.6 per cent in 1981. Manufacturing industry made increasing contributions to GDP, from

14.2 per cent in 1963 to 21.0 per cent in 1973 and 21.4 per cent in 1980, while the proportion of employed in manufacturing rose from 12.9 per cent in 1961 to 19.3 per cent in 1981, but was still far below that of agriculture. The output of modern manufacturing sectors rose relative to that of the traditional ones (Tables 11.2 and 11.3).

Table 11.2: Sectoral Shares in GDP in Greece, 1970 Prices

	1963	1973	1980
Manufacturing	14.2	21.0	21.4
Primary	23.2	14.9	13.7

Source: OECD, National Accounts 1963-1980, OECD, Paris, 1982

Table 11.3: Gross Value Added by Manufacturing Sectors

	1964	1977*
Food, drinks, tobacco, textiles, clothing, wood, furniture, paper, printing, publishing, leather, fur	53.8	54.9
Non-metallic minerals	8.8	5.9
Chemicals, rubber, plastic, oil refining, metals, metal products, machinery, electrical equipment and machines, transport equipment	37.4	39.7
Total	100.0	100.0

* establishments over 10 employees

Source: National Statistical Service of Greece, Annual Survey of Manufacturing Establishments, 1964 and 1977, Athens.

Capacity was built in newly-developed sectors of medium technology - oil refining, petrochemcials, electrical engineering and steel products - by some of the world's largest MNEs such as Pechiney (Aluminium de Grèce), Exxon (Thessaloniki Refining,

Esso Chemicals, Esso Industrial), Ethyl (Ethyl Hellas), Siemens (Siemens Industrial, Siemens Teleindustrial, VIEM), Philips (Philips Industrial), Nippon (Hellenic Steel Company) and Rhône-Poulenc (SICNG).

During the 1960s and until 1976, manufactured exports of Greece (Standard International Trade Classification 5-9 minus 68) grew annually on average 10.7 per cent between 1960-70 and 12.3 per cent between 1970-76; the share of manufactured exports as a percentage of all Greece's merchandise exports rose from 9 per cent in 1960 to 48 per cent in 1975 (Hamilton and Linge, 1981, p.19). Agricultural products in processed and unprocessed form were reduced in their importance in exports after 1960; however, in the 1970s they still remained the source of more than half of Greece's trade receipts (Table 11.4).

Table 11.4: Commodity Trade Structure of Greece, Percentage

	1962	1970	1977
Food and beverages, SICT 0, 1, 22, 4	58.7	41.2	32.6
Non-food agricultural, SICT 2, minus 22, 27, 28	23.2	9.8	3.4
Fuels and minerals, SICT 3, 27, 28, 68	7.3	14.5	14.2
Machinery and equipment, SICT 7	2.0	1.5	5.2
Other, SICT 5, 6, minus 68, 8, 9	8.9	33.1	44.5
Total	100.0	100.0	100.0

Source: World Tables 1980, World Bank

Greece's share of world manufactured exports improved considerably from 0.04 per cent in 1963 to 0.15 per cent in 1973 and to 0.22 per cent in 1976; her industrial output as a share of the world's industrial production rose from 0.19 per cent in 1973 to 0.25 per cent in 1970 and to 0.33 per cent in 1975 and 1977 (Hamilton and Linge, 1981, pp.17-18). However, Greece ranks very low in the above respect when compared with other newly-industrializing countries. Despite her impressive transformation rates from a rural country, Greece ranked in 1975 second lowest among 10 newly-industrializing countries in the percentage of manufactures in all merchandise exports, below Spain, Portugal, Yugoslavia, Mexico, Hong Kong, South Korea, Taiwan and Singapore (Hamilton and Linge, 1981, p.19).

The first oil-related international recession in 1974 was a turning point in the progress of the Greek economy, which was deeply affected by the international slow-down of trade and the global restructuring of mature industries. The growth of investment and output decelerated and the pace of rural transformation slowed down. The rate of growth of the share of manufacturing in the GDP slowed, and the agricultural production regained in the 1980s its pre-1960s' importance as a principal force in financing growth (OECD, 1982, 1983).

Manufacturing industry increasingly specialized towards low technology traditional sectors such as foods, textiles, clothing, wood, furniture, paper, printing, leather and non-metallic minerals which concentrated in 1977 60.0 per cent of manufacturing industry's gross output (Table 11.3). One of Greece's important advantages, cheap wages, diminished due to a fourfold increase in the index of gross average hourly earnings of industrial workers from 1975 to 1982, a rise which was the highest amongst the 10 EEC countries (Statistical Office of the European Communities, 1982). Nevertheless, Greece maintains cheaper wages compared with those of her wealthier EEC partners.

CHANGES IN THE STRUCTURE AND DESTINATION OF COMMODITY EXPORTS

As Table 11.4 shows, exports from Greece became more diversified in the 1970s than they had been in the 1960s. However, they exhibited a sectoral dependence and a concentration in few companies. Food, beverages and agricultural products declined as a proportion of the value of Greece's commodity exports from 81.9 per cent in 1962 to 51.0 per cent in 1970 and to 36.0 per cent in 1977 (Table 11.4). Machinery and equipment and other manufactured products increased their share from 10.9 per cent in 1972 to 34.6 per cent in 1970 and to 49.7 per cent in 1977, a more than fourfold increase, compared with only a reduction of less than half in the share of exports of agricultural products.

Six traditional commodities of low and medium

technology - textiles, clothes, cement, aluminium, iron and steel and fuels - constituted in 1978 41.5 per cent of the value of commodity exports (Table 11.5). In 1963 this percentage was only 3.0 per cent.

Table 11.5: Share of Selected Products in Greece's Exports

	1963	1978
Textiles, SITC 651-658	2.2	9.0
Clothing and shoes, SITC 831-851	0.2	9.0
Cement, SITC 661	0.2	5.8
Aluminium, SITC 684	0.2	4.2
Iron and Steel, SITC 671-675	0.1	4.2
Fuels, SITC 33	0.1	9.3
Total	3.0	41.5

Source: National Statistical Service of Greece, Statistical Yearbook, various years, Athens

Foreign investment in the late 1970s in terms of the proportion of total assets owned by subsidiaries of MNEs was significant in 5 of these 6 commodities. Subsidiaries with a shareholding by MNEs over 15 per cent accounted in 1979 for 9.2 per cent of assets of textiles firms; 9.6 per cent in clothing; 61.7 per cent in basic metals; 35.7 per cent in chemicals; and 10.2 per cent in oil and coal products (Dokopoulou, 1985, p.52).

In 1983 the top ten mining and manufacturing exporting companies produced 9 standardized technology products. The list is found in the top 200 exporting mining and manufacturing companies, published annually in the Bulletin (Deltion) of the Federation of Greek Industries. Four of the top 10 exporters in 1980 were foreign: Aluminium de Grèce (aluminium and alumina), Thessaloniki Refining (oil products, in 1983 was sold to the State), Biokat (construction) and Hellenic Steel (steel products). The other 6 major exporters amongst the top 10 - which were all Greek-owned - produce cement, minerals, cotton textiles and fertilizers.

As Table 11.6 shows, between 1970 and 1980, a period which largely comprised the international recession and restructuring of standardized

Table 11.6: Distribution of Greece's Commodity Exports by Area - 1970 and 1980; currency US$*

Area	1970		1980	
	US$ m	%	US$ m	%
World	642.5	100.0	5,141.6	100.0
Developed economies	487.1	75.8	3,080.0	59.9
Developing economies	48.3	7.5	1,446.8	28.1
Centrally planned economies	106.5	16.5	603.8	11.7
Other	0.6	0.2	11.9	0.3
USA [1]	48.3	7.5	290.3	5.6
Middle East [2]	26.2	4.1	842.7	16.4
Europe	487.6	75.9	3,156.0	61.4
(EEC) [3]	(335.5)	(52.2)	(2,447.8)	(47.6)
(Centrally planned) [4]	(72.0)	(11.2)	(458.5)	(8.9)
USSR	34.5	5.4	90.1	1.7
Africa	21.1	3.3	539.5	10.5
(Africa, North) [5]	(15.7)	(2.4)	(223.0)	(4.4)
Other	24.8	3.8	223.0	4.4
World	100.0	100.0	100.0	100.0

* There are no comparable figures for 1963

1 USA in 1980 includes Puerto Rico.

2 Middle East countries in 1970 include Cyprus, Iran, Iraq, Jordan, Kuwait, Lebanon, Saudi Arabia, Syria and Turkey. In 1980 Bahrain, Cyprus, Iran, Iraq, Jordan, Kuwait, Lebanon, Oman, Qatar, Saudi Arabia, Syrian Arab Emirates, Turkey, Yemen, United Arab Emirates.

3 EEC in 1970 and 1980 includes 9 countries.

4 Centrally planned economies of Europe in 1970 include Bulgaria, Czechoslovakia, DDR, Hungary, Poland and Romania. The 1980 figures include the same countries, plus Albania.

5 Africa North includes in 1970, UAR, Tunisia, Sudan, Sahara, Libya, Morocco and Algeria. In 1980 it includes Tunisia, Libya, Algeria, Morocco, Sudan and Egypt.

Source: United Nations Commodity Trade, various years

production, the geographic distribution of Greece's commodity trade changed substantially. The proportion of commodity exports destined for developed countries and centrally-planned economies, declined considerably from 92.3 per cent in 1970 to 71.6 per cent in 1980. EEC countries, the main destination in the developed world, took a diminishing proportion of Greece's commodity exports. This became even more marked towards Greece's full membership of the EEC in 1981. By contrast, the share of commodity exports bought by developing world countries increased from 7.5 per cent in 1980 to 28.1 per cent in 1980, so that by the latter date the Middle East and North African countries absorbed more than a quarter of Greek commodity exports. This suggests an increasing investment in export platforms in Greece, while the expectations were that a full membership into the EEC would be concluded.

The industrial sectors in which Greece specialized in exports shown in Table 11.5 have suffered effects from the slow-down of world trade and from the international restructuring of standardized processes. Four out of the 6 major products exported from Greece shown in Table 11.5 - textiles, clothes, aluminium and iron and steel - belong to the so-called 'problem industries' internationally, experiencing low profitability and severe international competition from low-cost producers (Plant, 1981). Moreover, governments of the Western countries have employed policies to try to restore the competitiveness and profitability of these 'problem industries' through restructuring; and to protect them from foreign competition with high import tariffs. These measures have broadly affected Greek exports which are also subject to competition in both home and export markets from the low-cost producing countries. Besides, the real prices of the major exported commodities listed in Table 11.5 have, with the exception of fuels, been in long term decline (World Bank, World Tables 1980).

THE POLITICAL BACKGROUND OF EXPORT PLATFORMS IN GREECE

Exports to the EEC countries from Greece developed after her association in 1962, as duties on manufactured imports from Greece into the EEC were phased out in 1968. The value of manufactured exports to the EEC as a proportion of Greece's total

EEC exports rose from 1.8 per cent in 1962 to 60.3 per cent in 1977 (Zolotas, 1978, p.21). The association agreement provided also that Greek tariff barriers on most industrial products had to be phased out by 1984; and that the country should adopt a common external tariff which was substantially lower than the Greek tariff on imports from non-EEC countries. However, there are still sectors, such as food, textiles, clothing, electrical appliances, accumulators, cables and transport equipment, which enjoy substantial protection through non-tariff barriers (Mitsos, 1981, pp.139 and 141).

Manufacturing firms had to modernize their equipment therefore to take advantage of both exports to the EEC and to be competitive in cheaper imports - most of MNEs' subsidiaries establishing export platforms in Greece sell also to the host market a proportion of their output (Dokopoulou, 1985, p.159). In response to this, modernization and restructuring occurred in the 1970s and 1980s in processes and products where Greece traded mostly with the EEC countries: textiles, steel, aluminium and fruit and canning (IOBE, 1981, 1982; Volos Cotton S.A., Annual Report 1981-1982). New capacity was built in sectors subsidized by the EEC: fruit and vegetable processing (Hellenic Food Industry, ELVAK, Georgoviomichaniki Pierias) and also in labour-intensive activities: clothing (Saron, the largest foreign clothing firm employing 850 in 1982, was established in 1976), assembly of telecommunications equipment and TV, cables and assembly of transport equipment. A large proportion of manufacturing investment came from West German firms establishing subcontracting, export platforms in Greece (Siemens in telecommunications and TV assembly; West German investment is prominent in clothing and textiles, also).

Because Greece's trade with the developed world has been 90% dependent on the European countries (Table 11.6), it possibly suffered greater impacts from the slow economic recovery of Europe relative to the USA in the early 1980s (as for example in aluminium, see Aluminium de Grèce, Annual Reports, 1981-1983).

Economic development policies of Greece regarding trade have never mentioned the USA as an important export market, and in contrast the USA has been viewed rather more as a potential source of foreign direct investment, to which most favourable concessions were from the 1950s to 1974 almost unconditionally offered (Benas, 1978). On the other hand, great emphasis was placed on the trade with the Arab countries, a much closer market, a fact partly related to transport costs on exported manufactures.

The Middle East and African countries have been expanding as export markets since the 1970s (Table 11.6). They purchase from Greece standardized products with high transport costs, especially asbestos and aluminium fabrications. The growth in the importance of the Arab region in Greece's exports increased according to interviews through foreign investment. However, several factors constrain the expansion of Greece's exports to Middle Eastern and African countries: (1) Middle Eastern and some African countries are not open economies and they import manufactured goods under inter-governmental agreements. (2) The war between Iraq and Iran has halted trade to these countries. (3) There is an embargo on the products of firms whose parents export to Israel. (4) Attitudes of Middle Eastern rulers vary towards the socialist policies manifested by the government of Mr. Papandreou, but are generally 'cool'. (5) The complex political environment of the whole Mediterranean region, which embraces both the competitors and export markets of Greece.

As Luciani (1984) points out, the countries of the Mediterranean basin are interdependent in a process of conflict and cooperation. There are conflicts of an international nature as, for example, over sea control, and resources over which confrontation arises and increases the risks of investments. This is certainly true of the marine border areas between Greece and Turkey.

Full membership of Greece in the EEC required that after 1981 her agreements for barter trade with the centrally planned economies should be abolished. This caused a change in her economic relationships. From the 1950s Greek governments had concluded bilateral agreements with East European Socialist countries for selling Greece's surplus agricultural production and minerals in exchange for capital goods to be used by the public corporations running the railways, ports, urban transport, energy and telecommunications in Greece. This policy, which has been operating since 1957, due to the liberalization and expansion of world trade under the auspices of the GATT (General Agreements on Tariffs and Trade), aimed partly to reduce the political cost of maintaining a surplus agricultural production in

Table 11.7: Distribution of Exports of a Sample of Foreign Subsidiaries in Greece by Sectors: in Dr. Billion

Sectors	No. of firms		1973		1980	
	1973	1980	Billion Dr.	As % in top 200	Billion Dr.	As % in top 200
Synthetic and cotton yarns; knitted garments	4	9	0.35	1.5	3.93	3.8
Clothes	3	3	0.28	1.2	1.41	1.4
Oleaginous foods	1	1	0.31	1.3	0.06	..
Paper sacks*		1			0.93	0.9
Rubber tyres	1	2	0.10	0.4	0.69	0.7
Plastic containers*	1	1	0.009	..	0.12	0.1
Petroleum products*	1	1	0.69	2.9	3.82	3.7
Chemicals						
Petrochemicals*	2	2	0.66	2.8	2.16	2.1
Pharmaceuticals	1	2	0.16	0.7	0.62	0.6
Fertilizers*	1	1	0.31	1.3	1.05	1.0
(Total Chemicals)	(4)	(5)	(1.13)	(4.8)	(3.82)	(3.7)
Asbestos-cement products	*1	1	0.63	2.7	0.19	0.2
Metal Products						
Aluminium	1	1	3.03	12.8	6.78	6.7
Aluminium fabrications	2	2	0.23	1.0	2.24	2.2
Copper fabrications	1	1	0.11	0.5	0.95	0.9
Steel plates, galvanized and tinned plates*	2	2	1.33	5.6	4.18	4.1
Open top tins*	2	2	0.38	1.6	0.71	0.7
(Total metal products)	(8)	(8)	(4.73)	(20.0)	(14.85)	(14.5)

Diamond tools		1			0.14	0.1
Electrical engineering, telecommunication switching	3	3	0.30	1.2	0.70	0.7
Batteries and switches	2	2	0.03	0.1	0.35	0.3
Cables*		1			1.50	1.5
(Total Electrical engineering)	(5)	(5)	(0.33)	(1.0)	(2.55)	(2.5)
Construction	1	1	3.18	13.5	3.23	3.2
Top 200 exporting	200	200	23.6	100.0	101.9	100.0
Total foreign subsidiaries	31	41	7.94	33.6	35.74	35.0

* High transport cost
.. Negligible

Source: List of top 200 major exporters in the Bulletin (Deltion), Federation of Greek Industries, various issues, Athens

Greece and partly to reduce the trade deficit created from importing capital equipment from western industrialized countries. The objective was not only to ensure imports from countries purchasing Greek products but also to increase exports to countries from which purchases of Greek products were made as the centrally planned economies of Eastern Europe.

Such a policy had another political cost: the loss of orders to industrial plants located in Greece in the metal working, mechanical, electrical and transport engineering sectors. This resulted in closures, redundant capacity and reduction of the scale economies of plants of both Greek-owned firms and MNEs' subsidiaries which were operating partly as export platforms, too, and specialized in products competing with imports from socialist countries (telecommunications components and transport equipment assembly). It must be noted that the production in these sectors suffers from smallness of scale, overcapacity and admittedly uneconomic production. For this reason exports are heavily subsidized and sales in Greece protected from cheaper imports.

EXPORTS OF FOREIGN SUBSIDIARIES

Table 11.7 shows the changes in the exports of a sample of MNE manufacturing subsidiaries taken from the list of Greece's 200 major exporting mining and manufacturing companies found in the Bulletin (Deltion) of the Federation of Greek Industries. The 1973 figures included 31 subsidiaries which continued to be on the list until 1980, while the 1980 figures contain 10 more, which were all the new exporters established after 1976.

The figures of exports from the list of the 200 major exporting mining and manufacturing companies are not comparable with the export statistics of the National Statistical Services because of the different methodology followed in their collection. Table 11.7 shows that during 1973-80 the share of subsidiaries in the exports of the leading 200 increased from 33.6 per cent to 35.0 per cent, while their number increased from 31 to 41 correspondingly. This could possibly imply a deconcentration of foreign investment in Greece's exports, but an increasing interest for the establishment of export platforms by a larger number of smaller subsidiaries. It could also imply an increasing concentration of Greek-owned and state-owned firms in Greece's exports. If we anticipate the transfer pricing (underpricing of exports) we could conclude that the share of the foreign subsidiaries in Greece's exports of the major mining and manufacturing 200 is more than that of 35.0 per cent and that certainly foreign investment in export processing in Greece has significantly increased during the period of recession.

There was loss of export shares, most noticeable in the capital intensive and energy-consuming sectors like petrochemicals, fertilizers, aluminium, steel products, tin, asbestos materials and construction equipment. The share of petroleum products exports increased, as did that of labour-intensive and assembly industries in which Greece has a comparative advantage: clothing (due to low labour cost), electrical cables (using local aluminium as raw material), textiles (using cotton) and aluminium fabrications.

COMPARATIVE ADVANTAGES AND DISADVANTAGES FOR EXPORT PLATFORMS

Table 11.8 summarizes the answers of 60 exporting MNE subsidiaries from the sample of 118 (exporting and non-exporting), regarding the comparative advantages and disadvantages of establishment of export platforms in Greece.

The Role of Transport Costs

The commodity trade structure of Greece shown in Tables 11.4 and 11.5 reveals a specialization in products with high transport cost, such as food products, cement, clothing, steel products and fuels. High transport cost may explain the predominance of the markets in proximity to Greece as Middle East, EEC and Eastern Europe, while the USA's share is as little as 5.6 per cent of Greece's commodity exports. A similar pattern is exhibited by the exporting subsidiaries in Table 11.8. The Annual Report, 1983 of Aluminium de Grèce refers to 90 per cent of aluminium quantities being exported in 1983 to the EEC; the Annual Report 1980 of Hellenic Steel refers to 55 per cent in volume of steel product exports from the company being delivered to Eastern Europe, 24 per cent to the EEC and 21 per cent to the Middle East and North Africa. Ethyl sold in the 1970s 60 per cent of anti-knock fluid exports in value to the EEC and 40 per cent to the Middle East and Eastern Europe (reference 15 Chronia Ethyl Hellas 1964-79). The advantage of low transport

Table 11.8: Comparative Advantages and Disadvantages for Exports of Foreign Subsidiaries from Greece, 1981

Advantages	Disadvantages
Low transport costs; export subsidies.	Competition from Centrally Planned Economies and countries with higher export subsidies; bureaucracy in the collection of subsidies.
Market sharing and price fixing agreements with other subsidiaries of MNEs located in other Mediterranean countries.	None.
Foreign policy.	Sub-national conflict in the Mediterranean region; inter-governmental agreements are needed for purchases of States in Middle East.
Urban infrastructure and external economies not available in the Third World countries.	None.
Exports to countries with poor safety regulations on health and products.	None.
Integration with resources.	Scale of output; overcapacity; cost of exploitation; restrictions on remittance of profits; small concessions compared with other developing countries; nationalisation.
Low wages; low production costs.	Increases in labour costs; intensified competition because of outmoded technology and poor product quality; in branded goods origin is important (cosmetics and perfumes).
Specialization in small scale orders.	Infrequent sea transport for small deliveries.

Table 11.8 (continued)

Advantages	Disadvantages
Barter trade agreements between Greece and Centrally Planned Economies.	Against EEC regulations.
	Low percentage of profits allowed to be remitted; parent plant policy; dumping.

Source: Interviews with personnel of 60 MNE manufacturing subsidiaries operating in Greece in 1982

costs is enhanced by the export subsidies, which enlarge the boundary of markets.

The forces that reduce Greece's advantages of proximity to main export markets are:

1. Higher export subsidies from other, more distant, countries to their own firms. These outweigh transport cost differentials between Greece and these countries. The subsidies to exporting firms from Greece were in 1981 6 per cent of the FOB value. This was given to recover the loss to the exporters who, in any case, have to deposit with the Bank of Greece an amount equal to the value of firm's exports until the remittance of the exchange. Exporters are not entitled to any interest on such deposits; the amount of subsidies in Greece is far below the banking interest rate and inflation (17.8 per cent annual rate between 1975-81, OECD Economic Surveys, Greece, 1982, OECD, Paris, 1983).

2. Export subsidies are not automatically given to exporters. They have to be collected by the firms, so they are costly, especially when offered to the smaller firms. Some small subsidiaries reported labour costs for subsidy collection to be higher than the subsidy itself.

3. There is competition from East European plants (socialist countries) especially in electrical goods and asbestos materials; and prices quoted by plants in Socialist countries do not reflect actual production costs.

Market Sharing Agreements
Sometimes a spatial monopoly may be created by an arrangement between MNE subsidiaries and national firms located in various countries around a market area, with the intention of achieving an agreement on low prices to eliminate competition from other firms located in countries in proximity. Such a case was referred to by a firm producing asbestos-cement products. The management were said to have come to an agreement with Turkish firms to arrange a common price against Egyptian and Spanish competitors selling to Middle Eastern and North African countries.

Foreign Policy
Favourable foreign policies of Greece towards countries with which Greece trades in the Mediterranean region and Middle East may not be very influential to establish export platforms. Some clients regard, for instance, as most important the reliability of deliveries, product quality and competitive prices. The growth of Arab markets in consumer and capital goods during the 1970s stimulated competition from advanced countries, the low-cost newly industrializing countries and the centrally planned economies. Besides, influences on the decision to establish export platforms originate in:

1. The decisions of parent plant managements which, during the period of slowdown in world trade, had priorities to sell their accumulated stocks rather than to export from Greek affiliates. In certain products (transformers, pumps, electrical distribution panels) exports for local production were reduced and even replaced by imports.

2. The procedures required for exports and the political environment of the Mediterranean region, as discussed earlier.

MNEs assess the potential of national political conflicts in countries where they establish export platforms and also the risks of nationalization of their assets without compensation in Third World countries. This is important because Greece is the country where export platforms were relocated due to nationalization of assets from less-developed countries, such as Egypt, in sectors like cotton textiles and asbestos products during the late

1950s.

External Economies
The advantage of establishing export platforms in Greece, as against some other, less developed countries in North Africa (like Morocco), lies in external economies which can be gained. These are obtained from the existence of urban infrastructure, services and linkages between plants selling inputs. Clothing subsidiaries' managements explained that the disadvantage of industrializing low labour-cost countries *vis-à-vis* Greece is their underdeveloped urban infrastructure. Foreign plants in this case would have to internalize the services that are already available in Greece's urban areas and thus production costs would be increased.

Low Product Standards
Greece is suitable as an export platform to countries with permissive environments, lacking codes and controls for products. This is because Greece also has low standards in safety regulations and thus low production costs. Harmful products are withdrawn from the market only when there is a campaign. Respondents from pharmaceutical firms pointed out:

> MNEs in the pharmaceutical industry prefer to export drugs from subsidiaries located in Greece to Arab and African countries because Greece and these countries either lack or have low standards in safety regulations on production and imports, and this lowers production cost. Import penetration of drugs in Greece was facilitated by the fact that only a certificate was required by the authorities on tests which were undertaken during their production abroad. Low production costs of drugs in Greece result from the low standards of regulations of preparation; few batches of pharmaceutical production are tested and even fewer are rejected relative to the standards in more advanced countries. In this respect there is also little transfer of technology. Moreover, there is poor State control to ensure that even the essentially required tests are carried out.

Burstall et al. (1981) mention that safety regulations in the USA drug industry have not only increased production costs but also caused the rate of new product introduction to decline considerably, so that US-based MNEs try to sell in countries where regulations are more permissive (i.e. EEC); US firms market first a high proportion of their new products abroad rather than at home because of the higher acceptability in the countries of Europe than in the USA.

Resource Endowment

MNEs can be influenced by the resources which a country possesses. However, an important problem in the development of minerals for export processing by MNEs in Greece has been the large spending on infrastructure which MNEs require the government to undertake. Such is the case of aluminium smelting by Pechiney, which uses domestically-mined bauxites. The government in Greece in 1960 had undertaken the construction of a hydroelectric project on the river Acheloos for the supply of electric power to the smelter. The cost of the project undertaken by the Public Power Corporation in Greece was estimated in the early 1960s at US$49m. and equivalent to 65.3 per cent of Pechiney's investment in the smelter of US$75m. (Benas, 1978, p.65). In the 1960 contract between Pechiney and the State in Greece, it was concluded that the State would supply its subsidiary, Aluminium de Grèce, with loans at an interest rate of 4.5 per cent for infrastructural projects, like housing for workers, for expenditure in excess of US$1m.

Strategy of the Parent Plant

The parent plants have constrained exports of their subsidiaries located in Greece for several reasons. First, MNEs have penetrated Third World markets where they established sales subsidiaries with a contract to operate only for a number of years; however, these markets can be served from export platforms in Greece after these contracts expire.

Secondly, MNEs have developed between them links for technology exchange and joint production. As a consequence the management of subsidiaries in some developing countries may agree on market sharing in countries and products. Thirdly, parent plants may set priorities in exporting their surpluses in periods of recession.

Scale of Production

Small subsidiaries in Greece are more flexible in their ability to undertake small volume deliveries, whereas larger affiliates are more efficient in large scale orders, as this is dictated by scale economies and higher technology equipment of the parent abroad. These small scale deliveries may be specialized and custom-made products. The disadvantages of meeting small scale orders is the infrequent transport in small countries like Greece.

Low Production Costs
Greece enjoys a relatively low cost of production in wages and employers' contributions, despite the increases of the former, as pointed out earlier. Disadvantages include: rising costs of materials and services, and intensified competition in export markets because subsidiaries in Greece produce goods of outmoded technology. Country of origin is an important constraint in the exports of some branded goods. For example, cosmetics and perfumes are best marketed if they are manufactured in one of the advanced countries (i.e. France).

Barter Trade
Barter trade between Greece and East European countries has been the incentive for the establishment of export platforms in Greece for these countries. But contracts for exports under this scheme could be concluded after Greece's full membership in 1981.

THE CASE OF THE ALUMINIUM INDUSTRY

Pechiney, one of the major world aluminium producers, had achieved in 1960 favourable concessions, with a 50 year contract with the Greek state for cheap electric energy rates to install an aluminium smelter to produce 53,000 tonnes of aluminium and 100,000 tonnes of alumina. For this reason its subsidiary, Aluminium de Grèce, was set up. Until 1973, the capacity in the aluminium production trebled to 150,000 tonnes but since the recession it has remained stable; that of alumina rose by 5 times to 500,000 tonnes in 1980 and to 600,000 tonnes in 1984 (Aluminium de Grèce, Annual Report, various years).

The aluminium industry in Greece has suffered repercussions in the 1970s and 1980s from the international restructuring of the sector. The world aluminium industry was in the 1970s characterized by a surplus capacity as it was hit by a decline in demand due to recession in business cycles, the changes in the final use of the metal and its replacement by other materials. Changes in the cost structure of the aluminium industry were taking place also because of the sharp rise in energy prices since the early 1970s. As smelting is energy intensive, the economies in the industry were considerably altered (IIASA, 1984). As a result, world capacity in the 1980s was reduced, as less competitive electrolytic units shut (half of Japan's smelters, the third largest aluminium producer, were closed). When more modern smelters operate in the late 1980s, they will only replace the lost capacity of the 1970s (Aluminium de Grèce, Annual Report, 1982, 1983).

The comparative advantage of certain countries endowed with cheap energy resources determined the industry's costs and shifted geographically the locations of aluminium smelters. The advantages of Japan, the USA and a number of European countries that have been major aluminium producers declined, while other countries built new capacity in aluminium smelters, because of their advantage in cheaper energy: hydroelectricity in Canada, and coal in Australia (IIASA, 1984). The largest aluminium producers which were vertically integrated sought low-cost input locations to supply their aluminium fabricating plants.

The repercussions in the aluminium industry from the fall in demand were a decline in the price of aluminium from US$2,000 per tonne in 1980 to US$950 in 1982. A recovery from the crisis in the aluminium industry did not appear until 1983, but was much slower in Europe, the major export market of Greece, than in the rest of the world (Aluminium de Grèce, Annual Reports, 1980-82).

The international crisis in the aluminium industry affected Aluminium de Grèce. Its production costs, it was stated, rose during 1980-82 on average by 22 per cent per annum, basically because of the oil price increases. The subsidized energy rates by the Greek government, US$ 0.019 per KW per tonne of aluminium, determined the company's profits (Aluminium de Grèce, Annual Report, 1983). To reduce its production costs, the company had improved the smelter's energy consumption; this was 18,000KW per tonne in 1966, and it was expected that by 1983 this would have been lowered to 14,500KW per tonne. Aluminium de Grèce also invested in protection of the working environment. The electrolytic basins were covered with lids to protect the atmosphere and raise workers' productivity.

As Table 11.9 shows, the capacity of Aluminium de Grèce's smelter has remained stable since

Table 11.9: Production and Exports of Aluminium Products from Greece, 000 tonnes

Year	Primary aluminium		Deliveries	Exports of	Output of
	Production	Exports	in Greece*	Fabrications	Fabrications
1	2	3	4	5	6
1963	0.09	..	..	..	4.0
1964	0.08	..	..	..	4.3
1965	0.09	..	..	..	6.0
1966	37.4	27.6	9.8	..	8.7
1967	72.5	..	10.7	..	9.2
1968	78.4	..	12.8	..	6.4
1969	80.3	..	16.6	..	11.5
1970	87.2	..	25.2	..	14.5
1971	112.8	..	18.8	..	10.7
1972	131.2	101.0	21.9	..	19.7
1973	141.3	116.3	34.9	..	29.4
1974	146.5	101.7	39.5	..	25.2
1975	136.0	89.1	38.2	..	27.0
1976	134.3	88.9	48.1	19.0	40.8
1977	131.4	80.3	50.9	25.2	47.4
1978	145.6	83.0	66.6	29.1	56.4
1979	141.7	75.0	76.1	34.1	58.9
1980	146.5	58.4	83.6	35.6	..
1981	147.4	82.2	63.2	..	..
1982	136.7	67.3	70.0	..	..
1983	137.0	54.0	87.0	..	..

* from Aluminium de Grèce to Greek fabricators

Primary aluminium: Standard International Classification of Trade (SICT) 3720221; fabrications: SICT 372025, 372028 and 372034.

Sources: Columns 2-5, Aluminium de Grèce, Annual Reports 1973-83
Column 6, United Nations _Yearbook of Industrial Statistics_, various years

the recession in 1974, almost 10 years after its operation, while its utilization declined until 1983. One strategy of the company to halt increasing production costs was to raise the capacity uutilization by securing a larger share in the domestic aluminium fabricating industry, which was threatened by import competition in Greece. The subsidiary's exports declined from a peak of 116,000 tonnes in 1973 to 54,000 tonnes in 1983 but the demand from the domestic fabricators rose.

The Case of Greece

As shown in Table 11.9 output of the aluminium fabrications rose from 4,000 tonnes in 1963 to 14,500 tonnes in 1970 and to 58,000 tonnes in 1983. Deliveries of aluminium ingots from Aluminium de Grèce to domestic fabricators rose from 9,800 tonnes in 1966 to 25,200 tonnes in 1970 and to 87,000 tonnes in 1983. Some of the largest fabricators (Fulgor, Manuli, Aluminium Profile) had a foreign shareholding from MNEs other than Pechiney. But two other large producers, ELVAL and Aluminium d'Athènes, have a shareholding partly from Aluminium de Grèce and partly from the Belgian Lambert. The above 5 subsidiaries had taken advantage to export to the expanding Arab markets in the 1970s. Aluminium de Grèce delivered to the domestic fabricators in 1970 29 per cent of its aluminium output in weight; in 1980 this was increased to 57 per cent and in 1983 to 63.5 per cent. As shown in Table 11.9 the sales in weight of Aluminium de Grèce to domestic fabricators, 76,000 tonnes, surpassed the exports of the company in 1979, 54,000 tonnes. The exports of fabricated products doubled in tonnes between 1976 and 1980, from 19,000 tonnes to 35,600 tonnes, as exports of aluminium from Aluminium de Grèce declined in the early 1980s. These exports of fabricated products were delivered to the Middle East.

The advantages of Greece in the supply of cheap primary aluminium is shown in Table 11.10 which compares the average annual prices of aluminium delivered from 1976 to 1981 from Aluminium de Grèce to fabricators in Greece and to export markets, with average international prices. Indeed, for five years, from 1977 to 1981, plants in Greece purchased aluminium from Aluminium de Grèce at cheaper than the international prices per tonne and for only two years between 1976 and 1981 were these prices above export prices.

The advantage of Greece for the establishment of aluminium processing has certain limitations. First, it was pointed out by the respondents that the size of market in relation to the economies of scale required is small. The largest aluminium fabricating plants in Greece had modernized to widen their market area but they suffered from overcapacity and high costs until the 1980s. The respondent from a cable producing subsidiary said that their plant employing 450, although included amongst the largest in the sector in Greece, was below minimum optimum scale and depended on export subsidies to compete in export markets. The lack of

Table 11.10: Comparisons of Average Prices from Aluminium de Grèce for Primary Aluminium, US$ per tonne

Year 1	International 2	To Greek firms 3	To export markets 4
1976	890	916	874
1977	1,144	1,098	1,075
1978	1,325	1,134	1,157
1979	1,549	1,342	1,440
1980	1,884	1,643	1,776
1981	1,647	1,381	1,386

Source: Column 2, World Bank, World Tables
Column 3 and 4, Aluminium de Grèce, Annual Reports, various years

integration of most fabricators with the raw materials makes their position vulnerable vis-à-vis the monopoly supplier in Greece, in case the non-integrated fabricators compete with integrated fabricators' subsidiaries of the monopoly in export markets. This was the evidence from three non-integrated respondents.

CONCLUSION

Greece plays a role in the southern EEC periphery as an export platform for MNEs attracted there by the country's comparative advantages in low-cost labour and resources. This role has expanded since the international recession of 1974. The share of products manufactured by MNEs amongst Greece's leading exporting mining and manufacturing companies rose from 1973 to 1980 towards Greece's full membership of the EEC, and the rise was pronounced in labour-intensive operations, whereas capital and energy-intensive operations lost shares.

The case of the aluminium industry drawing from locally-mined bauxites indicates that, during the recession and slow down of world trade and as costs were rising in the capital-intensive and energy-consuming operations in Greece, the parent MNE modernized operations and became more market-orientated. A great cost of this restructuring was borne by the public sector, which subsidized cheap electricity rates and the exports of apparently uneconomic production of forward linked aluminium fabricators.

The role of MNES in the export of manufactured goods from the southern periphery of the EEC needs to be seen in the framework of international political relations within the Mediterranean region, which increases or decreases risks of investment.

BIBLIOGRAPHY

Benas, D. I Isvoli tou Xenou Kefalaiou stin Hellada (Papazisis, second edition, Athens, 1978)

Burstall, M.L., Dunning, J.H. and Lake, A. Multinational Enterprises, Governments and Technology, Pharmaceutical Industry (OECD, Paris, 1981)

Caves, R. Multinational Enterprise and Economic Analysis (Cambridge University Press, 1982)

Dokopoulou, E. Foreign Investment in Manufacturing in Greece. Linkages and Spatial Impacts (Ph.D. thesis, University of London, 1985)

Dunning, J.H. and Pearce, R.D. The World's Largest Industrial Enterprises (Gower Press, Farnborough, 1981)

Giannitsis, A.K. 'Ekonomeki Oloklerosi tis Helladas stin EOK ke Xenes Ameses Ependeses', in Nikolinakos, M. (ed.), E.O.K., Hellada, Mesogeios (Nea Synora, Athens, 1978)

Hamilton, F.E.I. and Linge, G.J.R. Spatial Analysis, Industry and the Industrial Environment, Vol.2 - International Industrial Systems (John Wiley, 1981)

Hood, N. and Young, S. The Economics of the Multinational Enterprise (Longman, London and New York, 1979)

Hood, N. and Young, S. Multinational Investment Strategies in The British Isles. A Study of MNEs in the Assisted Areas and in the Republic of Ireland (Department of Trade and Industry, HMSO, London, 1983)

IIASA (International Institute for Applied Systems Analysis) Structural Change in the Aluminium Industry, 183/4, (Laxenburg, 1984)

IOBE (Instituto Ekonomikon ke Viomichanikon Erevnon), Tomatopoltos, Kladiki Ekthesis, Omada Erevnas Trofima-Pota (Athens, 1981)

IOBE Metapoiemena Frouta, Omada Erevnas Trofima-Pota (Athens, 1982)

Luciani, G. The Mediterranean Region (Croom Helm, Kent, 1984)

Mitsos, A., 'Eleftheri Kycloforia Viomichanikon Proionton', in Mitsos, A. (ed.), I Proschorisi stes Europaikes Koinotites (Ekdoseis Synchrona Themata, Athens, Thessaloniki, 1981)
Murolo, A. 'The Greek Economy: The Role of Transnational Enterprises and the EEC', Mezzogiorno d'Europa, 2/1982, pp.197-219
OECD, OECD Economic Surveys, Greece, 1981, 1982, (OECD, Paris, 1982, 1983)
Plant, R. Industries in Trouble (International Labour Office, Geneva, 1981)
Roumeliotis, P. Polyethnikes Epichereses ke Yperkostologises-Ypokostologises stin Hellada (Ekdoses Papazisi, Athens, 1978)
Rugman, A.M. Inside the Multinationals (Croom Helm, Kent, 1981)
Rugman, A.M.'Internationalization and Non-Equity Forms of International Involvement', in Rugman, A.M. (ed.), New Theories of the Multinational Enterprise (Croom Helm, Kent, 1982)
Rugman, A.M. (ed.) Multinationals and Transfer Pricing (Croom Helm, Kent, 1985)
Statistical Office of the European Communities Hourly Earnings Hours of Work, 1-1983
Tsoukalis, L. The European Community and its Mediterranean Enlargement (G. Allen and Unwin, London, 1981)
Vaitsos, C. 'Corporate Integration in World Production and Trade', in Seers, D. and Vaitsos, C. (ed.), Integration and Unequal Development. The Experience of the EEC (The Macmillan Press Ltd., London, 1980)
Vaitsos, C. 'Transnational Corporation Behaviour and the Enlargement', in Seers, D. and Vaitsos, C. (eds.), The Second Enlargement of the EEC, Integration and Unequal Partners (The Macmillan Press, London, 1982)
Zolotas, X, The Positive Contribution of Greece to the European Community, Papers and Lectures, no.40 (Bank of Greece, Athens, 1978)

CHAPTER 12

INDUSTRIAL LOCATION - PRODUCT OF MULTIPLE 'FACTORS': THE TOBACCO INDUSTRY IN GREECE

Lois Labrianidis

INDUSTRIAL LOCATION APPROACHES

This chapter is based on the following main set of assumptions. The industrial location phenomenon is a social process: the determinants of a firm's locational decision lie not only within the firm but also in the social structure of which it constitutes an integral part. In capitalist societies industrial location decisions are 'taken' by the owners of the means of production and are constrained by their productive priorities. These decisions are a product of a multiplicity of 'factors', such as the economic, political, ideological and cultural conditions prevalent in the country and, most important of all, of their spatial differentiation; the position of particular fractions of capital within those conditions, the personal attitudes of individual capitalists and the labour process and manufacturing techniques employed by the specific industry under question. Hence, since the interchange of the above 'factors' does not only allow for single solutions but for a range of options on behalf of the individual capital, the process is in a sense flexible: it can have many different outcomes. Moreover, the State cannot alter the above-mentioned nature of the industrial location process because, being a social relation, it is itself shaped by the very balance of social relations.

That is, there is a close interaction between the actions of firms and their social environment, hence, to understand its essential components and the hidden reality that lies within it there is a need for an analysis encompassing society as a whole: including economics, politics, culture, ideology and so on. Moreover, since industrial location phenomena are contradictory and complicated, their particular outcome cannot be predicted in advance on merely theoretical grounds. The specific locational decision of a firm, let alone of all industrial firms in a capitalist social formation, cannot be known in advance on the basis of theoretical knowledge of necessary social relations alone. It can only be the product of particular theoretically informed empirical inquiries. To understand fully the process of the location of industrial plants in any particular time, theoretically informed empirical work (in the sense of being historically specific and not empiricist) is necessary. There the key factors which influence the process can be traced and analysed in the context of the theoretical approach.

This is not a plea for empiricism, it does not lead to a chaotic approach. It simply advocates that it is only the general 'laws' that govern industrial location in capitalist societies as well as a methodology to study them that can be taken for granted. Based on these, particular cases can be studied, and this will help to advance the theoretical understanding. Analysis must be holistic (it will take as an integral part of the explanation such considerations as the economic, social and political situation in the country and the role of the State) and dialectical and, for a particular understanding of historical and spatial reality, be based on quite detailed historical research.

This chapter studies the development of the spatial distribution of the tobacco industry in Greece from the time that it started having some importance (1880) up to modern times (1980), passing through three main stages: 1880-1922, 1922-40 and 1940-80. Throughout that period Greece's international position with regard to the tobacco industry was very important. In particular, Greece was one of the principal tobacco leaf exporting countries (e.g. in 1935-39 it was the second most important tobacco leaf exporting country, with 8.4% of the 528,000m. tons of tobacco leaves traded internationally; in 1946-49 the fifth, with 4.7% of the 409,000m. tons; in 1950-54 the fourth, with 6.6% of the 606,000m. tons [Koutsoyianni, 1962, pp.25, 98, 195]).

DISPERSED LOCATION OF THE TOBACCO INDUSTRY: 1880-1922

At first (1880-1913) the plants of both tobacco

trading-processing (kapnamagaza) and tobacco manufacturing (kapnergostasia) firms were quite evenly distributed within Peloponessos, Central Greece and Thessaly. There were 23 main processing centres, the most important being Hermoupoli, Piraeus, Volos, Lamis, Agrinio and Xanthi, and 80 public kapnergostasia, the most important being in Athens, Kalamata, Patra and Piraeus. Later on (1913-22) the spatial distribution of kapnergostasia remained much the same, while that of kapnamagaza changed substantially, with Drama, Kavala, Serres and Thessaloniki, situated in central and eastern Macedonia, coming into operation and soon becoming the most important processing centres in the country (Figures 12.1, 12.2 and 12.3).

Tobacco Trading by Small, Highly Dispersed Firms

The role of the tobacco leaf merchants consisted of three main activities: purchasing the leaves, processing them and finally exporting them. After their purchase from the farmer, the tobacco leaves were transferred into the merchant's warehouses (kapnomagaza) where they were stored and processed commercially. This was a highly skilful job, hence, the availability of a skilled labour force was a very important location 'factor' for kapnomagaza. The skilled labour force required was readily available within the tobacco leaf producing areas, where people were already involved in the agricultural processing, itself quite similar to commercial processing. This fact in itself helps to explain to a significant extent the location of kapnomagaza within the tobacco leaf producing areas. An additional factor which contributed to the selection of those areas was the need to use large amounts of tobacco leaves. Hence, the kapnomagaza up to 1913 were located in the main tobacco producing areas of the then independent Greek state, that is in the regions of Thessaly (mainly in the departments of Domokos, Kardhitsa, Trikaoa and Farshala), Central Greece and Peloponessos. Macedonia, which included very important tobacco producing areas (such as Drama, Kavala, Serres and Thessaloniki) became after its annexation (1913) the most important tobacco producing region and one of the important processing centres in the country (Figures 12.1 and 12.3).

Tobacco trading firms sold their produce to other trading firms, operating either in the country or abroad, and to foreign manufacturing firms. The large outlay of capital which had to be faced in the purchase and sale of leaf tobacco, the heavy expense of its processing which was characterized by a peak period of labour employment, and the risk involved in buying a stock which could only be disposed of during the following year, were serious obstacles to the tobacco trading being carried out by small firms. However, the majority of firms were small. The co-existence of these numerous small firms with a few large ones was mainly due to the wide variety of tobacco leaves produced in the country. Another factor was that tobacco manufacturing was dominated internationally by small firms which used a wide variety of leaves, and hence trading firms competed for different markets. A final factor was that there was no systematic intervention of the State in the market, so as to transfer resources from small to large firms, as was to happen in later periods.

The numerous tobacco trading firms that existed were independent personal companies that operated their business in the owner's home town; there were no multi-plant firms yet. Thus not only was the particular locational choice in effect fixed, but the question of any location, let alone of any alternative location, quite simply never really came up - a point also made by such writers as Hamilton (1974, p.6) in theoretical terms, and Onyemelukwe (1974) for Nigeria.

Tobacco leaves were exported directly by sea, for shipping was the most effective means for transporting the merchandise available. Up to 1890, the export trade of tobacco leaves took place primarily from Hermoupoli, which was the most important exporting port in the country, and Volos. Since then it has taken place directly from the ports of the tobacco producing areas: Volos, Nafplio, Messologhi, Stylida and Piraeus (Table 12.1 and Figure 12.1). This partly accounts for the concentration of kapnomagaza in the above mentioned ports and adjacent areas.

Up to the 1910s there was no trade-union movement of kapnergates, which meant that 'labour militancy' could not have been a major factor in the locational decision of trading firms at this point, as it was to become in the next two periods. The lack of trade-union movement was mainly due to the fact that each kapnergatis was attached to a particular firm and in a sense was treated as being semi-permanent staff, to the job security and satisfactory remuneration of kapnergates, to the lack of significant trade-union movement in the country and to the enormous political and economic

Figure 12.1: Main tobacco processing centres, Greece: 1885-1919

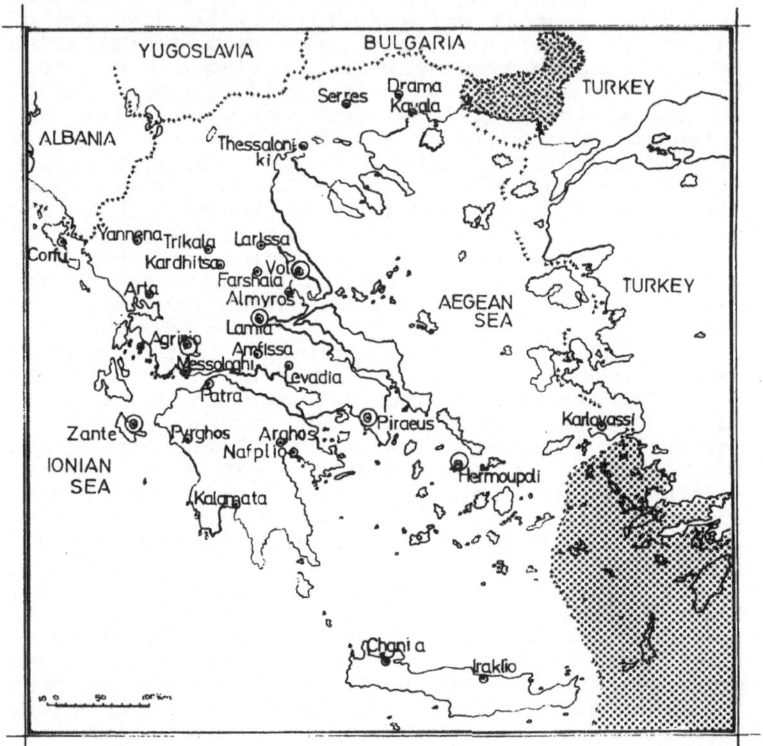

◎ Main centre

• Ordinary centre

Area not yet liberated

Source: Labrianidis (1982, p. 86)

Table 12.1: Volume of Tobacco Leaf Exports by Main Custom House, Greece: 1885-1979 (Averages by Period, in %)

Custom House	1885-89	1890-1919	1925-29	1945-49	1950-59	1960-69	1970-79
Thessaloniki	''	0.8	19.7	29.7	42.1	59.1	76.6
Kavala	''	0.4	30.2	63.4	38.0	23.4	15.8
Volos	30.4	39.0	15.7	1.5	6.1	6.6	2.6
Piraeus	7.4	3.8	7.3	4.5	7.5	6.3	2.2
Patra	0.4	0.8	6.7	0.1	2.3	1.9	1.2
Nafplio	-	20.0	4.0	-	0.9	0.6	0.1
Hermoupoli	32.3	3.1	-	-	-	-	-
Messologhi	-	10.6	-	-	-	-	-
Stylida	-	5.3	-	-	-	-	-
Various	29.5	16.2	16.4	0.8	3.1	2.1	1.5
Total in %	100.0	100.0	100.0	100.0	100.0	100.0	100.0
in a.n. (m.tons)	3,700	9,700	50,800	18,800	52,500	68,700	88,000

Note: '' areas not yet liberated

Source: Labrianidis (1982, pp.103, 115, 164)

power of tobacco trading companies.

Things were to change quite substantially from the 1910s when the attempts of merchants to reduce their production costs radicalized kapnergates. Since then the kapnergates' trade-union movement enjoyed considerable bargaining power. There are several factors which contributed to this. Firstly, tobacco processing, especially the most complicated types that were almost exclusively used at that time, needed highly skilled personnel. This made kapnergates difficult to replace, and hence employers were obliged to be more conciliatory towards them. Secondly, there was the seasonal unemployment in tobacco processing. This was compensated by high wages during employment periods, when workers enjoyed a relatively high standard of living. Therefore, during their periods of unemployment (from August-September, when the processing of the previous year's crop ended, to February, when the processing of the new year's crop began, all kapnergates were unemployed) not only did they have no incomes but also they were used to a standard of living higher than that of other workers (BTPT, 1929, pp.39-41). A third factor was that their working conditions were ideal for consciousness-raising (as they sat in rows facing one another, selecting and packing tobacco leaves, they could easily chat with each other: Jecchinis, 1962, p.92). A final factor was that the kapnergates became even more militant after 1909 because, after then, their jobs were constantly under serious threat and at the same time they received added support from the growing labour movement.

The kapnergates demanded an improvement in their remuneration and working conditions, as well as protection of their jobs. Working conditions were very important, since they had to sit in the same corner of the same room day after day, and a clean, bright and comfortable workplace was a great benefit. This was anything but the case, however, in the kapnomagaza. The fact that tobacco trading firms could use almost any warehouse made them footlose in this respect.

As for the efforts of kapnergates to 'protect' their jobs, these were orientated towards the prohibition of the export of unprocessed or inadequately processed tobacco. The use of simpler processing methods meant for merchants lower costs, while for kapnergates increasing unemployment. These efforts changed substantially during this period. In the 1909-16 period, the conflict was between a few belligerent merchants and the bulk of merchants and workers, while in the 1918-22 period the conflict was between workers and merchants. The conflict only stopped with the publication of an Act (L.2869/16.7.1922) which prohibited the export of unprocessed oriental tobacco (BTPT, 1925, pp.48-9; Mantzaris, 1927, pp.18-19). Thus after a prolonged and bitter struggle the kapnergates won their case.

However, the rise in the kapnergates' militancy from the 1910s did not result in any spatial manifestation: there was a considerable time lag between the actual rise of kapnergates' militancy and any shift in the locational distribution of kapnomagaza which might have been due to that militancy. Up to 1922 kapnomagaza were still located in towns. The workers employed only came to the processing towns during the period of employment, while during the rest of the period they lived in the adjacent agricultural areas and were occupied primarily in the harvesting and agricultural processing of tobacco leaves.

Tobacco Manufacturing by Small, Dispersed Firms

There was a predominance of family workshops; it was only during the later part of the period that some non-family workshops appeared. The proliferation of small firms was mainly due to the very low level of mechanization of manufacturing firms: they depended heavily on the skills of those involved in production. There was, however, some sort of mechanization by the end of this period, which was sufficient enough to put out of business a very important number of firms (e.g. in 1914 there were more than 600, while by 1920 their number had fallen to 300 - Fortounas, 1933; Varveropoulos, 1935, p.63). Also the production of a wide variety of commercial types of leaves in the country helped the survival of small firms since each one had its own blends by using small quantities of the different commercial types and hence had its own specific set of consumers. Furthermore, the State policy and, more particularly, the establishment of public kapnergostasia, permitted the proliferation of small firms. Eighty such kapnergostasia were established in 1883, and all manufacturing firms were obliged to operate there. These public kapnergostasia as well as the tools used in them belonged to the State; firms had been obliged to sell all their tools to the State, and they operated with public employees.

The existence of numerous small tobacco manufacturing firms might have led someone to expect that their industrial location pattern, the result of a myriad of decisions taken by the owners of these firms, would have been very diverse. However, this was not the case: the tobacco manufacturing firms were located in few factories (public kapnergostasia) which were evenly spread within Old Greece (Figure 12.2). This was due to the fact that, though firms were obliged to locate in public kapnergostasia for two brief periods only (in 1883-85 and 1887-92), they remained there, with only very few exceptions, throughout the whole of this period (1883-1922). Hence, the location of tobacco manufacturing firms during this whole period can, by and large, be assessed from the location of the public kapnergostasia. The public kapnergostasia (80 in 1883 and 79 in 1887) were located on the basis of being situated within the main consumption centres of the country, notably in the capital cities of all departments (market orientation). Also they were located 'exceptionally' in Piraeus and Lavrio, which were next to the most important agglomeration (Athens), as well as in Astakos, Aetoliko (Aetolia-

Figure 12.2: Public kapnergostasia, Greece, 1886-1922

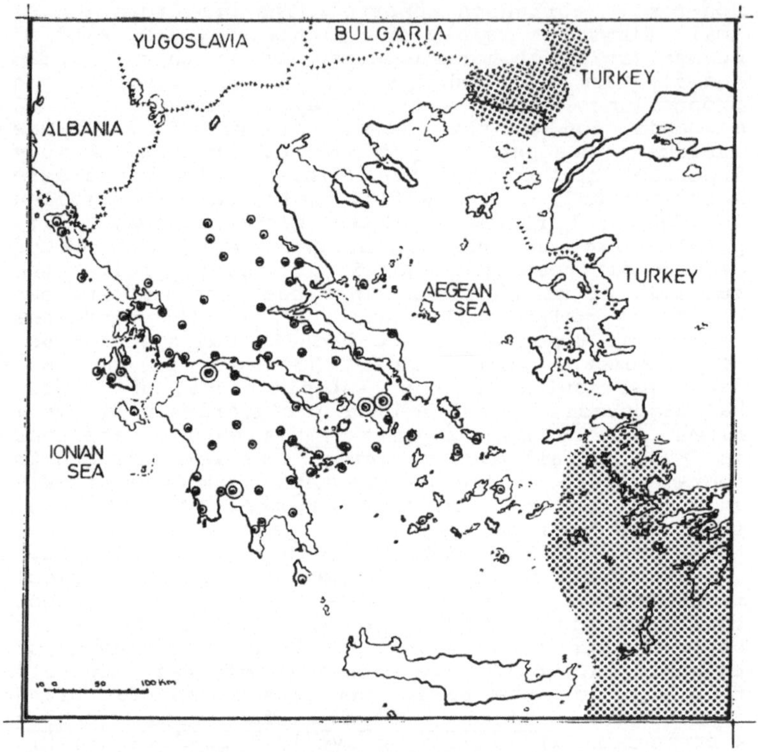

Most important Kapnergostasia

Ordinary kapnergostasia

Area not yet liberated

Source: L. ΑΡΚΣτ/27.4.18883 and L. ΑΥΚ/12.4.1887 Gazzette of the Greek Government

Akarnania), Aghios Georgios (Magnissia) and Filiatre (Messinia), all important tobacco leaf, primarily for home consumption (destined to be consumed in the country) and not for export (destined to be exported), producing areas.

With the liberation of the new areas in 1913 (Figure 12.3) one might have expected that some new manufacturing firms were going to be established there. However, this did not happen. Up to 1913, the population of this area consumed manufacturing goods made, with the varieties of oriental tobacco produed there, by the kapnergostasio of Regié in Thessaloniki. With the liberation of this area, this factory ceased to operate. The companies of Old Greece took advantage of the temporary lack of any firm there and managed to spread their products in this area too, and soon changed the customs of the smokers to like the taste of manufactured goods produced with the tobacco from Old Greece. This, coupled with the fact that the tobacco leaves of the new, liberated area, could easily be exported at a much better price than that of Old Greece, prohibited any significant attempt to create a new factory operating with locally-produced leaves. Also the establishment of a factory which was to operate with tobacco from Old Greece was considered as out of the question, being an economic adventure that was apparently bound to fail. Last, but not least, the small size of the overwhelming majority of tobacco manufacturing firms did not permit them even to contemplate operating on a more than one plant basis and to establish a branch of their factory in the newly liberated areas. In short, one might argue that the exclusive location of kapnergostasia in Old Greece was circumscribed, to a significant extent, by the gradual liberation of the Greek territory itself.

Up to the early years of the 20th century there was no trade-union movement of tobacco manufacturing workers. From that time things changed substantially. They were mobilized, other than for wage demands, around the appalling working conditions in the kapnergostasia. The public kapnergostasia were established in private rented buildings which were usually damp, sunless, dark and filthy, with wooden floors and no proper ventilation (Kordhatos, 1972, p.220; Papastratos, 1964, pp.159-60). To make things worse, each firm was installed in its separate compartment within these buildings, and the employees worked in small and crowded rooms. These conditions, as well as the

Figure 12.3: The unification of Greece 1832-1947

Source: Labrianidis (1982, p. 90)

actual nature of the tobacco leaves themselves, were very bad for the workers' health. They were mobilized around an even more serious problem: the import of cigarette-making machines, from 1895 onwards. The workers quickly realised that these machines were going to put them out of work, and they made every possible effort to stop their introduction.

The labour militancy of workers was not a major factor in the distribution of kapnergostasia. Up to the early years of the 20th century this was so because their trade-union movement was almost non-existent. After this, though, it became an important factor. There were other counteracting forces, mainly the need of the firms to locate in the public kapnergostasia, that prohibited their locational shift so as to avoid the 'trouble' areas.

INCREASE OF SPATIAL CONCENTRATION 1922-40

There was a marked spatial concentration of both kapnomagaza and kapnergostasia. The former were concentrated primarily in the north (mainly in the regions of Macedonia and Thrace). The foremost important tobacco processing centres were those of Kavala, Thessaloniki, Volos, Piraeus, Agrinio, Xanthi, Serres and Drama (Table 12.2 and Figure 12.4). One of the main characteristics of their spatial distribution was the co-existence of a few, very important, processing centres, along with many insignificant ones. That is, while more than 85 per cent of the total amount processed and of working days in tobacco processing were concentrated in just 8 centres, the remainder was distributed among more than 40. The kapnergostasia were quite dispersed spatially, within the southern part of the country. Although there was a fair number of manufacturing centres, around 90 per cent of production was concentrated in just 8 centres (Athens, Piraeus, Volos, Kalamata, Thessaloniki, Pyrghos, Patra and Xanthi). There was a marked shift in the importance of some centres: a significant increase in the importance of Piraeus, a less important increase for Volos, and a decrease for Athens (Table 12.3 and Figure 12.5).

Decline of Independent Tobacco Trading Firms and Spatial Concentration of Kapnomagaza

The elastic international demand for tobacco leaves and the fact that the largest part of the volume of their exports was absorbed by very few countries

Figure 12.4: Main tobacco processing centres. Greece: 1928-39 (% of total realised working days)

◎ (large)	18.0 - 29.9 %	⊙	2.0 - 4.9 %
◎	5.0 - 9.9 %	·	0.0 - 1.9 %

(shaded) Area not yet liberated

Source: Labrianidis (1982, p. 140)

Table 12.2: Amount of Processed Tobacco Leaves among the Main Processing Centres, Greece: 1939-79 (Averages by Period, in %)

Processing Centre	1939	1945-49	1950-59	1960-69	1970-79
Thessaloniki	29.0	31.1	38.9	51.5	64.9
Kavala	21.9	35.4	26.6	19.5	10.9
Xanthi	5.0	6.5	5.8	5.3	3.0
Serres	4.6	6.0	3.6	3.1	1.0
Drama	3.8	5.9	4.7	3.2	0.8
Agrinio	6.1	3.1	4.3	3.7	7.7
Volos	8.5	4.1	7.3	6.8	5.0
Piraeus	8.3	4.7	4.9	4.0	0.2
Various	12.8	3.2	3.9	2.9	5.5
Total in %	100.0	100.0	100.0	100.0	100.0
in a.n. (m. tons)	49,000	19,000	106,000	151,000	162,000
Number of centres	60	17	17	14	13

Source: Labrianidis (1982, pp.137, 170

(where often tobacco was controlled by only a handful of firms or by a state monopoly), meant that merchants were virtually at the mercy of their clients. Their position weakened further with the international economic crisis of 1929-30, which hit most severely the export trade of luxury products, such as tobacco. Ultimately this created a very unfavourable climate for independent tobacco merchants in Greece and brought about their disappearance from the trade. The trade was gradually dominated primarily by foreign companies, and to a lesser extent by Greek trading companies that were affiliated to a particular buyer.

Up to this period merchants had operated as intermediaries between farmers and foreign buyers (manufacturers or merchants). They had been the ones to decide on the methods of commercial processing to be used so that the product corresponded to their prospective clients' tastes and requirements. Furthermore, it had been they who, by controlling large quantities of capital (either personal or borrowed), had taken the risk of regulating the stocks of tobacco leaves that determined the balance of supply and demand. Instead the tobacco trade gradually came to be dominated by merchants who operated with definite orders or with 'encouragement' from foreign companies. The 'independent' merchants either reduced their operations drastically or abandoned the profession altogether.

The kapnomagaza were established primarily in the main regions that produced tobacco for export: East Macedonia - Thrace and Central-West Macedonia (Figure 12.4), so as to purchase directly the quantity of leaves they needed. Also, since the output of these firms was exported and shipping was the main transport means used, location next to a port was of primary importance. Significant processing centres were created in such ports as Kavala, Thessaloniki and Volos (Tables 12.1 and 12.2). The increase in the size of tobacco trading firms and primarily the fact that most of them were gradually either affiliated to a foreign buyer or were branches of international firms, as well as their low levels of mechanization, which meant that they could still use almost any warehouse as a processing plant, permitted a significant number of them to start operating on a multiplant basis.

From the time of the introduction of the 1922 Act, merchants did everything that they could to abolish it. In 1925 they had already achieved their aim with the introduction of the 'Act on tonga' which permitted the processing of all tobacco leaves with tonga (the simplest processing method). This was a major blow to the interests of workers and very much in favour of the merchants, because thus the latter could achieve a decrease in the number of wage-days as well as a 'deskilling' of their workforce, both of which meant a drop in their wage bill.

After 1925 there was an abrupt decrease in the use of classical processing methods in favour of tonga (e.g. in 1925 only 10 per cent of the total amount of tobacco processed was done with tonga while in 1939 this had risen to 78 per cent - Mantzaris, 1927, p.42: TAK[a], 1939). However, the fact that the productivity of the tobacco processing industry remained steady throughout the period indicates that the reaction of kapnergates was quite effective. That is, tobacco merchants throughout this period tried to change the processing methods used but they found immense resistance from their workers. As will be seen in the next section, what they so strongly strived to achieve in this period, namely to implement changes in situ (with only an insignificant spatial shift of kapnomagaza to small villages), they subsequently managed to achieve 'simply' by shifting their operations to other cities.

The reaction that merchants had to face was due to the fact that up to 1936 kapnergates were very militant. This was due to four main factors. Firstly to the constant threat to their employment opportunities since the introduction of the 'Act on tonga'. Secondly, to the decrease in the proportion of male kapnergates in the total labour force employed by merchants since the introduction of the 'Act on tonga'. This had two major advantages for merchants since it allowed them to cut down their costs immensely (the wage of female workers was around 44.5 per cent of the male wage), and to get rid of male workers who generally tended to be more unionized than women. This major blow to the employment opportunities of male kapnergates only, resulted in a series of mobilizations in the period from 1925. These lasted up to the introduction of L.5817/1933 which determined that, if commercial processing was to be done with the tonga system, in each kapnomagazo at least half had to be male workers. The main reason why the kapnergates' trade-union movement had not split into two opposing factions, one protecting the interests of women and the other of men, in its policy towards the above issue was that the unions were entirely dominated by male workers and their interests went undisputed. A third factor was the decrease in personal relations between kapnergates and their employers which encouraged increased dependence on unions. This was due to the increase in the size of firms and to the fact that workers did not consider themselves as attached to a particular firm, since they were no longer paid during unemployment periods by 'their' firm. Finally, to the general political situation in the country, which was favourable for the development of trade-union movement. The kapnergates had the most organized trade-union movement in the country (Fakiolas, 1978; Jecchinis, 1972, esp. p.91; Tsoukalas, 1974, p.170).

To counterbalance the significant rise in unemployment among kapnergates, a direct result of the merchants' new fredom to use the much simpler tonga processing method, the 1926 Act (L.3460) was introduced. This Act founded an organization for the insurance of tobacco workers, introduced a form of social insurance for kapnergates and made the profession of kapnergatis a closed shop: no worker was allowed to be employed in tobacco processing unless he was insured in that organization or had permission from it. The number of free workers of the total number employed fluctuated at very low levels (around 6 per cent). The number of realized working days by free workers was slightly higher (around 15 per cent).

There was a concentration of the majority of tobacco processing in the kapnoupoles: a very important part of the economic active population of those towns consisted of kapnergates, and their whole economy was heavily based on tobacco processing. The kapnoupoles of Kavala, Volos, Xanthi, Drama and Serres had the majority of the amount of processed leaves and of realized working days in the country (Table 12.2). A vital factor in this concentration was the existence of kapnergates there. Up to 1925 this was essential because of the high levels of skill required for tobacco processing, since then the profession of the kapnergates had in addition become a closed shop.

One of the tactics used by trading firms to curb the militancy of kapnergates was to divert an insignificant part of their operations (around 90 per cent of the total amount processed was still concentrated in 8 centres only! Table 12.2) during the last part of this period, to a number of centres, some of which were small villages. This shift, which also allowed merchants to exploit the abundant labour reserves of tobacco farmers, was made possible because firms could use almost any warehouse as kapnomagazo.

Decline of Small Tobacco Manufacturing Firms and Spatial Concentration of kapnergostasia

The tobacco manufacturing industry used virtually entirely leaves that were produced in the country. The overwhelming majority of kapnergostasia were located within the most important regions producing tobacco leaves destined for home consumption, namely Central Greece, Euboea, Peloponessos, Thessaly and Epirus (Tables 12.4 and Figure 12.5). They continued not to use Macedonian leaves, for the same reasons as in the previous period and hence the concentration of kapnergostasia in Old Greece was, to a significant degree, due to the gradual liberation of the country. However, the spatial distribution of tobacco leaves, though it was an

Figure 12.5: Main tobacco manufacturing producing cities, Greece: 1925-1939 (per cent of total tobacco manufacturing production)

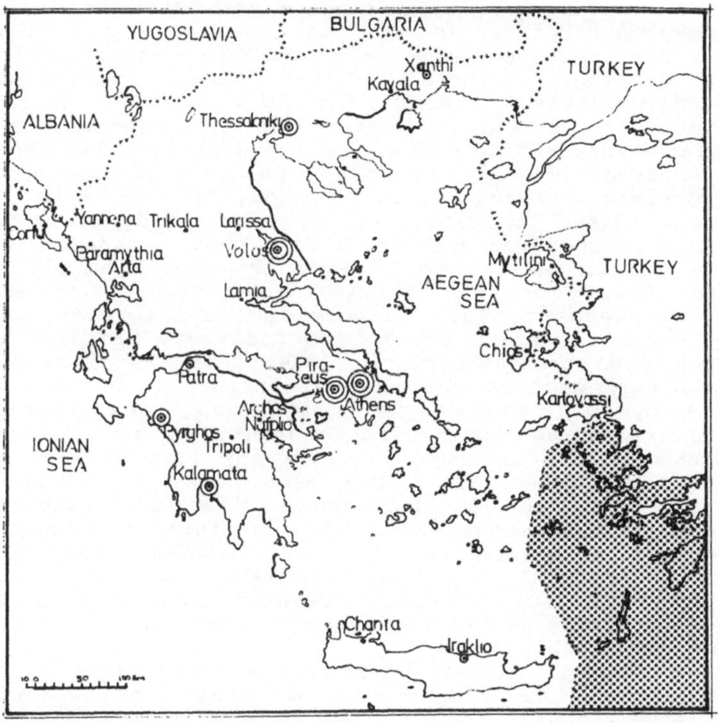

◎	19.0 - 26.9 %	●	1.0 - 3.9%
◎	4.0 - 5.9 %	·	0.0 - 0.9%
▒	Area not yet liberated		

Source: Labrianidis (1982, p. 143)

important factor, was not a determinant one; for example, in the department which produced almost half of the total production of leaves destined for home consumption (Aetolia-Akarnania) there was no such factory.

The wages of tobacco manufacturing workers were very low because of the high unemployment in this profession, due particularly to the mechanization of production. There was also widespread underemployment: apart from those employed in the factories of Athens, Piraeus, Pyrghos, Thessaloniki and Volos, who worked six days a week (in 1932 these factories employed around 32 per cent of the total workforce - Serraios, 1934, pp.82, 92), those in the rest worked for five, four or even two days a week. As a consequence workers, afraid that they might be thrown out of work since they could easily be dismissed for the first 'misbehaviour', allowed their wages to fall to very low levels. Also, the clear-cut distinction in the positions occupied by men and women (Serraios, 1934, pp.62-7) allowed a further decline in the remuneration of female employees. Since the employees of tobacco manufacturing firms neither presented any serious trade-union challenge nor had any rare skills, it may be argued that they were not particularly important as a locational 'factor'. Tobacco manufacturing continued to be orientated towards the domestic market which may account for the concentration of kapnergostasia in the most important consumption centres and of the overwhelming majority of them in the Athens-Piraeus complex (Table 12.3).

Although numerous tobacco manufacturing firms existed, the majority of them were very insignificant; indeed, less than 10 firms covered more than 65 per cent of total production. The number of firms was reduced quite dramatically: while in the 1920s there were more than 300 firms, by 1940 there were only 43! This monopolization trend was not due to international competition, since firms were fully protected by the State in this respect. Three main reasons may help to explain this monopolization. Firstly, the increasing mechanization of the manufacturing process rendered those firms that could not use the latest machinery uncompetitive.

Secondly, there was the role of the State. A major blow to the existence of small firms was the prohibition in 1925 of the production of hand rolled ready-made cigarettes and of cut tobacco for

Table 12.3: Main Tobacco Manufacturing Cities: The amount of Cigarettes Produced, Greece: 1925-79 (Averages by period, in per cent)

City	1925-29	1930-39	1944-49	1950-59	1960-69	1970-79
Piraeus	5.2	35.2	40.1	63.5	68.5	55.8
Athens	40.0	19.8	16.1	3.1	4.3	12.5
Volos	15.0	21.7	24.2	18.1	9.3	0.1
Kalamata	4.7	4.4	6.9	12.6	16.2	31.4
Thessaloniki	6.6	3.8	6.1	0.3	-	-
Pyrghos	6.3	5.9	0.3	0.3	-	-
Xanthi	2.9	1.6	0.2	0.3	0.5	0.1
Patra	3.2	2.9	1.3	0.1	-	-
Various	16.1	4.7	4.8	1.7	1.2	0.1
Total in %	100.0	100.0	100.0	100.0	100.0	100.0
in a.n. (m.tons)	4,700	5,100	8,70	10,800	14,700	21,800
Number of cities	32	24	15	11	7	5

Source: Labrianidis (1982, pp.132, 142, 289-93)

cigarettes to be rolled by the consumer. This simply meant that firms that could not introduce mechanization had to cease their operations completely. Then there was the State's decision to urge the non-competitive firms to stop their operations and grant them compensation (L.5352/30.3.1932). Another blow was that in 1938 the State forced firms to move out of the public kapnergostasia. Perhaps most important however were the inelastic profit margins set by the State (it fixed the retail prices of tobacco manufacturing products, the remuneration of wholesalers and retailers and the consumption tax) which were the same for all firms, even though they had a wide variety of production costs. This, in combination with the absolute freedom of most components of production costs, led small firms from one cul de sac to another.

Finally, the competition between tobacco manufacturing firms in the supply of excessive profits to the retailers of their products and the huge amounts of money spent on advertising in order to ensure brand sales (Thassitis, 1962, pp.42-4) resulted in the triumph of those firms that had the largest amount of capital at their disposal.

Thus, the most important factor that had caused the spatial concentration of kapnergostasia was the heavy reduction in the number of firms. In terms of the particular spatial pattern produced, this was primarily the result of the fact that firms which had survived the competition 'happened' (in the sense that this is related to their location but is not determined by it) to have their plants located there.

UNPRECEDENTED SPATIAL CONCENTRATION: 1940-80

The kapnomagaza were heavily concentrated in the northern parts of the country. More than 75 per cent of the total amount of processed tobacco leaf and realized working days in processing were concentrated here. Only three quite important centres (Volos, Piraeus and Agrinio) and some very minor ones were located elsewhere. Eight centres (Thessaloniki, Kavala, Volos, Xanthi, Drama, Serres, Piraeus and Agrinio) covered around 95 per cent of wage-days in tobacco processing and of the total amount processed; the first two alone covered around 70 per cent. While all processing centres remained steady or witnessed a decrease in their importance, that of Thessaloniki and Agrinio increased (Table 12.2 and Figure 12.6).

The kapnergostasia were also quite concentrated in a few cities only, and this concentration increased dramatically. Within the five most important tobacco manufacturing cities two opposite developments occurred: while production in Piraeus and Kalamata increased, that in Athens, Volos and Thessaloniki decreased (Table 12.3 and Figure 12.7).

Elimination of Independent Tobacco Trading Firms

There was a significant trend towards the elimination of independent tobacco trading firms. By the end of this period most of the firms were operated as assignees to foreign buyers. This was primarily the result of the crisis in tobacco exports during this period. Specifically, the crisis was due: at first (1940-49) to the 'extraordinary' conditions of the country (World War II, occupation and Civil War); later on (1949-53) to the loss of old consumption markets and the inability to create new ones; and at the end (1953-80) to the

Figure 12.6: Main tobacco processing centres, Greece: 1945-1979 (per cent of total realized working days)

23.0 - 47.9%	1.0 - 3.9%
4.0 - 5.9%	0.0 - 0.9%

Source: Labrianidis (1982, p.83)

Figure 12.7: Main tobacco manufacturing producing cities, Greece 1944-1979 (per cent of total tobacco manufacturing production)

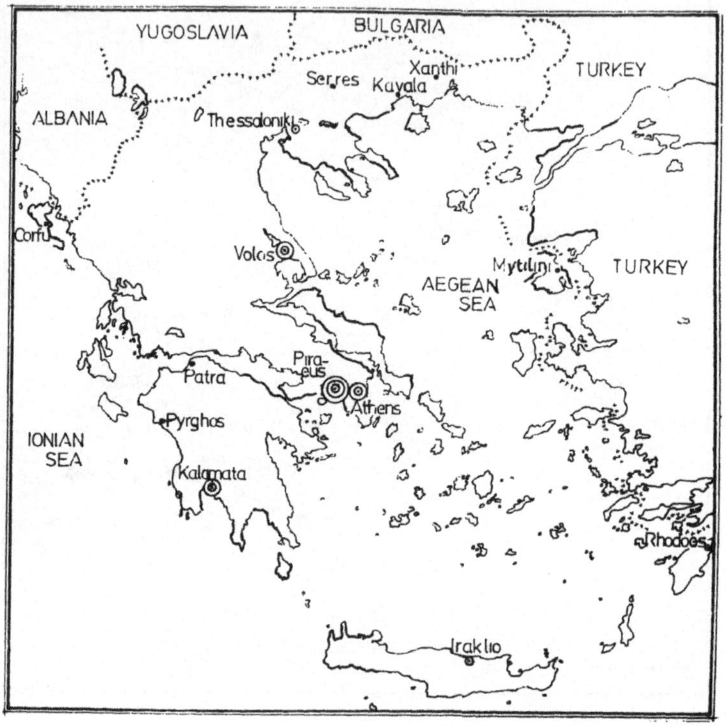

◎	57.0%	•	0.6 - 1.9%
◎	9.0 - 16.9%	·	0.0 - 0.5%

Source: **Labrianidis** (1982, p.184)

international crisis of oriental tobacco in general (and not to high processing costs or at least not simply, as merchants argued in their attempts to suppress wages even more). Moreover, the elimination of trading firms was accelerated by the policy of the State, which always favoured the foreign tobacco trading companies and those operated as agents of them, rather than those that operated freely. However, there was no significant trend towards monopolization (Table 12.4). One of the causes that permitted many small tobacco trading firms to stay in business was that, mainly since the mid-1950s, which was a period marked by the acceleration of the mechanization of commercial processing of tobacco, they ceased to do the commercial processing and they operated as 'purely' commercial firms. That is, a number of trading firms could not afford to have their own processing plants; they usually tended to have a kapnomagazo that was used as a warehouse only and they left it to other firms to undertake the commercial processing of their tobacco leaves.

Trading firms were in cut-throat competition, driving prices down in an attempt to secure new orders. As a consequence of this their profits decreased, though they still remained high. Their high profits were mainly due to the State policy. That is, not only were they financed by the State, using 10 to 15 per cent of their own capital, but further the State, with its heavy intervention in the tobacco leaf market (since 1955), tried to socialize the losses and to ensure that the profits would be reaped by merchants and domestic manufacturers.

None the less, firms, in their attempt to restore profitability to the unprecedented pre-war levels, made every effort to reduce their production costs through, for example, the simplification of commercial processing methods and mechanization and intensification of the labour process. As a consequence the cost of kapnergates' wages was reduced from being 16-29 per cent of total costs at the end of the 1940s to 4 per cent in the 1960s (Andreadis, 1967, p.155; Christoula and Grigorogianni, 1953; Decade of Greek Tobacco, 1955, p.74; Kapniki Epitheorissis). By the late 1960s some tobacco trading firms started to diversify their operations, mainly in other trading areas and tourism, due to the long term insecurity of both the volume of their exports and their profit margins (ICAP).

In this period there occurred, with State

intervention, a gradual shift away from the cultivation of the most oriental towards more neutral types of tobacco, as well as the introduction of burley tobacco. This shift was necessary because the monopolization of international tobacco manufacturing industries increased the standardization of each blend, reduced their numbers and converged their characteristics. Thereafter, the emphasis was placed on the provision of a standardized quality of each variety every year and on maintaining a low price. Consequently the comparative advantages of Greek tobacco leaf production (the existence of a wide variety of high quality and highly priced products), was turned into a major disadvantage.

As a result of this shift there was a parallel shift in the spatial distribution of tobacco production and particularly of that destined for export, which influenced the location of kapnomagaza. Thus, while up until then tobacco destined for export had been produced in the regions of East Macedonia - Thrace and Central-West Macedonia, which were equally important, from the mid-1960s, with the increase of burley production, which was produced mainly in Central-West Macedonia, this region easily superseded the East Macedonia - Thrace. In particular, it put the processing centres of East Macedonia - Thrace (Kavala, Xanthi, Serres and Drama) in a disadvantageous position and contributed to their decline, while it rendered the position of Thessaloniki more favourable, being situated between Central-West Macedonia and East Macedonia - Thrace (Table 12.2 and Figure 12.6).

The kapnergates' trade-union movement, which up to 1936 was the avant garde of the trade-union movement in Greece, was to face several major setbacks, and by 1954 it was almost completely eradicated. This defeat was the result of the general political situation prevailing in the country, which was far from favourable for workers, and of particular developments in the tobacco trade. Specifically the 1940-49 period was marked by World War II, the occupation and the Civil War and was particularly unfavourable for the development of genuine trade-union movement. In the 1949-52 period political suppression reached paramount levels. The police and parastate organizations created a climate of 'white terror' which further assured the absolute defeat of any opposition. Particularly acute was the persecution of the communists and their sympathizers and consequently of the communist-dominated trade-union movement of kapnergates.

In 1952 the State had abolished the Act (L.5817/ 22.9.1933) which obliged merchants to employ male workers in at least 50 per cent of their work force (Avgi, 18.2.1953). Subsequently, the percentage of working-days realized by men was reduced significantly. The State gave the final blow to the trade-union movement with the introduction of the 1953 Act (L.2348/1953) which abolished the closed shop of kapnergates. Following this the Union of Tobacco Merchants advised their members to reduce workers' wages as well as to employ exclusively new workers (e.g. for northern Greece, Avgi, 16.4.1953 and 17.4.1953). Also, with this Act 5370 kapnergates were forced to retire and their insurance organization was amalgamated with the main social security organization. It further determined that, in order for someone to be employed in a tobacco trading firm, he first had to be approved by the Security Police and that he would be employed on a six-day basis.

Another major blow to kapnergates' bargaining power came with the steady and dramatic increase in productivity of tobacco processing (7.4 kg/wage day in the 1940-49 period, 11.8 in 1950-59, 35.8 in 1960-69 and 71.8 in 1970-79! - NTG, b; Kapniki Epitheorissis; Panhellenic Organization of Kapnergates, 1951). This was mainly due to the mechanization of the process; to the intensification of work, the result of the introduction of a more strict legislation on labour relations; to the almost exclusive use of the simplest processing method (tonga), that was made possible by the defeat of the trade-union movement; and to the more scrupulous agricultural processing, which was made obligatory in 1925.

All these developments, which led to the reduction of the remuneration of workers in tobacco processing (since the wages of workers non-insured in the kapnergates' organization as well as of women were much lower than those of men) and to a considerable increase in unemployment of kapnergates, aimed at the reduction of the cost of tobacco trading firms by reducing the labour cost.

The kapnergates reacted to the attack on their status quite strongly throughout the tobacco processing centres (e.g. Thessaloniki, Kavala and Piraeus), during 1953. However, by the beginning of 1954, they were to face major setbacks. There was a number of reasons for this defeat, such as the general, political situation which was anything but favourable to the workers' demands, as well as the high unemployment and deskilling of kapnergates which made them particularly vulnerable.

At the beginning of this period the spatial distribution of kapnomagaza was influenced heavily by the existing pattern: there were cumulative advantages for kapnoupoles. This represented a form of inertia; the existence of an adequate infrastructure in terms of material reality (e.g. kapnomagaza), of human skills (e.g. tobacco entrepreneurs and workers) as well as of transport and engineering companies specializing in tobacco processing. Soon these same factors that accelerated the concentration in the kapnoupoles started having a reverse effect. In particular, merchants wanted to restructure tobacco processing in order to lower costs to cope with the difficult conditions that they had to face in the international market. This led them to pursue the 'deskilling' of kapnergates after the 1930s and particularly from the mid-1950s and was facilitated by the further mechanization and the abolition of the closed shop. The 'deskilling' process had two sets of consequences: it both enabled and 'forced' firms to move out of the kapnoupoles where kapnergates were concentrated; the restructuring meant fewer and lower paid jobs and hence it was very difficult to implement in cities heavily dependent on kapnergates' income. The 'moral' pressure that was exercised on merchants from the community in the kapnoupoles, along with the albeit weak trade-union pressure to employ as many workers as possible led them to want to abandon these cities. That is, the specialization of kapnoupoles was turned from a major advantage for the further spatial concentration of kapnomagaza there to a great disadvantage. As a result many kapnoupoles (e.g. Drama, Kavala, Kilkis, Serres and Xanthi) were led to wither economically (Avgi, 28.9.1952). The very fact of the movement of tobacco processing firms allowed them to overcome reactions to changes in the labour process. What the firms had strived for so long, at least since the 1930s, to achieve in situ, they managed to do by moving to other locations.

There was also a concentration of tobacco processing in fewer cities (Table 12.2) due to the realization of the advantages offered by such a move (i.e. provision of more adequate common facilities), to the concentration of processing in fewer firms and most important to the concentration of the operations of each firm in one city rather than a few, as well as in one kapnomagazo due to the mechanization of the process, and the evolution from handicraft to manufacturing. The decrease in the importance of kapnoupoles of East Macedonia - Thrace coincided with the rise in the importance of Thessaloniki, which soon became the most prominent tobacco processing centre. The increase in the weight of Agrinio was rather 'accidental'; it was entirely due to the growth of one firm, Papastratos.

The increase in the importance of Thessaloniki was due to the decline of all the other centres but most crucially of Kavala (Table 12.4). Specifically, as it was argued above, there was a need for tobacco trading firms to move away from kapnoupoles. Also, firms wanted to move away particularly from Kavala where there was a tradition of kapnergates' militancy. Kapnergates in Kavala were highly influenced by communist ideas from the 1920s, the city was considered as a stronghold of the Communist Party. Although this was an important factor in the tobacco trading firms' decision to move away from Kavala, one must view with scepticism the fact that merchants presented it as the most important cause of their shift (see several articles in Kapniki Epitheorissis in the late 1950s); they probably used this argument in order to scare kapnergates away from trade-union activities in the future. The move from Kavala to Thessaloniki, which had a much higher economic active population and was not dependent on employment in tobacco processing, offered them more opportunities to find the low paid labour force they needed. Finally, Thessaloniki was much more important as an international centre and more adequately supplied with services. In particular its port, which had become the second most important port of the country was much more favourable for tobacco exports than that of Kavala. By 1950 the port of Thessaloniki overtook in importance that of Kavala with respect to their tobacco exports (Table 12.1).

The above described need for a spatial shift of tobacco processing firms in the late 1950s was facilitated by the conditions that prevailed with regard to the kapnomagaza that they used. In particular most firms did not have their own kapnomagaza, but usually rented one. Moreover, even those firms that did have their own kapnomagaza, wanted to rebuild them since they were inadequate for the use of the new machinery; and/or in order to benefit from increases in land values caused by urban

Table 12.4: Number of Tobacco Trading Firms per City, Greece: 1946-1979

City	1946	1955-6	1958	1970	1979
Thessaloniki	102	56	78	68	84
Athens	46	17	29	34	38
Volos	25	10	10	12	17
Kavala	56	33	39	19	25
Lamia	2				
Piraeus	5	5	5	5	3
Drama	2	5	7		
Larissa	1				
Xanthi	25	3	11	8	11
Agrinio	10	4	6	10	12
Mythilini	8	2	8	1	1
Katerini			1	2	1
Komotini			3		
Nafplio	4	2	1		
Kardhitsa	1				
Serres	1	1	1		
Trikala		1	1		
Samos	2	1	1		
Patras			1		
Total	290	140	202	159	192

Source: Labrianidis (1982, p.233)

land and property speculation by realizing the values of their existing site.

<u>Monopolization of Tobacco Manufacturing and Spatial Concentration of kapnergostasia</u>

Up to 1960, manufacturing firms continued to use almost exclusively tobacco leaves destined for <u>home consumption</u>. Later the abandonment of the protectionist policies of the State was followed by a marked preference of Greek consumers for foreign goods; in this case through the increasing influence of blended cigarettes on Greek smokers. This alarmed manufacturing firms, which reacted by trying to convert their oriental cigarettes to the blended ones by using 'mixed' blends (i.e. both leaf destined for <u>home consumption</u> and <u>for export</u>). Hence, both the amount of imported tobacco leaves and of leaves <u>destined for export</u> used by manufacturing industry increased considerably (<u>Kapniki Epitheorissis</u> 399, Feb.1980; NTB, a). This meant a spatial shift in the areas from where manufacturing firms purchased their tobacco leaves. That is, while up to 1960 they purchased it mainly from the southern part of the country (i.e. Aetolia-Akarnania, Fthiotida-Fokida, Peloponessos and Thessaly), which gave locational advantages to the kapnergostasia that were located within these regions (e.g. in the Athens-Piraeus complex, Kalamata and Volos); subsequently they purchased it from Central-Western Macedonia, which gave advantages for a location in northern Greece.

This change in the tobacco leaves used, which was expected to be enhanced with the entry of Greece into the EEC in 1981 (manufacturing firms would not be obliged to make their blends with tobacco destined for home consumption, and that soon consumption would change completely into 'blended' cigarettes) which shifted the centre of tobacco leaf production used by domestic manufacturing to the north, may account for the location in 1980 of the kapnergosatsio of a new tobacco manufacturing firm (SEKAP) in the industrial zone of Xanthi. This, as well as the fact that Xanthi offers low paid and abundant labour reserves and the presence of Moslem minorities with no trade-union organization to promote their interests, may account for the otherwise 'odd' location of SEKAP in Xanthi. Furthermore, a significant factor for such a location might have been the regional incentives given by the State in the area (the highest in the country)! However, since there were important factors that, most probably, would have led SEKAP to locate in Xanthi anyway, one might argue that the incentives given were in a sense wasted.

The spatial concentration of kapnergostasia reached paramount levels and it was mainly due to the further monopolization of the industry (for the same reasons as in the previous period). The fact that the Athens-Piraeus complex was the most important consumption centre for tobacco manufacturing products (e.g. in 1950-80 in the Greater Athens area was consumed 34-36 per cent of total cigarette consumption - Ministry of Economics) may account for the concentration of the largest part of manufacturing production there (Table 12.3). Moreover, the fact that, up to the end of the Civil War, the tobacco manufacturing products were in danger of being destroyed or being stolen when transported, must have contributed to the concentration of kapnergostasia in Athens and other consumption centres. Finally, the concentration there was increased because the Athens-Piraeus complex had the highest percentage of specialized workers, managerial and clerical staff as well as the best service industries, factors that were of the foremost importance for the automated production of tobacco manufacturing.

CONCLUSIONS

The case study that this chapter deals with is by no means a typical representative of a generalized theoretical structure of industrial location in capitalist, social formations, or a 'sample', in the sense of being 'representative' or 'typical', of the characteristics of industrial location of either all capitalist social formations, or Greece. However, some generalizable conclusions can be derived from it, the most important being that the location of industry is a social process, the product of a multiplicity of 'factors', the importance of which cannot be predicted in advance on merely theoretical grounds. Numerous particular examples have indicated that. For instance the importance of labour militancy changed between and within periods, as well as between the two sub-branches of the tobacco industry. The gradual liberation of the country's territory was vital for the understanding of the lack of <u>kapnergostasia</u> in the areas liberated after 1913, while the <u>kapnomagaza</u> were spread there, too. The specialization of <u>kapnoupoles</u> in tobacco processing was turned (late 1950s) from being an advantage for the further concentration of this industry in that area to a major disadvantage. The spatial distribution of <u>kapnergostasia</u> in the last period was 'accidental' in the sense that the firms that survived the competition 'happened' to be located in some areas rather than others. The abandonment of the protectionist policies of the State was necessary to understand why the tobacco manufacturing firms started to produce blended cigarettes in the 1960s, which in turn was very influential on their spatial distribution. The political suppression that was particularly acute in the 1940s and 1950s was vital for any understanding of the smashing of the powerful trade-union movement of <u>kapnergates</u> by the early 1950s, which was very influential in the shift of <u>kapnergostasia</u> that occurred then. It must not be taken for granted that social conflicts occur on a class basis: e.g. in the 1909-16 period there was a conflict with regard to the tobacco processing method used between on the one hand a few belligerent merchants and on the other hand the bulk of merchants and workers; also kapnergates, throughout the period studied, were divided along sex lines. The above conflicts had important consequences for the spatial distribution of kapnomagaza. The significance of the State policy was not always the same, for example in the first period the creation of the public kapnergostasia determined the spatial distribution of kapnergostasia. Finally, the operation of a firm either on a single plant or on a multi-plant basis can be the product of a host of different causes. For example, the operation of by far the great majority of tobacco trading firms on a single plant basis in the first and in the last period was the outcome of completely different factors. That is, in the first period it was primarily the result of the fact that they were small personal companies that they could not even contemplate operating on a multi-plant basis, while in the last period it was the result of the fact that the increasing mechanization of the process rendered extremely expensive the preservation of more than one processing plant. As for the operation of manufacturing firms on a single plant basis throughout the whole study period, this was due at first to the fact that they were small personal companies which again could not even contemplate operating on a multi-plant basis. Later on, the increase in the size of tobacco manufacturing firms was coupled with increases in the levels of mechanization which in turn prohibited (made it unreasonably expensive) the operation on a multi-plant basis.

BIBLIOGRAPHY

Andreadis, Th., Thoughts around the Contemporary Problem of Greek Tobacco (Athens, 1967)

Bureau of Tobacco Protection of Thessaloniki (BTPT), The Question of Compulsory or not Processing of Tobacco Leaves (Serres/Thessaloniki, BTPT, 1925)

BTPT, The Tobacco Question (Thessaloniki, BTPT, 1929)

Christoula, P. and Grigorogianni, G., 'The problem of tobacco', Archion Ekonomikon ke kenonikon Epistimon, 34 (1), 1-59,(1953)

'Decade of Greek Tobacco', Compiled by the Newspaper Kapnos and a Team of Experts,

(Athens, Newspaper, Kapnos, 1955)
Fakiolas, R.E., Labour Trade-Unionism in Greece, (Athens, 1978)
Fortounas, A., 'Why more appreciation and respect towards the national tobacco manufacturing is necessary', Efimeris tou Kapnou, 8.5.1933
Hamilton, F.E.I., 'A View of Spatial Behaviour, Industrial Organizationás and Decision-making', in F.E.I. Hamilton (ed.), Spatial Perspectives on Industrial Organization and Decision-making (London, Wiley, 1974) pp.3-43
Jecchninis, C., The Development of Greek Trade-Unionism, with Special Reference to the Period of Reconstruction 1945-55 (London, Ph.D. thesis, University of London, 1962)
Kordhatos, J., History of the Greek Labour Movement, (Athens, Boukoumanis, 1972)
Koutsoyianni, A. An Econometric Study of the Leaf Tobacco Market of Greece (Manchester, Ph.D. thesis, University of Manchester, 1962)
Labrianidis, T., Industrial Location in Capitalist Societies; The Tobacco Industry in Greece 1880-1980 (London, Ph.D. thesis, University of London, 1982)
Mantazaris, A., The Question of Kapnergates (Athens, 1927)
Onymelukwe, J.O.C., 'Industrial Location in Nigeria', in F.E.I. Hamilton (ed.), Spatial Perspectives on Industrial Organization and Decision-making (London, Wiley, 1974), pp.461-84
'Panhellenic Organization of Kapnergates', paper given by the Executive Committee to the 4th Tobacco Congress (1951)
Papastratos, E., The Work and Its Pain: From My Life (in Greek), Athens, 1964
Serraios, I., For the Introduction of Tobacco Monopoly in Greece (Athens, National Press, 1934)
Thassitis, V., The Greek Cigarette Industry (Athens, Kapniki Epitheorisis, 1962)
Tsoukalas, K., The Greek Tragedy (Athens, Olkos, 1964)
Varveropoulos, V., The Monopolistic Character of the Economic Organization of Tobacco (Athens, 1935)

Magazines, newspapers, official and collective documents and publications:

Avgi (Dawn), Daily, 24.8.1952 - 30.12.1953
Charitakis, V., Kalliavas, A. and Mikelis, N.

Economic Review of Greece, 1928-39
ICAP, Financial Directory of Greek Companies (tobacco trading - processing) Annual, 1967-81
Kapniki Epitheorissis (Tobacco Review), monthly: 1946-81
Ministry of Economics, Archives of the Department for the Control of Tobacco Manufacturing
National Tobacco Board (NTB), (a) Consumption of Tobacco Manufacturing Products in Greece, annual: 1956-80
NTB, (b) Data on Kapnergates (Department of Commerce, Archives), annual: 1959-78
Treasury for the Insurance of Kapnergates (TAK), (a) Report and Account of Administration, annual: 1937-39
TAK, (b) Labour Statistics of Men and Women Tobacco Workers, annual: 1927-28

CHAPTER 13

INDUSTRY AND THE HUMAN AND ECOLOGICAL TRAGEDY OF CUBATÃO (SÃO PAULO, BRAZIL)

Léa Goldenstein and Stela Goldenstein Carvalhaes

The industrialization of Cubatão can only be understood in the context of the historical and economic processes by which São Paulo was formed, and hence only in terms of production within the organization of the Brazilian society in question. Those processes operating within the capitalist system were the international and technical divison of labour.

The international division of labour is based on the principle that countries which can produce at lower cost reserve for themselves the most sophisticated work processes and transfer the simpler ones to others. At the same time, monopoly capitalism relocates industries with a high organic composition of capital to the dependent countries, and unequal exchange becomes more and more heavily sustained by the cost of the reproduction of labour.

The technical division of labour creates the need for infrastructure and brings into being a complex market for labour and services with a spatial definition.

Development along late-capitalist lines causes and accentuates territorial inequalities, leading to the formation of one, a few, or several urban-industrial agglomerations.

THE STAGES IN BRAZILIAN DEVELOPMENT

In the stage characterized by an agricultural export economy, Brazil's national territory was unarticulated in the sense that the various regions were not interconnected amongst themselves but were linked directly to the centres of world capitalism. The expansion of coffee created a dynamic economy and located accumulation above all in the south-east, as agricultural production became organized for export and consumer goods industries for the home market were set up. The corresponding infrastructure began to be constructed (railways, roads, power lines, banks) in ways which defined the basic profile of the inter-regional division of labour. The main feature of this profile was the major concentration of industry in the city of São Paulo, which produces for the national market. Cubatão can only be seen as part of São Paulo's industrial complex. São Paulo first became linked directly to the Port of Santos, and São Paulo-Santos-Cubatão then became a single entity.

Yet the process of import substitution was stopped after World War II, when a political decision was taken to give financial support from governmental credit institutions and to grant a varied range of tax exemptions to monopoly groups. The State also participated to meet the need to set up simultaneously a complex capital goods industry as a support for the durable consumer goods industry. This could only be done by mobilizing enormous amounts of capital. The 1950s were the period of this decisive change in the pattern of accumulation.

A process of integration of the national economy was then unleashed, entailing fresh and profound changes in spatial organization. As industrialization proceeded, new areas were integrated, markets created and urban spaces and economies developed, all at an extraordinary pace. The whole process was underlain by a common denominator: the degradation of the environment and the deterioration of natural resources.

The problem of pollution and of the misuse of natural resources, including those which are non-renewable, was - and is - closely connected with the political option to favour rapid development at any cost, involving the sacrifice of nature and people alike. Not that those countries where industrialization was first introduced were able to save their countryside from similar degradation - yet the historical process of this industrialization led to such a huge accumulation of capital that it was possible for them to face up to the cost of what the so-called 'environmental question' represents. More recently industrialized countries, however, are subject to exactly the reverse. Their economies have developed as complements to those of already industrialized countries.

Since the 1950s Brazil moved on from a raw-material export stage to one of exporting semifinished and even finished products. The industrialization to achieve this has been based on imported technology, most of which is already in widespread use in the world and sometimes even out-of-date. The equipment imported in the world is often considered obsolete in the country of origin and amounts to a massive transfer of environmental problems. Highly sophisticated high-technology industries based on advanced, extremely costly, scientific research in developed countries generally cause less pollution. Production of intermediate goods starting with the raw material is the stage which most degrades the environment, particularly ore reduction, metal refining and petrochemicals - industries which typify modern Brazil.

The advanced capitalist countries are driven to export capital, mainly in the form of technology, including capital goods, technical services and patents, all directed towards manufacturing industry. They thus generate and absorb innovations, and then proceed to disseminate them, thereby determining patterns of dependence. Urbanization and industrialization thus not only take place without eliminating dependence but even aggravate dependence. Innovations reach the periphery much later on, representing an advantage for the core regions in terms of marketing of their goods and controlling innovations. Given the speed at which innovation takes place, the domination of the core regions over the periphery can only tend to increase, a process which the latter's huge balance-of-payments deficit perpetuates by stimulating a further influx of foreign capital, both directly and in the form of loans.

To become viable internationally, this industrialization process must be based on two favourable prerequisites: first, cheap labour and, secondly, the absence of any obligation to preserve the environment. Inequality of the terms of trade has not diminished but is rather worsened during the present stage, insofar as new, more intricate relations of dependence have grown up between the rich and poor countries as the latter industrialize.

The Brazilian federal government's Five-Year Plan (Plano de Metas, 1956-60) was the landmark for the introduction of global planning in that country. It was chiefly concerned with industrial growth and led to the acceleration of the concentration of economic activities, above all in São Paulo. Industrial structure became more and more dominated by sectors producing consumer durables, capital goods and intermediate products. Foreign monopoly capital bought up or associated with local firms in dynamic sectors of industry but in recent years has shown greater interest in the more traditional sectors. The State, as a financing body or an entrepreneur in its own right, or again on account of the infrastructure it provides - water, power, roads, services in general - became the most powerful influence on the direction taken by local industrialization and on the conditions in which spatial production takes place.

In the 1970s, when a new policy aimed at production for export was introduced, the representatives of the Brazilian government at the Stockholm Conference stated that they were interested in industrialization and could not concern themselves with pollution, ignoring the resulting social cost. This attitude and policy have since been put into practice during the twenty years of a dictatorial regime, under which both civilians and the working class have been denied any access to decision-making.

The Brazilian industrialization process has not, in general, been shaped by any substantive policies geared to developing regions outside the metropolises (except for the unsuccessful example of SUDENE). Frontiers have been pushed back and new areas settled, often directly related to serve the international centres, with the Brazilian metropolises as 'relais'.

THE EXPERIENCE OF CUBATÃO

Cubatão reflects this economic policy, aggravated by immense environmental problems which by now are virtually insoluble. The industrial centre is over 30 years old, and was set up without either any spatial development policy framework in the broader sense or even a policy controlling local territorial organization and industrial location in the narrow sense.

In spite of the physical barrier represented by the Serra do Mar escarpment, the presence of transport arteries justifies the statement that it is the industrialization of São Paulo which has extended to the foothills, where a highly industrialized space exists in complete symbiosis with the industrial complex of the Metropolis, from the standpoint of production decisions, marketing and distribution. Cubatão's vast chemical and iron and steelmaking complex is an integral part of greater São Paulo: together with the Metropolis it represents a single economic unit and is characterized as an expansion area.

When industry was introduced there it was based on a transport infrastructure which was considered pre-existing: a port, railways and road access. This infrastructure, however, was highly problematic. The rail system of São Paulo State, created by the coffee industry, converged on the capital like a great fan and then extended on down like an umbilical cord to the coast. This short but tricky route had been wrested from the mountain range by a funicular railway in 1867. Technical factors, allied to serious problems of ecological equilibrium, have made it hard to put even the equipment already installed to full use. There are two roads: the 'Achieta' highway, built in 1948, and the modern 'Imigrantes'.

Even before industrialization was fully under way, Santos had already become the country's largest port. It handled coffee until the Second World War, when it became an oil port. By then its major problems had been solved: lack of depth congestion, high running costs, and unsuitability for use by large bulk vessels. It was run under lease by the Companhia Docas de Santos, a private company without any interest in investing in expansion or improvements, and was one of the last, if not indeed the last, remaining privately-owned ports in the world, but the Company's lease has recently run out. The local physical conditions produce considerable silting of the port area, greatly aggravated by human intervention, making costly maintenance work a continuous necessity. Nowadays only shallow-draft shipping can enter the various canals.

The Oil Refinery

The decision to locate the Refinery in Cubatão was a political option taken in the name of national security. Aside from this justification, never properly elucidated, it was based on the existence of the nearby port for receiving oil and on the availability of power supplies. Such location criteria, however, proved to be ill-justified, as the power generated in the coastal region is the same as the supply available up in São Paulo, and at the same price. As to the oil supply, a pipeline was built from the port storage tanks to the refinery and from there another set of pipes conveys the oil and the various by-products up the mountain range to São Paulo. If the refinery had been built up on the Planalto, a single pipeline to convey the crude oil would have sufficed. The waste does not stop there. At the end of the 1960s this product accounted for about 70 per cent of imports. All tankers which were bigger than the port's capacity were obliged to undertake expensive offloading operations at sea. The ocean pollution rose to unacceptable levels, and the price of such operations became uncomfortably high. The inappropriateness of its location was so great that in 1969 work began on the construction of a new pipeline from Cubatão to an ocean terminal equipped for the big tanker vessels but located 120km. offshore. The cost of these duplicated investments has never been reckoned.

The refinery began operating in 1955. The plant was assembled from a dismantled facility sold by a United States corporation, with 1930s technology. Its economic importance was considerable, not just for the region but for the whole country. Initially equipped to process Venezuelan and Arabian oil, as more and more oil began to be produced in Bahia it had to be redesigned in accordance with the national petroleum policy, and partly converted for handling ever larger amounts of oil from Bahia.

The left bank of the river Cubatão became the site of a growing chain of plants, taking on all the characteristics of a modern complex - high industrial output, a certain level of integration and a dense mass of production plant, capital and labour. The refinery thus had a multiplying effect. A large number of petrochemical plants followed in its wake, mostly subsidiaries or affiliates of large US corporations (Copebrás, Union Carbide, Estireno and others). They remained relatively small for around ten years, since oil refining is a State monopoly and there was as yet no defined policy regarding derivates. When the petrochemical industry was opened up to private enterprise in 1965, the existing plants expanded, and new facilities were also installed.

Iron and Steel

COSPIA (Companhia Siderúrgica Paulista) is the major iron and steelmaking complex of the Baixada (coastal region). Situated at the end of an arm of the sea connected to the port estuary, it was designed to be a marine steel mill, dependent on transport by sea, but rail eventually became the preferred means, owing to the insufficiency of the port facilities, the limitations imposed by the shallowness of the estuary, and the disputes between the company engaged in building a terminal and the dock company which owned the lease to run the port.

Both Brazilian and foreign-produced coal were unloaded at the port of Santos and from there conveyed onwards by road or rail. Only in 1969 did the specialized terminal begin to be used, following an agreement with Companhia Docas. As regards the ore brought down from the 'Iron-bearing Quadrilateral' of Minas Gerais, COSIPA conducted cost studies which led it to opt for rail transport.

The mill was built on marshlands which could only be occupied by means of huge earthmoving and piledriving operations costing a fortune in time and money. These and other factors, linked to problems with stagnation or contraction of the national and international markets for iron and steel, have all had their influence on the organization's financial difficulties.

It cannot be repeated too often that the Baixada has no raw materials. It is a centre for the production of intermediate raw materials made entirely from feedstocks brought in from the outside: oil, coal, naphtha, iron ore, limestone, dolomite, salt, ethyl alcohol, clinker for cement, sulphur, some quantities of chlorine. Most of its production is taken up to the Planalto, mainly to the São Paulo metropolitan region. Thus, millions of tons are brought at high cost down the mountains, only to make the journey back up again once they have been transformed in the Baixada.

Intractable Environmental Pollution

Cubatão is an example of the industrial occupation of an inadequate site. The municipality (administrative district) of Cubatão comprises 58 per cent mountains and hills, 18 per cent alluvial piedmont plains and filled-in mangrove swamp, and 24 per cent mangrove swamp. It was a sparsely populated rural area, occupied by banana plantations without even the need for agricultural labour. Cubatão thus developed as an industrial satellite of the São Paulo metropolis without account being taken of the limited space, consisting of narrow stretches of sandy and swampy soil resulting from fluvial and marine sedimentation processes, with practically no slopes, and receiving enormous torrents of water flowing down from the Serra do Mar. The rich but ill-defined hydrographic network produced by this situation was therefore unable to control the flow of water. The area is made up of mangroves and meandering rivers, subject to the influence of the tides and situated close to the escarpment of the Atlantic arm of the Serra do Mar, which represents a barrier to expansion and an interference with the climate. This area could only be occupied by moving huge amounts of earth to fill in the sites in question.

Altogether there are 23 large industrial firms, making up an industrial complex dominated by petrochemicals and steel manufacturers. The municipality has no more than 85,000 inhabitants but levies more Valued Added Tax (ICM) and has a higher per capita income than any other region in Brazil.

Air pollution is generally serious in the urban-industrial areas of Brazil. Cubatão is the most serious case, or at least the most notorious, as the physical factors act in conjunction with social and political factors. The town has become a research and analysis laboratory since government bodies and scientific institutions from Brazil and abroad have begun to take an interest in it. Successive surveys have been made of its geomorphology, vegetation, atmospheric circulation, population and health. Its problems have begun to be public knowledge and many campaigns have been launched to publicize and protest against all these problems. The local people have begun to organize themselves, too.

Yet, in spite of all this, little action has been taken. Capital interests are very powerful, and it is very expensive to stop pollution in an area with adverse natural conditions. Yet it is not only costly, but difficult to undertake such expenditure at a time which is admittedly one of hardship for industry, with reduced profit margins and, in some cases such as the iron and steel industry and the fertilizer industry, serious economic and financial problems.

In addition, there is the institutional neglect of pollution and related problems. Suffice it to say that it was not until 1976 that legislation was approved in São Paulo to regulate air and water quality standards with regard to certain pollutants. Nothing is said in the law, however, on the matter of solid waste. At the Federal level, the environmental issue only became the subject of regulation in 1971, with the creation of ecological stations and environmental protection areas. In 1973, a Federal Decree, which has not yet been made binding, outlined the National Policy for the

Environment.

Until very recently, industrial firms had no pollution control equipment at all. It is estimated in Cubatão that around one thousand tons of pollutants in the form of gas and particles are discharged into the atmosphere every day. Every year, Cubatão's industry generates 1.5 million tons of solid waste, which is not only not properly disposed of but most of which is simply dumped in the open or, worse still, discharged into the mangroves, rivers and lagoons.

The complexity and expense of pollution control in this case is due to the fact that most of the industrial processes involved are obsolete and relatively unprofitable, yielding to still higher levels of emission of pollutants. The explanation for this situation can be found by examining the origins of industry in Cubatão and, it can be contended, of Brazilian industry as a whole. There is no doubt that only the mastery of the technical processes used in industry and of the risks of critical episodes resulting from accidents with these processes or from natural factors, can lead to systematic supervision and inspection, with gradual control.

The atmospheric conditions are extremely unfavourable and aggravated by a relief arrangement - the escarpments of the Serra do Mar surrounding the valleys in which the town and the industrial facilities are located - which hinders the dispersal of pollutants. Environmental pollution, especially air pollution, is undeniably favoured by the local meteorology. When the wind blows from the industrial areas towards the residential districts, the concentration of pollutants is extremely high in these places. The prevailing winds are south-westerly, south and south-easterly, blowing towards the escarpment. This is why the degradation of the hillside vegetation is so great and so visible. When the so-called 'thermal inversion' occurs, the pollutants are trapped in the two basins, one of which corresponds to the refinery and the urban area, and the other to the area of the steelworks and Vila Parisi. Pollution is worse in this latter basin, where sulphur dioxide and dust predominate. The situation is aggravated by the heavy rains which fall with frequency in the area and which, among other consequences, contribute to the impregation of the soil and raising of the water level in the rivers and swamps.

Pollution has caused serious and irreparable

damage to the region's people and vegetation, as well as corroding materials. The consequences, in fact, reach beyond Cubatão's industrial and residential areas. SO_2 emissions by industry are far greater than can be measured in the atmosphere: sulphur dioxide is probably being dispersed to other more distant areas, or giving way to the formation of other elements.

The concentration of petrochemical plants, steel mills, fertilizer factories and others is responsible for the release of calorific energy which, accentuated by the absence of vegetation, leads to the formation of a mass of heat hovering over the industrial area and functioning as a concentration of pollutants which reflect the sun's rays and can cause 'thermal inversions', preventing the pollutants from being dispersed. When the air cools down at night, the particles retained by the heat may then be precipitated in the form of acid rain. The humidity in the air leads to a higher level of absorption of these particles by the respiratory apparatus.

The problems are all the more serious owing to the diversity of their origins. The escarpment which hems in the coastal region, known as Baixada Santista, is steep, the soil is decomposed and fragile, and the vegetation covering it is essential to its stability. It began to be inhabited by workers, living in what purported to be provisional housing, towards the end of the 1940s when the first modern road was built to connect the Planalto to the Baixada. Settlements expanded when the new highway was built in the 1970s. From then on, coinciding with the worsening recession, the shanty towns have sprawled even further, and land use has spun out of control.

Land use in Cubatão is characterized by a lack both of planning and infrastructure. The occupation is intense, involving powerful economic interests on the one hand, and chaotic occupation giving rise to major social problems on the other. Attempts to intervene, by controlling pollution, evacuating dangerous hillside settlements, avoiding the spread of the shanty towns up the slopes and the filling in of mangroves, have run up against these opposing interests.

The degradation of the escarpment vegetation began to be described and criticized ten years ago by specialized bodies and scientific institutions. Aside from people's deforestation with a view to making a home, the destruction of the foliage, degradation of the vegetation and gradual disappearance of the tropical forest covering the foothills are a direct consequence of exposure to the pollutants from the industrial complex lying below. Since the equilibrium of the slopes has been destroyed, landslides are common, and the resulting problems for the people living and the civil infrastructure built there, are always serious.

No less problematic is the build-up of waste material and detritus at the foot of the hills and in the Baixada's rivers and mangroves. The mangrove and marsh vegetation has been submitted to sweeping changes over the last few decades. The few remaining spots of cropland bear inescapable witness to the effects of pollution.

The material coming down from the Serra, on the other hand, also aggravates the problems related to silting in the port and coastal region - all the more so because the indiscriminate landfills carried out in the mangroves to expand the areas to be occupied by industry and by the population have eliminated major functions performed by these mangroves. Their presence limited the silting up of the estuary in which the port is situated, since the submerged part of the vegetation retained the material washed down from the hillsides. It has become far more difficult and expensive now to keep the port channel clear, and more than one million cubic metres of mud and silt have to be removed every year. The silting process is all the more serious when it is recalled that the port of Santos may well continue to expand towards the inland end of the estuary, precisely into the mangroves of Cubatão.

On the other hand, as far as pollution is concerned, the fact that the mangroves retain sediments means that they also trap the pollutants, especially the heavy materials, and this also harms fishing. The lack of basic sanitation (sewage collection and treatment), pollutants, silting and successive landfills have all virtually killed off any remaining life in the region's mangroves. Measurements are being conducted to check the level of lead, mercury, cadmium, copper and zinc to correlate the presence of these substances with alterations in the flora and the possible contamination of the fish consumed by the local population.

Water pollution is easier to control, and most plants treat their liquid effluents. Yet this is offset by the fact that in the town itself there is not a single domestic sewer, in addition to the fact that the river Cubatão receives water from the Billings Reservoir, which in turn receives a large part of the waste water from the metropolis in natura. As if this were not enough, the waste from the port of Santos is washed by the tide into the mangroves, where it stays for good.

The Housing Problems

There are a few large firms in Cubatão which employ 25,000 workers at most. The great majority of jobs are temporary, offered by contractors performing construction and expansion work and by firms providing services. The recession has led to a contraction in this labour market, which anyway was characterized by high turnover and low pay. A large army of unemployed has therefore appeared, to whom must be added the unemployed workers from other towns along the coast. The result has soon made itself felt: 50 per cent of the population are estimated to be living in shanty towns and in tenement districts without adequate health provisions or even in areas considered to be high risk.

Three different examples of the housing situation can well illustrate this point:

a. Shanty towns on the hillsides. There are known as bairros cotas (literally 'contour districts'), referring to the altitude at which they are located. They were originally made up of relatively sound wooden shacks for the men working on the roadbuilding, but they have now burst their bounds under the pressure of people coming in after losing their jobs or houses in Cubatão and other towns in the Baixada region. Altogether there are more than seven thousand dwellings, occupied by at least thirty thousand people, making up an unknown number of favelas (shanty towns) in conditions considered highly dangerous by the authorities and by specialists, on account of the geotechnical fragility to which the clearing of the forest has left these slopes exposed.

b. Shanty towns in the mangroves. The best known of these is Vila São José, or Vila Socó, made up of houses on stilts in the middle of the mangroves. Criss-crossed by oil pipelines, these areas became pathetically notorious early in 1984, when leakages in the pipes caused explosions and fires which partially destroyed them, leading to the death of an unknown number of people. These shanty towns are relatively old and well-structured, but the extreme poverty of the inhabitants, and perhaps a concern to conceal the true dimensions of the tragedy, prevented a proper count of the real number of victims.

c. The largest of the unsanitary residential districts is Vila Parisi. A former rural plotland (hence not covered by the constraints imposed on urban plotlands by the legislation of the 1950s, the period in question) next to the steel mill, this area was a residential option for most of the unskilled workers in the region. It is worth recalling that the skilled workers mostly live in the centre of Cubatão or, even more often, in the neighbouring municipalities along the shore. Vila Parisi is a former mangrove swamp and is still subject to frequent flooding. It has no public sewers. Surrounded on all sides by industry, it is the district most degraded by atmospheric pollution.

Groups of physicians who supervise the population's health consider the area to be well below the minimum standards of public health. They have detected high levels of contamination by a whole range of pollutants, and an excessively high rate of mental illness and congenital malformations. All this is of course made still worse by the low levels of income and nutrition of this population.

A zoning law passed in 1982, reserving the area strictly for industrial use, has led to violent controversy and long heated debates. No concrete option has been offered to the residents who are forced to move out. The offers made to date by the official agencies are unacceptable. On the other hand, it would seem obvious that the industrial firms have an interest in dislodging the population and using the area to expand, thus also eliminating the evidence of the damage caused to the population.

Cubatão grows and industrializes, increasing its contribution to the GDP. Meanwhile, poverty is also increasing, with all the misery represented by the visual sores of spreading shanty towns, refuse dumps and industrial waste disposal sites, earthworks, landslides, air pollution, giving the permanent mist its own peculiar colour and density, and destruction of the forest and mangrove vegetation. All this dissociates the economic from the social. The very low socio-economic level of the population and the lack of any basic sanitation accelerate the deterioration of the environment.

The Conflict of Capital, the State, and Labour in the Organization and Reorganization of Space

In this historically defined area, which is limited in size, there is an evident conflict between capital and labour. It is possible to observe in almost schematic form the dynamics of construction (production) of space and its reorganization. Vila Parisi was the required 'pocket' of labour. Now, under the pressure of lack of space, industry needs the area. Vila Socó was a mangrove swamp, but now that it has been burnt, it is claimed as private property. The hillside shanty towns were created by the governmental Highways Department, and now they are a source of considerable concern and objections. By correlating time and space, it is possible to accompany the agents who interfere in the process of spatial production. Space is organized and reorganized as a function of forms of production.

Cubatão preceded even the ABC, Osasco and Guarulhos (densely industrialized municipalities within greater São Paulo) as the flagship of monopoly capital in Brazil at the production level, represented both by the State-owned corporations and by the multinationals - the refinery and the steel mill on the one hand, and the petrochemical plants on the other.

There are the industrial establishments which, with the full support of government, were to be responsible for an unplanned occupation and organization of space. Since the State was unable to undertake global aspects of the required infrastructure, each establishment in isolation took into account the factors considered favourable to setting up in the area: proximity to the Metropolis, proximity to the port, available power supply, plenty of water. The absurdly low value of land during this first stage seemed to offset the difficulties of building on such inappropriate land. Few of these firms were bothered about the problems which would result from premature saturation of the traffic routes, and the air circulation problems in this patch of land were equally blithely ignored, shut off as it was by the cliffs of the Serra do Mar. Less attention still was paid to problems related to industrial waste disposal. Man - the worker - always crops up in the underdeveloped countries. Where there is demand, migratory currents appear in the search for a place to settle down.

The State has played a major role in the industrialization process, not only as regards the large-scale national programmes symbolized by the Companhia Siderúrgica Nacional, by the Five-year Plan, by SUDENE, but also in the Sectorial Programmes (for steel, pulp, alcohol), or again in tax incentive and exemption policies at the municipal, state and federal levels. These policies were introduced at various moments in an effort to attract industry to the metropolises or induce them to move away, through what was publicized as decentralization, de-concentration, or other such slogans. These were in fact different ways of producing and reproducing space. Cubatão cannot be understood and interpreted unless the role of government is fully examined, either directly as planner and investor, or indirectly as legislator and underwriter.

And this space, in which a major part of São Paulo's most advanced industry was installed and organized, entailed no thought of, or provision for, man. The space was appropriated and organized in terms of production relations. A confrontation between production and social interests soon emerged. Conflict was postponed in different ways and at different times: the firms undertook costly systems to transport people to and from the residential areas in other coastal towns; Vila Parisi became the home of more than 15,000 people with lower purchasing power or without any certainty of finding work on this new labour market in the large corporations, with the contractors (temporary work), or even in the service sector. The interference of social relations as a variable in the occupation of space was unforeseen, and the confrontation rapidly emerged. The economic crisis of the 1970s, which has now reached a crescendo, only aggravated the existing conflict. On the one hand, waves of under-employed, unemployed and employed but impoverished people came looking for a place to live in the existing districts or the shanty towns which had already begun to proliferate in the mangroves and up the hillsides. On the other, there were the industrial firms, supported and shielded by the spectre of the crisis, refusing or delaying investment in facilities which could protect the health of their employees and the surrounding population and prevent the degradation of the rivers, forests and mangroves. Finally, there was the degradation of the space, organized by and for industry itself from the 1950s onwards.

Cubatão is a component of the industrialization of the metropolis of São Paulo itself. Part and parcel of this whole are two antagonistic realities - capital and labour. Production is placed in opposition to social need. What happens there is paralleled in any place where industrial or agro-industrial, or even agricultural, activities have progressed along the lines proposed and introduced by industrial monopoly capital. It has some serious aggravating factors of its own, however, which have made it wretchedly notorious and give it specificity: the limited amount and inadequacy of the space reserved for industrial production and the difficulty of properly structuring the urban agglomeration.

The controversy concerning land use in Cubatão centres on two fundamental points. The first is the conflict around the value of the land and the State's relation to this conflict. The State is unable to mediate, and hence becomes enmeshed in anti-social and costly projects such as the urbanization of steep hillsides or the construction of low-cost housing on recently filled-in mangroves which have not yet stabilized. This mediation should come about through standardization of land use, guaranteeing the various uses by building the infrastructure required to ensure the welfare of the population, as well as effective concrete action to oblige the industrial establishments to control pollution. The second is Cubatão's political and social status: since 1968 it has been classed as a national security area, which means political tutelage by central government, so that its governing officials are appointed by the Federal administration. This fact has now led to an even more serious impasse, as the São Paulo State government, with the opposition party in office, has only limited means for local action. Moreover, the industrial establishments operating in Cubatão are also considered 'national security' plants for the purposes of intervening in the production process to contain pollution. Only the Federal administration can have the factories shut down even in an emergency.

Cubatão is a town of poor workers where even the more skilled individuals live; this is why the trade unions participate less than would be expected in an industrial town with regard to local problems. It is thus a struggle by poor people, unskilled workers, shanty town dwellers. For all these reasons it has taken so long and proved so difficult to solve the problems of Cubatão. And it is because of all this that, to begin to solve them, the population must be considered a valid interlocutor, by creating an institutional structure at the political level which is effectively prepared to face up to such immense problems in an objective and decisive manner.

CHAPTER 14

INDUSTRIAL DYNAMICS OF NEWLY INDUSTRIALIZING COUNTRIES IN EAST AND SOUTH-EAST ASIA: A REAL PATH TOWARDS A NEW INTERNATIONAL ECONOMIC ORDER

Mahindar Santokh Singh

The objectives of a New International Economic Order (NIEO) have been outlined in the Charter proclaimed by the United Nations General Assembly of 1974. The level of success and/or failure achieved has been a much debated topic, pregnant with contradictory possibilities. In this context, the newly industrializing countries of East and South-east Asia are the focus of international economic development, more so in recent years, when international economic development has been characterized by industrial expansion of these peripheral areas, in contrast to the uneven growth, sluggish and recessional conditions in established western industrialized centres. Is the development of these nation states really marked, as it seems to be, by a readiness on their part for integration into the international division of labour? If so, how has this readiness been acquired?

This chapter intends to investigate the reality of the development path followed by newly industrializing countries in East and South-east Asia. It is a focus on the 'processes of social and economic engineering' (Wiseman, 1979) to achieve a higher value for their raw natural resources, a new push into export-oriented industrialization geared to the developed country markets, effective contribution to international trade in industrial output and a new approach to improving the industrial performance through technological advancement and structural change in industry. It boils down to an analysis of the purposive attempt in industrial rationalization. The economic and disciplinarian role of government institutions in the promotion of high speed growth in these countries is analysed in accordance with the explicitly set out social and economic targets in time-specific development plans.

METHODOLOGY

In this analysis of the role of strategies posed by governments we advocate utilization of the trajectory model in order to learn more about the dynamics of policy intervention from 'inception to completion' (Wiseman, 1979). The term 'trajectory' is borrowed from sociological literature. The German sociologist, F. Schuetze, defines trajectories as 'rounded, sequentially ordered structures of crystallised situational chains of events' (Schuetze, 1971). We have adopted the concept to apply to the entire experience of development policy intervention in a representative number of young, newly industrializing countries in East and South-east Asia after the Second World War. South Korea, Taiwan, Hong Kong, Singapore, Malaysia and Thailand are chosen as a representative sample of the newly industrializing countries in this region.

The first step in the individual nation state's development policy trajectory is the collection of historically ordered purposive attempts to create a situation or to institute reform. It is a comprehensive record of chronologically ordered, enlarged state functions which incorporate economic, technological, institutional, organizational, social and political changes that are tied up into the broader development strategies to bring about 'deliberate societal change' (Etzioni, 1976).

From here we progress to another plane of analysis. The trajectories of industrial intervention in the five countries and one colony (Hong Kong) are pieced together. There is no denying that each nation state's trajectory of developmental policies possesses its own uniqueness. However, there are underlying structures and patterns which can be isolated and developed into what may be termed 'ideal type' trajectories of 'societal guidance approach' to plan-rational development that enhances the nation's international competitiveness. By focusing on characterizing changes we realise that each subsequent stage or milestone in the policy intervention represents generally a sequence of change in institutional involvement. These begin with indirect assistance in fostering the appropriate climate for industrial development. It is followed by a proclamation of an official policy of industrial development and advances on to the creation of an institutional entity for engineering the course of its industrial rationalisation and recognition of the importance of the international division of labour in industry.

The ideal type trajectories have highlighted the advantage of the individual industrial policy trajectories in that these trajectories are not static, not time specific, nor are they contemporaneous. They are superimposed by features unique to each nation. The same stage or phase is experienced by each nation at a different period of time in correlation with its stage of maturation in the production system. Furthermore, common time frames or phases depict characterizing changes in the multiplicity of forces and processes of social and economic engineering that are operational. These characterizing changes provide a framework within which organizational and behavioural decision-making processes operate to create the means and the patterns. We have isolated a number of common phases which will be described and analysed as aspects of economic reality of these newly industrializing countries.

BRIEF BACKGROUND OF THE SAMPLE OF COUNTRIES SELECTED

An outstanding feature of historical similarity of the six countries chosen is that apart from Thailand all the newly industrializing countries under discussion share a common epoch of colonialism. South Korea and Taiwan were under nearly half a century of Japanese control before they emerged after World War Two, while Malaysia and Singapore were British colonies. Hong Kong is still a colony. They inherited economic systems in which foreign trade, especially export of primary products, is a key element in their economic structure (Table 14.1). For all of them the respective colonial power or the United States had featured as the dominant market for their exports. They all have a relatively small population compared with other Third World countries, with a total population of 2.4 million in Singapore, 5.15 million in Hong Kong, 14.5 million in Malaysia, 38.7 million in Korea and 48.2 million in Thailand. The gross national product per capita varies from the lowest US$590 in Thailand to US$3,830 in Singapore. Their agricultural system, with the exception of city-states of Hong Kong and Singapore, is based on monsoon rice culture and plantation crop cultivation. They have all operated as free enterprise economies. All possess enterprising populations with literacy rates that

Table 14.1: Statistical Information on Individual Countries

Country	Area (Sq.Km.)	Total Population in millions	(Dollars) 1979 GNP per capita	Total Employment	Employment in industry (per cent)	Contribution of manufacturing to GDP (per cent)		Primary Product Export as per cent of Total Exports	
						1960	1978	1960	1978
Hong Kong	1,045	5.15	3,760	1,717,000	54.9	22	34	*20.0	* 3.0
Malaysia	329,749	14.51	1,370	5,093,500	15.8	7	19.6	97.2	84.0
South Korea	98,484	38.72	1,480	14,775,000	19.3	14	27	96.0	12.0
Singapore	581	2.47	3,830	1,142,400	29.5	12	26	*74.0	*54.0
Taiwan	35,961	18.57	637 (1977)	2,087,000 (1967)	50.0	17	35	57.6	15.0
Thailand	514,000	48.18	590	19,890,000	21.6	13	19	98.8	81.0

* Entrepot trade not local production, as land is scarce

Source: Area and Population - 1981 Statistical Yearbook, 1979 Yearbook of National Accounts Statistics, vols. 1 and 2, 1979, United Nations.

fall somewhere between 60 and 90 percent - uniformly high by less developed country standards.

THE COLONIAL ECONOMY'S STRUCTURE

The colonial economy's structure and mode of operation may be pictured in terms of intersectoral relationships among its key economic sectors (Paauw and Fei, 1973). Structurally, the open dualistic economy was compartmentalized into two insulated parts: a modern export-oriented enclave and a large, backward, traditional, agricultural sector. In Hong Kong and Singapore the entrepot trade replaced this sector. The dominance of agriculture is discernible from its role in all the major aspects of the economy, namely the creation of employment, production of exports, contribution to gross domestic product and savings, financing of imports and transfer of profits abroad. Income generation was dominated by the export of land-based resources. The non-agricultural sector was characterized by the provision of commercial services to facilitate primary exports or entrepot port functions. Investments were concentrated in the plantation sector, and the pace of investments was controlled by foreign market demands.

It cannot be disputed that these nations' functions as world producers and/or exporters of primary resource products brought them definite advantages. By Asian standards they had achieved relatively higher levels of per capita income at the time of independence. Founded on a relatively prosperous primary export sector the people became accustomed to a high standard of living and a free flow of a wide range of manufactured goods. But spatial and structural imbalances prevailed. It is important to stress that, although the markets for manufactured goods were created, production of these goods locally was limited to a very narrow range of consumer goods, handicrafts and ancillary industries which sprang up with, and were dependent upon, the primary industries of agriculture and mining. Cottage industries were devoted to the production of hand-made consumption goods in every day use. They also satisfied meagre needs of the rural population but, all in all, manufacturing activity was not an important sector in the economy.

The cause of industrial backwardness lay in the international division of labour which made these countries economically dependent upon the industrially developed countries and turned them 'into buyers of industrial goods and suppliers of raw materials' (Cukor, 1974). In fact the policy of comparative advantage in primary production and situational imperatives such as their location along east-west trade routes was carried to its extremes by maintaining conditions of laissez-faire. Absence of protective measures led to the decline and disappearance of the cottage industry when factory-made manufactured goods began to flood the market.

From the economic point of view, specialization on just a few primary products or on entrepot trade, had the resultant effects that domestic economies in these countries were vulnerable to fluctuations in world trade. Deteriorating terms of trade of primary products relative to manufactured goods and declining prices of land-based commodities meant that development was often impeded. In addition, planning for long term development was almost impossible when countries did not have control over the quotation of prices of primary export commodities.

Hence structural transformations of the economy seemed a prerequisite for balanced and self-sustained growth. The timing seemed most appropriate after independence. From the social and political point of view, too, the isolated and poverty stricken traditional agricultural sector could not be further ignored.

Supported by the above arguments for a structural change in the economy, planners in these countries looked upon industrialization together with agricultural development as solutions to the weaknesses in these economies. Modernization of agriculture was emphasized alongside the development of the manufacturing industry. The exceptions were Singapore and Hong Kong, where such development was constrained by size of land. The primary task of the post-independent growth plans was to integrate the two halves of the agricultural sector into the national economy by emphasizing self-sufficiency in staple food production (rice) and an aggressive policy of diversification of primary exports. Emphasis on new crops and water resources with an export potential saw the development of fisheries and fresh-water resources in Taiwan; rubber, sugar cane and timber in Thailand; palm oil, tobacco, pepper, timber and petroleum exploration in Malaysia.

The agricultural export sector became the foundation for industrialization and modernization of the traditional good crop agricultural sector in the financial sense, in terms of markets and as a source of capital. Agricultural export surpluses continued to be the major source of the economies' savings fund. Through a combination of rural development strategies - new regional agriculture schemes, intensive research into output and productivity, land reforms, reduction of foreign ownership and control - returns from the sector were enlarged and profits mobilized as investments into the manufacturing sector.

The non-agricultural (commercial) sector had not developed an internal growth momentum of its own, apart from serving the primary export sector or the entrepot trade in Singapore and Hong Hong. The post-independence growth era aimed at overcoming these deficiencies by introducing an official industrial policy in which continuous development of the manufacturing activity would focus on the relatedness of the major functions - production, consumption, savings, investment, exports and imports.

INDUSTRIALIZATION THROUGH A POLICY OF IMPORT SUBSTITUTION

Crises, such as embargoes on Hong Kong's entrepot trade with China and balance of payment problems in primary export dependencies, marked the beginnings of the policy in which industrialization was spelt out as the sector to spearhead economic progress. The policy of industrialization was based on the conditions of free enterprise and laissez-faire. This approach originated from 'the outward looking' ideology on which the past development of these nations rested. A policy of import-substitution was embarked upon. Although investment in manufacturing embodied both public and private investments, the role of the public sector was restricted to providing the necessary infrastructure and a suitable climate for industrial growth.

The success of the policy so outlined thus rested on the initiative of both domestic and foreign entrepreneurs to invest. The 1950s and 1960s saw the implementation and growth of import-substituted industrial projects through a wide range of fiscal and physical incentives. These included tax holiday, pioneer status, emergence of industrial estates (developed sites) near urban centres or in rural areas. Moderate tariffs and quotas were imposed over a wide range of consumer imports to protect nascent domestic consumer industry. One third to half the investment budgets in five year Development Plans were allocated for the development of basic services - electric power, water supply, transport and communication networks. In all these countries an official body, namely a Division of Industrial Development or Economic Planning Board, was created to institute and review the protective measures and incentives from time to time. In addition, governments undertook the responsibility to maintain as far as possible a stable monetary and financial climate free from restrictions, controls and uncertainties.

In summary, the role of indirect participation found expression through (a) public expenditure on social and economic infrastructure; (b) fiscal and tax incentives; (c) protective tariffs; (d) creation of industrial estates; (e) industrial research and training facilities and (f) man-power training with a movement from a literary education towards an education with a technical bias.

The import-substitution phase of industrial development led to some increase in the share of manufacturing to gross domestic production. Improvements in per capita income stimulated a change in demand in favour of non-foodstuffs and boosted domestic demand for those industries.

The structural patterns of manufacturing, however, revealed that the process of import-substitution substituted domestic production for imported manufactures, mainly for consumer non-durable goods based on existing patterns of demand. It failed to extend into the production of advanced resource-based goods and intermediate products. Industrialization was entirely dependent on the import of capital goods.

Within the broad context of import-substitution the growth of manufacturing industry was not spread out over the entire group of industries. Industries under pioneer status and other tax incentives showed up predominantly as industries displaying rapid growth. Failure of manufacturing industry to create employment and absorb surplus labour from the agricultural sector and new entrants into the job market was indicated. The rising rate of unemployment reflected on the capital-intensive technology adopted by the manufacturing sector in conflict with the factor endowment - surplus labour situation prevalent in these nations. It was clear that foreign investors chose to adopt capital-intensive modes of production with which they were familiar in the

West. Further, the fallacy of the assumption that rapid industrialization would automatically bring about the required spread effects spatially became evident with growing disparities in regional development. In addition, the mushrooming of factories of small and very small size in the same activity led to duplication, intense competition among units and resultant wastage of resources. The unguided policy of free enterprise and a liberal flow of foreign capital into these countries posed problems of ownership and control since repatriation of profits led to a slowing down of reinvestments in the sector. Above all, the smallness of these national markets was the limitation to the continuous growth of the import-substitution form of industrialization. These aggregate social and economic problems posed themselves as a crisis situation, once again demanding alternative approaches to development.

EXPORT-ORIENTED INDUSTRIALIZATION

These new states faced the crisis of economic survival and national building. The mode of crisis management chosen was to discard the passive roles of the governments. A new strategy of export-oriented industrialization was initiated in the newly industrializing countries in east and south-east Asia as the next milestone in industrial promotion with direct government participation. In Malaysia, the government introduced a twenty-year perspective plan outlining the 'New Economic Policy' of the government (Malaysia 1970). A wide range of investment incentive acts were passed to provide not only financial incentives but to spell out priority projects, incentives for increase in domestic value added in manufacturing and greater use of local raw materials. Export processing platforms, or free-trade zones as they are called in some countries, were set up to encourage multinational corporations to transfer their semi-skilled, labour-intensive operations off-shore to these countries. This open door policy to multinational corporations came at the time when the latter were confronted with high cost, militant labour problems in their own countries.

Furthermore, loans and private domestic investments were channelled into the manufacturing product export sector. In South Korea one third to 48 per cent of all loans by banking institutions were channelled into the manufacturing sector. The textile industry recorded the largest amount of outstanding loans.

Preferential interest rate systems, preferential domestic taxes for promotion of exports and creation of government developmental banks were some attempts to institutionalize the flow of capital and loans into the export industries.

This phase marked the period of buoyancy for export-oriented industries such as textiles, clothing, footwear; other consumer goods like toys, electronics; wood, rubber, oil palm and other resource-based industries. Unemployment fell drastically to below 5%. Many countries like Singapore began to face labour shortages.

In Hong Kong the decline in the entrepot trade brought about by the fostering of direct-trade links by nations in its hinterland and the stream of refugees from China, turned enterprising businessmen into industrial entrepreneurs. They excelled in the production of consumer and intermediate goods for export under the Commonwealth tariff preferences and import quotas to the United Kingdom. Knitted goods, rubber footwear, hats, toys - practically most labour-intensive goods - began to be exported. Subsequently the market was enlarged to the United States. Under government promotional schemes, business organizations began training in overseas markets. A Federation of Hong Kong Industries was instituted to train, promote and plan public and private joint ventures.

In the realm of finance, Export Credit Insurance Corporations were set up in many newly industrializing countries. These enable exporters to offer credit terms comparable to credit terms of competitors. Through merchant houses, export markets for Hong Kong products were enlarged to western Europe. Germany became her third largest market for textiles, after the United Kingdom and the United States of America. The Netherlands, Scandinavia, Switzerland and Italy were also incorporated. Finally, she made inroads into Canada and Australia.

In Taiwan, Thailand, South Korea, Singapore and Malaysia free trade zones of 'export platforms' were sited near airports and seaports, i.e. primarily low-wage semi-skilled labour surplus zones. Production - partial, in bits and pieces - was wholly dominated by multinational corporations - a strategy commonly referred to as 'redeployment' (S. Amin, 1984) for production of cheap, labour-intensive, manufacturing goods for export to core capitalist countries. While the packages of economic incentives differ among developing countries, most involve duty free export and import, property tax reductions and some form of income tax holiday (Borrus et al., 1983). These incentives have been ranked second behind the availability of low-cost labour among reasons cited by industry executives for shift to off-shore production. From the standpoint of these countries, it provided an opportunity for governments to utilize multinational capital and surplus petro-dollars to create employment and to initiate an entry into export production and western export markets. By 1978, the top nine United States' integrated circuit manufacturers together had 35 off-shore assembly facilities in ten developing countries in south-east Asia (Borrus et al., 1983). Taiwan, Hong Kong, Malaysia, Singapore, Korea and the Philippines led this list.

External factors, such as the political structure of international trade, have also helped to boost south-east Asia's position in manufacturing for export. United States' firms prior to 1974 had used off-shore assembly affiliates in the developing countries of south-east Asia as export platforms to the Japanese market to circumvent the Japanese 12 per cent ad valorem tariff on imports of integrated circuits from the United States. Imports into Japan from an affiliate located in a less developed country were duty free (Borrus et al., 1983). Thus, while United States' re-exports of finished integrated circuits out of south-east Asia serve four markets: Britain, France, West Germany and Japan, the United States' exports of unfinished integrated circuits (chips, dice and wafers) go primarily to Malaysia, Singapore, Hong Kong and the Philippines for final assembly and packaging by United States' affiliates located there (Borrus et al., 1983). In this process 80 per cent of the local assembly operations are conducted under the auspices of United States' affiliates in south-east Asia.

The other major advantage that these countries had was that, after Japan joined the Organization for Economic Cooperation and Development in 1964, it began to gain ease in floating its securities in overseas markets. It also became a major investor in Korea, Taiwan and south-east Asia. It enabled these countries to work out new strategies of meeting world competition in terms of products (quality, design, price) by importing technology from Japan, combining it with labour power and then offering to the market products that were able to compete profitably with those of other countries (Zysman and Tyson, 1983).

INTER AND INTRA-INDUSTRY STRUCTURAL CHANGES AND MANAGEMENT STRATEGIES WITHIN EXPORT-ORIENTED INDUSTRIALIZATION

Having launched successfully export-oriented industries, the newly industrializing countries in south-east Asia did not find themselves in a static and stable situation of growth and development. It is imperative here to unravel the dynamics and competitive character of the processes by which national competitive and comparative advantages were created. Comparative advantage is not simply the effect of resource endowments in capital and labour (1983). A clear-cut interplay of market and political factors which accompany well conceived intervention policies underlie the adjustments and shifts described below. Effectiveness is the criterion of evaluation of goal-oriented strategic activities. Effectiveness implies an understanding of the competitive market dynamics. Examples would be selected to reveal the effectiveness of measures taken to promote structural adjustments required to maintain the growth momentum of these economies under changing international economic conditions.

In international competition South-east Asian nations are confronted with two major external pressures. First, in the lower rungs of international industrial division of labour exists a very large number of Third World countries with extensive labour surpluses and much lower labour costs than the South-east Asian countries. In contrast, in South-east Asia intense labour demands in export-assembly industries automatically have led to upward shifts in wages and labour costs and signs of labour shortages are beginning to appear in these countries. Secondly, in the West over the last twenty-five years industry and labour groups in the textile and apparel industry, steel industry, footwear and semiconductor industry, responded to global market changes by attempting to insulate their domestic markets from international competition; arguing that low profits, unemployment and plant closures are due to imports. They have insisted that the governments impose quotas. By 1982 the United States, for example, had severely restricted the imports of cotton, wool, man-made fibre textiles and apparel under the Global Multi-fibre Arrangement, which controlled virtually the whole world trade in textiles and apparel (Aggarwal and Haggard, 1983).

The relative weakness of the state *vis-à-vis* business interests contributed to the success of the Western protectionist coalition and the construction of import barriers. This was adverse to the United States' government's aid programmes of the 1950s and 1960s that helped to foster the growth in particular of the textile industries in Japan, Korea and Taiwan. This was made possible through the sales and grants of raw material under Public Law 480 and aid through Community Credit Corporation: aid for machinery requirements under loans from the Export-Import Bank International Cooperation Administration and the Development Loan Fund: and technical assistance to the industry under the Mutual Security Act (Aggarwal and Haggard, 1983).

Diverse strategies were employed by the east and south-east Asian suppliers to counter the switch from 'trade not aid' to international protectionist movements mooted by the United States. As noted earlier, the individual trajectories are not contemporaneous. 'Voluntary' export restraints by one country have led to a shift in sources of supply and exports from other south-east Asian countries lower down in the production system. For example, the Japanese 'voluntary' export restraint in the 1960s had merely resulted in the shift in the sources of supply to Hong Kong, Taiwanese and South Korean textile and apparel industries. These components were developed by Japanese expertise and local and Japanese joint-ventures in Japanese off-shore production.

After the Long Term Arrangements were signed by nineteen countries to be in force for five years, with a growth provision of five per cent in restricted categories of cotton textiles and cotton apparel exports in 1962, East and South-east Asian producers made a concerted effort to overcome the adverse impact of these regulations by diversifying production to wool, man-made fibres and silk divisions within the industry. These exports were not covered by the import restrictions on cotton textiles and apparel. In this effort involving technological change, East and South-east Asian suppliers displaced the Europeans as major exporters of wool and man-made fibre products to the United States (Aggarwal and Haggard, 1983). In response, the United States in 1971 imposed a 10 per cent import surcharge on textiles and apparel imports and followed it by the Multifibre Arrangement in 1973. In this spate of protectionist movements, the European Economic Community (EEC) was slow to negotiate its bilateral trade agreement under the Multifibre Arrangement. The east and south-east Asian countries thus sought a new solution by fragmenting their export markets and diverting from the effectively controlled United States' market to the EEC. It did not take long, however, for the EEC to institute changes and a stricter accord when the Multifibre Arrangement came up for renewal in 1977 and 1981. Renegotiations in 1981 marked a sharp upturn to increased protectionism against textile apparel exports from these countries.

Another strategy employed by south-east Asian newly industrializing countries was to branch into a wide range of products from the low-priced, low-quality to expensive, high quality textiles and apparel. This gave them a new thrust in their export promotion strategy. This approach was launched to take advantage of the selective agreements concluded by the EEC with Hong Kong, Korea, Singapore and Japan. Exporters diversified exports among EEC member countries since restrictions to specific products were applied separately by each country.

Recently the United States' customs has set up pre-emptive quota restraints on seven new made-in Singapore garments (Newsletter of the Singapore Textile and Garment Manufacturers Association, 1984). It said that, although the new curb would have no immediate impact on Singapore, as these articles were not yet in production, it constituted a warning should they decide to make these items for export to the United States later on.

Intra-industry adjustments discussed above have failed to allow the protectionist coalition to freeze the industry. In the first two months of 1984 alone, Singapore's exports of textile and garment products recorded an increase of 26 per cent (Newsletter of the Singapore Textile and Garment Manufacturers Association, June 1984).

The footwear industry is another industry in which south-east Asian producers, faced with quantitative limits of the volume of exports through the Orderly Marketing Agreements, scored a success through intra-industry production and sales strategies that left them in even stronger positions in the Western export markets (Yoffie, 1983).

Since 1974 Korea and Taiwan had accounted for 100 per cent of the increase in imports into the

United States. In 1977 the Carter administration negotiated for export restrictions with Taiwan and Korea but, despite these restrictions, by 1979 half the United States' domestic market was supplied by exports from these countries. The Orderly Marketing Agreements negotiated with Korea and Taiwan were selective restraints that limited the quantity of exports of only a few dynamic producers. These restrictions by their very nature tend to facilitate adjustments by the exporters. Taiwan and Korea through an 'incentive system' were forced to upgrade and diversify their product lines into the strength of the American producers' market (Korea Herald, 1977). New producers in low-wage countries like Hong Kong, unrestrained by Orderly Marketing Agreements, made an easy entry into the low-priced products which are homogeneous and require very low skill and small amounts of capital. As a result exports from Hong Kong jumped by 225 per cent in one year.

Quantitative restrictions had another positive effect on east and south-east Asia. It compelled restrained producers in these countries to keep down the cost of production by improving the productivity of labour. Secondly, to avoid long-term losses in revenue, these countries moved into dynamic markets - through deliberate government export promotional tours to East European and African countries. These unrestricted markets provided high levels of profits compared to the restricted markets.

The period of much needed adjustments to these industries to sustain their comparative advantage has also led to the third phase of industrialization with an emphasis on heavy industries. Malaysia, on the basis of her petroleum reserves, instituted a Malaysian Corporation of Heavy Industries (HICOM). In South Korea, the government invested US$6 million with chemical, basic metal and machinery industries in the latter part of the 1970s, fulfilling 97 per cent of the target set out in the fourth Five-Year plan. In South Korea, the proportion of total value added in manufacturing contributed by the heavy industry group increased from 21.6 per cent in 1954 to 52.9 per cent by 1981 (Development Bank of Korea, 1982). The need to move into skill-intensive and capital-intensive heavy industries was also recognized in Taiwan. Under this category steel, non-ferrous metals, basic petrochemicals and their derivatives, such as fertilizers, were emphasized. The contribution of heavy industries to total value of manufactured products increased from 32.7 per cent in 1954 to 62.2 per cent in 1981 in Taiwan (Statistical Yearbook 1983).

Consensus within the government of each country, namely of South Korea, Taiwan and Singapore, was reached that there was need to step up their development of high value added technology-intensive industries that are small users of labour. In Singapore investment commitments indicate a trend towards restructuring into higher value-added and technology-intensive products, such as wafer diffusion in the semiconductor industry, computers and computer peripheral equipment, directional drilling equipment and CNC lathes (Ministry of Trade, 1981). Census of industrial production 1980 also reveals that capital-intensive industries employed 18 per cent of all Singapore's industrial workers (Department of Statistics, 1981). In Korea the Eight Year Electronics Industry Plan (1969-1976) was set up (Development Bank of Korea, 1980). With the assistance of the plan the electronics industry recorded an average annual growth rate of 45 per cent and more than 50 per cent of annual export growth rate during the 1970s. In 1981 exports of the electronics industry accounted for 10 per cent of total national exports. In Taiwan, the 1980s are also earmarked for research and development and the introduction of advanced technologies. Taiwan's current Ten Year Economic Development Plan (1980-89) will have a marked influence on government investments with 34 per cent of the fixed capital investments allocated to manufacturing (Samuel Ho, 1981). In 1983, 1.06 per cent of Gross National Product in Korea, too, was spent on research and development (Ministry of Science and Technology, 1983).

In these, East and South-east Asian countries' attempts are under way to identify avenues of backward and forward linkages with the earlier labour-intensive assembly plants. The liberal free enterprise, but local-foreign joint-venture, strategy is indicative of the recognition of the economic power of present day multinational monopolies and the catalytic promotional role of foreign investment in drawing domestic capital and entrepreneurs into new production lines and processes. These countries state explicity that learning from scratch is a costly business. Singapore's petroleum refining and Malaysia's Bintulu liquid natural gas projects are testimony to this trend of thought and action.

SOCIETAL GUIDANCE APPROACH TO ECONOMIC AND SOCIAL POLICY INTERVENTION

The history of these newly industrializing countries after World War Two has been one of continuous enlargement of government functions in the economic realm. This priority defines 'their essence' (Johnson, 1982). First priority is given to economic development and to industrialization as a means of achieving a higher rate of economic development. 'Consistency and continuity of their top priority generated a learning process' that has made each state much more effective from the second phase of development when they became directly involved in industrial activity. The varying levels of involvement and success achieved within this group at the time of the 1980s reflect the degree of effectiveness of the adaptation process to the series of crises that assail the individual nation.

The high-growth systems, like the basic priorities of the states, have been a matter of deliberate choice based on the past economic record and success of the Japanese model of development. Nevertheless they do not lend themselves to mere institutional abstraction. The ideal trajectories reveal that the timing, the creation and the combination of institutions, financial, investment and control devices lead ultimately to the sum total of the states' adaptive process through the collective wisdom of their bureaucrats.

Developmentalism had its roots in the characteristics of the countries discussed earlier. It emerged with the elite national leaders who were trained abroad. The apprehensions of vulnerability of newly independent, small peripheral states pointed towards the goal of economic strength and the futility of military build up. A rational economic approach seemed in order. Managerial skills of the nations were tested in each subsequent time-specific plan and evaluated in the mid-term reviews. But policy intervention cannot take place in a value free context. It invokes the ideological position of the state. Acceptance as a criterion of evaluation of goal-oriented activity poses the social problem of what ideological route to pursue to solve these problems and to build a viable nation. Etzioni's conceptual contribution to societal guidance approach is most relevant to the discussion on these nations, as it attempts to answer in what ways and under what circumstances people understand and control their collective conditions (Etzioni, 1976). Two basic assumptions are followed in the approach adopted by these nations. The awareness that human needs are universal and, secondly, that different societies differ in the extent to which they are able to satisfy members' needs. Societal guidance approach involves 'upward processes' of three basic elements, state's responsiveness to basic human needs, formation of an authentic consensus and an egalitarian distribution of power. In other words it involves deliberate societal change (Stella R. Quah, 1984).

The ideological route pursued by these newly independent nations is to combine social displine on the basis of authentic consensus. Three alternatives pursued by industrialized nations and other Third World nations are democracy, various styles of socialism and others unwilling or unable to create authentic consensus have resorted to totalitarianism (Stella R. Quah, 1984). In the industrialized nations, democracy incorporates the requirements of building 'an authentic consensus'. Democracies first seek to build up a consensus before acting. In a societal guidance approach Etzioni is aware of the unequal distributions of power among a plurality of social 'groups' in society. He credits the government with significant capacity for autonomous action as long as such autonomy in power is derived mainly from the 'principle of legitimation for replacing sheer force with authority that can command the loyalty and willing compliance of those subject to it' (Etzioni, 1976). These nations are distinct from both totalitarian and typical present day democratic societies. We are all too familiar with the characteristics of democratic government, as a political system in which the rule of law sustains public liberties under a government elected by universal suffrage. In these new nations periodic free elections contribute to human freedom as they serve to check the power of executive and legislative officials.

Trajectories of newly industrializing countries are relevant as they show the presence of crisis situations and of timing. The crisis-economic survival and nation building; the dilemma of timing poses the question of whether a democratic regime can survive in nations with stagnant economic development or whether the society must undergo a basic economic revolution first before a democratic regime can be implemented. Barrington Moore discusses the 'democratic route to modern society'

that economic development derived from a revolutionary break with the past is a precondition for the development of democracy (Moore, 1966). How do you maintain individual freedom and initiative and yet have centralized social control and planning of the economic life of people (Mecord, The Springtime)? The questions alert the predicament of leadership committed to democratic principles and pressed to attend to economic survival of the nation-states.

The approach devised by these nations is one based on social discipline and rational planning. Social discipline with rational planning can be defined as a compliance with guidelines of behaviour, i.e. policies established by democratically elected decision-makers and designed to attain national goals (Quah, 1984). This compliance defined by Quah 'implies the acceptance and upholding of the principles of self-restraint in favour of the common goal wherever the implementation of means to attain national goals requires it'. Social discipline facilitates consensus building since 'a variety of conflicting groups manage to submerge, at least in part, opposing values and interest' beneath a sense of shared concern. What is in the 'public interest' or 'fair' is therefore accepted.

The technical amplification in the analysis process of social discipline brings to the forefront the issue of 'infliction of pain - active infliction or the passive acceptance of pain' (Berger, 1974). Proponents of individualism would assert that social discipline defined above does involve 'passive acceptance of pain'. When a society is motivated to comply with policies aimed at solving social and economic problems, 'the boundary between self-restraint and passive acceptance of pain is not easily identifiable' (Quah, 1984). We could argue that the question of value judgement is present here but that in the newly developing countries it is possible to conceive as morally acceptable policies designed to satisfy the basic needs of the majority of the population, although it requires the temporary (short or medium term) postponement of satisfaction of high-level needs of some individuals or a minority of the population. Following also this line of argument, the prospect of gratification of one's needs - in terms of higher income and higher standards of living - i.e. effectiveness of the policy motivates the individual to take a given course of action. In other words, when a policy is perceived as the most effective means of achieving high-level of economic (material) performance, people are likely to comply with the requirements of such a policy collectively in a disciplined manner.

Delving into the 'meaning of life' beyond the functional rationality of public institutions is the issue of how individual members of society are provided with an opportunity to satisfy their high-level needs and aspirations through participation in the nation's decision-making process (Quah, 1984). The trajectories indicate the importance of the democratic procedures in the planning and implementation of national development. Empirical illustrations emphasize the continuing of democratic elections - optimum participation in decision-making for the total population to select those in power, to retain and expel them subsequently.

Social discipline and rational planning have been in action in these states in all spheres, social and economic. Problem-solving takes the form of swift policy intervention producing radical changes in the population attitudes and behaviour and structural changes in the economy, while maintaining a stable political regime. Apart from the changes in the economic front, social problems are tackled with equal vigour.

Singapore's housing policy continued to be one of the top priorities in the government's development plan after 1965 when it realized that it was a serious social problem. Well before 1965, 250,000 people were living in slums and another 250,000 were squatters. The government created a suitable implementation mechanism by establishing the Housing and Development Board (HDB). Vast sums of money have been injected by the government to secure the success of the scheme. Even in 1980, a third of the total government development estimates for the financial year 1980/81 were allocated to the HDB. By 1980, 346,371 HDB apartments had been built, accommodating 68 per cent of the total population and 42 per cent of the total population are proprietors of the HDB built, subsidized houses (Quah, 1984).

Population control policy has also followed the same guidelines. In Singapore, for example, the average population growth rate from 1947 to 1953 was 4.2 per cent; from 1956 to 1965 it declined slightly to 3.6 per cent, but it was brought down to 1.28 per cent from 1980. The population control policies illustrate institutional interventions through a conscious and calculated action by government bodies through disincentives and incentives to change the people's attitude and behaviour regarding fertility and family size.

The very combination of authentic consensus, social discipline and rational planning represents a difficult and constant challenge. The challenge is threefold - to continue and expand the democratic process of decision-making, maintain people's voluntary compliance with national policies, and select appropriate rational policies for attaining industrial development corresponding with satisfaction from basic lower needs to higher-level needs of the majority population.

Participation in Decision-Making

Technically, elections represent the electorate's participation in decision-making. The general elections and by-elections provide the citizen with the opportunity to confirm or withdraw his support for the political leadership in power. Even subsequent elections reaffirm the popular contentment with the government's programmes and the people's identification with the policies of the party in power. These periodic opportunities are not allowed to lose their significance as instruments of participation in decision-making. They are followed up by fostering private sector participation and implementing private sector joint-ventures with government agencies.

An empirical viewpoint of the system in action reveals a possible shortcoming of situational imperatives of high growth plant-rational, social disciplined societies. The shortcoming is the impossibility of a long-term coexistence of strong technocratic leadership wielding direct government intervention and using effectively mechanisms of consensus and egalitarianism distribution of power. The Malaysian and Singapore experiences are discussed to show how consensus is achieved.

By 1955 the Alliance party included the United Malaya National Organization (UMNO), the Malaysian Chinese Association (MCA) and Malayan Indian Congress (MIC). It had the support of all the different ethnic communities to qualify for prospective government when the British handed over power in 1957. It has been the party in power ever since and has won elections in 1955, 1959, 1964, 1974 and 1979, providing the much needed political stability.

Apart from the ruling party as an alliance of

the three major communal parties, there is a number of parties in opposition but none had a national spread. The 1969 elections gave the Alliance a reduced Federal majority. At the State level, Alliance lost to opposition parties or opposition party coalitions in a few states.

With the growing Malay nationalism the need for political consensus in the sense of broadening the base of the alliance was sought. The western model of democracy was adjusted to local conditions. Elements of ambiguity in political relationships between various ethnic groups were eliminated through a pattern of extensive coalition of opposition parties from 1972 onwards. The term 'National Front' was formulated. It was a national front among political parties to work together in facing national development problems. It was a formal organization which would create permanent coalition. The common National Front symbol was used in the 1974 elections and it was registered as a confederation of political parties. Thus, UMNO became the decisive political power in Malaysia. The stable socio-political situation through political consensus was created as a prerequisite for planned socio-economic revolution to be spearheaded through the New Economic Policy. Parliamentary elections are more in the form of a referendum, and the Federal Government device is the instrument by which development is induced and channelled. The Malaysian Development Policy System contains the elements in a vertical array where development policy, the money, power and information that are its impulses, are moved through Federal institutions to and through area units of organization - State, District and urban centres.

Likewise, Singapore has maintained a parliamentary system, and parliament is elected every five years. The People's Action party recorded success in all six general elections since 1959 and, apart from 1959, it has won all the seats in Parliament. It has had a de facto one party system since it has won all the seats in parliament since 1968, and the absense of opposition in parliament may be interpreted as a demonstration of the popular support of the government's policies, rather than an intolerance of opposition and tendency towards authoritarianism.

CHANGES IN THE INTERNATIONAL DIVISON OF LABOUR

In their process of economic engineering it has been

proved that in the newly industrializing countries the state does 'not stand above society' nor does it have its own 'logic or momentum' (Petras, 1984). The strength of the state can only be understood in terms of its capacity to motivate and generate, through social discipline and plan rationality, productive forces and convert them into productive activity for the satisfaction of the majority. The priorities are shaped by mass organizations and relative egalitarian norms (Petras 1984).

This size and scope of state activity associate with 'free enterprise'. The complementarity of state interventionism and private enterprise is clearly evident. The growth of autonomous public corporations, para-statals and state investment and trading houses are part of the new empire. Joint business ventures between private and public, local and foreign are the order of the day.

Growth of international finance capital as western banks recycled petro-dollars and surplus profits of multinational corporations create a vast source of direct financing for new state activity. The growing state debt and the financial ties of all peripheral states to the private money markets is another feature. Loans go to finance productive activity. The public sector has grown in these capitalist societies, the private sector continues to draw substantial personnel, resources and subsidies from the public sector. There is a tendency for employees and executives, who gain power and wealth in the public sector to convert these resources to the private. The interchange of roles (between private and public) and the linkages between the two contribute to the subordination of the public to the private sector.

As public enterprises become profitable there is a tendency to sell off the profitable public firms and for the state to remain with the less lucrative operations. Through linkages with multinationals, the peripheral state forges an alliance to promote industrial exports. In these combined forces, state and local capital seek to modify their role in the world division of labour, entering into competition with imperial countries for industrial markets. Joint venture industrial activity, where local capital is spawned by the multinationals became the agents of competitive capitalism in the world.

The push for industrial results from a programmatic position, or in part because of conversion of merchant groups to industrial entrepreneurs or because of various crisis situations outlined earlier, has led to extensive industrialization in these peripheral states. These revolutionary regimes depended on external financing and technology for developing their capacity for production. As seen from the trajectories the society must produce efficiently and at competitive costs with other countries at the international level. Under peripheral capitalism the state sector is growing in the high cost - low profit upstream and infrastructural sectors, while the low cost - high profit downstream manufacturing and processing sectors are in private hands. The process of comprehensive socialization undertaken by societal guidance regimes ensures that these occurrences are reduced.

While these nations stand at the periphery of technico-economic development the more complex position of the state - being socio-political centres and technico-economic centres - requires some conception of the world order and an evaluation of their industrial performance and their role in the world-wide transition to a new economic order.

There has emerged a number of theorists who have called into being a 'New International Division of Labour' in which the old colonial division of labour involving Third World exports of raw materials and importation of finished goods has been transcended (Martin Landsberg, 1970). The proponents of the new division of labour argue that the accompanying industrialization of the Third World reflects the new world capitalist rationality and logic. We will examine the performance of these newly industrializing countries over the twenty year period 1960 to 1980 to assess these assertions.

In 1960 the percentage share of primary commodities to total exports of the countries discussed varied from a high of 98 per cent for Thailand, 96 per cent for Korea, to 94 per cent for Malaysia. Even three-quarters of Singapore's entrepot trade was mainly in primary export commodities. Twenty years later, apart from the two resource rich nations, where primary exports still account for 80 and 84 per cent of exports, the positive role of manufacturing exports is discernible in all these newly industrializing countries. Percentage differences in the two decades of manufacturing exports vary from 74 per cent in South Korea, to 17-20 per cent in the rest. In the Malaysian situation, the high percentage of primary exports needs to be qualified in that rubber, which accounted for 33 per cent of the exports, declined in importance to 17 per cent by 1980. Mineral exports took its place, accounting for one-third of the exports. In mineral exports, 73 per cent of the increase is attributed to the export of crude petroleum; 25.5 per cent of total commodity exports is crude petroleum. The 8-10 per cent or more level of development in the national economy is also a good indicator of the propensity of these countries to shift their role in international division of labour. South Korea, Hong Kong and Taiwan are three leading countries in the industrial exports of textiles, clothing and footwear. They show a definite shift in exports towards non-primary goods between 1960 and 1980.

The actual growth of industrial exports indicates that all these countries demonstrated substantial growth. Non-primary products accounted for 50 per cent of total exports in Hong Kong, South Korea, Taiwan, and Singapore in the 1980s. Thus the trend towards a new international division of labour is evident, although critics modify this view with the comment that consumer non-durables comprise the bulk of industrial exports. Textiles and clothing account for 36 per cent of South Korean, 30 per cent of Taiwanese and 44 per cent of Hong Kong's industrial exports. Essentially this category of products is hardly a basis for sweeping assertions concerning a new international division of labour. But such conclusive remarks obscure the fundamental issues that confront the newly industrializing countries in south-east Asia.

The real issue is the very limited opening of industrial markets in the western industrial countries, the constraints on industrial financing and the constriction to the transfer of technology. Hong Kong, South Korea, Taiwan and Singapore's experiences and success are laudable, since they have been achieved in the face of extreme odds discussed earlier. The problem at hand is not the incapacity of East and South-east Asian countries to break into new markets but the formidable walls and intransigencies of the metropolitan countries in resisting the creation of a New International Division of Labour. Their resistance to industrial change has been discussed earlier. The level of industrial exports that have taken place from these countries is largely the result of revolutionary policies of successful economic engineering and adjustment and the assistance of competitive capitalism, namely the role of multinationals in seeking out genuine comparative advantages at global scale. In the newly industrializing countries of east and south-east Asia, multinational capital seems to have played a major role in redefining the region's participation in the International Division of Labour. They have extended their sphere of influence from the traditional International Division of Labour with the concentration on primary product exports to the New Division of Labour, with emphasis on the export of manufactured goods. Competitive capitalism has also paved the way for national capital and local big business and public corporations to transform more and more the economic structure of these countries. The state and multinational capital thorough a policy of joint-ventures (that define ownership and control, with the latter leading in new technologically-advanced ventures and the former in technologically-simple ventures, where technology transfer has taken place) have become increasingly important in defining the durability of their new position in the International Division of Labour.

BIBLIOGRAPHY

Aggarwal, V.K., Stephen Harrard, 'The Politics of Protection in the United States Textile and Apparel Industries', in American Industry in International Competition, (Cornell University Press, 1983) pp.249-312

Berger, P.L., 'Pyramids of Sacrifice', Political and Social Change, (Penguin, Middlesex, England, 1978)

Borrus, Millstein and Zysman, 'Trade and Development in the Semi-Conductor Industry', in American Industry in International Competition (Cornell University Press, 1983)

Byung-Kwon Cha, 'Import Substitution and Industrialization: The Korean Case', in Asian Economies, Seoul, Korea, Dec. 1972

Cukor, G. Strategies of Industrialization in the Developing Countries (G. Hurst & Company, London, 1971)

Etzioni, A., Social Problems (Prentice Hall, Englewood Cliffs, N.J., 1976)

Gavan McCormack and Jon Halliday, 'The Tokyo-Taipei-Seoul Nexus', in Journal of Contemporary Asia, vol. 2, 1971

Glaser, B. and Strauss, A. The Discovery of Grounded Theory, Strategies for Quantitative Research,

1967

Harold Ha Kwon Sunoo, 'Economic Development and Foreign Control in South Korea', in Journal of Contemporary Asia, vol. 8, no.3, (Stockholm 49, Sweden, 1978), pp.322-37

Johnson, Chalmers, MITI and the Japanese Miracle (Stamford University Press, Stamford, California, 1982)

International Financial Statistics, IMF, in Data Asia, 30 November - 6 December 1981, vol.X, no.49

Landsberg, Martin, 'Export-Led Industrialization in the Third World: Manufacturing Imperialism', The Review of Radical Political Economies, vol.II, no.4, 1970, pp.50-63

Lim, David, 'Export-oriented Industrialization: A Case Study of Malasia', in Kajian Ekonomi Malaysia, vol.3, no.2, 1970

Moore, B. Social Origins of Dictatorship and Democracy (Beacon Press, Boston, 1969)

Paauw and Fei, The Transition in Open Dualistic Economies - Theory and Southeast Asian Experience (Yale University Press, 1973)

Petras, James, 'The "Peripheral State": Continuity and Change in the International Division of Labour', Journal of Contemporary Asia, 1984, pp.415-31

Quah, S.R., 'Social Discipline in Singapore: An Alternative for the Resolution of Social Problems', Journal of Southeast Asian Studies (Singapore University Press, September 1983)

Samir Amin, 'After the New International Economic Order: The Future of International Economic Relations' Journal of Contemporary Asia, vol.12, no.4, 1984

Samuel Ho, P.S. 'South Korea and Taiwan Development Prospects and Problems in the 1980s', in Asia Survey, vol.XXI, no.12, (University of California Press, December 1981), pp.1175-95

Sano, J.R., 'Foreign Capital and Investment in South Korean Development in Asian Economies' Research Institute of Asian Economies, no.23 (Seoul, Korea, December 1977)

Sharon Siddique, 'Family Trajectory: An Alternative to the Family Life Cycle Model', paper presented at Research Seminar on Third World Urbanization and the Household Economy, June 1983

Singapore: Report on the Census of Industrial Production 1980, (Department of Statistics, Singapore, December 1981)

East and South-East Asia

Strauss, Anselm and Glaser, Barney Anguish *A Case History of a Dying Trajectory*, 1971

The Korea Development Bank, *Industry of Korea*, Seoul 1980

Tyson, L. and Zysman, J. *American Industry in International Competition* (Cornell University 1983), pp.15-59

Wiseman, of Policy Intervention in Social Problems', *Social Problems*, 21, 1, 1979

Wong, John, *Asean Economies in Perspective 3*, (The MacMillan Press Limited, London, 1979)

World Bank Development Reports 1979, 1980 (Washington, World Bank)

Yoffie, D.B., 'Adjustment in the Footwear Industry: The Consequences of Orderly Marketing Agreements', in *American Industry in International Competition* (Cornell University Press, 1983), pp.313-49

CHAPTER 15

REGIONAL CHANGES IN THE INDUSTRIAL SYSTEM OF A NEWLY INDUSTRIALIZING COUNTRY: THE CASE OF KOREA

Sam Ock Park

This chapter sets out the results to date of an ongoing research project, analyzing the dynamics of operating units in the industrial system and particularly the influence of large enterprises on regional development in the Republic of Korea. About one hundred 'Groups' (conglomerates) have been organized in Korea during the last decade. These groups altogether control more than 800 firms which operate on a national or multinational basis. Firms in a 'group' are officially independent of each other, are controlled directly or indirectly by the group headquarters and are more or less interrelated with each other within the group. Leading and shaping Korean industrial growth and dynamics, it is not surprising that 10 of the groups are included in Fortune's 500 largest world enterprises (1983) outside the USA and, being international in their activity space, have helped make Korea one of the newly industrializing countries (NICs) in the world industrial system.

The major research questions addressed in the present study are as follows: how do the large enterprises in an NIC affect locational changes in manufacturing? Do the large national firms contribute towards Korean regional and local economies? What are the roles played by the firms in moulding and shaping spatial division of labour? How are operating units interrelated within a large enterprise, and what are the major processes of locational changes in the operating units?

There has been increasing recognition in the last decade that local industries are becoming more and more linked with regional, national and international economic systems, a trend which may support or may conflict with the need for a new international economic order (Hamilton and Linge,

1979, 1981). It has been a rather common phenomenon that, as large enterprises have increased their dominance in most national economies, both they and the government have often reformulated their industrial policies and shifted decision making to keep up with their changing roles in the national economy. Such changes of policies and strategies have resulted in turn in further changes in the industrial systems.

The behaviour of multiregional firms has become an important research theme, and many have urged studying 'the influence of the policies and organizational structures of large enterprises on changes in industrial location and on processes of regional economic development' (Hayter and Watts, 1983, p.157). In addition, the rise in the share of the NICs in the international trade in manufactures has been regarded as the most significant aspect in the operation of global industrial systems in the 1970s (Linge and Hamilton, 1981, p.19). Despite the recognition of these issues, there remains a dearth of empirical studies. While several research efforts have been made to identify the impacts of large enterprises on the regional economy in developed countries (e.g. Bade, 1983; Blackbourn, 1978; Kemper and Smidt, 1980; O'Farrell, 1980; Watts, 1979), their findings cannot be directly applied to the NICs.

DATA AND METHODOLOGY

Most data for this study were derived from directories of Korean business published in 1979 and 1982/3 and from a questionnaire survey conducted during the period April - June 1984. The directories of Korean business contain, for each firm, information on the locations of firm headquarters, plants and branch offices, current employment sizes and product types. The directories also have a list of organized 'groups' and the firms which belong to each of the groups.

A questionnaire was mailed to each of the 100 groups, followed up by a telephone call reminder to all non-responding groups. A total of 45 groups (45 per cent of all groups) answered the questionnaire. The survey revealed that 32 of these groups were set up before 1978, and these were chosen for the study of the dynamics of operating units. The responses of the 32 groups yielded 315 firms, of which 194 firms are in manufacturing, operating 324 plants and 121 branch offices.

Operating units in an industrial system can be divided into: (1) production units: (2) associated units such as offices, laboratories and research and development facilities; and (3) industry-related units such as those selling manufactured goods and providing after-sales services (Hamilton and Linge, 1979, p.6). In this study, manufacturing plants and headquarters are regarded as production units and associated units respectively. Branch offices, which perform sales and after services in separated locations, are industry-related units. However, some branch offices in Seoul conduct information-gathering and some decision making, and their roles resemble those of the associated units.

Primary information on operating units was examined to identify how the groups performed during the recent recession and political fluctuations in Korea. Opening and closure of each unit in each group were examined from both spatial and temporal perspectives. Previous studies have shown that larger, multiregional firms, in general, represent the leading firms in locational dynamics and that branch plants are a major mechanism of locational dynamic process (Erickson, 1976, 1981; Erickson and Leinbach, 1979; Park and Wheeler, 1983). Assuming that most of the products of national firms in Korea are highly standardized, it is hypothesized in this study that the groups have contributed to the establishment of the spatial division of labour and to the filtering down process within the Korean urban system.

Decision makers in group headquarters and the proportion of intra-group material linkages were also investigated in the questionnaire survey. Firm headquarters are most likely to have authority in higher-order decision making, while the production units of multiregional firms have only very limited decision making authority (Watts, 1981; Wheeler and Park 1984), and this hypothesis is accepted here.

To examine the spatial dynamics of operating units, Korea is divided into five areas: Seoul and Kyŏnggi Province; Pusan and South Kyŏngsang Province; Taegu and North Kyŏngsang Province; 'other cities' larger than 100,000 in population; and other small cities with less than 100,000 population and rural areas ('other rural counties'). Even though there is no official definition of metropolitan areas in Korea, Seoul and Kyŏnggi, Pusan and South Kyŏngsang, and Taegu and North Kyŏngsang are regarded for convenience as the Seoul, Pusan and Taegu metropolitan areas respectively (Figure 15.1)

Figure 15.1: Cities over 100,000 persons and Provinces in South Korea

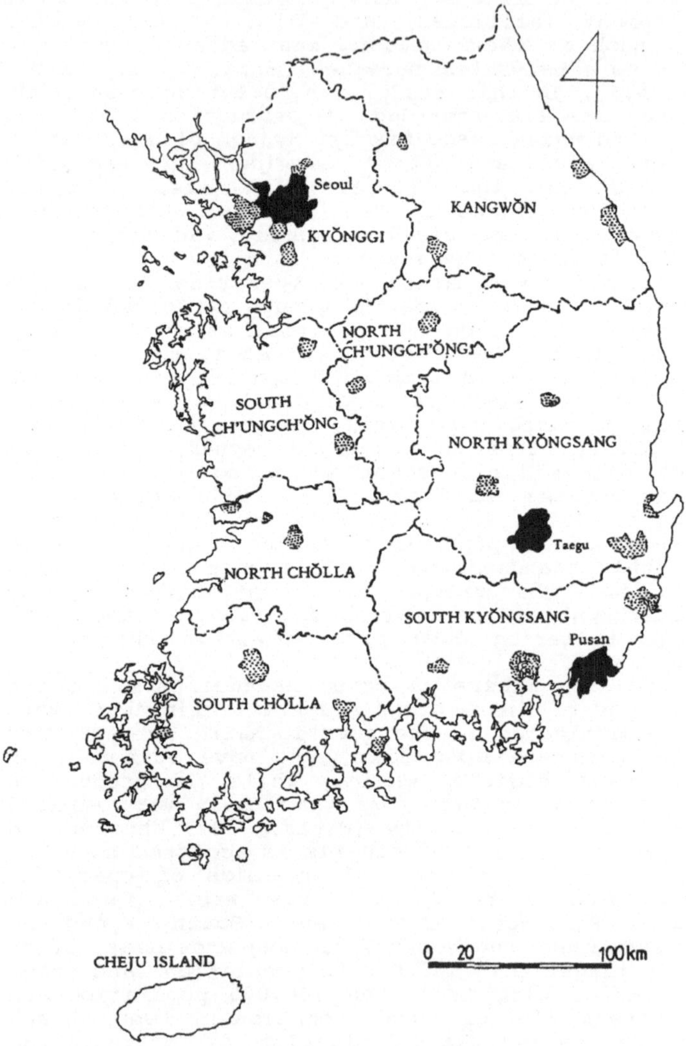

A BRIEF HISTORY OF INDUSTRIALIZATION AND INDUSTRIAL STRATEGIES IN KOREA

Korea has experienced rapid economic growth and industrialization during the last three decades (Table 15.1), generally related to a high growth of manufacturing. Since the First-Five-Year Economic Development Plan, launched in 1962, industrialization progressed rapidly, with considerable changes in industrial structure and development of new industries. Exports have grown with annual growth rates of more than 35 per cent since the late 1960s, a trend related to the structural changes in exports associated with the expansion of manufacturing.

Rapid industrialization and structural change could not be achieved without government support and industrial strategies in Korea. Industrial strategies during the 1950s were domestic-orientated, and import substitution of consumer goods was emphasized. The reconstruction of the economy from the destruction in the Korean War was one of the major tasks of the government. In the early 1960s, the government felt that its input substitution policy would not be able to achieve rapid economic growth, even though it would contribute to some increase in the share of manufacturing to GNP. Accordingly, export promotion began to be emphasized in accordance with selective emphasis of input substitution during the first half of the 1960s, which can be characterized as a transition period (Kim, 1980).

Export-orientated industrialization has been the major industrial strategy since the late 1960s. Then and the early 1970s unbalanced growth in sector as well as in space was emphasized (Park and Wheeler, 1983). In the early state of export-orientated industrialization, textile and apparel were the key industries for export growth, but later the development of heavy and chemical industries was greatly emphasized. Spatial policy designs for industrial location were introduced in the early 1970s. The Local Industrial Development Law (1971) was the result of the first specific policy to address industrial dispersion. The First Ten Year Comprehensive National Land Development Plan (1972-81) intended to disperse industrial plants from Seoul to designated areas throughout the nation.

The sectoral and spatial industrial policies and a rapid economic growth, however, resulted in

Table 15.1: Major Statistics of Industrialization in Korea

		1964	1966	1971	1976	1981	1982
Industrial origin of GNP (per cent):	(primary	46.5	34.4	26.8	23.5	16.2	14.8
	(mining & manufacturing	17.2	20.2	22.3	28.4	30.2	29.5
Persons employed by industry (per cent):	(primary	61.9	57.9	48.4	44.6	34.2	29.7***
	(mining & manufacturing	8.8	10.8	14.2	21.8	21.3	23.3***
Per cent of heavy industries* to total manufacturing value added		26.3**	34.1	39.3	46.8	52.9	-
Export by products:	(agriculture and marine products	30.3	24.2	10.5	9.1	6.5	5.2***
	(manufactured goods	51.6	62.4	86.0	89.	92.9	94.4***

* Heavy industries include chemicals, petroleum, primary metals, machinery and transport equipment
** Value of 1961
*** Value of 1983

Source: Economic Planning Board, Major Statistics of Korean Economy, 1984

bipolar concentration of population and economic activities in the Seoul and Pusan metropolitan areas. Furthermore, investments in heavy and chemical industries were generally in larger enterprises, and accordingly these benefited from the unbalanced sectoral strategy, while small and medium-sized firms were in comparatively unfavourable situations (Nam, 1981).

Over-concentration of population and economic activities in Seoul is now an urgent issue in view of both economic efficiency and equity. With the problems of over-concentration, the Second Comprehensive National Physical Development Plan (1982-91) focuses on a balanced national land development through harmonizing industrial dispersion with agglomeration economies. The industrial distribution plan comprises: (1) industrial redistribution in the Seoul and Pusan areas; (2) expansion of the south-eastern coastal industrial belt and consolidation of existing industries in the belt; (3) industrial expansion in provincial medium-to-large cities; and (4) industrial development of rural supporting centres.

The export-orientated industrial strategy in the 1980s emphasizes development of technology-intensive industry and high quality products with increasing R&D investments. The percentage of R&D expenditure to GNP was quite low, but recently the share is considerably increasing (Table 15.2). The government encourages investments in new technology development and in technology-intensive industry, with planned establishment of 'technopolises' in provincial medium cities.

LOCATIONAL PATTERNS OF OPERATING UNITS OF THE 32 'GROUPS' IN 1984

More than 96 per cent of all headquarters spatially separated from their plants (separated HQs) in the 32 'groups' are concentrated in the city of Seoul, representing marked spatial division of labour (Table 15.3). The rate of concentration of separated headquarters in the prime city is much higher than the rates in Japan and other developed countries (Abe, 1984; Stephens and Holly, 1980; Strickland and Aiken, 1984). Headquarters unseparated from their plants (unseparated HQs), or plants unseparated from their headquarters (unseparated plants), show a similar locational pattern to plants separated from their headquarters (separated plants). However,

Table 15.2: R&D Expenditure in Korea

Year	1972	1974	1976	1978	1980	1982	1983	1984	1986
Percent of R&D Expenditure to GNP	0.31	0.52	0.46	0.67	0.62	0.95	1.06	1.46	2.00*

* projected value

Source: Ministry of Science and Technology, _Science and Technology Annual_, 1983

Table 15.3: Location of Firm Headquarters (HQs) and Plants of the 32 Groups

Employment size	Separated HQs					Unseparated HQs (Unseparated plants)					Separated plants				
	≥500	100-499	10-99	subtotal	%	≥500	100-499	10-99	subtotal	%	≥500	100-499	10-99	subtotal	%
Seoul and Kyŏnggi	56	39	17	112	(98.2)	15	26	1	42	(52.5)	68	33	12	113	(46.3)
Seoul	55	38	17	110	(96.5)	7	8	.	15	(18.7)	25	8	1	34	(13.9)
Cities*	1	1	.	2	(1.8)	4	11	1	16	(20.0)	27	11	7	45	(18.4)
Rural counties**	.	.	.	.		4	7	.	11	(13.8)	16	14	4	34	(13.9)
Pusan and S. Kyŏngsang	.	.	.	.		14	8	.	22	(27.5)	43	19	5	67	(27.5)
Pusan	.	.	.	.		3	2	.	5	(6.2)	18	10	1	29	(11.9)
Cities*	.	.	.	.		9	4	.	13	(16.3)	17	4	4	25	(10.2)
Rural counties**	.	.	.	.		2	2	.	4	(5.0)	8	5	.	13	(5.3)
Taegu and N. Kyŏngsang	.	1	.	1	(0.9)	1	7	1	9	(11.2)	17	5	1	23	(9.4)
Taegu	.	.	.	.		.	4	1	5	(6.3)	5	2	1	7	(2.9)
Cities*	.	.	.	.		1	2	.	3	(3.7)	10	2	1	13	(5.3)
Rural counties**	.	1	.	1	(0.9)	3	1	.	1	(1.3)	2	1	.	3	(1.2)
Other cities**	.	.	1	1	(0.9)	3	.	.	3	(3.7)	14	5	3	22	(9.0)
Other rural counties**	.	.	.	.		.	2	2	4	(5.0)	8	9	2	19	(7.8)
Total	56	40	18	114	(100.0)	33	43	4	80	(100.0)	150	71	23	244	(100.0)

* Cities more than 100,000 population in 1980

** Rural counties represent small cities less than 100,000 population and rural areas

Source: Compiled and calculated from the questionnaire survey by the author

separated plants are more dispersed to 'other cities' and 'rural counties'. The three metropolitan areas, Seoul, Pusan and Taegu, account for about 83 per cent and 91 per cent of locations of separated plants and unseparated plants, respectively. This 8 percentage point difference of the plant concentration in the metropolitan areas reflects the greater diffusion of separated plants amongst lower-order urban centres and dispersion to 'other rural counties' than the unseparated plants. Compared with the locational pattern of all the separated plants in Korea, the separated plants of the 'groups' are less located in small cities and rural areas of the Seoul metropolitan area (Table 15.3) and are more diffused within the national urban system than those of non-'groups'.

To examine the dynamics of plant location of the groups, the separated plants are classified according to the year of establishment in four time periods: before 1960; 1960 to 1969; 1970 to 1979; and 1980 to May 1984. The locations of separated plants controlled by the headquarters in Seoul are illustrated in Figure 15.2. Generally the older plants are larger employers. About 50 per cent of the separated plants were established during the 1970s, reflecting the rapid industrialization during the 1970s in Korea. Industrial diffusion from Seoul to lower urban hierarchies has been the most continuuous process of industrial dynamics over the four time periods. New industrial investments in the Pusan metropolitan area from Seoul had much advanced during the 1960s and the 1970s. Emphasis on heavy and chemical industries during the late 1960s and the 1970s is responsible for these new industrial investments in the Pusan metropolitan area and especially along the south-eastern coasts of the Korean peninsula.

Another distinctive process is the industrial decentralization within the Seoul metropolitan region. Small cities and rural areas within the metropolitan area have increased their share of manufacturing plants over time, and during the 1980s more than half of the new separated plants established in the metropolitan area have been located in rural counties. The outer suburbs of Seoul experienced rapid industrialization during the 1980s, a trend which was predicted by an earlier analysis of locational preference of multiplant firms in Korea (Park, 1981).

The diffusion of operating units of the groups can be clearly identified through the locational

Figure 15.2: Location of plants headquartered in Seoul by the year of establishment (A: before 1960; B: 1960 to 1969; C: 1970 to 1979; D: 1980 to May 1984)

Source: Compiled from the questionnaire survey by the author

pattern of branch offices. The numbers of branch offices in major cities correspond well with the hierarchy in the Korean urban system (Table 15.4). Industrial firms headquartered in Seoul usually selected regional (provincial) centres for the location of their branch offices. In Kangwon province, however, the firms selected Wŏnju for their regional branch office location instead of Chunchon, the provincial capital, because of Wŏnju's superior access to Seoul and the rest of the country both by highways and rail.

The concentration of the branch offices of the 32 groups in Seoul is far less than that of branch offices of non-group firms. This difference is not surprising because most of the firms of the groups have headquarters in Seoul and they have established branch offices in provincial cities, mainly for sales of products and services. However, branch offices headquartered in areas other than Seoul are naturally concentrated in the city of Seoul, and their function is similar to that of headquarters.

DYNAMICS OF OPERATING UNITS IN THE INDUSTRIAL SYSTEM

Overall Changes

The locational pattern of groups examined in the previous section is the result of dynamics of industrial organization.

The 32 groups have experienced considerable changes in their industrial organization since 1979. The 32 groups controlled 335 firms, 336 firms and 315 firms at the end of 1978, the end of 1981, and in May 1984 respectively. However, this seemingly small change in the total number of firms concealed the actual change of industrial firms. During the period of 1979 to 1981 (the first period), 39 firms were merged or newly established and 38 firms were closed or reorganized in the groups. During the period from 1981 to May 1984 (the second period), 31 firms were added to the groups, while 52 firms were closed or reorganized (Table 15.5).

The higher rate of firm closures in the second period resulted from consolidation of firms to improve the financial structure of the enterprises. The world-wide recession and political instability in Korea at the end of the 1970s did not immediately affect group organization. With the internal recession and political upheavals, however, firms began to perform poorly in the ealy 1980s. The government forced the groups to consolidate their firms with poor performances. Accordingly the number

Table 15.4: Location of branch offices of Manfuacturing Firms in the 32 Groups

	Total number of branch offices (%)		Headquartered in Seoul (%)		Headquartered in other areas (%)	
Seoul	42	(34.7)	7	(8.6)	35	(87.5)
Pusan	23	(19.9)	20	(24.7)	3	(7.5)
Taegu	13	(10.7)	12	(14.8)	1	(2.5)
Kwanju	9	(7.4)	9	(11.1)		.
Taejon	9	(7.4)	8	(9.9)	1	(2.5)
Wŏnju	7	(5.8)	7	(8.6)		.
Chŏnju	6	(5.0)	6	(7.4)		.
Masan	3	(2.5)	3	(3.7)		.
Kyŏngju	2	(1.7)	2	(2.5)		.
Other cities	7	(5.8)	7	(8.6)		.
Total	121	(100.0)	81	(100.0)	40	(100.0)

Source: Compiled from the questionnaire survey by the author

of firms in the groups decreased considerably in the second period.

Dynamics of manufacturing firms in the groups show a similar pattern of change in the overall firms, including financial firms, construction firms, etc., in the groups. The numbers of manufacturing firms in the 32 groups were 218, 217 and 194 at the end of 1978, the end of 1981, and May 1984, respectively, representing more than a 10 per cent decrease in the number of manufacturing firms in the second period. The rates of closures and additions of the manufacturing firms were more than 10 per cent in each period, and the closure rate of the second period was about 21 per cent, a higher rate of change than the case of all firms in the groups.

The number of plants of the firms in the groups was considerably increased from 310 to 340 during the first period, while there was a decrease from 340 to 324 in the second period. More than 25 per cent of the total plants of the groups had been newly established or merged by the groups in the first period, a fairly high rate of change in production units. In the second period, plant closures exceeded the addition of plants because of consolidation of firms in the groups. Most of the closed plants were in textiles, while most new plants were related to electronics or technology-

Table 15.5: Changes of Operating Units of the 32 Groups

Period	1979-1981				1982-May 1984			
Employment size	≥500	100-499	10-99	subtotal	≥500	100-499	10-99	subtotal
Firms*								
Additions	11	21	7	39 (11.6)**	9	13	9	31 (9.2)**
Closures	17	11	10	38 (11.3)	17	28	7	52 (15.5)
Manufacturing firm headquarters								
Additions	9	12	5	26 (11.9)	6	11	6	23 (10.6)
Closures	16	7	4	27 (12.4)	18	23	5	46 (21.2)
Relocations	1	4	0	5 (2.3)	1	5	0	6 (2.8)
Plants								
Additions	39	29	11	79 (25.5)	21	27	8	56 (16.5)
Closures	27	15	7	49 (15.8)	35	31	6	72 (21.2)
Relocations	4	3	3	10 (3.2)	2	7	0	9 (2.6)
Branch offices								
Additions				10 (8.3)				17 (14.0)
Closures				11 (9.1)				16 (13.2)

* Non-manufacturing firms are also included

** Values in the parentheses are percentages to total existing units of the 32 groups at the beginning of each period.

Source: Compiled and calculated from the questionnaire survey and Directory of Korean Business, 1979 and 1982/3 by the author

intensive industries, reflecting the reorganization of the industrial structure of the groups.

The change in the numbers of branch offices since 1978 has been less than significant, but the rate of change is higher in the second period than in the first period. Generally, the rate of change (births and closures) is higher amongst production units than amongst associated units or industry-related units. Within a same type of operating unit, small units tend to have higher rates of change.

Regional Dynamics

As the separated HQs have concentrated mostly in Seoul, additions and closures of separated HQs occurred mostly in Seoul in both time periods (Table 15.6). Additions of unseparated HQs extended to the three metropolitan areas but 'other cities' or 'other rural counties' have no additions during the the two time periods. Closures of unseparated HQs, however, reveal contrasting patterns in the two time periods. In the first time period, closures of unseparated HQs were limited to the Seoul and Pusan metropolitan areas. The city of Seoul experienced considerable loss of unseparated HQs, while the small cities and rural areas within the Seoul metropolitan area had considerable additions of unseparated HQs. This change in the first time period reveals an accelerating decentralization from the city of Seoul to medium cities within the metropolitan area by single plant firms which have unseparated HQs (or plants).

By contrast, in the second period, the closures extended to the 'other cities' and 'other rural counties', while the Seoul metropolitan area as a whole recorded a comparative gain of unseparated HQs. These contrasting patterns of dynamics during the two time periods possibly indicate that firms which have unseparated HQs and located in areas other than Seoul metropolitan area were in unfavourable conditions to survive during the second period when the groups were asked to consolidate their firms with poor performances.

During the second period most of the closures of branch offices were in the city of Seoul. The closures of branch offices in Seoul appear to be related to the closure of firms which have unseparated HQs in areas other than Seoul. Most of new branch offices in the second period were located in the 'other cities', representing a filtering down of the industry-related units (such as those selling manufactured goods or providing after-sales

Table 15.6: Additions/Closures of Headquarters and Branch Offices of the 32 Groups by Regions

	1979-1981						1982-May 1984					
	Separated HQs		Unseparated HQs		Branch Offices		Separated HQs		Unseparated HQs		Branch Offices	
	A	C	A	C	A	C	A	C	A	C	A	C
Seoul and Kyǒnggi	100.0	80.0	58.3	76.5	60.0	45.4	92.9	94.7	66.7	44.4	17.6	93.8
Seoul	100.0	80.0	16.7	52.9	50.0	45.4	85.7	94.7	22.2	14.8	17.6	87.5
Cities*	.	.	33.3	17.6	10.0	.	.	.	22.2	14.8	.	6.3
Rural counties**	.	.	8.3	5.9	.	.	7.1	.	22.2	14.8	.	.
Pusan and S.Kyǒngsang	.	20.0	16.7	23.5	30.0	36.4	7.1	5.3	11.1	18.5	23.5	6.3
Pusan	.	20.0	.	5.9	20.0	36.4	.	5.3	.	3.7	11.8	6.3
Cities*	.	.	8.3	17.6	10.0	.	7.1	.	.	7.4	11.8	.
Rural counties**	.	.	8.4	.	.	.	.	.	11.1	7.4	.	.
Taegu and N.Kyǒngsang	.	.	25.0	.	10.0	9.1	.	.	23.2	25.9	5.9	.
Taegu	.	.	8.3	.	10.0	9.1	.	.	11.1	14.8	.	.
Cities*	.	.	.	.	.	.	.	.	11.1	7.4	5.9	.
Rural counties**	.	.	16.7	.	.	.	.	.	.	3.7	.	.
Other cities*	.	.	.	.	10.0	.	.	.	.	3.7	52.9	.
Other rural counties**	.	.	.	.	.	9.1	.	.	.	7.4	.	.
Total	100.0	100.0	100.0	100.0	100.0	100.0	100.0	100.0	100.0	100.0	100.0	100.0

(Values are in percentages) A: Additions, C: Closures

* Cities more than 100,000 population

** Rural counties represent small cities with less than 100,000 population and rural areas

Source: Compiled and calculated from the questionnaire survey and Directory of Korean Business, 1979 and 1982/3 by the author

services to regional cities from the city of Seoul.

The dispersion process of manufacturing plants of the groups is distinguishable during the first period. The city of Seoul recorded a considerable decrease of manufacturing plants as a result of many plant closures and relocation, while most medium cities and rural counties of the country increased their manufacturing plants by more plant additions than closures (Table 15.7). Manufacturing decentralization to smaller cities and rural areas within the Seoul and Pusan metropolitan areas is also recognized.

This trend of industrial dispersion and decentralization in the first period, however, did not continue in the second period because most medium cities and rural counties exhibited more plant closures than additions. Only those small cities and rural areas within the Seoul metropolitan area experienced considerable additions of plants. This disturbance in the plant location dynamics is mostly related to the closures of firms during the consolidation period. Plant closures in the areas other than Seoul appear to be a result of changes in the internal allocation of activities among operating units in a multiplant enterprise as suggested in previous studies (Townroe, 1975; Steed, 1971; Erickson, 1981).

Dynamics of the Alpha Group* in Korea: A Case Study

* A fictional name has been used to preserve the anonymity of the group, which is one of the largest in Korea.

Alpha Group, founded in 1967, controls 29 firms in the fields of trade, construction, manufacturing, leisure, shipping and finance. Alpha extended its manufacturing activity through mergers with firms in the field of light industries in the first half of the 1970s. In the second half, it took over firms in the heavy machinery, automobile, shipbuilding and plant facilities, and chemical industries, followed in 1983 by the acquisiton of three firms in consumer and industrial electronics. At present Alpha controls 17 manufacturing firms which operate 47 manufacturing plants in Korea, and 62 branch offices overseas.

Alpha has established a solid foundation for coping more flexibly and effectively with the rapidly changing international situation, for maximizing scope and for internationalizing structure. In recent years, Alpha has taken the lead, following the national directions, in the

Table 15.7: Additions/Closures of Manufacturing Plants of the 32 Groups by Regions

	1979-1981		1982-May 1984	
	Additions (%)	Closures (%)	Additions (%)	Closures(%)
Seoul and Kyŏnggi	28 (35.4)	28 (57.1)	35 (62.5)	42 (58.3)
Seoul	7 (8.9)	17 (34.7)	8 (14.3)	12 (16.7)
Cities*	14 (17.7)	8 (16.3)	8 (14.3)	23 (31.9)
Rural counties**	7 (8.9)	3 (6.1)	19 (33.9)	7 (9.7)
Pusan and S. Kyŏngsang	24 (30.4)	9 (18.4)	9 (16.1)	11 (15.3)
Pusan	7 (8.9)	5 (10.2)	4 (7.1)	3 (4.2)
Cities*	9 (11.4)	4 (8.2)	1 (1.8)	2 (2.8)
Rural counties**	8 (10.1)	0 (0.0)	4 (7.1)	6 (8.3)
Taegu and N. Kyŏngsang	9 (11.4)	8 (16.3)	6 (10.7)	11 (15.3)
Taegu	3 (3.8)	1 (2.0)	1 (1.8)	7 (9.7)
Cities*	4 (5.1)	7 (14.3)	5 (8.9)	2 (2.8)
Rural counties**	2 (2.5)	0 (0.0)	0 (0.0)	2 (2.8)
Other cities*	7 (8.9)	3 (6.1)	1 (1.8)	2 (2.8)
Other rural counties**	11 (13.9)	2 (4.1)	5 (8.9)	6 (8.3)
Total	79 (100.0)	49 (100.0)	56 (100.0)	72 (100.0)

* Cities more than 100,000 population

** Rural counties represent small cities of less than 100,000 population and rural areas

Source: Compiled and calculated from the questionnaire survey and the _Directory of Korean Business_, 1979 and 1982/3 by the author

rapid development of the heavy and chemical industries, and at the same time continues its efforts to upgrade the production of light industry goods through modernized production facilities and development of higher quality merchandise.

RELATIONSHIPS OF OPERATING UNITS AND REGIONAL DEVELOPMENT

The results of the analysis of locational dynamics in the operating units of the groups suggest that the groups contributed to diffusion of the units within the Korean urban system, decentralization of manufacturing within the large metropolitan areas, and recent dispersion of manufacturing to 'other rural counties'. However, it cannot be yet concluded that the groups contributed to the regional development of peripheral areas through industrial investments. To examine this issue, an analysis of the questionnaire survey is presented briefly here.

According to the questionnaires answered by 45 groups, the average number of firms belonging to a group is about nine. Meetings of firm presidents within a group average about 12 a year. Ten per cent of the total materials needed by plants in a group are supplied by other plants within the same group.

The relationships among the operating units within a group can also be examined by the analysis of decision-making authority (Table 15.8). The authority of decision making, such as for investments in new manufacturing plant, facility relocation or expansion, new plant location and investments for high technology developments, in most cases resides with the group headquarters. On the other hand, the authority of decision making in the selection of general material supplies for plants, marketing strategies and specialist labour recruitment, is mainly with the firm headquarters. Decisions on investments and plant location are regarded as very important ones which should be made at the group headquarters.

In general, decision-making authority is almost negligible at plant level. In a regional context, 'the extent to which investment, purchasing and marketing decisions can be made at plant level has been regarded as an important issue with relation to external control' (Watts, 1981, p.5). The preliminary results of the survey, however, show that individual plants of the groups have authority only in the selection of low-level production

Table 15.8: Percentage of Decisions made at Group Headquarters or at Individual Firm Headquarters

Decisions are made at	Mostly Group HQs	Group HQs & Firm HQs	Mostly Firm HQs
Investment for new manufacturing plant	89.7	7.7	2.6
Plant relocation or expansion	76.9	17.9	5.1
Investment for high technology development	66.7	15.4	17.9
Selection of new plant location	61.5	23.1	15.4
Promotion and salary increase for personnal of section chief chief and higher ranks	59.0	17.9	23.1
Investment for general technology import and development	41.0	20.5	38.5
Regular appointments of new workforces	35.9	30.8	33.3
Selection of technical or managerial consultants	33.3	30.8	35.9
Promotion and salary increases for general and production workforces	33.3	28.2	38.5
Selection of bank services	33.3	17.9	51.3
Selection of attorney services	28.2	25.6	46.2
Pricing policy	25.6	30.8	43.6
Selection of the most important material sources for plants	15.4	30.8	53.8
Marketing strategy	15.4	28.2	56.4
Irregular appointments of new workforces	12.8	17.9	69.3
Selection of general input material sources for plants	7.7	12.8	79.5

Source: Compiled and calculated from the questionnaires by the author

workers. The plants have little authority on decisions such as R&D investments, marketing, new investments on plant or technology development, promotion and salary increases for personnel at plants. Thus, the groups in Korea control firms and plants directly or indirectly and local plants of the groups have little autonomy. Furthermore, promotion and appointments of section chief and higher ranks of firm HQs or plants are decided in the group HQs, located in Seoul. Most staff were educated in Seoul and live in the same city. In the case of plants located in the suburbs of Seoul (Kyŏnggi Province), most staff either commute from Seoul or live in lodgings, while their family members remain in Seoul. Even in the case of plants located at a greater distance from Seoul, about 30 per cent of the section chief and higher ranks still maintain their residences in Seoul and send their pay cheques to their families in Seoul.

Thus the employment effects of a plant of a group on the local area is limited to only low level production workforces and accordingly the monetary flow impacts on the local area are minimal. Forward and backward material linkages within a local area by a plant of a group are also almost negligible. The groups' firms or plants located in the provincial areas, of course, may perform better than the average total industry in terms of wages, employment size and employment growth, as investigated elsewhere (Bade, 1983). However, as long as the firms or plants located in provincial areas have little autonomy, as in the present circumstances in Korea, the contribution of the groups to the regional development seems to be below expectation.

CONCLUSION

This chapter reports one of the very few empirical investigations into the dynamics of operating units in the Korean industrial system, focusing on the role played by large enterprises (groups) in shaping the spatial division of labour and regional development. Locational patterns of operating units of the 32 groups, in comparison with non-group firms, show more concentration of separated headquarters in Seoul and more diffusion and dispersion of production units to areas other than Seoul, showing that the spatial division of labour is more advanced in the groups. Groups' branch offices headquartered in Seoul are also filtered down to lower urban hierarchies from Seoul, while most of branch offices headquartered in areas other than Seoul are concentrated in Seoul.

The operating units of the groups have experienced a considerable change during the period of 1979 to 1984. Production units show higher rates of change than associated units or industry-related units. The second period (1982-84) experienced more changes than the first period (1979-81), especially amongst smaller units, reflecting the fact that the world-wide recession and political fluctuation in Korea in the late 1970s did not immediately affect the organization of the groups, which during the second period were forced by the government to consolidate some of their poorly performing firms. This latter process disturbed the progress towards industrial decentralization within the large metropolitan areas, diffusion within the Korean urban system, and dispersion to non-metropolitan areas identified during the first period. During the consolidation period, firms which have unseparated headquarters in areas other than Seoul, especially in textiles, accordingly closed. Many branch office closures in Seoul during the second period are also related to the firm closures in areas other than Seoul.

Even though there has been some disturbance in the trends of industrial dynamics, it is clear that the organization of the groups is an important variable in understanding the Korean industrial system. Yet the groups' industrial dynamics appear to have few links with the economic growth in peripheral areas as, in general, the limited autonomy at the local plant level and the over-concentration of decision powers in Seoul seemingly result in the low level of employment effects, monetary flow impacts and linkages by the plants of the groups in their localities. Without autonomy, the plants of the groups have little potential for innovating, generating local multiplier effects and for regional development. Further in-depth study is needed, however, to examine the social and economic impacts of external control so as to derive amenable policy implications for regional development of peripheral areas in Korea.

BIBLIOGRAPHY

Abe, K., 'Head and Branch Offices of Big Private Enterprises in Major Cities of Japan', Geographical Review of Japan, Vol.57(B) (1984), pp.43-67

Bade, F.Z., 'Large Corporations and Regional Development', Regional Studies, Vol.17 (1983), pp.315-26

Blackbourn, A., 'Multiregional Enterprises and the Regional Development: A Comment', Regional Studies, Vol.12 (1978), pp.125-7

Erickson, R.A., 'The Filtering-down Process : Industrial Location in a Non-Metropolitan Area',

Professional Geographer, Vol.28 (1976), pp.54-60
Erickson, R.A., 'Corporation, Branch Plants, and Employment Stability in Non-Metropolitan Areas', in Rees, J., Hewings, G.J.D. and Stafford, H.A. (Eds.), Industrial Location and Regional Systems (J.F. Bergin Publishers Inc., Brooklyn, N.Y., 1976), pp.135-54
Erickson, R.A. and Leinbach, T.R., 'Characteristics of Branch Plants Attracted to Non-Metropolitan Areas', in Lonsdale, R.E. and Seyler, H.L. (Eds.), Non-Metropolitan Industrialization (Winston/Wiley Publishers, Washington, D.C. 1979)
Hamilton, F.E.I. and Linge, G.J.R. (Eds.), Spatial Analysis, Industry and the Industrial Environment, Vol.1 - Industrial Systems (John Wiley & Sons, Chichester, 1979)
Hamilton, F.E.I. and Linge, G.J.R. (Eds.), Spatial Analysis, Industry and the Industrial Environment, Vol.2 - International Industrial Systems, (John Wiley & Sons, Chichester, 1981)
Hayter, R. and Watts, H.D., 'The Geography of Enterprise : A Reappraisal', Progress in Human Geography, Vol.7 (1983), pp.157-81
Kemper, N.J. and de Smidt, M.,'Foreign Manufacturing Establishments in the Netherlands', Tijdschrift voor Economische en Sociale Geografie, Vol.71 (1980), pp.21-40
Kim, K.S., Patterns of Factors of Korean Industrialization, (Korea Development Institute, Seoul, 1980), (in Korean)
Linge, G.J.R. and Hamilton, F.E.I., 'International Industrial Systems', in Hamilton and Linge (Eds.), Spatial Analysis, 1981, pp.1-117
Nam, J.H., 'The Heavy and Chemical Industry', in Park, J.K. and Lee, K.O. (Eds.), National Budget and Policy Targets : Evaluating the 1981 Budget, (Korea Development Institute, Seoul, 1981), pp.172-95 (in Korean)
O'Farrell, P.N., 'Multinational Enterprises and Regional Development : Irish Evidence', Regional Studies, Vol.14 (1980), pp.141-50
Park, S.O. Locational Change in Manufacturing : A Conceptual Model and Case Studies, Ph.D. Dissertation, University of Georgia, Athens, 1981
Park, S.O. and Wheeler, J.O.,'Industrial Location Policies and Manufacturing Employment Change : The Case of the Republic of Korea', Regional Development Dialogue, Vol.4 (1983), pp.45-64

Park, S.O. and Wheeler, J.O., 'The Filtering Down Process in Georgia : The Third Stage in the Product Life Cycle', Professional Geographer, Vol.35 (1983), pp.18-31

Steed, G.P.F., 'Forms of Corporate Environmental Adaption', Tijdschrift voor Economische en Sociale Geografie, Vol.62 (1971), pp.90-4

Stephens, J.D. and Holly, B.P., 'The Changing Patterns of Industrial Corporate Control in the Metropolitan United States', in Brunn, S.D., and Wheeler, J.O. (Eds.), The American Metropolitan System : Present and Future, (Edward Arnold, London, 1980), pp.161-80

Strickland, D. and Aiken, M., 'Corporate Influence and the German Urban System : Headquarters Location of German Industrial Corporations, 1950-1982', Economic Geography, Vol.60 (1984), pp.30-54

Townroe, P.M. 'Branch Plants and Regional Development', Town Planning Review, Vol.46 (1975), pp.47-62

Watts, H.D., 'Large Firms, Multinationals and Regional Development : Some New Evidence from the United Kingdom', Environmental Planning, A. Vol.11 (1979), pp.71-81

Watts, H.D., The Branch Plant Economy : A Study of External Control (Longman, London, 1981)

Wheeler, J.O. and Park, S.O., 'External Ownership and Control, the Impact of Industrial Organization on the Regional Economy', Geoforum, Vol.15 (1984), pp.243-252

CHAPTER 16

DEVELOPING REGIONAL INDUSTRIAL SYSTEMS IN THE PEOPLES' REPUBLIC OF CHINA

Li Wen-yan

An industrial system is composed of a set of operating units with the functions of industrial management, research, production and services (Hamilton and Linge, 1979), and it can refer to a large one like a national industrial system, or a small one like an industrial combine. A regional industrial system, in the author's opinion, is an industrialized area with diversified industrial structure and close organizational and techno-economic linkages among the population of units, thus forming a territorial industrial integration of a certain level with special features. A regional industrial system is dynamic in both capitalist and socialist countries, yet once it comes into being it will be relatively stable. Only when sudden changes occur in some factors can qualitative changes in the whole system be expected.

For a developing country, with vast territory and huge population like China, where the marked differentiation of natural and social conditions is very obvious, it is of great significance to study the factors that shape the formation of its multi-level regional industrial systems, their inherent features of sectorial structure and spatial pattern, existing problems and trends of development. The hierarchy of industrial systems in China can be viewed as comprising five orders: (1) the industrial systems of macro-economic regions; (2) industrial region (base); (3) industrial centre (nodes); (4) industrial district; and (5) industrial point (estate). This chapter focuses on the first two levels.

MACRO-ECONOMIC REGIONAL SYSTEMS

Given the circumstances of China, the formation of

the industrial system of a macro-economic region requires that five prerequisites should be met. First, there should be a relatively integrated sector structure in which not only several specialized sectors play an important role in the regional division of labour of the whole country, but where there is also a comprehensively coordinated development between light and heavy industries, and between mining, raw materials and manufacturing industries. Labour-intensive, capital-intensive and technology-intensive types of industry should all attain certain levels of development.

Secondly, a sufficiently strong economic base and large consumer market should exist. The general means of both subsistence and production should reach a level adequate to support the population and scale of construction in the region. The capacity of the market should be large enough to support the economic distribution of key industrial products.

Thirdly, it is necessary for there to be many industrial bases and a batch of industrial centres. There should be more than one comprehensive or specialized basis (energy, in particular), and a number of industrial centres linked together by developed transport and power networks and able to sustain a definitive division of labour and close cooperation among them.

Fourthly, reliable resource basis is essential, comprising such natural resources as are diverse in variety, large in amount and spatially well-combined (especially the mineral and energy resources) as well as adequate social resources comprising labour and especially sufficient, qualified manpower and financial sources. Utilization of resources should be as full as possible and the potentials for future resource exploitation should also be large enough.

Fifthly, an effective production, organization and management system is required which is scientific, a rational form of social production organization adapted to the level of the regional productive forces, which comprises the relevant design and research institutions for forming and running a large regional industrial system.

Applying these requirements, one can identify that regional industrial systems of the first order have basically taken shape in three regions of the Chinese Peoples' Republic: the north-east, north and east. Initial forms may be found in south-west, central and south China, while they are embryonic in north-west China. The following sections will examine the first three regional basic data which are set out in Table 16.1.

North-east China

This consists of the most important integrated industrial base of central and southern Liaoning Province, comprising the Daqing oil base, eastern Heilongjiang coalfields, greater Hinggan mountains, forests and a few industrial centres scattered beyond these resource areas. The main specific features are:

1. Rich natural resources in favourable combinations. Verified reserves of iron ore in this region account for one quarter of the country's total and nearly half of its petroleum. There are also in excess of 60 billion tons of coal reserves and several other mineral deposits.

2. Preferential development of heavy industry in the region was based on original development during the first half of he 20th century and especially through the planned construction in the 1950s and 1960s, focusing on metallurgy and the oil industry respectively. The result has been to diversify and integrate the industrial structure of north-east China, which now possesses highly developed iron and steel, machine-manufacturing, chemicals, energy and building materials industries. Its annual output value from heavy industry is 20 per cent of China's total, while the region's population is only 9 per cent. Light industry, relatively weak in the past, has recently been strengthened.

3. Fairly precise relationships are evident in the division of labour and cooperation among provinces (autonomous regions) and industrial centres. The specialized sectors in Liaoning Province are iron and steel, petroleum-refining, chemical raw materials and machine-manufacturing industries; in Jilin Province, automobile manufacture and chemical industries; in Heilongjiang petroleum, coal, forest and machinery industries; in the eastern Nei Mongol, forest and coal industries. Heilongjiang and eastern Nei Mongol provide coal and timber to Liaoning and Jilin;

Table 16.1: Basic Facts of Three Macro-economic Regions

Items	North-east China	North China	East China
Population (millions)	91.3	170.9	162.1
Verified reserves of key minerals:			
Coal (billion tons)	175	276	26
per cent of China's total	23.6	37.2	3.5
Petroleum (mill.tons)	3,629	2,431	22
per cent of China's total	47.5	31.8	0.3
Iron ore (bill.tons)	11	13	3.2
per cent of China's total	24.6	28.9	7.2
Bauxite (mill.tons)	8	603	-
per cent of China's total	0.6	44.2	-
Annual industrial output value (billion RMB)	88.8	117.1	151.6
Percentage of sector's industrial output value in the regional total:			
Metallurgy	11.8	7.2	7.4
Coal mining	2.8	5.1	0.7
Petroleum	15.0	4.6	2.0
Chemicals	9.0	13.2	12.8
Machine-manufacturing	20.6	20.8	24.8
Textiles	9.1	15.8	22.8
Foodstuffs	10.5	11.1	11.2
Total industrial firms (000s)	43	53	89
of which, state-owned (000s)	10	13	16
Industrial employees (state-owned firms) (000s)	6,283	6,914	6,057

Note: North-east China and north China do not include Inner Mongolia, except for coal reserves

Source: Statistical Yearbook of China, 1983

Heilongjiang and Jilin supply non-ferrous metal ore to Liaoning (accounting for a quarter of its requirement); Daqing's crude oil is transported from Heilongjiang to Liaoning for refining (70 per cent of the total amount refined annually), while Liaoning supplies other provinces with most of the oil products they need. As for the machinery industry, every province has its own specialization, but three provinces cooperate closely to produce complete sets of equipment of many kinds. Several management units have been put in charge of the industrial activities of the whole region to ensure that organizational relationships among the populations of units within every main sector become closer than before.

4. North-east China is a clearly defined geographical region with a fairly complete and relatively separate transport network. Therefore a regional industrial system of this macro-economic region is already a reality.

East China

This region consists mainly of the most integrated industrial base of the Changjiang (Yangtze) Delta, the significant industrial area of Nanjing-Wuxi with a developing heavy industrial base, the coal resource base of Huaibei and Huainan and several scattered industrial centres. The main features of this regional industrial system are:

1. Specialization in the predominant development of intermediate and processing industries. Before liberation in 1949, this region had well developed textile and light industries, with machine-repairing concentrated in Shanghai and a few adjacent cities. During the 1950s and 1960s, this region, the people of Shanghai and Jiangsu Province in particular, carried out a technical transformation of the machine-manufacturing and textile industries and greatly extended metallurgical and chemical industries, thus achieving basically the transition from a backward to modern system. At the beginning of the 1980s, apart from continuing to reinforce the steel and petrochemical industries, new sectors began to develop vigorously, such as the production of electronics and durable consumer goods.

2. A lack of natural resources is offset by a superior geographical location and good social conditions. Although most industrial sectors and centres have to rely on the supply of raw materials and energy from outside east China, favourable transport conditions and the comparatively high technical level and infrastructure provision of the region have enabled them to grow at rates which have long been above the national average. Even heavy metallurgical and chemical industries have also greatly developed in the coastal cities. To meet the demand there, coalfields and several other mineral deposits in Huaibei and Huainan, far less important than the large ones of other regions in terms of reserves, have been exploited to much greater scale because of their proximity to the coastal industrial area.

3. Close and intricate economic and technological cooperation results from industrial specialization. Generally speaking, Jiangsu province supplies processed agricultural and farm by-products, pig iron, spare parts and fittings to Shanghai, while this coastal metropolis absorbs from Zhejiang province supplies of processed foodstuffs and hydro-electric power and, from Anhui province coal, pig iron and copper. Shanghai in turn offers relatively advanced technology in many industrial sectors to the other provinces.

Although Shanghai's industry has made much progress in the past decades, the proportion it accounts for in the whole country is falling. Zhejiang and Anhui provinces, previously very backward in industry, have experienced much more economic growth, while Jiangsu has developed much more swiftly since 1970 and its annual industrial output value was roughly equivalent to 80 per cent of that of Shanghai in 1982 compared with only 33 per cent in 1965.

North China

This region embraces the most important integrated industrial base of Beijing-Tianjin-Tangshan as the core region, the heavy industrial bases of central Shandong and central Shanxi, light industrial bases of southern Hebei and other industrial centres.

North China has three extraordinary advantages for the development of industry: a nodal geographical position centred on the capital and hub of China's transport network; abundant and spatially well-combined mineral resources in the form of large reserves of coal, iron ore, bauxite, petroleum, limestone and salt; and a fairly concentrated scientific and technical labour force.

Three decades of construction have ensured the formation of mainstay industrial sectors like iron and steel, coal, machine-manufacturing, textiles and chemicals. Recently, petrochemicals and electronics industries together with an expansion of coal mining have been the main foci of construction in this region. By comparison with the north-east and east China, the industrial system of north China enjoys an even richer resource base. Development is relatively well coordinated, especially between light and heavy industry and among mining, raw materials and manufacturing. Energy resources are especially abundant and fairly comprehensive, while the distribution of industry is also relatively harmonious, or even.

Apart from the national core region of Beijing-Tianjin-Tangshan, which is the leading industrial area in north China, the region contains other important zones such as central Shandong, central Shanxi and southern Hebei, which are also developing. Shanxi is China's largest coalfield, while Hebei and Shandong provinces are not only also important producers of coal but supply crude oil, too. They supply the needs of energy-consuming centres and oil to be transported to the south of China. Three of the major iron and steel bases in China are located in the region: Beijing-Tianjin-Tangshan; Taiyuan; and Baotou. The raw materials and fuel they need come primarily from within the region and the resources are ample for a long time to come. Petrochemicals in Beijing, Tianjin and Zibo, coal-chemicals in Beijing and Taiyuan and other chemicals industries in Qingdao provide the whole region with sufficient industrial chemicals and various chemical products. Machinery industries in Beijing, Tianjin, Taiyuan, Jinan and Qingdao, especially those producing the motor vehicle, heavy-duty machinery, universal machinery and railway rolling stock, have very close ties of cooperation amongst themselves. The development of sections of the power grid system within north China are beginning to be linked up to improve operational efficiency.

INDUSTRIAL REGIONS AND THEIR PROBLEMS

An industrial region, the second level of the

hierarchy in the Chinese industrial system, is in essence the subsystem of a macro-regional system, the core of a large economic region. It may be termed a 'regional territorial industrial complex', as it: comprises industries concentrated in a compact area (varying in size from a few thousand to tens of thousands of square kilometres); has great economic strength rooted in more than one specialized sector of national importance; several industrial centres with nationwide significance, and, at the same time; close economic linkages between these centres. Besides, all industrial centres and urban settlements within the region usually share a common infrastructure and constitute a relatively complete urban system (Probst, 1976).

Generally speaking, the chief factors forming the base of an industrial region are:

1. The natural resources and environmental conditions. Primarily, the mineral, land and water resources supplying the raw mineral materials for heavy industry, and energy inputs to industries and urban settlements. Some metalliferous ore deposits like iron, copper and bauxite, and energy resources such as petroleum, coal and hydro-electricity all play an outstanding role in the development of the industrial system. On the other hand, the distribution of surface and ground water acts as a constraint on the location and construction of industrial bases in the vast arid and semi-arid regions of China, while the limited availability of flat land usually restricts development in mountainous southern China.

2. Geographical position and transport conditions. A macro-geographic situation of a region may be measured in terms of its location relative to: the national political centre, the economically most developed regions of the country, big seaports or other important windows of foreign trade, and energy sources (Li Wen-yan, 1982). The density of transport network and number of interregional trunk lines are also useful indicators.

3. The existing levels of economic development. This factor refers to the characteristics of the structure of the regional economy, the level of its production technology and

management, national income generation and local financial resources, the extent of urbanization and status of local infrastructure.

4. Social and cultural factors depend primarily on the amount of quality of the labour force, the scale and level of science and technology, education and culture at its disposal, as well as the customs and habits of the local people.

To date about a dozen industrial bases have been formed or are taking shape in China. Among them are the Changjiang Delta, the regions of Beijing-Tianjin-Tangshan, central and southern Liaoning, east Hubei (Wuhan and surrounding cities), southern Sichuan (Chongqing and adjacent areas) and the Zhujiang Delta, which are all of nationwide significance and act as core areas of their respective macro-economic regions. These fall into three different types, those based respectively on resources, markets or both.

Resource-based Industrial Regions

These are based in areas with an abundance of natural resources, particularly with concentrated key mineral deposits, advantages of external links and transport facilities and adequate water supplies.

Central and southern Liaoning (see Table 16.2) is a representative of this type of industrial region. Its main manufacturing cities comprise Shenyang, Anshan, Fushun, Benxi, Liaoyang and Dalian. The region boasts some 22 per cent of the known reserves of iron ore in China and also a substantial amount of high-grade coal and metallurgical auxiliary raw materials. Over a ladder-shaped area (Figure 16.2) are distributed more than 20 large mines for coal, iron ore and magnesite, the foundations for the development of four mainstay industries (iron and steel at Anshan and Banxi; coal mining at Fushun; machinery at Shenyang) and railway transport since early in this century. After reconstruction in the 1950s, central and southern Liaoning became the leading heavy industrial region of China, and it still retains this importance. Following the development of the Panjin oilfield in the adjacent area and crude oil transported from Daqing, oil refining and petrochemicals have swiftly developed, making this region more complete in industrial structure and economically stronger.

Table 16.2: Basic Facts of Three Major Industrial Regions of China (1980)

Item	Beijing-Tianjin-Tangshan	Changjiang Delta	Central & Southern Liaoning
Land area (000 km²)	52	84	58
Population (000s)	26,518	48,478	19,562
Urban population (000s)	10,578	11,362	8,438
Annual industrial & agricultural output value:			
total (bill.Y)	52.36	114.24	38.82
per capita (Y)	1,974	2,356	1,984
Annual industrial output value:			
total (bill Y)	47.5	99.86	33.64
per capita (Y)	1,791	2,059	1,771
per capita (urban) (Y)	4,490	8,785	4,105
Ratio of light to heavy industry:	45:55	55:45	30:70
Total industrial firms in major cities (1983)	10,923	38,927	9,322
Annual output of coal per capita (tons)	1.11	-	0.77

Source: Calculated from Statistical Yearbook of China, 1983

Resource-based raw materials-processing industries including metallurgy, oil refining, basic chemicals and building materials still claim the major proportion of total industrial output value. Yet local intermediate raw material supplies are also an advantage for the development of metal-consuming machinery industries.

The region produces 27 per cent of China's pig iron, 23 per cent of steel, 20 per cent of rolled steel, 22 per cent of petroleum, 8 per cent of cement, 40 per cent of soda ash, 15 per cent of machine tools and 9 per cent of electricity. The six cities noted above from the nuclei of this region constitute an integrated territorial industrial complex with close economic and technological connections, a dense transport network, integrated power system, unified water conservancy agency and heavy commuting between neighbouring cities.

The two main problems of the industries in the region are the increasing shortages of coal supply and their outdated equipment. With the exhaustion of the reserves in two old coal mines, the advantages of the natural resources have begun to weaken. Moreover the predominance of 1950s technological equipment requires replacement to raise the intensity of resource utilization and productivity of labour.

Central Shanxi province is another example, though it is both a small-sized and newly-built industrial region particularly abundant in coal. There, iron and steel, machinery and chemical industries have grown to form industrial centres at Taiyuan (a wide range of industries), Yuci (machinery and textiles, and Gujiao (coal). The sectoral structure of central Shanxi is more or less similar to central Liaoning, though the petro-chemicals industry is absent. Compared with central Liaoning, however, the water resources of central Shanxi are more restricted and its economic-geographical position and social and cultural conditions are no better. However, as long as appropriate measures are taken, this zone is expected to become an important industrial region in the near future.

Market-orientated Industrial Regions

Despite poor natural resources, some regions can become nationwide industrial bases on account of their superior geographical position, convenient transport and communications facilities, abundant and highly-skilled labour force. Changjiang Delta industrial base is the most typical of these.

Shanghai became the biggest commercial and industrial centre of the region from early this century. Textiles and machine-assembly used to be the major sectors and were concentrated mainly in Shanghai and a few other nearby cities. Now, however, the region's production units manufacture various machines, equipment, consumer goods, chemicals and rolled steel. Since 1960 industries have expanded in the suburban districts of Shanghai city, its outlying counties and adjacent medium and small-sized cities.

As the major industrial area of China, the Changjiang Delta includes ten cities (and their affiliated counties) covering an area of 84,000 sq.km., with a population of 50 million. Data are presented in Table 16.3 for the 7 biggest cities of the region.

In industrial output value it accounts for 20 per cent of China's total, and it concentrates 20 per cent of the country's metallurgy, 30 per cent of machinery, over 50 per cent of shipbuilding and 38 per cent of textiles. Changjiang industrial area is thus the leading one in variety and quality of products, the size and skill of the labour forces and productivity.

Shanghai localizes a total of 8,300 industrial enterprises employing a labour force which exceeds 2.6 million. These produced 11.4 per cent of China's industrial output value in 1982. Shanghai's annual output of steel is about 5 million tons which meets 90 per cent of the rolled steel needed in the city's industries. Its chemical industries produced over 20,000 categories of chemical products and, of these, 90 per cent are manufactured in their entirety in Shanghai. More than 1,800 types of machinery are produced, 90 per cent of the output comprising fully assembled machines, over 80 per cent of which are heavy-duty machines for use in metallurgy, mining, chemical fertilizer plants and power stations. While Shanghai's major industrial products supply between 10 and 30 per cent of their respective national markets, one-third of the total daily necessities handled by the state comes from Shanghai. The city is thus the core of both the Changjiang Delta industrial region and east China. Moreover, as the hinterland gravitating to the Delta region comprises several provinces with a population of 160 million, the scale and future absorptive capacity of the market for this base is very large. Besides, as the biggest harbour in China, Shanghai can also export a great amount of products manufactured in the Delta to the outside world.

A major problem in this industrial region, however, is that its structure does not correspond to the needs of Chinese modernization drives. For example, the technology-intensive industry of Shanghai accounts for only 17 per cent of its total industrial output value while resource-based industry is still more important. Another problem is that the sectorial structure of the region's ten cities is very similar, with textile and light industries predominating, creating unnecessary duplication and competition between the cities.

Table 16.3: Industrial Sectorial Structure and Productivity of the Major Cities of the Changjiang Delta

Items	Shanghai	Suzhou	Wuxi	Changzhou	Nantong	Hangzhou	Ningbo
Annual industrial output value (1982: bill. RMB)	63.67	3.44	4.82	3.86	2.28	7.35	2.39
All light industry (1982: per cent)	56	67	66	61	73	62	61
All light industry (early 1950s)	77	98	97	93	-	96	-
Textiles industry	24.5	29.1	36.3	41.6	45.2	-	17.3
Total industrial employees (1983: 000s)	3,062	485	494	343	438	610	314
Average productivity (RMB per person per a.):							
State-run firms (1983)	29,496	17,371	20,110	24,488	22,643	17,859	19,464
Collective-owned firms (1983)	12,091	12,522	14,227	15,133	13,908	12,201	13,574

Source: Calculated from Statistical Yearbook of China, 1983 and local sources

According to the statistics for 1982, the proportions of the output value of light industry in the different cities range mostly between 50 and 70 per cent, with textiles accounting for 24-25 per cent.

To solve these problems, urgent tasks lie ahead in: adjusting the regional economic structure, strengthening division of labour and economic cooperation among respective cities, accelerating technology transfer from Shanghai to other cities within the Delta region and further beyond it, and directing the production profiles of manufacturing industries in the Delta region towards overseas markets.

Another typical industrial region of market-orientated type is the Zhujiang (Pearl River) Delta. This industrial area, with Guangzhou as its nucleus, embraces the cities of Foshan, Jiangmen, Shenzhen and Zhuhai and 20 or so surrounding counties, and has developed rapidly in recent years. Thanks to the numerous overseas Chinese residents living in the region, proximity to Hong Kong and Macao, and the recently opened special economic zones of Shenzhen and Zhuhai, this Delta region possesses some advantages which other industrial areas do not have in China. Manufacturing and tertiary activities are expanding as its products penetrate world markets to an appreciable degree. Yet raw materials' supplies and energy resources are far from adequate within this region and constitute two weaknesses in the chain of the regional industrial system.

Mixed Type Industrial Regions

This type combines abundant resources with vast local markets. The Beijing-Tianjin-Tangshan region is a good example. It possesses 12 per cent of the country's iron ore, high quality coking-coal, considerable anthracite, reserves of petroleum and non-metallic minerals. The spatial combination of mineral resources in this region, and hence the prospect of development of steel and chemical industries, resembles those in central Liaoning. In addition, there are in adjacency the energy resources of Shanxi and cash-crop supplies from eastern and southern Hebei. These all combine, therefore, to form a good basis for the development of various resource-intensive industries. On the other hand, the market potential is much larger than that of Liaoning because the hinterland of this industrial region covers the large area of Hebei, Shanxi, western Inner Mongolia, northern Shandong and Henan, even part of north-west China. Besides, population density is high, and here is the political and cultural centre of the whole country, so the conditions for developing light and technology-intensive industries are as favourable as in the Changjiang Delta.

As a result, during the past 30 years, this region has progressed through several stages of development from (1) light industry and coal to (2) iron, steel and machine-manufacturing to (3) petrochemicals, electronic products and durable consumer goods as the contemporary lead (pilot) industries, so forming a comprehensive industrial base with relatively well coordinated light and heavy industries.

Tianjin is the oldest industrial centre and large port city in China so that its sectorial structure resembles that of Shanghai, though the conditions of its port, economic base and urban water supply are not as good as those in Shanghai. Nevertheless, the availability of resources, particularly petroleum, is much better than in Shanghai, offering greater advantages for the development of the petrochemical and shipbuilding industries. At present, Tianjin sends 70 per cent of basic and light industrial goods out, primarily to north China, in contrast to Shanghai, which supplies a much broader local market.

Beijing, however, exhibits the characteristics of having both light and basic industries, with iron and steel, machine-building and petrochemical industries as the leaders. The annual production of rolled steel in Beijing is less than that of Shanghai, but as it relies mainly on the mineral resources within the surrounding area, its scale of iron-smelting is much larger.

Similarly, the leading industrial sectors of iron and steel, coal and building materials in Tangshan are all based on local resources but can easily supply products mainly to the market of the Beijing-Tianjin-Tangshan region.

Light industry in this region depends mainly on the raw materials of north China, including some from north-west, north-east and central China, but its manufactures are sold locally.

At present, though, economic development in this region still lags behind the Changjiang Delta. Economic and technological linkages among Beijing, Tianjin and Tanshan are still underdeveloped and comprise predominantly the transport of minerals and raw materials, fuels, metals and semi-products.

Technology transfer and cooperation within the region are much weaker than in the Changjiang Delta, yet with the development of newly emerging industries such as electronics and petrochemicals and the transformation of the traditional industries by the influx of new equipment, this status will surely undergo considerable change.

ALL CHANGE ON THE EASTERN FRONT

To speed up the modernization drive, China is carrying out a series of major institutional reforms to reconstruct its economy. Decentralization of the power of economic planning and management to local authorities will definitely promote the formation, dynamics and diversification of regional industrial systems. Furthermore, China is implementing an open-door economic policy, especially in industry and trade. Apart from the current four Special Economic Zones in south China, 14 port cities have been opened recently to the outside world. Peculiar measures and regulations have been or will be adopted in these cities and zones to stimulate the construction of joint ventures, cooperative enterprises and plants operated exclusively with foreign investment. As a result of the more flexible policy towards foreign trade, existing major industries in these cities will have more opportunities to transform themselves into truly modern production units. Under these circumstances, it is to be expected that established coastal industrial centres and regions will be strengthened and new ones will emerge. Some important industrial bases or centres located inland in areas including Chongqing are also carrying out economic reform experiments so as to develop their economy vigorously. Frontier regions are also exploring ways to get rid of backwardness through the exploitation of their rich resources.

Everything in China has been changing recently, and it is expected that a multi-level regional system, coordinated in structure and rational distribution will take shape before the end of this century.

BIBLIOGRAPHY

Hamilton, F.E.I. and Linge, G.J.R. (1979) 'Industrial Systems' in F.E.I. Hamilton and G.J.R. Linge (eds.), Spatial Analysis, Industry and the Industrial Environment : Industrial

Systems, Wiley, Chichester, pp.1-23
Li Wen-yan (1982), 'Provincial Differentiation of the Mineral Resources and Geographical Position within China', in Geographical Research (in Chinese) 1 (1), pp.8-19
Li Wen-yan, and Chen Hang (1983), 'A Preliminary Study on the Energy-economic Regionalization of China', Acta Geographica Sinica (in Chinese) 38 (4), pp.7-19

INDEX

NB Authors listed here are those named first in each entry in the references.